QUALITY CONTROL
IN FOODSERVICE
REVISED EDITION

QUALITY CONTROL IN FOODSERVICE

REVISED EDITION

Marvin Edward Thorner, Ch.E., FCSI

Consultant in Chemical Engineering and
Food Technology
M.E. Thorner Associates
Hollywood, Florida

Peter Burnam Manning, Ph.D.

Professor of Foodservice
Department of Hotel, Restaurant, and Travel
Administration
and Food Science and Nutrition
University of Massachusetts
Amherst, Massachusetts

AVI PUBLISHING COMPANY, INC.
Westport, Connecticut

Front Cover Photograph Courtesy of Wine Institute

*Frontispiece Photograph Courtesy of the
Louis Rich Company, Madison, Wisconsin*

Library of Congress Cataloging in Publication Data

Thorner, Marvin Edward.
    Quality control in foodservice.

    Bibliography: p.
    Includes index.
    1. Food service—Quality control.   I. Manning.
Peter Burnam.   II.   Title.
TX911.3.Q34T48   1983   642'.5   83-12651
ISBN 0-87055-431-X

Printed in the United States of America

Contents

Preface to the Revised Edition   ix

1   Scope of Quality Control in Foodservice   1

  What Is Quality Control?   1
  The Meaning of Quality   2
  Factors Affecting Food Quality   3
  Developing a Comprehensive Program   4
  Basic Segments of a Program   5
  Examples of Quality Control Projects   6
  Location and Space Requirements for Quality Control
    Activities   8

2   Implementation of a Quality Control Program   11

  Basic Tools for Quality Determination   11
  Sensory Evaluation of Foods and Beverages   11

3   Purchasing and Specifications   35

  Purchasing   35
  Specifications   35
  Regulatory Food Standards and Grades   38

4   Receiving, Sampling, and Product Inspection Control   57

  Receiving   57
  Sampling Techniques   59
  Product Inspection Control   63
  Water Capacity and Fill of Container   64
  Determination of Drained Weight   66
  Determination of Percentage Breading   68
  Determination of Percentage Fat in Ground Beef   70
  Insect Filth in Foods   71
  Sensory Evaluation   71
  Packaging Inspection   75
  Inspection Control of Other Products   75

5   Storage and Issuing Control   77

Storage Categories   77
Definitions of Refrigerated Storage   78
Dry Storage Techniques   78
Handling Frozen Foods   80
Stability of Foods Under Frozen Storage   84
Effects of Storage on Foods   86
Effects of Light and Air on Foods   88
Storage Conditions for Foods   89
Issuing   93

6   Preparation and Production Equipment   95

Factors Related to Equipment Performance   95
Implements Required to Perform Evaluation Checks   96
Preventive Maintenance   97
Significance of Temperature Control   98
Significance of Timing   100
Equipment Requiring Performance Evaluation   101
Convection Ovens   102
Microwave Ovens   104
Deep Fat Fryers   111
The Frying Medium   114
Causes of Common Frying Problems   119
Daily Record of Deep Frying Operation   120
Steam Cookers   121
Tilting Skillets   126
Griddles   128
Blenders   129
Other Equipment   129

7   Precooking Quality Control   131

Recipes   132
Weights and Measures   132
Thawing   135
Salads and Salad Greens   136
Control of Sandwich Preparation   137
Quality Control of Egg Cookery   138
Cheese and Butter   141
Other Foods and Beverages   142

8   Cooking Quality Control   143

Vegetables   144
Meat   146
Poultry   148
Seafood   150
Pre-prepared Foods   151

9   Postcooking Quality Control   153

Postcooking Microbiological Contamination   154
Holding and Overproduction   154

Sauces and Gravies 157
Cheese and Cheese Cookery 159
Salads 160
Sandwich Control 161
Fruit 162
Syneresis 162
Summary 163

10 Desserts and Baked Products Control 165
Categories of Convenience Desserts 165

11 Nonalcoholic Beverages Control 173
Factors Leading to Poor Quality Beverages 173
Coffee 174
Soft Drinks 189
Dairy Beverages 202
Cream Dispensing 206
Nondairy Products 209
Juices 211
Tea 218
Cocoa Beverages 222

12 Food Spoilage and Sanitation Control 227
Food Spoilage and Contamination 227
Factors Causing Bacterial Spoilage 230
Introduction of Food Contaminants 231
Causes of Foodborne Illnesses 232
Sanitation Procedures 238
Cleaning and Care of Food Preparation Equipment 241
Cleaning and Care of Coffee Preparation and Serving
    Equipment 244
Carbonated Drink Dispensers 255
Bulk Milk Dispensers 256
Cream Dispensers 257
Dispensing Freezers 258
Juice and Still Beverage Dispensers 258
Iced Tea Dispensers 259
Teapots and Servers 260
Hot Chocolate Dispensers 260
Ice Making Machines 261
Control of Kitchen Air Pollution 262
OSHA 263
Vending 263

13 Water Quality and Warewashing Control 265
Properties and Sources of Water 266
Hard and Brackish Water 267
Impurities in Water 268
Water Treatment 271
Effects of Water Quality on Foods and Beverages 280
Warewashing 283

14   Quality Control of Vending Equipment   **287**

Classification of Vendable Services   287
Operating Principles of Vending Machines   288
Vending Machine Design   288
Coin-Operated Vending Machines   289
Quality Control Areas   292

15   Energy Management   **307**

Energy Supply and Demand   307
Energy Costs   309
Energy Control and Conservation   309
NRA Guidelines   310

16   Preventive and Corrective Maintenance   **321**

Developing the Program   321
Guide for Preventive Maintenance   325

**Appendix   USDA Standards for Prepared Meat and
            Poultry Products and Useful Tables**   **329**

Glossary   **347**

References   **353**

Index   **357**

Preface to the Revised Edition

The present day foodservice facility is a maze of complicated and sophisticated equipment that is usually installed to provide the most efficient preparation and production systems. In addition, food forms and their methods of handling, preparation, and production are rapidly changing to fit the needs of a growing industry.

Quality control is essential at each step of an operation—from the evaluation and development of food specifications through service to the consumer. Quality control procedures can spell the difference between substantial financial losses and profits. A properly administered quality control program will ensure customer satisfaction and increase employee morale and productivity.

This book is the first comprehensive treatment of quality control for the foodservice industry. It was organized and written as an on-the-job training manual, a textbook, and a guide for all categories of foodservice personnel.

It takes the reader step-by-step through every phase of a foodservice facility. It offers many simplified procedures applicable to all types of foodservice. Each phase is explored and coupled to experience of the past, so that it paves the way to a successful modern foodservice operation. This book will assist an operator in analyzing his present quality control program and improving it, so that it may become more meaningful and constructive. Each facet of foodservice is examined in detail, and the relationship and importance of quality control in developing a successful operation are emphasized.

Many of the subjects discussed in this book are known to a majority of personnel engaged in the foodservice industry; however, a partial or haphazard quality control program is useless. This book proves the reasoning behind this statement—if one or two steps are neglected or overlooked, the entire program will result in complete failure.

A comprehensive quality control program that includes analytical examination for all products and the monitoring of handling, preparation, and serving techniques is a most difficult and an almost impossible task to expect from the greater part of the industry. Full coverage is possible if a completely outfitted laboratory is available and staffed by highly trained technicians, skilled field inspectors, and instructors. The authors have recognized this problem in the treatment of the subject matter.

It is not the intent of this book to provide full, in-depth, detailed quality control procedures. The purpose of this text is to develop simplified inspection skills that may be used without prior technical training, and which can serve as an effective guide and instrument to check quality parameters at all stages of a foodservice operation.

It was not feasible to illustrate each and every procedural facet and food category encountered in foodservice. The examples presented serve as simplified guidelines for tracing poor quality food or faulty preparation and production techniques which are not discussed. This concept is especially evident in Chapters 7, 8, and 9 (Precooking, Cooking, and Postcooking Quality Control, respectively).

Chapter 15, newly revised, on Energy Management, is a timely subject. Most of the basic facts contained in this chapter are directly related to a quality control program. It was for this reason that it was included in the text. Additional material has also been added on the causes of foodborne illnesses. The new and final chapter on Preventive and Corrective Maintenance of foodservice equipment has been added for the purpose of emphasizing the role of maintenance in assuring food quality as well as in reducing energy consumption.

The authors wish to thank all those who helped make this book possible. Organizations that contributed tables and illustrations are given credit under the illustrated material.

MARVIN E. THORNER
PETER B. MANNING

Related AVI Books

BASIC FOOD MICROBIOLOGY
Unabridged Edition   *Banwart*
CONVENIENCE AND FAST FOOD HANDBOOK
Thorner
ELEMENTARY FOOD SCIENCE
2nd Edition   *Nickerson and Ronsivalli*
ENERGY MANAGEMENT IN FOODSERVICE
Unklesbay and Unklesbay
FOODBORNE & WATERBORNE DISEASES
Tartakow and Vorperian
FOODSERVICE FACILITIES PLANNING
2nd Edition   *Kazarian*
FOODSERVICE STANDARDS SERIES
Minor
ICE CREAM
3rd Edition   *Arbuckle*
JUDGING DAIRY PRODUCTS
Revised 4th Edition   *Nelson and Trout*
NON-ALCOHOLIC FOOD SERVICE BEVERAGE HANDBOOK
2nd Edition   *Thorner and Herzberg*
PRACTICAL BAKING
Revised 3rd Edition   *Sultan*
QUALITY CONTROL FOR THE FOOD INDUSTRY
3rd Edition   *Kramer and Twigg*
SCHOOL FOODSERVICE
2nd Edition   *Van Egmond-Pannell*
THE PASTRY CHEF
Sultan
THE PRACTICE OF HOSPITALITY MANAGEMENT
Pizam, Lewis, Manning
THE PSYCHOBIOLOGY OF HUMAN FOOD SELECTION
Barker
THE TECHNOLOGY OF WINE MAKING
4th Edition   *Amerine et al.*
WORK ANALYSIS & DESIGN FOR HOTELS, RESTAURANTS & INSTITUTIONS
2nd Edition   *Kazarian*

Scope of Quality Control in Foodservice

WHAT IS QUALITY CONTROL?

Quality control, or quality assurance, is an activity, procedure, method, or program that will ensure the maintenance and continuity of specifications and standards of a product within prescribed tolerances during all stages of handling, processing, preparation, and packaging, and will further ensure that all the original and desirable characteristics are sustained during storage, processing, or preparation and will remain unaltered until consumed.

The terms *quality control* and *quality assurance* are used interchangeably. The latter term is the more recent, and is gaining acceptance; however, both have the same meaning.

Quality Control in Foodservice

When the definition of quality control is applied to foodservice, it becomes the standard to which all steps of the operation must, of necessity, conform in order to ensure that changes in a food's characteristics do not take place.

This role promotes quality control to a broad, encompassing, and highly significant activity in the development of consistent and high-quality foods and beverages.

Quality control can achieve its maximum benefits only if it is instituted on all levels and sublevels of a foodservice operation.

Programs of this sort have rarely been expanded to embrace all the activities within the confines of a foodservice facility. They are usually developed for a small segment of the overall operation, e.g., the inspection of incoming products. To be meaningful, quality controls must be applied to all steps, areas, and equipment that come in contact with food and beverages.

Once a program is developed covering all edible products and their contact points, problems contributing to unsavory and unpalatable foods and drinks will be drastically reduced or completely eliminated. Moreover, a strong, thorough program will increase business and profits and result in greater customer satisfaction.

Management's Role

Management of small or medium-size establishments is generally averse to such a program because it feels incapable of directing and executing the required tasks intelligently. Others are of the opinion that quality control can be performed only by food technologists or highly trained technicians. Many multiple-unit organizations which operate fully equipped laboratories and personnel training schools have not developed strong and comprehensive in-store programs. In this respect, the emphasis has been placed on the formulations, specifications, and testing of incoming products, leaving a wide gap between the initial phase of quality control and service to the consumer.

On the plus side, however, is the current awareness by management that if a quality control program is not carried out to the fullest extent, especially where efficiency food items are the major source of revenue, growth will suffer and failure may result.

THE MEANING OF QUALITY

The word *quality,* with reference to edibles and beverages, has many significant meanings and interpretations. Two distinct and divergent definitions exist, one for the consumer or "end-user," and the other for the technician or technologist.

The Consumer's Interpretation of Quality

The average consumer associates quality with personal preferences, as something that is liked, disliked, excellent, superior, great, or good. These descriptions are both subjective and abstract and do not produce concrete evidence about the degree of quality from the standpoint of actual grade.

Many factors influence the consumer's decision, such as habit, locality, ethnic characteristics, advertising, "gimmicked" sales promotions, and price.

In addition to these psychological factors, positive sensory stimulation plays an important role in establishing quality parameters. These include an appealing flavor, a pleasing mouth feel or texture, an attractive natural color or appearance, general palatability, product consistency, and, to many customers, the nutritional value of the food. Additional factors that determine consumer quality preferences are the ambience or character of the restaurant, the type and efficiency of the service, plating methods, and cleanliness. These contribute to mood appeal and have a decided effect on the consumer's final determination of quality.

The Technical Interpretation of Quality

The analyst or technologist usually refers to quality as an index or measurement obtained by grading or classifying in accordance with explicit, predetermined specifications. These may be established by the U.S. Department of Agriculture, the Food and Drug Administration, other government agencies, trade associations, or a company's own testing and consumer evaluation panel.

Quality, from a scientific standpoint, can therefore be defined as an orderly classification of a product's chemical and physical characteristics. Flavor, texture, appearance, consistency, palatability, nutritional values, safety, ease of handling, convenience, storage stability, and packaging are the essential elements that must be evaluated in establishing a product's quality.

It is interesting to note the dictionary definition of quality as a characteristic, an attribute of something, a property or feature, or the degree of excellence of a product or thing. Regardless of the exact definition, there are two dominant factors in the evaluation of quality: the actual chemical or physical measurements of the product, and the acceptance of the product by consumers based on whether it will fulfill their "wants" with complete satisfaction.

Management's Interpretation of Quality

In addition to the foregoing definitions of quality, management relates quality to profits. Management equates quality with certain economic factors, such as the cost of the product, profits generated, and consumer acceptance within the intended selling price range. These economic factors are carefully weighed, so that a successful operation will not only produce an adequate return on its investment, but will also ensure healthy long-range growth.

FACTORS AFFECTING FOOD QUALITY

Many factors are responsible for poor quality food. Most of them can be traced to poor sanitation, faulty handling, malfunctioning equipment, incorrect preparation, and carelessness. Although additional elements exert deleterious effects on quality, only those that occur from in-store situations will be discussed here. For purposes of confining these problems to practical applications, it will be assumed that the food undergoing preparation was purchased according to predetermined and exacting specifications. When delivered, the products were checked and found to be in good condition and of the quality expected.

The properties of food considered when making a quality evaluation are: flavor, which is a combination of taste and aroma perception; nutritional content; texture; appearance; and consistency. In addition, attributes such as shelf-life, convenience, packaging, and price form a secondary group that tends to influence quality evaluation.

A feeding establishment, regardless of size, is a complex manufacturing center. From the time the food is delivered until it is served, a myriad of steps and handling operations is involved. The preparation center and adjunct operations can be compared with a highly organized food processing plant. Many of the physical and chemical unit operations and instrumentation that enter into the production of foods and food products are also involved in a foodservice facility. Most foods can be likened to delicate products such as perfume, where the valuable essences are easily destroyed by improper handling or processing. The following are the prime factors responsible for significant quality changes.

(1) Spoilage due to microbiological, biochemical, physical, or chemical factors
(2) Adverse or incompatible water conditions
(3) Poor sanitation and ineffective warewashing
(4) Improper and incorrect precooking, cooking, and postcooking methods
(5) Incorrect temperatures
(6) Incorrect timing
(7) Wrong formulations, stemming from incorrect weight of the food or its components
(8) Poor machine maintenance program
(9) Presence of vermin and pesticides
(10) Poor packaging

Any of these factors, either singly or in combination, will contribute to poor quality and effect changes that will be evident in the food's flavor, texture, appearance, and consistency.

DEVELOPING A COMPREHENSIVE PROGRAM

In the definition of quality control we find it expressed as an activity encompassing all steps involved with the handling of foods and beverages—from point of purchase until they are served to the customer.

An adequate quality control program can be implemented utilizing simplified procedures, without the service and expertise of skilled technicians. Many tests and controls may be competently performed and the resulting data evaluated by supervisory personnel. Special equipment and complicated instruments are not required. Items such as thermometers, timers, hydrometers, scales, standardized measuring devices such as scoops, simplified procedural instructions, testing kits for water analysis and fat content of ground meat, and the basic knowledge of sensory evaluation comprise the fundamental tools for a positive program.

The services of food technologists are needed for microbiological evaluations, special formulations, interpretations of governmental food regulations, and planning for quality control within a multi-unit company, especially where the operation includes a manufacturing commissary. In smaller operations, it would be beneficial to retain the services of a food technologist or independent laboratory on a call or *per diem* arrangement, depending on the scope and intensity of the program.

The Era of Efficiency Foodservice

With the advent and phenomenal growth of foodservice units handling and featuring convenience or pre-prepared foods, quality control assumes an added role, which is different from that in a conventional facility which converts its products from the raw to the finished state.

Where convenience products are prepared elsewhere and/or by other companies, there is no end-user control over their preparation or formulation, and tests must be performed to assure product consistency and expected quality. In addition, convenience food preparation, reconstituting, and heating involve techniques different from those used for traditional foods. Therefore, quality and consistent production are maintained by optimum equipment performance and exacting preparation techniques. This goal can be achieved only by a strong quality control program.

BASIC SEGMENTS OF A PROGRAM

The fundamental operational aspects of most feeding establishments are identical; though there are variations in volume, size, food preparation, and production, serving and sanitation are common to all foodservice units. However, differences will exist in the scope of a quality assurance program. The convenience food-oriented facility requires a more elaborate plan than the conventional restaurant.

The following are the basic suggested segments of an all-inclusive program.

(1) Purchasing
  (a) Prepurchasing: comparison shopping, price evaluation, quality grading, delivery efficiency, supplier reliability, and a continuing market survey to keep informed and abreast of all new developments
  (b) Establish specifications and formulations for each food and beverage item that will be purchased. Where U.S. Government Standards of Identity exist, they should be incorporated into each specification
  (c) Establish procedures for test panels and cooking tests
(2) Inspection of delivered products
  (a) Record temperature of the food, if frozen, and the condition and temperature of the refrigerated delivery truck
  (b) For fresh meat, poultry, and fish, inspect the truck for sanitary conditions. Inspect the packaging for signs of contamination. Inspect the product for visual signs of contamination and freshness

     (c)   For fresh fruits and vegetables apply the same procedure as for item (b)

     (d)   Run comparison tests to compare the delivered products with purchase specifications

     (e)   Product weight determination

     (f)   Product count determination

     (g)   Record pack date and code of products. Check coding to determine when the product was processed and packed

     (h)   Check canned merchandise for "swells" and dents

     (i)   Check label nonmenclature for conformity to labeling standards

(3)   Dry, freezer, and cooler storage

     (a)   Storage temperature evaluations

     (b)   Stock-rotating schedules

     (c)   Orderly stacking procedures

     (d)   Sanitation control

     (e)   Procedures for proper storage of leftover food

(4)   Food preparation and production

     (a)   Efficiency checks of all cooking equipment for timing, temperature, and physical condition

     (b)   Sanitation control to eliminate problems of off-flavors, off-tastes, and food spoilage

     (c)   Test quality of finished food, beverages, garnishing, and plating

     (d)   Control of warming and holding units to ensure against overcooked foods

     (e)   Update and review recipe cards and other data pertinent to the formulation and preparation of the food

     (f)   Ensure against overproduction

(5)   Warewashing control to assure that soap, grease, and soil residues are completely removed

(6)   Sanitation control for refuse collection and disposal area

(7)   Rodent and vermin control

(8)   Water quality determination and control

(9)   Review new procedures and methods that may pertain to food handling, production, and packaging

(10)   Review and disseminate local, state, and federal health codes and other regulations pertinent to the establishment

EXAMPLES OF QUALITY CONTROL PROJECTS

To acquaint the reader with the objectives and scope of the ensuing text, selected examples of quality control projects that are encountered within a foodservice establishment follow:

(1) Overcooking of poultry, meat, and fish may result in undesirable texture changes such as toughening, stringiness, or softening to the point where the products "fall apart."

(2) Dressings that are mixed with leafy vegetables long in advance of serving will cause the leaves to droop and the edges to darken.

(3) Adding milk to highly acidic foods will cause curdling.

(4) Bacteria growth is accelerated at temperatures between 45° and 140°F (7° and 60°C), especially if the foods are moist and nonacid.

(5) When thin and small slices of meat are fried and seared slowly, they may become burned and dried out due to a loss of moisture.

(6) Foods with incompatible flavors and odors, such as fish, potatoes, or chicken, should not be fried together or in the same frying medium.

(7) Temperature plays an important role in properly prepared deep fried foods. Low temperatures tend to increase the fat content, whereas temperatures above 385°F (196°C) accelerate fat breakdown.

(8) When meats are cooked, the degree of doneness may be properly checked by using an accurate thermometer designed for this purpose.

(9) Fish and other seafood that give off a decided "fishy" aroma characteristic of ammonia are not fresh and may have deteriorated.

(10) Aged eggs can be detected by an unnatural dark color and strong sulfury aroma.

(11) Overcooking and high heat will produce tough-textured eggs.

(12) Custards that are prepared rapidly by using "forced" or high heat will cause the eggs to curdle.

(13) Improper cooking of vegetables may create color changes and the loss of flavor and nutritive value.

(14) Objectionable changes occur in vegetables cooked in hard water. Texture is altered, resulting in an overly soft and spongy product. Color changes also develop, e.g., beets turn bluish-purple and cauliflower assumes a yellow hue.

(15) When preparing vegetables, select them for equal size to prevent over- or undercooking.

(16) To prevent disintegration or breakdown of sauces containing starch, the use of waxy maize or starches selectively modified for freezing should be considered.

(17) When oil and vinegar are added to salad greens, the oil should be added first so it will adhere to the surface of the leaves.

(18) When entrees are considered, the products used should have compatible tastes and flavors.

(19) Storage of pasteurized concentrated fruit juice above 35°F (1.7°C) for extended periods, or of canned juices at 70°F (21.1°C) or above for several months will create off-flavors and unpalatable products.

(20) Holding brewed coffee at 190°F (87°C) or above for extended periods will cause breakdown and decreased quality.

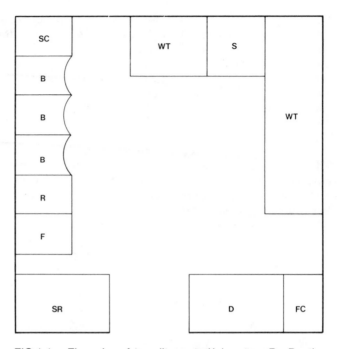

FIG.1.1.   Floor plan of a quality control laboratory. B—Booths for test panel. D—Combination desk and bookshelves. F—Freezer for sample storage. FC— Filing cabinet. R—Refrigerator for sample storage. S—Sink. SC—Storage cabinet. SR—Sample rack. WT—Worktables and/or laboratory benches with storage cabinets above and below the work surfaces.

LOCATION AND SPACE REQUIREMENTS FOR QUALITY CONTROL ACTIVITIES

The location of an appropriate area for quality control operations depends on several factors, such as type and size of the establishment, whether it is a single or multi-unit operation, and if it has a central commissary. The area devoted to quality control for a single unit facility requires consideration since space is usually limited and at a premium. A combination receiving and quality assurance office is feasible for a small-to-medium volume operation. The functions of both receiving and quality control can be handled by the same person. Usually the distance from the receiving section to the food preparation and production areas is small enough so that all activities may be performed without too much movement.

For larger installations or commissaries, a separate laboratory should be set up. The ideal location of such a laboratory would be between the storage areas and the preparation and production centers. Multi-unit establishments without commissary facilities should place their quality control facilities in or near the executive headquarters or purchasing and operations department.

The area needed is minimal unless a full laboratory program is to be instituted, including product evaluation, taste panels, spoilage studies, product development, and formulation, in addition to routine quality control work. For routine tests an area measuring 8 × 8 ft is ample. This will allow sufficient space to install the following equipment: small desk and chair, filing cabinet, bookcase, and a laboratory bench or worktable with stainless steel top 8 ft long and including a stainless steel sink. Cabinets should be installed under and over the counter area (see Fig. 1.1).

2

Implementation of a Quality Control Program

BASIC TOOLS FOR QUALITY DETERMINATION

The tools, apparatus, and equipment required to perform practical and reliable quality testing are basic and uncomplicated. Intensive training is not necessary to use them in a proper and constructive manner. Although the sophisticated testing equipment which is commercially available will yield results of high precision and accuracy, it is not required for the routine tests and simplified methods of evaluation common in foodservice operations.

If a program encompasses a wide range of control functions, including qualitative, quantitative, microbiological, and nutritional analyses, a fully outfitted laboratory is mandatory. However, for the simple routine evaluations that are the subject of this book, the following tools are considered to be ample and suitable: (1) human senses; (2) scales; (3) thermometers; (4) hydrometers or a hand refractometer; (5) stopwatch and timers; (6) sieves; (7) water analysis kit; (8) portable fat analyzer; (9) triers; (10) standardized measuring containers, spoons, and scoops; (11) pH meter; (12) standardized pressure gauges; (13) electrical test meter; (14) microwave energy leak detector; (15) carbonated water pressure tester; (16) soft drink, syrup-water ratio tester; and (17) periodicals containing the latest regulations and specifications.

SENSORY EVALUATION OF FOODS AND BEVERAGES

Sensory Evaluation—The Key to Quality Control

Sensory evaluation has numerous applications within a foodservice center. It is considered to be the "key" to an effective quality control program. Without a basic understanding and working knowledge of this subject, a quality control activity cannot be of value. The following list indicates the points where the employment of sensory evaluation is applicable:

(1) Evaluating supplier's samples, and comparison shopping
(2) Evaluating deliveries against specifications
(3) Checking flavor and taste deterioration resulting from prolonged storage
(4) Checking for superficial signs of food spoilage
(5) Checking and taste characteristics of deep fry fat
(6) Checking the degree of doneness from microwave oven preparations and from other equipment
(7) Checking the effects of food additives, such as spices, herbs, and garnishes
(8) Checking sauces and gravies
(9) Checking complaints
(10) Checking and investigating reasons for off-flavors and off-tastes
(11) Checking the taste and flavor of beverages, such as coffee and soft drinks

Development of Sensory Tests

Odor and taste play an important and almost indispensable role in the foodservice industry. The self-development of sensory determinations can be a long and arduous task. Without the full maturity and realization of this growth, foodservice personnel lack an essential working tool. Those who have mastered the culinary arts have done so because they have also mastered the art of precise identification of odors and tastes and have applied this knowledge to their craft.

Proper handling of foods and beverages of all categories requires a full understanding of one's smell and taste functions. Application of these senses will not only help to maintain the uniformity of the product but will forestall customers' complaints, and will make it easier to understand complaints if they arise. The economic aspects of our sophisticated food establishments make it mandatory to continually sustain and improve quality, thus maintaining and increasing both consumer satisfaction and profits.

Sensory perception is complex. It involves the senses of taste, smell, touch, and sight. According to experiments carried on by Georg von Békésy in 1964, hearing, the fifth sense, is also involved in combination with the other four. An important factor that contributes to customer dissatisfaction is excessive noise. Noise levels have a decided bearing on the customer's mood, so that high-quality food can be mentally downgraded if the decibel level is too high. However, for our purposes we shall consider only the senses of taste and smell, in conjunction with touch and sight, as the tools of self-evaluation.

The delicacy and receptivity of the human senses are yet to be fully duplicated by modern scientific means. Scientific instruments such as the gas chromatograph and mass spectrometer are being used successfully to identify and classify the chemical structure of many odors. However, the mechanisms of sensory perception within the human body are still considered to be the most sensitive and precise. Humans are able to identify and differentiate among odor-producing substances in concentrations as low as 1 part per billion. The average person can identify about 2000 odors and tastes, the trained technician, 5000 or more.

Proficiency in sensory evaluation is the result of habit and prolonged training. This can best be understood by tracing a sensory effect from source to recognition. Electrical impulses are transmitted from the point of reception to a central nerve area. Finally, it is supposed that, from this nerve center, the impulse is relayed to the brain, where the sensation is correlated and defined.

This physical process sets up within the body a conscious realization of the sensory event. In many instances a person cannot verbally define smell or taste, especially if it is a new experience. In such cases a mental comparison must be made to connect the sensation with a previous experience. For example, orange juice has its own characteristic flavor, and a mental imprint was probably developed in us during childhood. However, if the orange juice turns rancid, obliterating its true character, the mental imprint would be reclassified to a sensation of sourness or rancidity.

Various adjunct factors have an important effect on sensory evaluation. Sex, age, locality, ethnic groupings, income, and physiological and psychological influences all have a bearing on the process of sensory registration. Likes and dislikes play a major role in sensory orientation. Foodservice personnel whose childhood experiences led to a like or dislike of a certain food often reflect the same attitudes in adulthood. As an example, those restaurant managers who liked and enjoyed their own coffee were found to maintain the highest efficiency of coffee service, both in coffee brewing and sanitation.

Mechanisms of Sensory Perception

There is no chronological order in which a person reacts to a sensory experience. Since we are exploring the interplay of sight, touch, smell, and taste as determining evaluators, the sense that comes into action first is of little importance. It all depends on the substance under investigation.

Smell. The nose is the center of odor perception. A few molecules of an odor-producing substance will excite this organ sufficiently to yield a determination with speed and precision.

When we breathe or sniff, the air enters through our nostrils, which are separated by a thin wall of cartilage and bone, known as the septum. The air passes from the lower nostrils up through the two tunnels or nasal passages and down to the region of the throat.

Each nasal passage is lined with soft, moist, mucous membranes covered with fine hairs called cilia. The hairs act as an air filter. Tiny blood vessels located in the nasal passages warm the incoming air, increasing the volatility of odor-producing substances so that finer dispersion of the molecules results.

The area controlling the sense of smell is located in the highest part of the nasal cavity. This section is known as the olfactory bulb tract, a moist mucous membrane containing a large number of nerve fibers. The olfactory nerve connects with the olfactory lobe on the lower surface of the front part of the brain. This part of the brain registers and classifies incoming odor sensations.

Although the olfactory tract is the center of odor detection, the entire nasal cavity comes into play as an evaluator. The lower part of the nose perceives tactile sensations, such as cold, heat, and pain, and reacts vigorously to some substances (e.g., pepper) having unusual tactile properties.

Taste.   The cavity of the mouth, which contains the tongue, can be considered as the focal point for flavor or taste perception. Flavor is a complex sensation, encompassing the senses of taste and smell, together with the sense of touch.

The taste response is primarily sensed on the tongue. Items which are analyzed for taste must be in a moist state. If ingested dry, the saliva, acting as a diluent, suspends or dissolves them for sensory action. This sensory action is induced on receptors known as taste buds.

The function of the taste buds registers four sensations: sweet, salty, sour, and bitter. The sense of touch can act as an intensifier or limiter to the four basic sensations. Temperature gradients have a direct relationship to the resulting sensation. The sense of touch influences all areas of the mouth and throat. Figure 2.1, a diagram of the tongue, shows the location of the taste bud receptors for saltiness, bitterness, acidity, and sweetness.

The boundary or interaction surfaces bridge the taste sensations so that subtle stimuli result. However, unless the odor-producing areas are activated in combination, the complete sensory response will fall short of a true identification. Since flavor or taste is the nonvolatile portion of the item under identification, the volatile portion, even though it is not sniffed directly into the nasal cavity, will permeate into it through connecting channels located at the rear of the mouth (Fig. 2.2).

Touch (Feeling).   The sense of touch can be described as the threshold of pain. This response includes categories of temperature variation, texture, and sensations of burning or bite produced by spices or condiments.

The role of touch in odor and flavor identification is extremely important, since these senses are modified or intensified by it so that the final determination can be altered or misinterpreted.

The entire mouth cavity as well as the lower nasal cavity is affected by touch. Carbonated beverages, if tested when too cold (below 40°F, 4.44°C) will prevent subtle flavor detections. Coffee, if too hot (above 140°F, 60°C) or too cold, does not display its true and accustomed character. The acid-

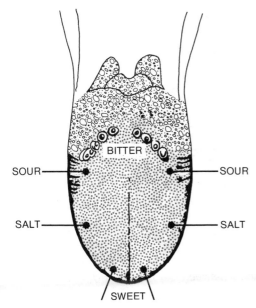

SOUR

SOUR

SALT

SALT

BITTER

SWEET

FIG. 2.1.   Areas of the tongue
that are sensitive to the four taste
sensations.
From Thorner and Herzberg (1979).

indicating area of the tongue will not give a true taste of sourness if the
temperature of a food is above 100°F (39°C).

If the food texture changes from its expected normal sensation, the difference is usually detected. The quality is downgraded and the consumer
becomes dissatisfied. Texture embodies such sensations as firmness, softness, juiciness, chewiness, and sandiness. Customer comments denoting
dissatisfaction may include such descriptive terms as tough, undercooked,
mushy, precast like iron, gristly, or hardtack.

Sight.   The sense of sight is useful in the evaluation of a number of
characteristics of the product being tested.

Color, density, texture, sanitation, and deterioration can be observed
visually before application of the senses of smell and taste. Spoilage can
often be pinpointed by the observation of mold formation.

The color of the food will influence quality determination and customer
reaction. Proper shape, natural color, particle size, visual consistency, and
sanitation are some of the factors influencing quality.

Techniques of Sensory Detection

Methods of sensory detection vary from person to person. However, several fundamental rules must be followed:

Concentration followed by repeated application is recommended, especially if the item under test is a new taste experience. Regardless of personal

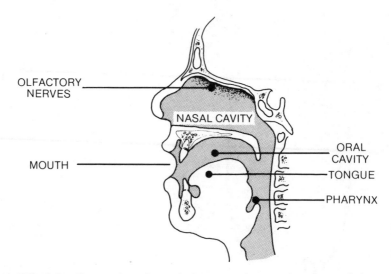

OLFACTORY
NERVES

NASAL CAVITY

MOUTH

ORAL
CAVITY
TONGUE
PHARYNX

FIG. 2.2.   Connecting channels between the nasal cavity and the
mouth.
From Thorner and Herzberg (1979).

likes or dislikes in the taste or odor of a certain food, each experience should
be concentrated upon so that an indelible imprint of its sensory character is
made.

Visual Observations (Appearance).   As a first step, the sample should be
observed for color, density, or viscosity, and visual evidence of spoilage.
Sanitary conditions should also be noted, such as cleanness of dishes and
dispensers.

Smelling Techniques (Aroma, Odor).   As indicated previously, flavor is
a combination of smell and taste. The smell or odor character is established
first, since this sense is the keener of the two, and will assure a more positive
as well as a speedier identification.

A deep sniff at short intervals using both nostrils is advisable. If possible,
the sniffing should be done with the mouth open, waving the sample from
the region of the nostrils to the mouth. This procedure will permit full
penetration of the volatile material into the entire sensory area, and will
ensure full coverage of the olfactory section of the upper nasal cavity. The
surrounding air should be still and free from interfering aromas.

If a comparison of similar substances is being made, a whiff of one sample,
followed by a whiff of the other (the sequence being repeated several times)
should be sufficient for positive identification. If a control sample is used,
this should be analyzed first, followed by the unknown.

Odor determination of dry substances can be made by first blowing on the sample with moist breath. The aroma of the dry material can then be studied since its volatiles will be released.

Tasting Techniques. Prior to the actual testing, an inexperienced taster should perform a series of examinations using solutions having the four basic tastes. Dilute solutions of pure substances exhibiting the effects of sweetness, sourness, bitterness, and saltiness should be prepared. As each solution is tested, a mental note should be made of the reaction and the location of the stimulus on the tongue.

Before actual testing, the mouth should be rinsed with warm water. This preliminary step will freshen the mouth cavity and prepare the taste buds for sharper perception.

The sample should be drawn into the mouth with a "slurp" or whirling action, so that all areas of the cavity are moistened. Immediately after the mouth is fully moistened and the sense registered, the liquid must be expelled. If the impression was not clear, a second or third test should be made. Between tests of the same or different substances, the mouth should be flushed with warm water.

The sense of touch plays an important role in taste evaluation. The temperature of the material must be noted and, if not in the proper range, it must be adjusted and controlled to meet its physical character.

Taste Panels

It is not unusual to find one person with the responsibility of selecting brands of food using his own personal likes or dislikes as the sole indicator. This system may once have been feasible for small restaurants or where a chef, by tradition, had the full authority to direct purchasing and preparation functions. However, if the scheme is used for a prepared food operation, it may lead to consumer dissatisfaction. Regardless of the size of restaurant, a taste panel consisting of three or more people should have the authority to make the necessary selections.

The subject of taste panel procedures, programming, and test evaluations is a broad one. Many procedures and methods of scoring are used. Professional tasters are employed in a number of industries, e.g., the coffee, tea, wine, and liquor industries. Federal and state agencies use highly trained personnel to test such products as butter and cheese. Occasionally, consumer panels are called upon to provide an insight into customer preferences for particular products.

Many companies operate taste panel laboratories provided with separate booths to isolate the panel members. Isolation prevents interaction, either by facial expression or conversation. Subdued or colored lights may be installed so that food color will not affect the final decision. Test or scoring reports have a wide range of formats. Some use a numerical ranking scale known as a *hedonic scale.* Descriptive terms such as *like definitely, like mildly, neither like nor dislike, dislike mildly*, and *dislike definitely* are frequently employed. The taster checks his opinion for each sample and may make additional comments. The terms are given number rankings, such as 5 for *like definitely*, down to 1 for *dislike definitely*. When the forms are completed, the results are averaged.

The *triangle* procedure test is another method that can be used when two samples are submitted for evaluation. This is practical for two- or three-member panel groups and can be readily adapted to a convenience food program. The samples are submitted to each panel member. Two samples are identical and one different. Each sample is coded and all are plated in the same way. The taster is asked to select the sample that is different. The panelist may be asked to indicate the samples or sample he prefers.

Taste testing may be exhausting, resulting in a gradual dulling of perception. For some highly flavored products, the limit of tasting endurance is about 5 to 6 samples. The time of day, ambient conditions, and the physical condition of the panelist should be taken into consideration when scores are evaluated. Professional panelists are most proficient during the early part of the morning.

Evaluation of Complaints

Perhaps the most difficult evaluation that foodservice personnel have to make are those related to complaints. Coping with customer complaints is considered an art. To understand customer reaction, and to judge the value of superficial descriptive statements, such as *no good, poor, doesn't taste right, lousy, not bad, not good,* and *can be better,* is frustrating and requires patience and knowledge of human reactions.

Complaints can be separated into three categories: (1) psychological, (2) physiological, and (3) pressure or business competitive patterns.

Psychological complaints are those which arise from the sensory effects of the product and involve the senses of touch, smell, sight, and taste. In this category, criticism may arise from the mode of service, incorrect temperature of the food, color or shade of the product, and texture (mouth feel). For example, a customer may be accustomed to a cup of coffee with cream added, exhibiting a straw-like color. If, for some reason, the color is darker or lighter than usual, a complaint may be lodged that the beverage is "poor" or "just not good."

Various food combinations which are not compatible will cause distressing reactions. Examples of this are maple syrup and coffee, a combination that causes a bitter aftertaste, and onions which will alter the flavor of coffee. Condiments and relishes can also create abnormal reactions.

Physiological complaints are those which arise from the physical condition or health of the customer. The customer may have a hangover, upset stomach, common cold, or other ailment which will completely change his typical sensory reaction. Foods or beverages consumed under these conditions will have an unusual taste, which may result in unmerited complaints.

Pressure or business competitive pattern complaints are annoying because they indicate problems which cannot be rationally traced or solved. These are an outgrowth of unethical business practices among vendors (suppliers) for the sole purpose of creating a beneficial atmosphere for their sales efforts. This is a form of business sabotage. Representatives or agents are sent to establishments to make unfounded complaints about a food or beverage. Tracing the source of complaints originating under this scheme can be difficult. However, if management has confidence in its ability to evaluate complaints through the process of sensory determination, then a solution becomes an easy matter.

Frequency of complaints must also be taken into consideration. If there is an abnormal number within a short period, a full investigation of possible causes must be made. Although there are no statistics available on this subject, a "rule of thumb" is that complaints should not exceed 1% of the average patronage.

Scales

Scales are manufactured in a variety of models, shapes, and capacities. Their uses are unlimited, not only for quality assurance programs, but for portion control, receiving, and production. Weighing devices have been used for food preparation since biblical times. They are a basic tool and, together with thermometers and timers, are essential for preparation and quality assurance.

Weighing devices are available to fill all needs, such as portion control scales, floor scales, hanging platform scales, built-in scales, table- or countertop devices and built-in conveyor or track units. Capacities range from 1 gram to several tons. There are types which print the weight on a tape and may be connected to computers for automatic portioning. Others register weight on a direct-reading dial, cast a magnified image of the weight, or indicate the reading by sliding a weight along a beam.

Scale Characteristics. Technical developments have provided the means of determining weight accurately, quickly, and simply. An association of scale manufacturers instructs the industry in the proper use and maintenance of weighing devices. Selecting scale equipment can become a burdensome and frustrating task because of the number of models on the market.

Good scales, regardless of capacity, are expensive. It is not advisable to purchase cheap weighing equipment. Scales can last indefinitely if they are used and maintained properly. In the long run, a few scales of high quality will prove more advantageous and less expensive than many inexpensive ones. A useful weighing device should have the following features: compactness, rust resistance, ease of cleaning and adjustment, durability, accuracy, quick readability, prompt damping action for speedy weighing, tare reset device, positive protection of parts from dirt and grease, and leveling adjustment for uneven surfaces. If necessary, they may be specified to be tamperproof and have built-in illumination.

Scale Location.   Scales should be placed in strategic locations so that they are a useful part of a forward flow system. They should not be installed in remote areas, since they are used frequently. Convenience food systems require the services of a number of portion control scales to check the weights of incoming products and to monitor production at various locations, including assembly and preparation areas. Quality cooking by microwave ovens can only be accomplished if the weight of the product is determined beforehand and the time cycle set accordingly. Subsequent weighing is then necessary to check the consistency of each portion. If changes in weight are observed, the cooking cycle must be increased or decreased. Scales have proved invaluable as a means of detecting weight shortages of delivered merchandise. They can also be used to determine shrinkage losses due to prolonged freezer storage, and to assist in securing an accurate inventory and cost-control schedule.

Portion control scales of various capacities are recommended for quality control tests, formulations, and portioning. Figure 2.3 shows one type of portion control weighing device. This scale has a 2 lb adjustable weight

FIG. 2.3.   Portion control scale, 5 lb capacity.
Courtesy of the Pelouze Scale Company.

capacity in ¼ oz increments. The knobs located at the center of the scale can be rotated to zero to compensate for the weight of a plate or platter. Similar models are available for dietetic control portions. These register in grams and have a 500 to 1000 g capacity with 1 g accuracy. Other portion control devices are available that register under- or overweight tolerances by means of a pointer encased in an upright housing. The weight is adjusted by means of a beam graduated in ¼ oz. For additional capacity, 1 or 2 lb weights are supplied for use as counterweights.

Scale Maintenance and Sanitation.   Scales that are dirty, dusty, or encrusted with grease and soot will not give accurate results. Scales should be kept clean and dry. A daily cleaning schedule is advisable to avoid buildup of foreign matter. Scales that are sealed require that all exterior surfaces and parts be cleaned. Those with exposed parts must be cleaned carefully, so that knife edges and other sensitive mechanisms are not disturbed. Never use force or pressure when cleaning or adjusting a scale. This may cause unrepairable damage and inaccurate results. Cleaning should be done with lint-free cloth and mild detergent solution. A low-pressure dry air hose can be used both for removing dust and drying.

It is recommended that a set of weights be purchased to check the accuracy of all scales. The test for accuracy should be performed monthly. Scales that have adjustable compensating or balancing devices can then be reset according to the inaccuracy indicated by the check weights. These check weights should be kept separately and stored in a dustproof box. Each scale should be tagged and the test date recorded.

Scale Requirements.   It is difficult to establish a plan detailing the number of weighing devices that are required. A fast food, portion control, and convenience food establishment may need many small scales and only 1 or 2 larger scales for receiving. For a medium-size operation the following scales may be required:

(1)   Receiving area: one platform scale of 500 or 1000 lb capacity and one counter scale of 50 lb capacity

(2)   Receiving office and/or quality control section: three portion control scales of 2, 5, and 10 lb capacity

(3)   Storage areas: one counter scale of 25 lb capacity and one platform scale of 500 lb capacity

(4)   Assembly: one counter scale of 25 lb capacity and several portion control scales

(5)   Preparation and garnishing section: one counter scale of 25 lb capacity and several portion control scales, such as one 32 oz by ¼ oz capacity and one 5 lb by ¼ oz capacity; one bean scale calibrated in grams, equipped with a pan to accommodate an 8 in. diameter sieve (an effective, inexpensive model is the Harvard Trip Balance single beam scale)

Thermometers

One of the basic tools used in the foodservice industry is a temperature measuring device or thermometer. Almost every function within a food serving establishment, regardless of size or mode of operation, is dependent on a thermometer. The demands of the culinary arts make it mandatory that temperatures be known, set, and held at required levels. Beverages (hot or cold), refrigerators, dishwashing operations, deep fryers, griddles, and storage facilities are but a few of the many areas where accurate temperatures must be maintained. Unfortunately, temperature-measuring devices are often taken for granted, and little thought is given to the possibility of inaccuracy. Unless an appreciation is developed for the applications, limitations, and accuracy of thermometers, inconsistent and erroneous readings will occur.

Testing for Accuracy.   One of the first rules governing thermometer application is accuracy. A new thermometer is not necessarily accurate. Both old and new instruments require periodic checks for accuracy. If an instrument is improperly handled, the readings will be affected.

Testing thermometer accuracy involves the use of elaborate equipment, such as a constant temperature liquid bath in which the device is suspended for a period of time. Although this method is highly accurate, it is unnecessary for the foodservice thermometer.

The simplest method is to check one instrument against another. The thermometer used in this procedure is a high-accuracy precalibrated bimetallic device. This thermometer should only be used for testing and, properly handled, will retain its accuracy indefinitely.

Another procedure which can be followed if the bimetallic thermometer is not available is the use of boiling water. However, there are limitations to this method. Even though pure water has a boiling point of 212°F (100°C) at standard pressure, altitude and impurities can alter this temperature.

Errors Caused by Improper Reading or Placement.   Errors of incorrect reading can occur, especially when the dial is small or the numbers have been rubbed off the glass column. Holding the instrument so that the eye is directly in line with the scale will reduce reading errors. Thermometers must also be placed correctly. Stems should be immersed sufficiently so that the entire bulb is completely covered. Time is an important factor. Readings cannot be rushed, as it takes time for the instrument to reach its maximum registration. There is no hard-and-fast rule to apply to the time factor; experience is the best guide.

Types of Thermometers.   (1) Those with a mercury or fluid column should be provided with the metal protecting case. Typical overall length is 6 in. (15 cm).

(2) The bimetallic, all-metal type, utilizes a precision bimetal helix which

responds quickly to changes in temperature. The coil is located in the end of the stem. Changes in temperature cause a rotary action of the helix, turning a shaft on which a pointer is mounted (Fig. 2.4).

(3) The cup-type measures the temperature of liquids in tanks, barrels, and similar vessels. The thermometer is lowered into the liquid, allowed to remain for about 1 min, and then withdrawn. The cup will bring up a small amount of fluid which prevents the reading from changing before it is observed.

Checking Thermostats and Built-in Thermometers.   In various sections of this book, thermometer applications are discussed and methods of reading the internal temperature of frozen foods are described. Accuracy testing of thermostats installed on such equipment as deep fryers, steam-pressure cookers, and other units containing these devices is essential to quality production. Tests of this sort should be put on a weekly schedule and records kept each time a test is performed. Built-in thermometers found on coffee brewers and refrigerators also require periodic checks. Many of these have a metallic stem or bulb; if dirt, grease, or salts resulting from hard water become encrusted on the stem, temperature accuracy will diminish.

Suggested Thermometer Requirements.   (1) Accurately calibrated thermometers are required to check the accuracy of those instruments employed for routine tests. One of each of the following is suggested: −30° to +125°F (−34.4° to 52°C), 0° to +230°F (−17.8° to 112°C), +20° to +500°F (−6.7° to 260°C). These should be long-stem mercury-filled devices. They should be used only for calibrating and should be stored in a safe place when not in use.

(2) For routine temperature readings the following are recommended: three thermometers −30° to +125°F (−34.4° to 52°C) for recording frozen food cooler storage temperatures; for frozen foods, metal-stem thermometers are needed to penetrate the product and to record its internal temperatures; three 0° to +230°F (−17.8° to 110°C) thermometers for routine check-

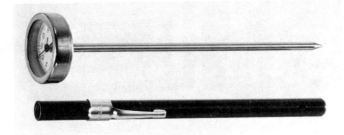

FIG. 2.4.   Bimetallic thermometer.
Courtesy of the Cooper Thermometer Company.

ing of coffee brew water and holding temperatures of foods stored in cabinets and steam tables; two deep fat thermometers, +20° to +500°F (−6.6° to 260°C); and a surface-activated pyrometer, used for checking griddle temperatures. Thermometers should be of high quality. The style is not important as long as they are accurate and easily read.

Figure 2.5 illustrates a temperature check kit designed for the foodservice industry.

Refractometers

Another instrument of value to the foodservice operator is the Abbe refractometer. With it, one can determine the percentage of sugar in syrup, total solids in juice products, and the purity of fats and oils used in food preparation.

The Abbe refractometer is comprised of two glass prisms between which the refractive index represents a measure of the "bending" or refraction of light as it passes through a fluid that is placed between the glass prisms. Under standard conditions of temperature and pressure, the refractive index will vary with concentration.

The principle of refraction, or bending of light, can be demonstrated by placing a pencil in a glass of water. When the glass is viewed from the side, the pencil appears to be broken at the surface of the water. This illusion is

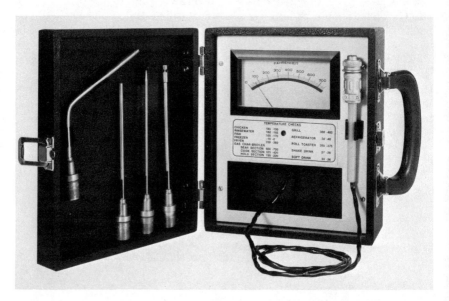

FIG. 2.5.   Temperature meter kit designed for the foodservice industry, Model 400.
Courtesy of Food Automation-Service Techniques, Inc.

caused by the fact that light travels at different speeds through the water and the air above the water.

The Abbe refractometer is composed of two glass prisms between which the sample is placed, a telescope for observing the extent of the refraction, and a scale on which the refractive index is read. Some refractometers also have a scale calibrated in sugar percentage, which saves the operator the time of converting refractive index to percentage of sugar.

The cost of a standard Abbe refractometer prevents its widespread use in foodservice establishments. However, a modified Abbe refractometer, called a hand refractometer, is inexpensive and within the budget of most. It is very simple to use and is sufficiently accurate for foodservice operations.

The hand refractometer consists of a prism, a prism cover, and a telescope with a built-in scale. The sample to be tested is placed on the prism and the cover is closed (Fig. 2.6). The instrument is held toward the light and the percentage sucrose (Brix) is read directly from a scale built into the instrument. Since the hand refractometer is not accurate over a wide range, four models are necessary to cover the complete range, 0–32%, 28–62%, 45–82%, and 58–92% sucrose.

FIG. 2.6. Hand refractometer with focusable eyepiece. Sample is placed on prism. Cover is shown closed. Scale reads directly in % sucrose.
Courtesy of Bausch & Lomb, Inc.

Using a refractometer and appropriate tables, the foodservice operator is able to rapidly determine the percentage of sugar in fountain syrups, maple syrup, and honey. The sugar content in premix and postmix carbonated beverages can also be checked to ascertain if dispensing equipment is operating properly. One quality factor of tomato products is total solids content, and this can also be measured with a refractometer. A foodservice operator who uses corn oil for salads can determine with this instrument if the oil is pure. In the field, crop maturity can be determined with a hand refractometer.

Hydrometers

A hydrometer is a weighted spindle with a graduated neck that floats in a liquid at a height related to the density of the liquid. The neck contains a numerical scale from which the measurement is read. This scale gives the percentage of soluble solids in the liquid. Hydrometers are available to measure many different solutions by various systems, such as Brix, Baumé, Twaddle, API, and Salimeter (Fig. 2.7).

Brix Hydrometer. The Brix hydrometer is used to measure the percentage of sugar by weight at a specified temperature. This device will produce the same results as a refractometer. The higher the Brix value, the greater the sugar concentration in the liquid. Hydrometers of this type are helpful in determining the density of fruit syrups and juices and the operating

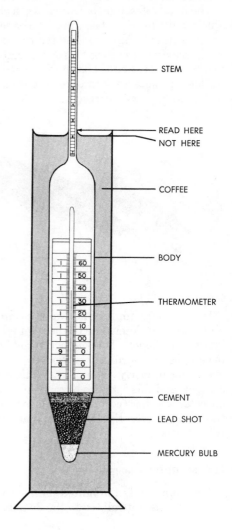

FIG. 2.7.   Example of a hydrometer.
Courtesy of Coffee Brewing Center.

efficiency of postmix soda and juice dispensers. Two of each of the following are recommended: scale reading 0° to 12° Brix, 9° to 21° Brix, and 0° to 35° Brix.

Readings on hydrometers, other than those used for coffee, are expressed in degrees. These are merely points of reference on an arbitrary scale, adopted to obtain uniformity of results. Two methods are employed: the Baumé and Brix. Bottlers of soft drinks express their results in degrees Baumé when measuring syrups. Soft drinks, juices, and light syrups are measured in terms of percentage sugar. For this purpose the Brix hydrometer is used, since 1 Brix degree is equal to 1% sugar by weight. Although refractometers can be used for the same purpose, they are expensive and are not always available.

A limitation on the use of hydrometers is temperature. The instrument is accurate only at the single temperature for which it has been designed. If the temperature varies more than a few degrees above or below the standard reading, errors will occur in the results. For this reason a temperature correction table has been developed (Table 2.1). This table will correct readings on instruments standardized at 68°F (20°C).

TABLE 2.1. Temperature Corrections to Readings of Brix Hydrometers Standardized at 68°F (20°C)

Temperatures		Observed Percentage of Sugar (°Brix)								
(°F)	(°C)	0	5	10	20	30	40	50	60	70
					Subtract					
32	0	0.30	0.49	0.65	0.89	1.08	1.24	1.37	1.44	1.49
41	5	0.36	0.47	0.56	0.73	0.86	0.97	1.05	1.10	1.14
50	10	0.32	0.38	0.43	0.52	0.60	0.67	0.72	0.75	0.77
59	15	0.20	0.22	0.24	0.28	0.32	0.34	0.36	0.38	0.39
68	20				No correction					
					Add					
77	25	0.27	0.28	0.30	0.32	0.35	0.38	0.39	0.39	0.40
86	30	0.61	0.62	0.63	0.68	0.73	0.78	0.79	0.80	0.81
95	35	0.99	1.01	1.02	1.10	1.16	1.20	1.22	1.23	1.22
104	40	1.42	1.45	1.47	1.54	1.60	1.64	1.65	1.66	1.65
113	45	1.91	1.94	1.96	2.03	2.07	2.10	2.10	2.10	2.08
122	50	2.46	2.48	2.50	2.56	2.58	2.59	2.58	2.56	2.52
131	55	3.05	3.07	3.09	3.12	3.12	3.10	3.07	3.03	2.97
140	60	3.69	3.72	3.73	3.72	3.67	3.62	3.57	3.50	3.43

Source: Tressler and Nelson (1980).

Directions for Using a Hydrometer.   The equipment needed for the measurement is: (1) Brix hydrometer, (2) glass cylinder, (3) thermometer (reading to 212°F, 100°C), and (4) several clean absorbent towels. Handle these pieces of equipment with extreme care to prevent breakage. They must also be kept clean. Fill the cylinder to the engraved line above the diamond with warm water containing a small amount of detergent and suspend the hydrometer in the solution. Force the hydrometer down into the solution by pushing gently on the top of the hydrometer stem. Remove pressure and let hydrometer rise. Repeat several times. Holding the hydrometer only at the very top, remove it from the solution. Rinse it thoroughly under warm, but not hot, running water. Dry with a clean absorbent towel. Do not touch the body of the hydrometer or any part of the stem except the top. Lay it down gently on a clean towel.

Pour the detergent solution from the cylinder. Rinse it out thoroughly with warm water.

The thermometer stem should be washed and rinsed also.

Now make sure the sample to be tested is well mixed.

Fill the hydrometer cylinder with the sample, then pour it out. This removes any traces of material that might affect the measurment.

Fill the cylinder with the sample to the engraved mark. Insert the hydrometer.

Check the cylinder to make sure it is standing on a level surface and that the hydrometer is floating without touching the walls of the cylinder.

Add more liquid until it fills the cylinder exactly to the brim.

Check the body and submerged portion of the stem to see whether any small bubbles are adhering to them. If any are seen, the hydrometer must be removed and wiped with a clean towel, and again lowered gently into the liquid.

After the hydrometer has been in the sample for at least 2 min, gently push it down into the cylinder nearly to the bottom and allow it to rise. Repeat this once or twice. On the last rise, stop the bobbing motion of the hydrometer with a finger. Read as rapidly as possible after the hydrometer stops. Precise reading, which is essential, comes only after much practice.

Notice that the liquid is drawn up slightly around the stem. Take the reading where the liquid meets the stem, not at the level of the liquid away from the stem. (Refer to Fig. 2.7.)

Immediately after taking the hydrometer reading, insert the thermometer and read it. Record both readings. (First reading.)

Mix the sample again and bring the hydrometer to a rest away from the walls of the cylinder. Take another density and temperature reading.

Record both readings. (Second reading.)

Repeat for a third reading.

Remove hydrometer, rinse it off, dry it, and lay it on the towel.

If other samples are to be tested, pour out the one already in the cylinder and rinse it out with the next sample. Proceed as before.

Average the three readings (hydrometer and temperature). Make a temperature correction by referring to Table 2.1. Add or subtract the figure found in the table. For example:

Average of 3 readings	20.00°	Brix at 86°F (30°C)
Add correction factor (Table 2.1)	0.68	
Percentage of sugar at 68°F (20°C)	20.68°	Brix

The FDA has designated four categories of syrup densities to be used for fruit products and sweet potatoes. Each category is determined by measuring the degree Brix of the syrup:

Extra heavy syrup means that a syrup tests at least 25°, but not more than 40° Brix.

Heavy syrup means that the syrup tests at least 21°, but less than 25° Brix.

Light syrup means that the syrup tests at least 16°, but less than 21° Brix.

Slightly sweetened water means that the syrup tests less than 16° Brix.

Although the categories are the same, the Brix scales for the syrups of various products differ. The examples shown apply to the syrup of canned apricots. USDA Quality Grade Standards designate the liquid media and Brix measurements for the product.

FIG. 2.8.   Solid state timer designed for precise control of cooking time, Model 20-99.
Courtesy of Food Automation-Service Techniques, Inc.

Stopwatches and Timers

Stopwatches and timers are essential for checking the timing cycle of equipment. Most equipment used for fast food preparation has built-in timing devices which require constant checking to assure accuracy. Microwave cooking, for example, depends on precise time cycles for the proper degree of doneness. It is not advisable to check automatic timers with an ordinary wrist watch, especially when the cycle is less than 1 min. Stopwatches are available that are graduated in 1/5 sec, 1/10 sec, and 1/100 min. A timer graduated in 1/5 sec is sufficient. Interval timers with an alarm are useful for checking longer cooking cycles. Figure 2.8 shows a preprogrammed product key timer for fast food operations.

Sieves

Sieves are required to determine drained weight. They are employed in USDA and FDA specification evaluations. Several sieves are required: two U.S. Standard No. 8 screens, one of 8 in. diameter, and one of 12 in. diameter. A No. 2 mesh screen is necessary for checking canned tomatoes. The 8 in. diameter sieve should be used for can sizes of No. 2½ or smaller, while the 12 in. diameter sieve is required for a No. 10 size can.

Water Analysis Test Kits

Water testing was once considered a task for analytical chemists. Although the chemist is still necessary for more sophisticated examinations, analysis kits are available that allow nontechnical personnel to make fast, simplified tests of water.

A number of manufacturers sell kits that cover a complete range of water conditions and analyses. Each test is devised for simplicity. Bottles of test solutions are numbered. By following the instruction sheet, numbered bottles are selected and used for each specific test procedure.

For example, the high and low range total hardness test employs three reagents: a buffer solution, a stable indicator, and a titrating solution. The latter is added drop by drop until a color change occurs. Water hardness is determined by counting the number of drops required to bring about the color change: 1 drop equals 1 ppm of hardness. See Chapter 13 for additional information concerning water quality and its effects on food and beverages. Figure 2.9 illustrates commercially available test kits.

Portable Fat Analyzer

A simplified method exists for measuring the fat percentage of ground beef. The Hobart fat percentage measuring kit is devised for simple, rapid, and accurate analyses (Fig. 2.10). Refer to Chapter 4 for an explanation of the operation of this analysis.

Triers and Specialty Sampling Devices

Depending on the scope and the extent of the organization and its relationship to the laboratory, it may be necessary to use a variety of sampling devices. One such specialty item is the trier, which is employed for sampling dried beans, spices, and green coffee from burlap shipping bags. A trier is a pointed, tapered tool with a hollow handle. The point is necessary to pierce burlap bags of merchandise. By turning the trier slightly to the left and right the product flows into the hollow handle. The trier is then withdrawn and the sample removed.

Butter sampling is also performed by means of a trier. If tub butter is to be sampled, the instrument is inserted diagonally, taking a plug extending

FIG. 2.9.   Test kits for water analysis.
Courtesy of Ecologic Instrument Corp.

from one side at the top, through the center, to the opposite side at the bottom. Three cores are usually taken. A butter trier is shaped in a true arc of a circle. In sampling pound print butter, two entire quarters, diagonally opposite each other, are taken.

Dry milk products and cheeses are also sampled by the use of specially designed triers.

Standardized Measuring Containers, Spoons, and Scoops

These tools are available in many sizes and are accurately manufactured and standardized to fit the needs of precise measurements of liquids and powders. They are used to sample incoming merchandise, especially for formulations and recipe development. See the Appendix for direct-reading tables for adjusting the yield of a recipe, with ingredient amounts given in weights and volumes.

FIG. 2.10.   Fat percentage measuring kit.
*Courtesy of the Hobart Manu-
facturing Company.*

pH Meters

An important factor in quality control is pH. Such measurements are used to determine the degree of acidity or alkalinity of a substance. The pH values are numbered from 0 to 14. Number 7 is the neutral point, the value of pure water. All pH readings below 7 indicate acidity, whereas those above 7 indicate alkalinity. The lower the number below 7, the greater is the acidity; the higher the number above 7, the greater the alkalinity.

Each number above or below 7 is divided into tenths. Small differentials in pH can indicate major differences in the degree of acidity or alkalinity of a substance. For example, a pH reading of 5.0 is 100 times more acidic than pure water at pH 7.0 (neutral point). A pH reading of 3.0 is 10,000 times more acidic than pure water at pH 7.0. Acidic pH values are indices of hydrogen ion (H^+) concentration, and alkaline pH values of hydroxyl ion (OH^-) concentration.

A table of pH values of selected foods is located in Appendix A.4. Throughout the ensuing text, examples of the use and effect of pH are shown and explained. A working knowledge of acidity or alkalinity of foods and beverages will help eliminate or control numerous storage, preparation, and spoilage problems.

The measurement of pH is relatively simple and can be done with instruments manufactured for this purpose (Fig. 2.11). Meters are obtainable from many sources and cover a wide range. A general purpose pH meter that registers values between 0 and 14 with an accuracy factor of 0.05 pH is recommended. Other instruments are available that are equipped with expanded scales, such as 0–7, 7–14, or limited to a smaller-scale segment within the acid or alkaline range.

Standardized Pressure Gauges

Standardized pressure gauges are useful for checking the accuracy of those installed on pressure cookers, steamers, and carbon dioxide cylinders.

Electrical Test Meter

A combination test meter that will measure voltage, resistance, and amperage is a useful instrument for checking the electrical current entering equipment. If a unit stops or malfunctions, an electrical tester will aid in pinpointing defects in motors and in tracing broken wires or loose connections.

Microwave Energy Leakage Detector

This instrument is necessary to determine radiation leakage from microwave ovens. Present Department of Health and Human Services regulations limit radiation leaks. An instrument of this type will detect leakage so that measures may be taken to correct the problem (Fig. 2.12).

Carbonated Water Pressure Tester

Determination of carbonation volumes can be made by a pressure tester designed for this purpose. The apparatus for this test is sold by the Bastian-

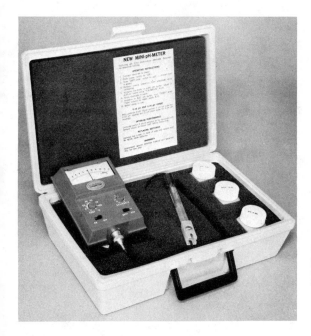

FIG. 2.11.   A portable pH meter.
Courtesy of Ecologic Instrument Corp.

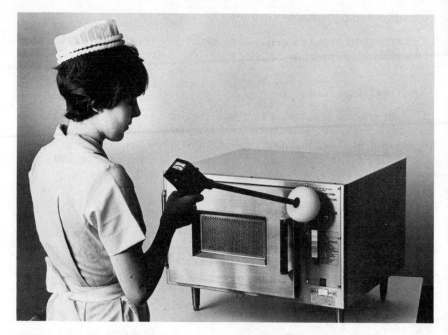

FIG. 2.12.   Microwave energy detector Micro-Guard™ Model MG-1.
Courtesy of Sage Laboratories, Inc.

Blessing Company and is called an Excelall carbonation tester. Additional information concerning the use of this tester will be found in Chapter 11 on beverages.

Soft Drink Syrup-Water Ratio Tester

Determination of the syrup-water ratio may be accomplished by a metal separator which is inserted in the nozzle or delivery head of a soft drink dispenser. The separator consists of two orifices, one for the syrup, the other for the carbonated water. A dual purpose plastic graduate, calibrated in ounces, catches the syrup in a small tube, while the carbonated water flows into the large tube. The ratio of syrup is then compared with the volume of carbonated water. A detailed explanation of this test will be found in the beverage chapter.

3

Purchasing and Specifications

PURCHASING

The initial phase of a foodservice quality control program is purchasing. Purchasing is a highly skilled activity requiring knowledge of products and market conditions. The common denominator for purchasing, regardless of volume, is obtaining the best value for the money. Buying requires much experience, many techniques, and a vast quantity of data. Due to the rapidly expanding sales of new products and prepared foods, the data required for foodservice purchasing today can fill a good-sized library.

Purchasing techniques include comparative shopping, evaluation of new products, wise judgment in timing large purchases of seasonal items, and selection of the most efficient purveyor. In addition, a buyer must understand foods, specifications, and formulations, and be able to evaluate these in terms of price, inflationary trends, and quality. Purchasing also requires integrity and the ability to cooperate with management, suppliers, kitchen employees, and the quality control center.

Effective purchasing paves the way for a successful foodservice operation. If it is realized, it means that the first step of quality control has been achieved.

SPECIFICATIONS

One of the means devised to assist purchasers is the specification. Specifications are important to both buyer and management. They are the guidelines detailing the characteristics of a product, including such properties as quality grade, weight, count, contents, and packaging.

Specifications make the task of comparison shopping easier, since the characteristics of a product are expressed in a common language and can be used as a basis for evaluation. They facilitate the submitting of purchase proposals to suppliers for quotations (bid purchasing). Specifications, if properly employed, provide an excellent means of improving cost control and product uniformity. The latter is significant when purchasing prepared food products. Pre-prepared foods should be bought according to specifications and nutrient content.

Specifications should be reviewed and revised periodically. During periods of short supply, revisions may be necessary to maintain the same food costs. In addition, new and improved products may be offered which are less expensive or possess some decided advantage over those in current use. Finally, specifications are management's silent guardian of security. Where large purchases are involved, management has the means at its disposal to cross-check price, quality, and other factors against the specifications.

Methods of Preparing Specifications

The first step in preparing a set of specifications is to list all the products that will be purchased. Menus should be used as a guide for buying foods. The list should be divided into various product categories, such as meat, dairy, desserts, beverages, etc. Subdivisions will be helpful to categorize products possessing similar characteristics. The meat list will show all the cuts of beef and pork products, followed by pre-prepared meat items and those entrées containing percentages of meat, e.g., stew and pot pies. Other food products may follow a similar pattern.

The second step is to compare the list with existing government and trade association specifications and standards. If these do not exist for specific items, they will have to be developed to complete the program. It is important to include all items to be purchased, such as paper goods, soaps, and detergents. Equipment specifications should also be considered, especially where repeat purchases are made for a multi-unit organization. If this is the first attempt at writing specifications, help may be required. One way of obtaining this assistance inexpensively is to start a collection or library of all regulatory food specifications emanating from governmental sources. This library will serve a dual purpose, as it will also assist in quality control testing.

At present a number of federal agencies in the United States are involved in the promulgation of food standards. Among these are: General Services Administration, Food and Drug Administration, Public Health Services, Department of the Interior, Department of Defense, and Department of Agriculture. Several of these agencies have overlapping regulations for identical foods. A detailed explanation of the functions of these agencies will be found in a later section of this chapter.

Product Grouping

The development of specifications can be a monumental task. At the onset of their preparation, specifications should be prepared for those products accounting for the largest volume of purchases. Simplification will result if all of the items are separated into various food groups. The following is an example of a product grouping list.

(1) *Milk and milk products*: Fresh fluid, processed milk drinks and soups; cream, frozen desserts, nonfrozen desserts, ice cream, milk desserts; cheese (all types)

(2) *Meat, poultry, fish*:
Beef; cooked, canned, dried, soups, mixtures
Pork; cooked, cured, fresh, mixtures
Veal, lamb; fresh, cooked, mixtures
Variety meat, liver, sweetbreads, fresh cooked mixtures
Lunch meats
Poultry: chicken, soups, mixtures
Fish, shellfish: soups, mixtures

(3) *Eggs*: Raw, cooked (scrambled)

(4) *Vegetables*: Potatoes, dark green, deep yellow, tomatoes, soups, mixtures

(5) *Condiments, pickles, olives*

(6) *Fruits*: Citrus, raw, processed, juice (single strength and concentrated), punches, dehydrated

(7) *Grain products (enriched and nonenriched)*: Flour, cereals, pastes, breads, rolls, biscuits, crackers, cakes, cookies, pastry

(8) *Fats and oils*: Butter, margarine, lard, vegetable fats, salad and cooking oil, salad dressings, imitation cream products

(9) *Sugars and sweets*: Syrups, jellies, candies, dessert powders

(10) *Beverages*: Coffee, tea, soft drinks, cocoa, and hot chocolate

(11) *Soaps, detergents, cleaning supplies*

(12) *Paper goods*

(13) *Accounting and office supplies*

Most of these groupings may also include the following subheadings: frozen, pre-prepared frozen, dehydrated, fabricated, and freeze-dried.

Specification Fact Form Sheet

The *fact form sheet* is the final version of a product's specifications. Certain details or headings will apply to all foods and nonfoods. These are: name or general description of the product; trade, brand, or generic title; packing, method, and type of packaging; quantity; cubic measurement (required for determining storage capacity); shipping instructions; primary supplier and alternate source; price and terms.

Depending on the product, the following are examples of pertinent data that will serve to further describe the merchandise.

(1) Federal or state grade
(2) Trade association recommendation
(3) Coding
(4) Count
(5) Weight per portion

  (6) Weight per case
  (7) Cubic size of case
  (8) Container size
  (9) Drained weight
(10) Moisture content
(11) Geographical location of food's origin
(12) Percentage of breading
(13) Percentage of principal ingredients per portion
(14) Percentage of other ingredients (spices, herbs)
(15) Percentage and types of additives
(16) Nutrient composition, such as number of calories per portion, and protein, carbohydrate, fat, mineral, and vitamin content
(17) Serving yield per can or container
(18) Serving size or portion
(19) Methods of preparation, reconstitution, or heating—conventional, convection, microwave, quartz, or infrared oven preparation
(20) Time cycle and temperature, and whether the product will be prepared from raw to finish, frozen, or defrosted state
(21) Anticipated flavor, texture, and appearance
(22) Special instructions pertaining to gravy, sauces, and kind of spices or herbs

The data pertaining to each product may be recorded on a suitable card and filed according to its group or category. Three sets should be made: one for purchasing, one for the control laboratory, and the third set for the receiving department. A fourth may be necessary for the kitchen.

REGULATORY FOOD STANDARDS AND GRADES

Federal Regulatory Agencies

Regulatory food standards and grades that are promulgated by federal agencies are an important source of information when preparing specifications or checking incoming merchandise. The following sources are recommended:

Food and Drug Administration (FDA). This agency has the responsibility for preventing adulteration and misbranding of foods. Its objectives are to assure that food is safe, pure, wholesome, sanitary, and honestly packaged and labeled. The regulations apply to food moving in interstate commerce. The agency also assists in the prevention of milkborne and shellfish diseases and in the control of sanitation related to shellfish production. The FDA sets and issues reasonable definitions and legal standards for most staple foods.

Department of Agriculture.   This Department has the responsibility for inspecting meat and meat plants. It aids both the consumer and the industry by disseminating food specifications and in quality improvement. It provides a basis for trading, using standards of quality or grades.

It issues guidelines on prepared meat and poultry products, and it inspects and grades poultry. These operations apply only to interstate transactions.

Department of Defense.   This agency is mainly concerned with military purchases. All food is purchased on specifications which are handy references and may be obtained from the Government Printing Office, Washington, DC. It also publishes menus and recipes which are available for a small fee. The Army operates a food research and development facility located in Natick, MA. Publications are issued which are available to the public.

Department of Commerce.   This department works with the fish industry and assists in quality improvement. It operates an inspection service and establishes grade standards for fishery products.

Local and Private Regulations

State and Municipal Laws.   All states and many municipalities have food laws and health codes. These supplement federal regulations, and apply only to intrastate transactions. These state and local laws usually follow federal regulations. Changes are made to provide enforcement for specific local situations.

Trade Associations and Other Agencies.   Many trade associations have self-regulatory, voluntary grading operations. Members agree to abide by these regulations and the association monitors the product accordingly. International food standards exist, established under the auspices of the United Nations through FAO/WHO; they are known as the Codex Alimentarius Commission. The Commission develops international and regional standards and publishes them in a food code form.

Food Laws and Regulations

Food Labels, an Important Source of Information.   The "Fair Packaging and Labeling Act" of 1966 and the recently enacted truth-in-labeling regulations are for consumer protection. These laws apply to all packaged food, regardless of where it is sold. Most labels list the ingredients of a food product, which provides a deeper understanding of product quality and contents.

Labels reveal whether or not spices, coloring, flavors, preservatives, or other additives have been added to the food. The ingredients contained in meat and poultry products must be listed in descending order of predominance, as used in the formulation of the product. Foods with geographic names must contain products from the stated locality, for example, Idaho potatoes must be grown in Idaho. A food is misbranded if its label expresses or implies a false geographic origin in words or pictures. Exceptions are made for geographical names indicating a class of food, rather than a place of origin, such as Swiss cheese, Irish potatoes, and Gouda cheese.

Recently the FDA proposed regulations to permit food manufacturers to disclose on labels the names and source of all fat ingredients, including the kinds of fatty acids that may be present. These regulations will allow the consumer to distinguish between foods high in "polyunsaturated" vegetable fats and low in, or free of, "saturated" animal fats. Another important feature of these laws would require all labels of processed foods to show the specific animal source, e.g., beef or chicken fat, or the specific vegetable origin, such as cottonseed or corn oil. At present, oils and fats are labeled as "shortening" or vegetable oil.

Additional information is required on labels, effective July 1, 1975. All fortified foods, and all foods for which a nutrition claim is made, must display nutrition information on the labels. Figures 3.1 and 3.2 are examples of the standard formats required for labels under these regulations.

Meat and Poultry Products Standards.   The United States Department of Agriculture has recognized the need for prepared meat and poultry products standards to protect both the consumer and the foodservice industry. Although hundreds of prepared foods are offered for sale, and new ones are introduced daily, standards are now available for many products. New standards are in constant preparation as new items emerge and new processing techniques are developed.

When federally inspected processed meat or poultry products are purchased, it is assured that they were examined by the USDA for wholesomeness and label accuracy. These inspections are performed at each step of the processing. The Consumer and Marketing Service branch sets standards and examines formulas for product characteristics and label description.

These standards describe the product's composition, such as the minimum amount of meat, the maximum amount of water, and other components contained in the item.

Exacting Procedures Followed to Prepare Standards.   The USDA test kitchens examine and test similar products processed by various manufacturers. The data obtained from these tests provide information about the product trend, general properties, and quality factors. Information is gathered from restaurants, cookbooks, and other reference materials. Test panels composed of representatives from different segments of the food industry are used. The data gathered from these sources are evaluated and a product standard definition is evolved.

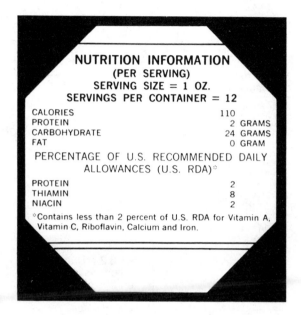

NUTRITION INFORMATION
(PER SERVING)
SERVING SIZE = 1 OZ.
SERVINGS PER CONTAINER = 12

CALORIES   110
PROTEIN   2 GRAMS
CARBOHYDRATE   24 GRAMS
FAT   0 GRAM

PERCENTAGE OF U.S. RECOMMENDED DAILY
ALLOWANCES (U.S. RDA)*

PROTEIN   2
THIAMIN   8
NIACIN   2

*Contains less than 2 percent of U.S. RDA for Vitamin A,
Vitamin C, Riboflavin, Calcium and Iron.

FIG. 3.1.   Nutrition information per serving.
Courtesy of FDA.

In addition, technical work is performed in laboratories to finalize the product's standard, based on such factors as allowable fat and moisture content.

If a manufacturer develops a new processing technique, it must be checked to determine whether it will produce a wholesome product. Additives, if used, must be safe and effective. All processors are required to register their complete formulas, which must be approved prior to commercial distribution. If a manufacturer markets a product similar to one for which requirements are established, but with some slight variation, then the new item must be labeled by another name.

Enforcement Activities of the USDA

USDA Performs Continuous Product Inspections.   Between the time a product's formula, label, and packaging are approved and the time it reaches its final destination, inspectors check all phases of processing. This procedure guarantees that the standard is followed, the label used correctly, and the product wholesome.

First, the inspector examines the raw meat or poultry that will be used to make the product to be certain that these perishable ingredients are fresh and wholesome. He also checks all the other ingredients, including spices and vegetables. During processing, the inspector follows the USDA-approved formula or recipe. He observes the measurement of ingredients to

NUTRITION INFORMATION
(PER SERVING)
SERVING SIZE = 8 OZ.
SERVINGS PER CONTAINER = 1

		FAT (PERCENT OF		
CALORIES	560	CALORIES 53%)	33 GM	
PROTEIN	23 GM	POLYUNSAT-		
CARBOHYDRATE	43 GM	URATED*	2 GM	
		SATURATED	9 GM	
		CHOLESTEROL*		
		(20 MG/100 GM).	40 MG	
		SODIUM (365 MG/		
		100 GM)	830 MG	

PERCENTAGE OF U.S. RECOMMENDED DAILY ALLOWANCES (U.S. RDA)

PROTEIN	35	RIBOFLAVIN	15
VITAMIN A	35	NIACIN	25
VITAMIN C		CALCIUM	2
(ASCORBIC ACID)	10	IRON	25
THIAMIN (VITAMIN B₁)	15		

*Information on fat and cholesterol content is provided for individuals who, on the advice of a physician, are modifying their total dietary intake of fat and cholesterol.

FIG. 3.2. Nutrition information listing optional items, e.g., cholesterol, fat, and sodium.
Courtesy of FDA.

make sure that the amounts added comply with the approved formula.

If the processing includes cutting, chopping, mixing, stuffing, slicing, or forming, the inspector watches each operation to assure that the formula is being followed. If the product is cooked, he checks the cooking time and temperature to ensure the proper degrees of doneness. Smoking and curing are also checked. The inspector continues his vigil during the freezing operation to see that the products are properly frozen.

Finally, the product's packaging material is inspected for soundness and safety. Can closures are inspected for proper sealing and soundness. The inspector follows the USDA's previously approved packaging specifications. Samples from each lot of canned products are tested for presence of microorganisms. These samples are incubated, or held for a specific length of time at elevated temperatures, to check for microbial activity.

Labels and weights are then checked to determine if they meet the standard. It was previously stressed that labels form a composite guide to the product's contents. The ingredient present in the largest amount is listed first, while that constituting the lowest percentage comes last. This scheme helps to evaluate the cost of the product. For example, the label of a certain brand of meat pie lists the water first, followed by potatoes, carrots, and, finally, the legal percentage of meat. Another brand lists the meat first, followed by carrots, potatoes, and beef stock. The net weight of both brands is identical; however, the latter brand costs 4¢ more because it contained a higher percentage of meat and carrots, and it was therefore considered the better value.

Labels should also be checked for the USDA stamp of approval (Fig. 3.3).

Grading. Grading of foods is a vast undertaking conducted jointly by USDA's Consumer and Marketing Service and the departments of agriculture of the various states. Grading is a voluntary service and is self-supporting. It is provided to those companies requesting it on a fee-for-service basis.

During the fiscal year 1970, the following products were certified: 80% of the poultry, 69% of the butter, 67% of the lamb and mutton, 64% of the beef, 50% of the fresh fruits and vegetables, and 20% of the shell eggs. During the same period, the following foods were certified for quality and/or wholesomeness: 87% of the dried eggs, 80% of the frozen fruits and vegetables, 77% of the processed liquid eggs, 46% of the nonfat dry milk, and 40% of the canned fruits and vegetables.

Grade Standards. Grade standards define differences in quality that affect the usefulness and value of a food. They cover the whole range of a product's natural qualities. The number of grades for a particular food depends upon its variability. For instance, eight grades are necessary to span the range of beef quality, while only three are needed for turkey. Beef and lamb grades usually encountered are USDA Prime, Choice, and Good. Choice is the grade most widely available; it denotes a high degree of tenderness, juiciness, and flavor. Chicken and turkey are often sold with the USDA Grade A shield affixed to the package. Lower grades, such as B and

FIG. 3.3. Typical USDA grade and inspection stamps.

C, are seldom offered for retail sale, but are used in soup, pies, etc. Grade A poultry has more meat and a better appearance.

Eggs are graded for both quality and size. Top quality eggs—USDA Grade AA and A—have a firm yolk and thick white and stand up well for frying and poaching. Grade B eggs may have a flatter yolk and a thinner white. Egg sizes are based on weight per dozen, such as Extra Large, weighing 27 oz per doz; Large, weighing 24 oz per doz; Medium, 21 oz per doz; and Small, 18 oz per doz.

Examples of FDA Standards of Identity

The increasing role of pre-prepared foods of all types in the foodservice industry has prompted increased policing activities by the Food and Drug Administration to protect the consumer against misbranding and adulteration and to assure wholesomeness. In order to give a clearer understanding of the Standards of Identity, selected examples follow.

§27.15 Canned prunes; identity; label statement of optional ingredients.
(a) Canned prunes is the food prepared from dried prunes, with or without one of the optional packing media specified in paragraph (b) of this section. Such food may be seasoned with one or more of the following optional ingredients:
(1) Spice.
(2) Flavoring, other than artificial flavoring.
(3) A vinegar.
(4) Citric acid.
(5) Lemon juice.
(6) Unpeeled pieces of citrus fruits.
Such food is sealed in a container. It is so processed by heat as to prevent spoilage.
(b) (1) The optional packing media referred to in paragraph (a) of this section are:
(i) Water.
(ii) Light sirup.
(iii) Heavy sirup.
(iv) Extra heavy sirup.
(2) Each of packing media in subparagraph (1) (ii) to (iv), inclusive, of this paragraph is prepared with water and one of the optional saccharine ingredients specified in paragraph (c) of this section.

§ 20.3 Ice milk; identity; label statement of optional ingredients.
Ice milk is the food prepared from the same ingredients and in the same manner prescribed in § 20.1 for ice cream and complies with all the provisions of § 20.1 (including the requirements for label statement of optional ingredients), except that:
(a) Its content of milk fat is more than 2 percent but not more than 7 percent.
(b) Its content of total milk solids is not less than 11 percent.
(c) Caseinates may be added when the content of total milk solids is not less than 11 percent.
(d) The provision for reduction in milk fat and total milk solids from the addition of bulky ingredients in § 20.1 (a) does not apply.
(e) The quantity of food solids per gallon is not less than 1.3 pounds except that when the optional ingredient microcrystalline cellulose specified in § 20.1 (f) (6) is used the quantity of food solids per gallon is not less than 1.3 pounds, exclusive of the weight of the microcrystalline cellulose.
(f) When any artificial coloring is used in ice milk, directly or as a component of any other ingredient, the label shall bear the statement "artificially colored," "artificial

coloring added," "with added artificial color," or "_____, an artificial color added," the blank being filled in with the common or usual name of the artificial color; or in lieu thereof, in case the artificial color is a component of another ingredient, "_____ artificially colored."

(g) The name of the food is "ice milk."

(h) If both artificial color and artificial flavoring are used, the label statements may be combined.

§ 19.525 Cottage cheese; identity.

(a) Cottage cheese is the soft uncured cheese prepared by the procedure set forth in paragraph (b) of this section. The finished cottage cheese contains not more than 80 percent of moisture, as determined by the method prescribed under "Moisture—Official," on page 210 of "Official Methods of Analysis of the Association of Official Agricultural Chemists," Ninth Edition (1960). [Ed. note, 10th edition, 1965, p. 247, 15.157.]

(b) (1) One or more of the dairy ingredients specified in subparagraph (2) of this paragraph is pasteurized; calcium chloride may be added in a quantity of not more than 0.02 percent (calculated as anhydrous calcium chloride) of the weight of the mix; harmless lactic-acid-producing bacteria, with or without rennet, are added and it is held until it becomes coagulated. The coagulated mass may be cut; it may be warmed; it may be stirred; it is then drained. The curd may be washed with water and further drained; it may be pressed, chilled, worked, seasoned with salt.

(2) The dairy ingredients referred to in subparagraph (1) of this paragraph are sweet skim milk, concentrated skim milk, and nonfat dry milk. If concentrated skim milk or nonfat dry milk is used, water may be added in a quantity not in excess of that removed when the skim milk was concentrated or dried.

(3) For the purposes of this section the term "skim milk" means the milk of cows from which the milk fat has been separated, and "concentrated skim milk" means skim milk from which a portion of the water has been removed by evaporation.

[24 F.R. 6482, Aug. 12, 1959, as amended at 28 F.R. 3022, Mar. 28, 1963]

USDA Standards for Prepared Meat and Poultry Products

Standards for meat and poultry products are pertinent guidelines in quality interpretation and cost evaluation. To meet these standards, a food must contain the *minimum* amount of meat or poultry prescribed by the USDA. For example, ready-to-serve chicken soup must contain at least 2% chicken. Condensed chicken soup must contain 4% or more, since it would then contain at least 2% when diluted with water. But chicken-flavored soup, which is not considered a poultry product, may contain less chicken.

The standards for meat ingredients usually are based on the fresh weight of the product, whereas those for poultry are measured on the weight of the cooked, deboned product. Since meat and poultry shrink during cooking, standards take this into account. For instance, beef pot pie must contain at least 25% fresh beef. Turkey pot pie must contain 14% or more cooked turkey. Chicken burgers must be 100% chicken; a product containing fillers must be called "chicken patties." Additional standards for prepared meat and poultry products will be found in the Appendix.

USDA Standards for Meat and Poultry

The Series *1000* Specifications.   There are so many different kinds and cuts of meat available that a new meat dish could be featured every day of the year. Since meat comprises a large share of total food purchases, it is important that exacting specifications be followed to ensure uniform quality and good value.

One method is to specify the quality grade of the primal cuts from which the individual portions will be taken; however, other considerations may arise when the primal cuts are processed. For example, what are the percentages of unwanted bone and fat? Another question concerns the substitution of cheaper cuts for more expensive ones.

The answers to these questions are provided by the USDA Institutional Meat Purchase Specifications Series *1000*, which have become the industry's guidelines for comparison. The following are several examples of these exacting guidelines: Porterhouse steaks may have no more than 4 in. tails and the diameter of the tenderloin muscle must be not less than 1¼ in.; T-bone steaks may have no more than 3 in. tails and the diameter of the tenderloin muscle must be not less than ½ in. of surface fat and a maximum thickness of ¾ in. at any one point.

Specifications are also designated for two styles of ground beef: regular and special. For both the fat content must not exceed 25%.

Portion-cut meats command a large segment of the foodservice market. Table 3.1 shows examples of a wide variety of portion-cut meats. Specifications should be adopted for all items in this meat category.

Poultry Products

Poultry is very popular in American meals. Convenient and convenience forms of poultry cover a wide range of products. With today's modern production, processing, and marketing methods, chicken, turkey, duck, and goose are available year round for roasting, broiling, frying, and stewing.

Packaged, cut-up poultry, heat-and-serve fried chicken, breaded uncooked frozen and freeze-dried products, turkey and chicken rolls, and roasts, stuffed or unstuffed, are just a small part of the vast convenient and convenience poultry market.

The classifications of poultry include *chickens, turkeys, geese, guineas, and ducks*. Broiler-fryer chickens are produced mainly in the Del-Mar-Va Peninsula, where Delaware, Maryland, and Virginia converge. Other growing areas include Georgia, Mississippi, Alabama, Arkansas, and the Carolinas.

Stewing hens, a by-product of the egg industry, are produced in the Southeast, Midwest, California, and parts of the Northeast. Turkeys are raised in Rhode Island, California, and the Midwest. The major producing area for ducks is Long Island, New York.

Some poultry is marketed at an early age. Broiler-fryers are ready for market in about 9 weeks and a 20 lb tom turkey in about 5 months.

Inspection of poultry and poultry products comes under the jurisdiction of the USDA. Congress has enacted two laws to protect the consumer against unhealthy and unwholesome poultry—the Poultry Products Inspection Act

TABLE 3.1.   Examples of Portion-Cut Meats

Cut or Description	Portion Size (oz)	Suggested Methods of Preparation
Strip loin, boneless	6 to 14	Broil, panbroil, panfry, or grill
Pinbone strip, boneless	6, 8, 10, 12	Broil, panbroil, panfry, or grill
Butt strip	6, 8	Broil, panbroil, panfry, or grill
Sirloin, butt	3, 4, 6	Panfry or grill
Sandwich cut, round or oblong	2, 3	Panfry or grill
T-bone	8, 10, 12, 14, 16	Broil, panbroil, panfry, or grill
Rib club, boneless	8, 10, 12	Broil, panbroil, panfry, or grill
Rib eye	4, 5, 6, 8	Broil, panbroil, panfry, or grill
Tenderloin (filet mignon)	4, 6, 8, 10	Broil, panbroil, panfry, or grill
Twin beef (filet mignon)	2, 4	Broil, panfry, or grill
Beef filet or sirloin	4, 6, 8	Broil, panbroil, panfry, or grill
Beef Swiss	4, 5	Braise
Sirloin beef cubed	3, 4, 5, 6	Panfry or grill
Floured beef steaks	4	Grill or panfry
Pepper beef steaks	2¼, 3, 4	Grill or panfry
Mushroom beef	2¼, 4	Grill or panfry
Pizza patties with cheese slice	3½	Grill or panfry
Chuck wagon steaks	2¼, 3, 4, 6	Panfry or deep fat fry
Cubed dinner beef steaks	6	Panfry or grill
Salisbury steaks	6	Panfry or grill
Chopped beef steaks	6, 8	Panfry, grill, or broil
Beef patties	2, 3, 4	Panfry or grill
Sirloin beef kabobs	6, 8	Broil, panfry, or grill

Source: Colonial Beef Company, Philadelphia, PA.

of 1957 and the Wholesome Poultry Products Act of 1968. The latter requires inspection of all poultry products whether they move in interstate or intrastate commerce. In addition, the USDA has specified minimum meat requirements for many processed products.

Poultry is graded for quality. After inspection, a USDA grade seal is affixed to the product. The top poultry grade is U.S. Grade A. To attain a Grade A rating, the poultry must have good overall shape and appearance, be meaty, be practically free from defects and have a well-developed layer of fat in the skin. Other grades, such as B and C, exist; birds receiving these ratings are used in processed foods. In 1965 grade standards were developed for raw, ready-to-cook poultry rolls, roasts, and bars.

Poultry is usually labeled according to age. This is important, since age indicates tenderness and suggests ways to cook the poultry. It is important to remember that cooking poultry in intense heat toughens the meat and causes abnormal shrinkage and loss of juice. The following are the age groups:

(1)   Mature chickens may be labeled *mature chicken, old chicken, hen, stewing chicken,* or *fowl.*

(2)   Mature turkeys may be labeled *mature turkey, yearling turkey*, or *old turkey.*

(3)   Mature ducks, geese, and guineas may be labeled *mature* or *old.*

(4)   Young chickens may be labeled as *young chicken, Rock Cornish game hen, broiler, fryer, roaster*, or *capon.*

(5)   Young turkeys may be labeled as *young turkey, fryer-roaster, young hen*, or *young tom.*

(6)   Young ducks may be labeled *duckling, young duckling, broiler duckling, fryer duckling*, or *roaster duckling.*

Although not included in the preceding categories, mention should be made of squab and squab chicken. These are popular gourmet items. Squab are immature pigeons weighing about ½ to 1 lb each. Squab chickens are young chickens, while Cornish hens are a crossbreed of a Cornish bird and a chicken.

Cuts and Forms.   Poultry is probably one of the most popular, convenient, versatile, and profitable foods served. Fried chicken with the bone in is accepted on a national scale. For the convenience, fast food operation, prepared raw or cooked poultry is available in a wide selection of cuts and forms. The basic forms are chilled raw poultry, frozen raw poultry, smoked poultry, freeze-dried products, and canned varieties. In addition, poultry cuts or parts are available, such as breasts, legs, splits, wings, and livers. Poultry is often boned and marketed in cans. Chicken, turkey, and game fowl are available in this form. Broilers or fryers are boxed one dozen to the case. Turkeys are usually dressed and ready to cook. Weights vary from 20 to 25 lb. Turkey rolls have a weight range of 8 to 10 lb and will yield about 30 to 35 servings.

Fish Products

Fish and shellfish products provide a wide variety of choices. There are more than 240 species sold in the United States, which puts this food group ahead of all others with regard to the number of products offered for sale. Fish and shellfish can be purchased frozen, canned, cured, fresh, and in a wide selection of convenience, convenient, and specialty items.

The number of fish and shellfish products which can be successfully handled and merchandised in a fast- and convenience-food operation is much less than for the general market. Frozen, canned, cured, and an interesting variety of pre-prepared frozen entrees that need only to be heated before serving are the main products used. In addition, there are frozen raw fish products that are stuffed or breaded and then baked or deep-fried.

Forms of Fish Products.   Whole fish are sold just as they come from the water. Before cooking they must be scaled, eviscerated, and the head, tail, and fins removed. Small fish like smelt are often cooked with only their entrails removed.

Dressed fish are scaled and eviscerated, and sometimes have the head, tail, and fins removed. The smaller fish are called *pan-dressed* (Fig. 3.4).

Steaks are cross-section slices from a large dressed fish cut ⅝ to 1 in. thick. A cross-section of the backbone is usually the only bone in a steak.

Chunks are cross-sections of a large dressed fish with a cross-section of the backbone included.

Single fillets are practically boneless and may be skinned. The most common type is with the sides of the fish cut lengthwise away from the backbone.

Butterfly fillets are the two sides of the fish cut lengthwise away from the backbone and held together by the uncut flesh and skin of the belly. These fillets are practically boneless.

Frozen raw or *fried breaded fish portions* are cut from frozen fish blocks, coated with a batter, breaded, packaged, and frozen. Portions weigh more than 1½ oz and are at least ⅜ in. thick. Raw portions must contain not less than 75%, and fried portions not less than 65%, fish flesh, according to U.S. Department of Commerce (USDC) standards. They may be purchased raw or partially cooked.

Frozen fried fish sticks are cut from frozen fish blocks, coated with a batter, breaded, partially cooked, packaged, and frozen. Fried fish sticks weigh up to 1½ oz, must be at least ⅜ in. thick, and contain not less than 60% fish flesh, according to USDC standards.

Canned fish are packed in a large variety of convenience and specialty products. These include three popular items; tuna, salmon, and sardines.

Tuna is packed from six species, namely, albacore, blackfin, bluefin, skipjack, yellowfin, and little tuna. Albacore has lighter meat than the others and is the only species permitted to be labeled "white meat" tuna. The others are labeled "light meat." Canned tuna is packed in oil or water. Solid packs are the most expensive, followed by chunk and flaked, while the grated is the least expensive pack.

Salmon, packed from five species, is sold by the name of the fish since there is a difference in the color, texture, and the flavor of each. Higher-priced varieties are deeper red in color and have a higher oil content. The most expensive is the red or sockeye; followed by the Chinook or king; the medium red, silver or coho; the pink; and the least expensive, the chum or keta.

Cured fish are processed from many different species. Some of the more common cured fish on the market are: pickled and spiced herring and salmon; salt cod and salmon; and smoked chubs, salmon, whitefish, and sturgeon. Cured fish have remarkable versatility. They may be served as hors d'oeuvres, in sandwiches, in salads, or as an appetizing entree. Smoked salmon or lox is highly regarded in many sections of the country. This product is available in cans and is packed in oil with protective paper separating each slice.

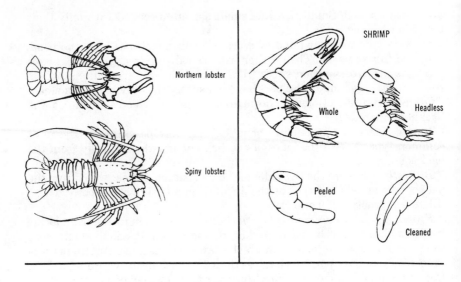

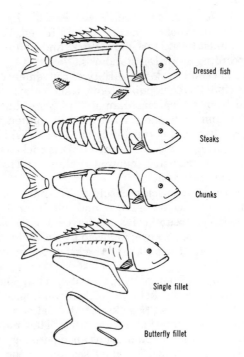

FIG. 3.4.   Market forms of fish and shellfish.
From Kerr (1969).

Forms of Shellfish. In the United States, shellfish means crustaceans and mollusks. Crustaceans include crabs, lobsters, and shrimp; mollusks are clams, oysters, and scallops.

Clams are available fresh in the shell or shucked, that is, the meat is removed from the shells. The meat is pale to deep orange in color and has a fresh, milky odor. Fresh, shucked clams are packed in little or no liquid. Frozen raw or fried breaded clams are shucked clams coated with a batter, breaded, packaged, and frozen. They may be purchased raw or partially cooked. Canned clams are sold whole, minced, or in chowder, bouillon, broth, and nectar.

Crabs consist of three principal species: blue, Dungeness, and king. Frozen crab legs are the legs of cooked king and tanner crabs which have been frozen and split or cut into sections. The meat is white, with an attractive red tint on the exterior. Crab meat is the meat removed from cooked crabs. The meat is packed and chilled, frozen, processed, and canned. King crab meat is primarily leg meat. The packs of blue crab are: lump meat, obtained from the two body muscles which operate the swimming legs; flake meat, small pieces of white meat from the body; a combination of flake and lump meat; and claw meat, brownish-tinted meat from the claws.

Lobsters consist of the northern variety and the spiny lobster. The northern lobsters have large, heavy claws, whereas the spiny lobsters have no large claws.

Lobsters in the shell are sold fresh, frozen, or cooked (Fig. 3.5). The cooked lobster should be bright red and have a fresh, milky odor. Lobster meat is the meat removed from cooked lobsters. The meat is packed and chilled, frozen, or canned. It is white, with an attractive reddish tint on the outside.

Oysters consist of three main species: Eastern, Pacific, and Western. The oyster meat is referred to as shucked and should be plump and have a natural creamy color and clear liquid. The meat is packed with little or no liquid. Oysters containing an excess amount of liquid should be avoided, as this indicates poor quality and careless handling. Frozen raw or fried breaded oysters are shucked oysters coated with a batter, breaded, packaged, and frozen. They are available raw or partially cooked. Canned oysters are sold whole and for stew.

Scallops are mollusks with two valve shells. They are active swimmers and move about the ocean bed freely. The two principal species marketed are the bay and the sea or giant scallops. The adductor muscle is excellently flavored and is the only part of the scallop eaten by Americans. The sea scallop's muscle may be as large as 2 in. across, whereas that of the bay scallop measures about ½ in.

Shucked scallops are the adductor muscles removed from the shells. The meat is a creamy white, light tan, orange, or pinkish. Fresh scallops should have a sweetish odor and be packed in little or no liquid. Fried scallops must contain not less than 60% scallop meat, according to USDC standards. They are available raw or partially cooked.

Shrimp as marketed in the United States are the common or white

FIG. 3.5. Preparing
herbed lobster tails for
heating.
*Courtesy of American Spice
Trade Association.*

shrimp, which is greenish-gray; brown or Brazilian shrimp, which is brown-ish-red; pink or coral shrimp; and Alaska, California, and Maine varieties, which vary in color and are relatively small. However, when cooked, all shrimp assume the same color—a reddish tint. There is very little difference in the appearance and flavor of cooked shrimp. Shrimp are sold according to size; the larger the size, the higher the price.

Headless shrimp are, as would be expected, shrimp with the heads removed. "Green shrimp" is a trade term used to describe raw shrimp.

Peeled and cleaned shrimp are headless shrimp with the shell and dark intestinal tract removed. They are sold raw or cooked, fresh, frozen, and canned.

Frozen raw or fried breaded shrimp are peeled and cleaned shrimp coated with a batter, breaded, packaged, and frozen. Breaded raw shrimp must contain not less than 50% shrimp meat according to USDC standards. They are available raw or partially cooked.

Shrimp vary in average count per pound from under 10 to over 70. Trade nomenclature for the different sizes are: under 10 to the pound, extra colossal; 10 to 15, colossal; 16 to 20, extra jumbo; 21 to 25, jumbo; 26 to 30, extra large; 31 to 35, large; 36 to 42, medium large, 43 to 50, medium; 51 to 60, small; 61 to 70, extra small; and over 70, tiny or tidi.

Grade Standards.   Grade standards have been established by the National Marine Fisheries Service, U.S. Department of Commerce, for a total of 15 processed fishery products. These include frozen raw and fried breaded fish portions, frozen fried scallops, frozen raw and fried fish sticks, frozen headless dressed whiting, frozen ocean perch fillets, frozen sole and flounder fillets, frozen haddock fillets, frozen fish blocks, and frozen raw or fried breaded shrimp.

Quality grades for fish products are Grades A, B, C, and substandard. When purchases are planned, specifications should include the USDC grade standard. In addition, the amount of fish or shellfish to buy per serving varies with the recipe to be used, size of serving, and amount of bone or shell in the product. Allow approximately 3 to 4 oz of cooked, boneless fish or shellfish per serving. Table 3.2 shows the many forms of fish and shellfish available to the foodservice industry.

Fruits and Vegetables

Vegetables are generally classified according to the section of the plant from which they are taken, such as the root, stem, leaves, flower, fruit, and seeds. Examples are: (1) *root*—carrots, beets, and sweet potatoes; (2) *stem* —potatoes and asparagus; (3) *leaves*—celery and rhubarb (leafstalks), spinach, and kale; (4) *flowers*—broccoli and cauliflower; (5) *fruits*—tomatoes, squash, cucumbers, peppers, snap beans, and snow beans; (6) *seeds*—corn, beans, and peas.

Vegetables may also be classified according to color, like green, yellow, orange, red, and white. They are also separated according to flavor and aroma intensity values. Onions and cabbage are in the strong family, while potatoes and corn fall into the mild-flavored category. Other factors are considered, such as high and low sugar, high and low fat, high and low protein, acidity, and mineral and nutritional content.

Federal grades are established for fresh fruits and vegetables. Copies of these standards are available from the Superintendent of Documents, Washington, DC.; Fresh Products Standardization and Inspection Branch, Consumer and Marketing Services, USDA, Washington, DC. Additional sources are the United Fresh Fruit and Vegetable Association, the Western Growers Association, and state university cooperative extension services.

Purchasing fresh fruits and vegetables should be performed on the basis of final use. Briefly, the following quality attributes should influence product selection: color, degree of ripeness, weight, size, count per serving, uniformity, and freedom from defects.

Fresh Fruit Standards.   There are several U.S. grades for fresh fruits. *U.S. Extra Fancy* is an extra-special grade that applies only to apples. This grade shows exceptional quality in appearance, color, shape, and lack of defects. *U.S. Fancy* is a top grade for most fruits. This grade indicates good color and good shape. The U.S. No. 1 and U.S. Extra No. 1 grades represent the top quality for many fruits and lower grades in the case of some fruits.

TABLE 3.2. Fish and Shellfish
Approximate yield and approximate amount to purchase per serving.

	Fish and Shellfish as Purchased	Yield (%)	Amount to Purchase (oz)
Fish	Whole	27	11
	Dressed or pandressed	38	8
	Fillets, steaks, and chunks	61	5
	Portions and sticks	90	3½
	Pickled and spiced	100	3
	Salted	72	4¼
	Smoked	66	4½
	Canned tuna	100	3
	Canned salmon	81	3¾
Clams	In the shell:		
	hardshell	14	21½
	softshell	29	10½
	Shucked	48	6½
	Breaded, raw or fried	84	3¾
	Canned minced	100	3
Crabs	In the shell:		
	blue	14	21½
	Dungeness	24	12¼
	softshell	66	4½
	king crab legs	52	6
	Cooked meat	97	3¼
	Canned meat	85	3½
Lobsters	In the shell	25	12
	Spiny lobster tails	51	6
	Cooked meat	91	3½
Oysters	In the shell	12	25
	Shucked	48	6½
	Breaded, raw or fried	88	3½
	Canned whole	100	3
Scallops	Shucked	63	5
	Breaded, raw or fried	87	3½
Shrimp	Headless	50	6
	Peeled and cleaned	62	5
	Cooked, peeled, and cleaned	100	3½
	breaded, raw or fried	86	3½
	canned whole	100	3

Source: Kerr (1969).

Fruits of these grades have a good appearance, but a few more defects are permitted when these grades represent the second or third highest grade.

Others grades for fresh fruits are U.S. No. 2 or U.S. combination. These are generally used for processing.

Fresh Vegetable Standards. *U.S. Fancy.* This is the premium grade for some vegetables. It means the vegetables have outstanding quality and appearance. Only a very small percentage of a crop qualifies for this grade.

U.S. No. 1. This is the highest grade for most vegetables. In a normal year, about two-thirds of a crop meets this standard. These vegetables have good quality and appearance, and few defects.

U.S. No. 2 or U.S. Combination. Other grades for fresh vegetables are used for processing and are generally not sold fresh.

Standards and Grades for Other Food Categories

Bakery Products and Frozen Desserts. Standards of Identity have been promulgated by the FDA for bakery products and frozen desserts. Bakery items are covered in Part 17 and frozen desserts in Part 19 of the Code of Federal Regulations (CFR), Title 21.

Standards of Identity are provided for the following bakery products:

(1) Bread, white bread and rolls, white rolls or buns, and white buns.
(2) Enriched bread and enriched rolls.
(3) Milk bread and milk rolls or buns.
(4) Raisin bread and raisin rolls or raisin buns.
(5) Whole wheat bread, graham bread, entire wheat bread, and whole wheat rolls, graham rolls, entire wheat rolls, or whole wheat buns, graham buns, and entire wheat buns.

Standards of Identity are provided for the following frozen desserts: ice cream, frozen custard, French ice cream, French custard ice cream, ice milk, fruit sherbet, water ices, nonfruit sherbet, and nonfruit water ices.

Milk and Cream. Standards of Identity for milk, cream, and related dairy products are listed in the Code of Federal Regulations, Title 21, Part 18. These include: low fat milk, skim milk, half and half, light cream, light whipping cream, heavy cream, evaporated milk, concentrated milk, sweetened condensed milk, nonfat dry milk, and nonfat dry milk fortified with vitamins A and D.

Additional Standards of Identity. Standards of Identity for additional products are listed in CFR, Title 21, and include: Part 14, cacao products; Part 15, cereal flours and related products; Part 16, macaroni and noodle products; Part 19, cheeses, processed cheeses, cheese foods, cheese spreads, and related foods; Part 22, food flavoring; Part 25, dressing for food, such as mayonnaise, mayonnaise dressing, French dressing, and salad dressing; Part 31, nonalcoholic beverages; Part 45, oleomargarine, margarine; Part 46, meat products.

Fruit drinks, frozen concentrated lemonade, fruit butters, and frozen strawberries are other products regulated under CFR, Title 21.

Frozen fruits and vegetable grades are listed under USDA Quality Grade Standards; items such as fruit jelly, preserves or jams, chili sauce, and peanut butter are also included.

4

Receiving, Sampling, and Product Inspection Control

RECEIVING

A concerted quality control system includes a highly organized receiving department. Well-formulated specifications will be of little value unless those people employed to operate the receiving department monitor receipt of all incoming merchandise thoroughly and systematically and use the skills and modern techniques available to promote an effective performance. To accomplish this significant task, receivers must possess a working knowledge of food specifications, those physical or chemical properties that may deteriorate due to mishandling, and the capability of coordinating the receipt of merchandise with available storage facilities and kitchen personnel.

Statistics gathered over the years reveal that poor receiving procedures have the following results: pilferage; accepting underweight merchandise; contamination; and waste because the product received did not meet specification. These factors in combination or individually have contributed to severe losses and even business failures.

When measurements are made to determine which step in a foodservice organization is the most important, the usual answer is that all are of the same magnitude and equally necessary for a team-oriented, profitable system. However, in too many establishments receiving activities are loosely knit, and these chores are delegated to menial labor without proper supervision or final inspection, and with substandard working conditions.

Thoughtful foodservice operators agree that a tightly controlled, highly organized receiving station is a prerequisite of a successful business. Regardless of the size or scope of a company, receiving requires quick handling, exacting quality control procedures, and trained personnel possessing good judgment and experience in interpreting specifications, coding, and temperature measurements. These factors are highly essential where receipt of fresh and frozen foods is concerned.

Receiving Procedures

The following procedures apply to frozen foods and other perishable items.

(1) Arrival of deliveries must be anticipated. Appointments should be made well in advance. Freezer and cooler space should be made available prior to arrival of merchandise. Assure stock rotation by moving aside or marking present inventory. Employ the "first-in, first-out" procedure (FIFO). This applies to all products, whether perishable or not.

(2) Mechanical moving equipment should be clean and ready for use.

(3) When the truck arrives, it should be inspected for cleanliness, freedom from foreign odors, and other contamination. Prior to removal of merchandise, packaging should be inspected for imperfections. Depending on the kind of perishable items, a check should be made of the truck's interior temperature. If the products are frozen, they must not be accepted if the truck's interior temperature is above 0°F (−17.8°C).

(4) Unloading must be accomplished quickly to minimize exposure to exterior temperatures. This task is essential in warm weather where frozen foods are involved.

(5) If frozen foods are received with product temperatures in excess of 0°F (−17.8°C), notification should be made to the manager or others in authority so that quick disposition of the shipment can be made. See Chapter 5, Storage and Issuing Control, for additional information concerning the handling and storage control of frozen foods.

(6) Separation of the merchandise or quality checks should not be made on the platform or in interior distribution areas. Merchandise must be moved into freezer or cooler space immediately, where segregation can begin.

(7) Weighing and counting should be done as rapidly as possible.

(8) Segregation within the freezer or cooler should start immediately. Lost time is costly, so orderly storage by commodity groups is essential to save labor, reduce handling, and maintain inventory control.

(9) Labels and case markings should always be visible. This will save time when stock is issued to the preparation center.

(10) Nonperishables may be checked at the receiving station and then taken to appropriate storage areas. Identical procedures should be followed for nonperishable items as for frozen products. These include check weighing, unit count per shipping container, quantity count of entire shipment, code evaluation, and conditions of the packaging or casing.

Record Keeping

The practice of maintaining receiving records varies from one organization to another. Record keeping is important for frozen foods; canned goods;

meat, poultry, and fish; fresh fruit and vegetables; and sundry items such as spices, coffee, tea, cereals, and flour. Regardless of the variations in record keeping, certain fundamentals are necessary. Methods of recording data are sometimes found to be highly personalized and irrelevant to the operation. Those companies that maintain computerized controls will require recording systems suited to their programming methods.

Specifically, receiving records should list the following data: name of purveyor, date and time of receipt of goods, description of the item, and brand name. When perishables are received, condition and temperature of the truck should be noted, as well as the temperature of the food. Cross checking the purchase order for quantity, weight, specifications, size of item, and pack date code, as well as making a visual examination for defects and damage, are also mandatory and must be made a permanent part of the record. These data are necessary for future reference in cases of contamination or hidden and unforeseen spoilage that should be attributed to the vendor.

Receiving Equipment

Basic equipment for receiving is scales of various sizes, movable bins, thermometers, and mechanical equipment needed to transport the merchandise to the various storage areas in an orderly rapid manner. The mechanical equipment may consist of conveyors, forklift trucks (battery-operated to eliminate noxious exhausts), hand trucks, dollies, movable shelves, and overhead trolleys. Storage areas that are a part of a central commissary or centralized warehouse are ideal for forklift palletized mobility. Figure 4.1 illustrates two types of scales suited for receiving. Figure 4.2 shows examples of mechanical equipment.

SAMPLING TECHNIQUES

Sampling is an important segment of quality control. Proper sampling is a specialized art and must be accomplished with extreme care. Many industries employ the services of professional samplers, who are licensed to perform their task. Rigid examinations are required by authorities before a license is issued. Commodities like spices, coffee, and tea are sampled prior to acceptance of an order. A sampling firm is given authority to draw samples of the product. These are then tested according to predetermined procedures.

Precise sampling procedures should be developed for each food category that will eventually undergo quality testing. These procedures should be made a permanent part of the receiving department's schedule of activities.

Sampling Schedule

Statistical sampling schedules should be established to ensure the removing of samples that are representative of a shipment. Usually, results of

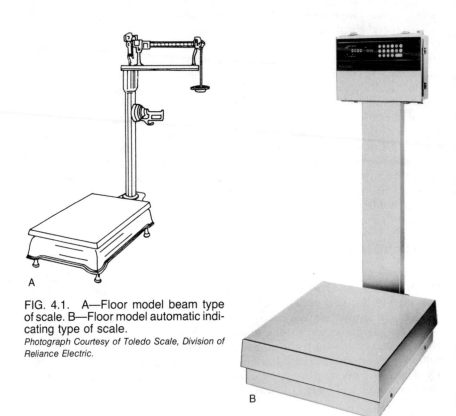

FIG. 4.1.   A—Floor model beam type of scale. B—Floor model automatic indicating type of scale.
Photograph Courtesy of Toledo Scale, Division of Reliance Electric.

inspections are taken at face value; for example, it may be assumed that test data are identical with the true average value of the lot examined. Further, it may be assumed that the item tested is identical in all respects to the entire lot of merchandise. It must be realized that inspection results become more representative as frequency and size of sampling are increased. The USDA, other agencies, and associations have instituted standard procedures for methods of sampling.

Definition of Sampling—Inspection Terms

Quality Control for the Food Industry, Vol. 2, by Kramer and Twigg (1973), employs the following definitions for terms encountered in sampling studies:

Attributes and Variables.   Inspection by attribute consists of classifying a unit of a product simply as acceptable or unacceptable, whereas inspection

FIG. 4.2.   Examples of mechanical equipment.

by variables refers to actual values obtained in terms of some scale used to establish a level of quality.

Critical, Major, Minor.   These terms refer to the importance of the quality characteristic to be inspected. In food products a *critical* characteristic may be defined as one which may constitute a health hazard to the consumer, such as the presence of a toxic substance. A *major* characteristic is one which, while not directly injurious to health, may cause the product to be unsuitable for human consumption, e.g., presence of insect material. A *minor* characteristic is one which might cause a change in the economic value of material that is fit for human consumption.

Risk Inspection.   The degree of risk that a buyer is willing to assume may be generated by confidence in the supplier, so that a greater than normal risk is taken by inspecting fewer samples. Where a buyer wishes to minimize risk, he will employ tighter inspection control and examine more samples, thereby reducing sampling error.

Bulk, Sublots.   These terms refer to the character of the lot. A *bulk* lot is one in which the units of the product are not packaged in any way; *sublots* refer to subdivisions of the lot in pallets, crates, cartons, and packages.

Factors Influencing Sampling Procedures

The factors that influence the sampling procedure to be selected follow:

(1)   Purpose for which the inspection is made
(2)   Nature of the material to be tested
(3)   Nature of the testing methods
(4)   Nature of the lots being sampled

Purpose of Inspection

Sampling plans must be selected that are capable of achieving a specific purpose since all inspections are not performed for the same purpose. Purposes for quality inspections may be to accept or reject a lot of merchandise, to evaluate average quality, or to determine uniformity.

Nature of Material

The size of the sample that is necessary to be representative of the lot is influenced by the following characteristics.

Homogeneity.   Where an essentially homogeneous material is to be sampled, such as a true solution, one small sample may be sufficient. As variability among units of a lot increases, there is need for increasing the number of units in order to have a representative sample.

Unit Size.   With liquid or semiliquid products, and with foods consisting of small particles, there is a need for establishing some definite sample quantity, such as volume of a container, or the contents of a probe or trier. Where the units are of intermediate size, such as an ear of corn, each piece may serve directly as a sample unit. Where the units are very large, such as a side of beef, it is necessary to determine exactly how, where, and how much of the unit is to be removed for the sample.

USDA Sampling Procedures

To illustrate the nature of sampling the USDA has provided detailed steps and procedures. This program is covered by the Regulations Governing Inspection and Certification 7 CFR, Part 52, and includes detailed sampling plans for canned and other processed fruits and vegetables. These regulations indicate the exact number of samples to be drawn from lots of a specific size for various size containers. These plans also denote the acceptable number of maximum number of deviants for specific lots.

> 2,400 or fewer containers   –   3 samples, 0 deviants
> 2,401 to   12,000 containers –   6 samples, 1 deviant
> 12,001 to   24,000 containers – 13 samples, 2 deviants

24,001 to   48,000 containers – 21 samples, 3 devi
48,001 to   72,000 containers – 29 samples, 4 devi
72,001 to 108,000 containers – 38 samples, 5 devi
108,001 to 168,000 containers – 48 samples, 6 devi..........

From 168,000 containers, the number of deviants increases by 1 for each additional 12 samples taken up to 216 (20 deviants).

The sample rate is increased for larger size cans and may be relatively higher for frozen foods and less for juices and comminuted products.

Simplified Sampling Procedures for Small Lots

When sampling a delivery consisting of several cases or cartons of a number of items, such as two cases of product A, three cases of product B, one case of product C, and five cases of product D, do not remove all the samples from the same carton if more than one is available. If three samples are needed, draw them from different containers. Always mark or label the sample with date and code. If the samples are not perishable, they should be stored in the control laboratory until tested. Perishable items should be kept in a refrigerator or freezer until inspected. It is advisable to set aside a shelf or some other specific space to store samples. This may prevent confusion or disappearance of samples. Samples should be inspected immediately upon their receipt and, if found defective, the entire lot can be set aside for eventual disposal or return.

PRODUCT INSPECTION CONTROL

Scope

A comprehensive inspection program, including analytical procedures for all products purchased by foodservice establishments, is a most difficult and an almost impossible task. Full coverage is possible if a completely outfitted laboratory is available. However, it is not the intent of this book to provide full and detailed quality control laboratory procedures. The scope of this text is to develop simplified inspection techniques that may be followed without prior technical training and that will be effective as a guide in checking quality parameters against actual specifications.

Inspection Tests and Procedures

Quality control inspection procedures considered to be essential for an effective foodservice program follow:

(1) Proper sampling techniques
(2) Sensory evaluation
    (a) Appearance of product (uniformity of size and color)

(b) Texture
(c) Flavor (taste and aroma) characteristics
(d) Evaluation of results with purchase specifications, USDA and USDC scoring methods
(3) Visual observation of defects [may be combined with (2a)]
(4) Determination of syrup density where applicable
(5) Determination of sugar content where applicable
(6) Determination of fill container and maximum headspace
(7) Determination of drained weight
(8) Determination of percentage breading
(9) Determination of percentage fat in chopped meat
(10) Determination of presence of insect filth (maggots, rodent hair, mites, and aphids on leafy fresh vegetables) by visual methods
(11) Determination of condition of container, carton, case, vacuum can, plastic film, or any other product used for a product's wrapping

WATER CAPACITY AND FILL OF CONTAINER

Purpose

Determination of water capacity and fill of container applies to foods packed in cans and glass containers. Both the FDA and USDA have published methods for these determinations. For example, the FDA requires that the fill of container test form part of a product's standard of identity. The standard of fill of container for canned applesauce is a fill of not less than 90% of the total capacity of the container, except that, in the case of glass containers having a total capacity of 6½ fl oz or less, the fill is not less than 85%. If canned applesauce falls below the standard of fill of container, the label shall bear the general statement of substandard fill.

Equipment Needed

Thermometer, 0° to 150°F (−17.8° to 66°C)
Can opener
Clean lint-free paper toweling
Distilled water (if available) or water free of foreign matter
Straight-edge stainless steel ruler with a scale calibrated in ¹⁄₁₆ in., plus one with a ¹⁄₃₂ in. scale
Scale such as Harvard Trip Balance, single beam

Procedures

The following is FDA procedure No. 10.6 for determining *water capacity of a container.*

(1) In the case of a container with lid attached by double seam, cut out the lid without removing or altering the height of the double seam.

(2) Wash, dry, and weigh the empty container.

(3) Fill the container with distilled water at 68°F (20°C) to ³⁄₁₆ in. vertical distance below the top level of the container, and weigh.

(4) Subtract the weight found in (2) from the weight found in (3). The difference is the weight of water required to fill the container.

If the container has a removable lid attached, in the case of glass jars, fill the container with water to the level of the top.

The following is FDA procedure No. 10.6 for determining *fill of container.*

(1) In the case of a container having a lid attached by a double seam, cut out the lid without removing or altering the height of the double seam.

(2) Measure the vertical distance from the top level of the container to the top level of the food.

(3) Remove the food from the container; wash, dry, and weigh the container.

(4) Fill the container with water to ³⁄₁₆ in. vertical distance below the top level of the container. Record the temperature of the water, weigh the filled container, and determine the weight of the water by subtracting the weight of the container found in (3).

(5) Maintaining the water at the temperature recorded in (4), draw off water from the container as filled in (4) to the level of the food found in (2). Weigh the container with remaining water, and determine the weight of the remaining water by subtracting the weight of the container found in (3).

(6) Divide the weight of water in (5) by the weight of water found in (4), and multiply by 100. The result shall be considered the percentage of total capacity of the container occupied by the food.

In the case of a container with lid attached (glass jar), remove the lid and follow the procedure shown in paragraph (4), but fill the container to the level of the top.

The following are USDA procedures for determining *Fill of Container* and *Maximum Headspace* of containers.

USDA grades recommend that cans be filled as full as practicable without impairment of quality and that the product and packing medium occupy not less than 90% of the water capacity of the container. Place a straight edge from which a scale is suspended across the top of an open can. The scale is lowered until it touches the surface of the product. The distance from the surface of the product to the top of the container is the headspace. To obtain percentage of fill, divide height of container minus headspace height by height of container.

A similar procedure is applicable to frozen, semimoist, or dry products packed whole or comminuted in any container that is not only rigid but has the same diameter throughout its length, e.g., cylindrical containers. Glass and some plastic containers and cartons do not conform to these requirements so that this simple method for determining percentage of fill cannot be applied, usually because of the narrow neck of the bottle.

When the product is packed in a translucent container such as glass, it may be filled to a uniform distance from the top, although individual units may contain substantially more material than necessary to satisfy the mandatory percentage of fill regulation. For this purpose the headspace technique is sufficient.

Table 4.1 gives the maximum gross headspace in thirty-seconds of an inch for various can sizes which is considered adequate to avoid slack filling.

TABLE 4.1. Maximum Gross Headspace for Various Size Cans

Can Designation	Trade Description	Maximum Gross Headspace, $\frac{1}{32}$ in.
8 Z Short	211 × 300	14
8 Z Tall	211 × 304	15
No. 300	300 × 407	19
No. 1 Tall	301 × 411	20
No. 303	303 × 406	19
No. 2	307 × 409	19
No. 2½	401 × 411	20
No. 3 Vacuum	404 × 307	16
No. 10	603 × 700	27

Source: U.S. Dep. Agric.

DETERMINATION OF DRAINED WEIGHT

Purpose

For fruits and vegetables packed in liquid, the drained weight of the solid product is more important than the total net weight. When comparisons are made among brands, the higher the drained weight, the greater the value of the product. This procedure is also employed for USDA grading of certain commodities.

Equipment Needed

U.S. Standard No. 8 circular sieve—12 in. diameter
U.S. Standard No. 8 circular sieve—8 in. diameter
U.S. Standard 2-mesh screen (for tomatoes)
Stopwatch or timer
Scale
Thermometer, 0° to 150°F (−17.8° to 66°C)
Rack or tripod ring

Procedures

The following procedures may be employed to determine the drained weight for most canned, glass-packed, and frozen fruits and vegetables (Fig. 4.3).

FIG. 4.3.   Items used in determination of drained weight.

(1) Quick Method (for Approximate Results). Empty contents of the container onto a previously weighed No. 8 screen and allow to drain for 2 min. At the end of 2 min the product remaining on the screen is weighed. The weight of the screen is subtracted, and the difference is the drained weight of the product. For frozen items, allow them to thaw completely before proceeding with the test.

(2) USDA Method. Evenly distribute the contents of the container upon a No. 8 circular sieve. A 2-mesh sieve is used for canned tomatoes. Without disturbing the product, the sieve is inclined so as to facilitate drainage. Allow to drain for 2 min. The drained weight is the weight of the sieve plus the contents, less the weight of the dry sieve.

An 8 in. diameter sieve is used for No. 2½ size cans and smaller, and a 12 in. diameter sieve is used for No. 10 size cans. Halves of apricots, peaches, and pears are turned "cups down" on the screen.

For recommended drained weights, see USDA grade regulations for individual commodities.

The following procedure is recommended by the USDA specifically for frozen fruits and vegetables.

(1)   Thawing: Thaw samples in the closed containers in such manner as to allow free circulation of air. Open the container periodically and take a reading of the temperature at the center of the mass. Drain the product as soon as possible after the temperature at the center of the container has reached 28°F (−2°C).

(2)   Draining: Open the container, and if the product is a fruit packed in syrup, remove any hard-caked sugar from the top. Do not disturb the product while removing the sugar cake. If any loose granulated sugar remains, gently stir the top of the liquid to dissolve it.

Place the screen or sieve, which has been previously weighed, in a horizontal position on the rack, tripod ring, or other suitable support, and pour most of the free liquid through the screen. Pour the remainder (balance) of the product uniformly on the sieve, and allow to drain for 2 min.

Weigh the product remaining on the sieve. Subtract the weight of the sieve. The difference is the drained weight.

Three tests should be performed. Average the results to calculate the drained weight of the shipment.

DETERMINATION OF PERCENTAGE BREADING

Purpose

The amount of breading that can be used to coat certain food products is regulated by the FDA and the USDC's National Marine Fisheries Service. Breaded shrimp, fish portions, fish sticks, oysters, and scallops are regulated by these agencies.

The percentage of breading is a troublesome area when costs between one brand and another are being evaluated and the price differences justified. It therefore becomes an important aspect of quality inspection control to determine the amount of breading, in order that cost evaluation can be made on the unbreaded product.

The FDA promulgated regulations for breaded shrimp in June 1965. This regulation refers to all forms of shrimp, such as "fantail" or butterfly; butterfly with tail off; round with tail; round with tail off; pieces; and composite units. Regardless of the form, the regulations limit the amount of breading to 50% or less of the raw shrimp. Frozen raw lightly breaded shrimp is another category. If the label states "lightly breaded," the product must the 65% shrimp material. Frozen fried scallops must contain a minimum of 60% by weight of scallop meat. Frozen raw breaded fish portions must contain not less than 75% by weight of fish flesh. Frozen fried fish portions must contain not less than 65% by weight of fish flesh. Frozen raw breaded fish sticks must contain not less than 72% by weight of fish flesh.

Exacting methods of analysis to determine the percentage of breaded material on a product have been established by the FDA; however, for routine purposes, simplified procedures have been developed by the National Frozen Food Association. These tests are suggested for spot cost evaluation and as a means to cross-check deliveries since the results will be reasonably accurate and can be performed without elaborate laboratory equipment.

Equipment Needed

Scale that is accurate to 0.1 oz
Thermometer 0° to 150°F (−17.8° to 65°C)
Ladle, large spatula, or paddle
Stopwatch or timer
Lint-free toweling or cloth

Tweezers
Bucket or large pot
Wire mesh aluminum screen (2 × 2 ft)

Simplified Procedure for Breaded Shrimp and Scallops

Select 1 lb of the product at random from several packages. If there is a significant amount of loose breading in the carton, include a portion of it with the sample. Weigh the samples immediately, before moisture condenses on them and before they thaw.

Place the weighed sample in a bucket or large pot that contains 2 or 3 gal. of tepid (70°–80°F, 21.1°–26.7°C) water. Gently stir the sample with a ladle, large spatula, or paddle for 10 min. This will separate the bulk of the breading from the seafood. If any of the breading remains, wash it off under a moderate spray of water. If necessary, gently brush off any remaining material with the fingers.

Next, lay the debreaded pieces on a sloping screen or paper towel and allow to drain for 2 min before weighing.

The percentage of seafood is calculated as follows:

$$\frac{\text{Weight of debreaded product}}{\text{Weight of breaded product}} \times 100 = \text{percentage of seafood}$$

The percentage of breading is calculated as follows:

100% minus the percentage of seafood = percentage of breading

In the case of shrimp, a cutback of 5 percentage points is allowed to compensate for "inaccuracy of method." This provision does not apply to breaded scallops.

Procedure for Breaded Fish Sticks

Select 1 lb of the product at random from several packages. Weigh the sample. Place each piece individually in a tepid (70°–80°F, 21.1°–26.7°C) water bath and allow to remain for 10 to 80 sec (the larger the portion, the longer the dip). Remove from the bath; blot lightly with a double thickness of paper toweling. Then scrape off or pick off the breading from the fish flesh with a small spatula or tweezers. Weigh the debreaded portions and calculate the percentage of breading by the preceding method used for breaded shrimp and scallops. Make no adjustment for "inaccuracy of method."

Procedure for Breaded Oysters

Breading percentages determined for frozen breaded oysters do not have too much significance because the raw shucked oysters, before being breaded, are both high in water content and highly variable in the amount of water content. The breading acts almost like a sponge, absorbing some of this water before freezing, so that the breading weights are correspondingly high and variable.

The following procedure is suggested by the National Marine Fisheries Service's Technological Laboratory on the basis of limited experimentation.

Weigh 1 lb of a randomly selected sample. Hold the frozen oysters individually under a stream of cold water and remove most of the breading by rubbing the surface. Stop washing before the oysters thaw. Blot quickly and weigh. After thawing, check for additional breading left in the folds. If a significant amount remains, weigh it and subtract this weight from the previously determined debreaded weight. Do not wait until oysters are thawed and breading has been removed from the folds to determine the debreaded weight. During thawing, the oysters will lose a considerable amount of fluid so that a weight determined after thawing will not be correct. Apply the previously described formula to determine the amount of breading. No allowance is made for "inaccuracy of method."

If specific procedures do not exist for products that require an evaluation of the percentage of breading, improvisations can be made by referring to the preceding methods. Once a procedure has been established, it should be closely followed, so that continuity and uniform results are obtained.

DETERMINATION OF PERCENTAGE FAT IN GROUND BEEF

A Hobart fat percentage measuring kit (see Fig. 2.10) can be used to determine and evaluate the fat content in ground beef so that comparisons may be made with specifications and/or the maximum percentages required by law.

The Hobart fat percentage measuring kit is designed for rapid, accurate, and simplified analyses. One kit will provide a continuous series of tests at 15 min intervals.

A 2 oz sample of ground beef is inserted in the kit under a heating element. The sample must be ground at least twice through a ⅛ in. plate. The heater is activated when the timer is set for a 15 min interval. The fat and juices are collected in a test tube located under the heater. A specially calibrated scale with a movable pointer is mounted vertically next to the test tube. This scale measures the column of fat and is expressed in terms of percentage fat in the meat. The heating element is automatically turned off at the end of the 15 min cycle. A bell is sounded indicating the end of the cycle.

The kit is manufactured to analyze ground beef samples containing 10 to 40% fat. Test results are within ±1% when the device is operated in accordance with suggested procedures.

The procedure for the determination of fat in canned and packaged meats makes use of a refractometer. This procedure may be considered a bit too complicated for the scope of this book. However, it may be necessary to employ this test to find out the percentage of meat in frankfurter and other packaged meat products.

The complete procedure can be found in *Food Analysis Laboratory Experiments, 2nd Edition* by Meloan and Pomeranz (1980).

Briefly, dry sand is added to the sample to serve as a grinding medium so that the fat will be exposed to the chemical solvent bromonaphthalene. Anhydrous sodium sulfate is added to absorb the moisture from the meat. Fat has a refractive index of about 1.49, and bromonaphthalene a refractive index of 1.65. Readings between these indices give the percentage of fat in the sample. This test can be performed and results calculated in about 15 min.

INSECT FILTH IN FOODS

Maggots and mites are sometimes found in flour, dried fruit, cereals, and in smoked and dried meats and fish. These mites are small (less than 1 mm) and usually whitish. They are referred to as "cheese mites," "flour mites," "bulb mites," and "dried fruit mites." Visual observation in many instances can be used to determine their presence. These foods are usually kept in dry-storage areas. Frequent inspection should be made to determine presence of these insects. If they are found, the food products must be removed and immediately discarded.

A maggot is the larval stage of a fly. In some foods like canned tomatoes, where it is difficult to determine their presence visually, a floatation test is used. Again we refer the reader to *Food Analysis Laboratory Experiments, 2nd Edition* by Meloan and Pomeranz (1980) for the complete procedure. Tests are also described for determination of insect fragments and rodent hairs in cornmeal, mites and aphids in leafy vegetables, and rodent urine on food containers.

SENSORY EVALUATION

The mechanisms of sensory evaluation have been discussed in Chapter 2. Sensory perception is a major laboratory tool for quality assurance. Once the art is mastered, it can be employed to good advantage at almost every phase of food handling. It is suggested that sensory evaluation procedures forming parts of the USDA and USDC quality grade standards be followed.

USDA and USDC quality grade standards are established by assigning grade scores to such factors as color, uniformity of size, defects, and product character. When an evaluation is made, the scores for many of the factors are determined by sensory analysis. *Appearance* characteristics are scored from a product's color, uniformity of size, and defects. The product's *character* is scored from an evaluation of texture, taste, and aroma. Each of the quality grade standards have incorporated in them factors that relate only to specific characteristics of the product.

The following example will serve to illustrate these points.

U.S. Standards for Grades of Frozen Whole Kernel (or Whole Grain) Corn—Color (Varietal)—Golden or Yellow; White

U.S. Grade A (or Fancy). Similar varietal characteristics, good flavor and odor, minimum score of 90 points for good or reasonably good color, practically free from defects, tender.

U.S. Grade B (or Extra Standard). Similar varietal characteristics, good flavor and odor, minimum score of 80 points for reasonably good color or fairly good color scoring no less than 7 points, reasonably free from defects, reasonably tender.

U.S. Grade C (or Standard). Similar varietal characteristics, fairly good flavor and odor, minimum score of 70 points for fairly good color, fairly free from defects, fairly tender.

Grade A. *Color (Quality Factor)*: Practically uniform, typical of tender sweet corn, product bright, practically free from "off-variety" kernels. *Defects*: Practically free from pieces of cob, husk, silk, and harmless extraneous vegetable matter; pulled, ragged, crushed, damaged, seriously damaged kernels, loose skins. *Tenderness and Maturity:* Kernels in milk or early cream stage of maturity, tender texture.

The standards for grades of frozen whole kernel corn show the extent to which sensory perception is employed. The senses of sight, odor, feeling, and taste are involved and must be applied if a meaningful evaluation is to be made.

Fish and Shellfish Grading

Fish and shellfish are graded by the U.S. Department of Commerce, National Marine Fisheries Service. This is a voluntary service offered to the fish industry. The basic techniques employed for fish and shellfish parallel those for vegetables and fruit. Sensory evaluation is required for scoring. For example, grades for frozen breaded fish sticks are U.S. Grade A and U.S. Grade B. U.S. Grade A requires good flavor and odor and means that the cooked product has the typical flavor and odor of the indicated species of fish and of the breading, and is free from rancidity, bitterness, staleness, and other off-flavors and off-odors.

Condition of the package, ease of separation, broken or damaged sticks, uniformity of size and weight, distortions, coating defects, blemishes, bones, and texture are the factors that require evaluation for grading.

Additional Applications

The ensuing examples illustrate the usefulness of sensory evaluation techniques.

Samples should be tested in the following order: (1) appearance, (2) aroma, (3) taste, (4) mouth feel, and (5) aftertaste.

The product should be examined in its usual manner of service, e.g., hot coffee in cups; cold drinks in glasses; mixed salad spreads or other foods on serving plates. When evaluating a beverage such as coffee, it should be sensed black without an adjunct, e.g., no milk, cream, or sugar. A carrier will dilute or alter the true sensory effect. If the evaluator's normal mode of drinking coffee is with an adjunct, then this additional procedure may also be followed.

Test of Coffee Bitterness Versus Strength. This illustration of a sensory examination is used, not only as an example of a typical application, but because it is one of the most misunderstood among foodservice personnel.

Temperature. Test should be made at 140°F (60°C).

Appearance. Coffee exhibiting strength and strength combined with bitterness will appear to have identical brew color, i.e., a deep brown.

Aroma. Both will show equal characteristics. The aroma will have a deep, full coffee character. Sniff deeply, holding the cup about 1 in. from the nasal cavities. Then lower the cup slightly and sniff again with the mouth open.

Taste. Both should be equal in taste character. Take a sip from one sample, swirl it around in the mouth, and expel the liquid. Rinse the mouth with warm water and repeat the procedure with the second cup.

Mouth Feel. Both samples should produce a thick full-bodied feeling, as opposed to watery.

Aftertaste. The sample of coffee being tested for strength will not leave a lingering sensation on the back of the tongue or the throat. The mouth will return to a normal clear tone almost immediately. The sample possessing the bitter character will retain its sensation. The aftertaste of bitterness will also have a tendency to clog the taste buds. The sensation of bitterness can be compared with the following substances: quinine, alum, hops, rind of a fresh orange, juice from a peach pit, or phosphate of soda.

Test for Spoilage of Milk. *Temperature.* 72° to 90°F (22.2° to 32.3°C)

Appearance. Observations should be made to determine presence of mold, separation, and stringiness.

Aroma.   Sniff the milk for presence of musty or fermented character.

Taste.   Sip a quantity of the milk and roll it slowly around in the mouth until the flavor is sensed, then expel the liquid. If the milk is spoiled, the acid area of the tongue will become activated, indicating sourness and resulting destabilization of proteins.

Test for Spoilage of Syrup for Carbonated Beverages.   *Temperature.* Room temperature.

Appearance.   Observations should be made to determine presence of mold and product separation. Product should appear clear and without sediment.

Aroma.   (1) Smell stopper (jar cap) and neck of bottle. Note presence of off-odor, e.g., mold, pungency, or sourness. (2) Take a small wooden stick, strip of blotter paper, or knife blade and immerse into the syrup and allow to drain. Smell the liquid for presence of musty or fermented character. Repeat this procedure with samples of syrup known to be free of contamination.

Taste.   Taste the sample of syrup on the stick, blotter paper, or knife. Bring it in contact with the saliva and make a solution of the two by slowly rolling the liquid in the mouth. After the character is sensed, expel. If spoilage is present, the tongue will indicate sourness.

Mouth Feel.   Since the sample under observation is small, the sense of feeling will not be activated.

Aftertaste.   If spoilage is indicated, a lingering sourness or off-taste will be sensed.

Test for Syrup:Water Ratio in Synthetic Sweetened Colas.   This test for incorrect syrup-carbonated water ratio can be applied when a hydrometer is not available.

Temperature.   The liquid should be brought to room temperature. This will reduce the fizz and still the liquid.

Appearance.   Hold the glass containing the sample in natural light, and note the color of the liquid. If possible, the sample should be compared with one of the correct syrup-carbonated water ratio.

Aroma.   Sniff deeply, holding the glass of liquid below the nose, and again slightly below the open mouth. Note the intensity of the aroma.

Taste.   Sip a small amount of the beverage, swirl it around the mouth, and then expel it. Determine the intensity of the flavor and the registration of the sweetness.

Mouth Feel.   Sliminess and a sticky feeling will be sensed if the syrup ratio is in excess of the recommended formula.

Aftertaste.   A pronounced lingering of sweetness on the tongue, upper palate, and throat will be sensed. Clogging of the taste buds will also result.

PACKAGING INSPECTION

Proper and secure packaging of all food is a prerequisite to wholesome and safe products.

Cans should not be accepted or used if they leak or bulge at either end. Bulging or swelling sometimes indicates spoilage. Dents in cans do not harm the contents unless they have actually pierced the can or sprung the seam. If many cans of a shipment are dented or the labels torn, it reflects poor handling and storage procedures on the part of the purveyor.

Packages of frozen food items should be solid. Packages that are limp, wet, stained, or sweating indicate that the frozen products probably were thawed at some point. They should be set aside and returned.

Thaw indicators are becoming widely used to detect the mishandling of frozen foods. These indicators are useful to prove thawing at any time during transit or transfer. For example, when a trucker receives merchandise from a frozen food packer, he is requested to sign a statement that the indicators are normal. When he delivers the product to its final destination, the receiver checks the indicator, and, if it is normal, he signs the receipt showing that the shipment was in good condition upon arrival.

Some states are requiring the affixing of thaw indicators to the package or container of certain frozen foods. A provision of one to these acts follows: "No person shall knowingly sell, exchange or offer for sale at wholesale or retail, in bulk or in package form any article of food which has been frozen, without affixing to the package containing the same as an irremovable part thereof, a device approved by the State Department of Health to provide an instant alert as to whether said frozen product has thawed."

INSPECTION CONTROL OF OTHER PRODUCTS

Inspection control features and procedures of other products will be found in subsequent chapters.

5

Storage and Issuing Control

Storage facilities are of major importance in a quality control program. Proper storage maintenance, temperature control, cleaning and sanitation, and stability are major considerations in such a program. Storage stability of food products has a significant role in preventing spoilage and changes in texture, flavor, and color. Each category of food, whether canned, dried, fresh, or frozen, requires special handling and astute observation to ensure that changes in quality attributes do not occur.

STORAGE CATEGORIES

Main storage areas fall into four categories: (1) receiving, (2) refrigerated, (3) dry, and (4) refuse. Supplemental or adjunct areas, consisting of small satellite units to facilitate localized production, are a subcategory. Under-the-counter coolers, dry food and nonfood cabinets, trash and garbage receptacles are examples of this subclass of storage space.

Following are the subdivisions of the four categories of storage areas:

(1) Receiving station
   (a) Loading and unloading dock
   (b) Interior distribution area
(2) Refrigerated storage
   (a) Freezers
   (b) Coolers
   (c) Thawing units

This category also includes such units as walk-in refrigerators (coolers and freezers), reach-ins, roll-in cabinets, pass-through refrigerators, and upright movable units.

(3) Dry storage
   (a) Food storage for canned, dry, and bottled items
   (b) Nonfood storage for linen, janitorial supplies, and locker and dressing rooms
(4) Refuse
   (a) Main refuse collection center containing compactors
   (b) Substations, trash cans, and bins

For purposes of quality control, refrigerated and dry storage are discussed in this chapter. Receiving was described in Chapter 4.

DEFINITIONS OF REFRIGERATED STORAGE

Storage Freezers. These are low-temperature units that maintain constant temperature in the range of $-10°$ to $0°F$ ($-23°$ to $-17.8°C$).

Processing Freezers. These units are used to perform the actual freezing of food at temperatures of $-20°F$ ($-29°C$) or below. They are specialty units, not generally used as storage freezers.

Coolers. These are medium temperature-range storage units that hold the temperature at a mean of $38°F$ ($3.33°C$), with a minimum of $32°F$ ($0°C$) and a maximum of $48°F$ ($8.9°C$). Coolers are used for thawing frozen foods; storing meat at $32°–38°F$ ($0°–3.33°C$); storing dairy products at $36°–40°F$ ($2.22°–4.44°C$); and storing vegetables and fruit at $44°–48°F$ ($6.67°–8.89°C$).

Thawers. These are specially designed to maintain a steady temperature of $40°F$ ($4.4°C$), regardless of room temperature or product load. Reverse-cycle refrigeration is employed, so that the refrigerant is used for both cooling and heating.

DRY STORAGE TECHNIQUES

Dry Storage Demands Exacting Procedures

Proper dry storage controls for the warehousing of semiperishable products are as important as those for frozen and perishable foods. Possibly because of more publicity, better training, or the knowledge that spoilage is likely to occur, personnel generally handle frozen foods with greater care than semiperishables. Foodservice personnel usually ignore proper storage techniques when handling canned products and other food items that do not require refrigeration. Too often dry storage areas in food establishments are a "catchall" for old equipment, junk, and a variety of material that should be either discarded or put elsewhere. Dry storage areas are often found in the boiler room, damp cellars, spaces that have hot water or steam pipes running through them, or the compressor room. These conditions will eventually result in damaged, spoiled, or unpalatable foods.

The following techniques should be followed to ensure that foods kept in dry storage will not deteriorate:

(1) Dry storage areas must be maintained at high levels of cleanliness, should be vermin- and rodent-proof, and should be constructed of materials that can be easily washed.

(2) Dry storage areas should be well planned. Shelving should be adequate and flexible, located away from machine vibrations, the entrance should be wide enough to allow passage of hand trucks and dollies, and aisles should be wide enough to allow passage of mobile equipment and freedom of movement when loading or unloading. Ample space will help in inventory control and stock rotation.

(3) Dry storage areas must be well ventilated and protected from drastic temperature changes. Measures must be taken to guard against freezing temperatures or temperatures exceeding 70°F (21.1°C).

(4) Dry storage areas should be provided with good lighting, so that labels and cartons can be readily identified; however, sunlight should be blocked to avoid deterioration from this source.

(5) Dry storage areas must be kept free from moisture from sweating pipes, high humidity, and dampness due to wet walls or seepage. Items such as cereals, tea, coffee, hot chocolate powder, and powdered creaming agents must be protected from abnormally high moisture conditions that could result in mold formation.

(6) Dry storage areas should be located in the vicinity of the main refrigerated components, so that the composite forms one operating entity in the production system.

(7) Dry storage areas should have sufficient height and space between shelves. Space should also be provided to pile full cartons or to permit the use of pallets.

(8) Dry storage areas should not be a "catchall" storage assembly warehouse. Items such as cleaning materials, soaps, paper goods (unless they are used for food preparation), and linens should be placed in separate storage places.

(9) Provisions should be made to enclose and segregate odor-producing items such as spices. Odors emanating from these materials could contaminate such foods as dried beans, coffee, and cereal.

Storage Control of Semiperishable Foods

Because practically every food item that is put into dry storage can deteriorate, break down, or spoil, stock movement must be monitored. It is as important to maintain the "first-in, first-out" (FIFO) rotation procedure with dry stores as with refrigerated items.

Supermarket Techniques. One method that will tend to prevent deterioration is the supermarket display technique. All cases should be marked, separated into categories, and dated. The date should indicate the arrival day. Codes on cans and packages should be understandable, so that some idea as to when the item was packed can be gained. Goods stacked on shelves should be uniformly stored. Each can or box should be stamped with the date of delivery.

Handling of Canned Foods.   If canned foods are subjected to prolonged storage or temperature extremes, deterioration becomes a possibility. For example, high temperatures will accelerate the reaction of acids present in some foods. This action may produce pinholes in the metal and darken the interior of the can. High temperature may also induce changes in the texture of some foods, cause development of off-flavors in fruit juices (especially citrus products), and emulsions may be destroyed, although this defect is more likely to occur with freezing temperatures. Mayonnaise, mustard, and salad dressing are examples of emulsions.

Canned foods should not be kept over six months even when stored under ideal conditions. It is difficult to determine the length of time foods have been canned prior to delivery, even with a knowledge of the coding data. For this reason, excess stock should be avoided. The advantage of purchasing large quantities to save money must be weighed against the possibility of spoilage. Other factors to consider with quantity purchases are the amount of money tied up and the storage space required.

The ideal holding temperature for semiperishables is 60°F (16°C). The higher the temperature, the greater the chance of deterioration. For example, at 100°F (37.8°C) the average shelf-life will be reduced by two-thirds. Although 70°F (21°C) is recommended for dry storage areas, the life of many foods can be extended by lower storage temperatures.

Several thermometers should be installed in various locations within the storage area, e.g., one hung near the ceiling and another midway from the ceiling to the floor. If adequate air circulation is maintained, temperatures should be about the same throughout the area. Windows facing the sun should be shielded or blocked to prevent deterioration from sunlight.

HANDLING FROZEN FOODS

The quality of frozen foods changes with time and temperature of storage. Once frozen foods have deteriorated or lost their original quality characteristics, they cannot be restored to their original state by refreezing.

The techniques of handling frozen foods so that they retain their quality must be mastered. This is a prerequisite to the success of the entire program. It is not easy to train personnel to handle, store, and control products efficiently. Often people assigned to these tasks are of marginal ability and in a menial classification, so that the results of their work follow a similar pattern.

The first step in meeting the goal of a well organized frozen food storage operation is to assign to one person the responsibility of running or directing it. In many establishments this assignment does not require the full time of one worker; nevertheless, the operation of the department should be carried out by one person, who must be responsible for ordering, or advising the purchasing agent, when the merchandise is low. His chores include stocking, rotating, and the care and cleaning of all food storage facilities, including those satellite units located in the production and serving areas. In addition, he should become familiar with the operation of the equipment, so that if mechanical problems arise he will be able to appraise the situation and call upon authorized repairmen to correct it. This is not a menial job, since it requires a person who is alert and efficient and has good judgment. A certain amount of training must be given the individual, so that he (or she) develops a thorough understanding of the reasons underlying proper frozen food storage control. This person should also be given authority to direct those people who may be assigned to help him.

Training and Management "Followup"

Management cannot assume a haphazard attitude toward the training program. After an individual has been taught the technical aspects of a position, he must be made to realize the importance of his work. If he is encouraged and motivated along these lines, success will be forthcoming. The importance of his department in relation to the overall operation and to his co-workers should also be emphasized.

Management then has the added responsibility of following up and evaluating his work by periodic checks and inspections to determine if the job is being properly performed. This step is especially significant during the early stages of employment, so that corrective measures can be taken immediately.

Deterioration Is Not Reversible

One of the cardinal rules for proper handling of frozen foods is to maintain the product temperature at 0°F (-17.8°C) or lower. A 10°F (5.6°C) rise in the temperature of the food can more than double the rate of spoilage; the higher the temperature, the faster the rate of deterioration. Many people are of the opinion that if food remains in a solid state it is acceptable. Unfortunately, this misconception can have dire consequences with regard to quality deterioration. If, for example, a frozen product is allowed to reach a temperature of 25°F (still the solid state for most foods) for just one day, the resulting loss of quality may be equivalent to one or more years of freezer storage. Once damage has occurred, it cannot be reversed by subjecting a food to proper storage temperatures.

Effects of Intermittent Thawing

Repeated freezing and thawing during storage is detrimental to the quality of frozen foods. As little as a 5°F fluctuation in freezer storage temperature above and below the zero mark can be damaging to many foods. Above 10°F (-12.2°C), thawing intensifies the concentration effect. Upon refreezing, water melted from small [ice] crystals tends to coat unmelted crystals, causing them to grow in size and form large clusters. This condition can cause physical damage to the cellular structure of food by rupturing and separating cells. Solid foods from animal or vegetable tissues, such as meat, fish, fruit, and vegetables, are of cellular structure, containing delicate cell walls and cell membranes. Within and between the cells is water. Upon freezing, water solidifies and increases in volume by 10%. The increased volume does not affect the cellular structure. However, intermittent thawing and freezing has an adverse effect on frozen emulsions such as butter, ice cream, puddings, and pie fillings.

AFDOUS Code Requirements

A significant development relevant to the proper control, handling, and storage of frozen foods occurred when a code of standards was issued on June 22, 1961, by the Association of Food and Drug Officials of the United States.

This code is not an official federal regulation, but it has been adopted by the frozen food industry as a basis for good handling and storage practices. Since its inception, a number of states have incorporated various features of the code into law. Those states with regulatory handling requirements are: Arkansas, Connecticut, Florida, Georgia, Illinois, Massachusetts, Maryland, Oregon, and Pennsylvania. Because of the important and increasing role of frozen foods in the domestic food markets, full regulatory measures are now being taken by the federal government, other states, and local agencies.

The code defines *internal product temperature* as the equilibrated product temperature of frozen foods. Temperature provisions of Section B, paragraph 1, are as follows:

(a)   All frozen food shall be held at an air temperature of 0°F (−17.8°C) or lower except for defrost cycles, loading and unloading, or for other temporary conditions beyond the immediate control of the person or company under whose care or supervision the frozen food is held; provided that only those frozen foods destined for repackaging in smaller units may be defrosted for such purposes in accordance with good sanitary precautions.

(b)   The internal product temperature of frozen food shall be maintained at 0°F (−17.8°C) or lower except when the product is subjected to the previously mentioned conditions; then the internal product temperature shall not exceed 10°F (−12.2°C), and such product shall be returned to 0°F (−17.8°C) as quickly as possible.

   1.   Internal product temperature for any case of frozen food shall be determined in accordance with the following procedure:

      (a)   Only when an accurate determination of internal product temperature fails without sacrifice of packaged frozen food shall representative packages or units be opened to allow for inserting the sensing element for temperature measurement to approximate center of the packages in question.

2. Internal product temperature of consumer packages of frozen food shall be determined in accordance with the following procedure:

(a) Open the top of the case and remove two corner packages.

(b) With an ice pick or similar tool punch a hole in the case from the inside. Do not use the stem of the thermometer.

(c) This hole is positioned so that, when the thermometer stem is inserted from the outside, it fits snugly between packages.

(d) Insert the thermometer stem about 3 in. Replace the two packages. Close the case and place a couple of other cases on top to assure good contact on the sensing portion of the thermometer stem.

(e) After 5 min read the temperature.

3. Thermometers or other temperature measuring devices shall have an accuracy of ±2°F (±1.1°C).

In addition, the code contains provisions for sanitation conditions of equipment, buildings, and grounds.

Temperature Measuring Techniques

The proper taking of temperature readings requires experience, patience, an understanding of the reasons for obtaining the data, and a knowledge of the product. In Chapter 2, a section is devoted to thermometers and their correct use.

Technical Service Bulletin 7, dated May 15, 1969, "Frozen Food Temperatures: Their Meaning and Measurement," should be obtained as a guide for this purpose. This useful information is issued by the National Association of Frozen Food Packers, Washington, DC. The bulletin outlines in detail correct methods for taking product temperature and describes appropriate equipment for the proper care and handling of frozen foods.

Receiving and Storage Guidelines for Frozen Foods

(1) Be ready to receive the merchandise and know what is being delivered. Have storage space available for immediate unloading.

(2) Unload the products quickly and move them directly into the freezer.

(3) Follow the instructions for taking temperatures of incoming food, and make a record of the data.

(4) Segregate the merchandise and stow it in its proper location.

(5) Inspect cartons for damage and use appropriate sealing tape to repair broken cases or packages. Proper packaging is mandatory for maintaining the original quality. Packaging materials should be moisture- and vapor-proof to prevent dehydration, discoloration, odor absorption, loss of flavor, and oxidation.

(6) Cases and packages should be stacked so that the labels or marks are visible. Additional marking may be necessary to supplement worn or torn labels.

(7) When loading or unloading the freezer, push carts all the way inside and work within the unit. This practice will help to maintain proper freezer temperatures and reduce the entry of moisture.

(8) Keep freezer absolutely clean, neat, and sanitary. Do not allow junk, old cartons, and other debris to accumulate. Remove and discard damaged food.

(9) Rotate the stock. Know the code or packaging date and receiving date. Combine rotation procedures with the stacking operation.

(10) When stacking shelves with small items, use dividers between different products to avoid mixing items. This scheme will save space and make inventory taking easier.

(11) When stacking satellite units or thawing boxes, make a list of items beforehand so that trips inside the freezer can be minimized.

(12) Record all box temperatures every 4 hr. Report any unusual changes.

(13) Display case types of freezers are being used to promote efficiency in the preparation area. These are open-top freezers, similar in design to those used in supermarkets. They expedite the production flow since the items can readily be seen and removed without stooping. One disadvantage is the need to defrost these open units frequently.

(14) If temporary power failures occur, do not open refrigerators or attempt to move the food. Depending on insulation, ambient temperatures, and degree of tightness of the door seals, temperatures should hold within an acceptable range for 18 to 24 hr.

STABILITY OF FOODS UNDER FROZEN STORAGE

Stability of precooked and other forms of processed food continues to be a major area for research and development. The amount of investigation that has taken place during the last two decades has provided the industry with a great amount of information on proper methods of storage, handling, and the maximum lengths of time foods can be held without affecting quality. The following will serve to illustrate the importance of stock rotation and proper temperature.

(1) Some doughs and batters, frankfurters, white sauces, and thickened wheat flour-based gravies do not hold up under ordinary freezer storage ($0°$ to $10°F$, $-17.8°$ to $12.2°C$).

(2) White sauce thickened with waxy rice flour will remain stable for 3 years at $-10°F$ ($-27°C$), 1 year at $0°F$ ($-17.8°C$), 2 months between $0°$ and $+10°F$ ($-17.8°$ and $-12.2°C$), and 3 weeks at $+10°F$ ($-12.2°C$).

(3) Soups, bread, and most meat entrees hold their original quality remarkably well if the products are properly packaged and stored at 0°F (−17.8°C) or below.
(4) Methods of packaging have an effect on foods stored in freezers:
   (a) Solid packed foods last longer since less surface is exposed.
   (b) Meats covered with gravies and sauces will retain their original quality for long periods of time.
   (c) Vegetables packed in liquid can be preserved for long periods.
   (d) Foods packed in a nitrogen atmosphere plus a tight vapor- and moisture-proof paper will be protected against oxidative deterioration.

Foods Having Short Storage Life

Although many precooked frozen foods and baked goods will remain in excellent condition for 6 months or longer, a few products have a short storage life (2 weeks to 2 months). The following is a partial list of such foods (Tressler *et al.* 1968):

Product	Maximum Storage Life at 0°F (−17.8°C)
Bacon, Canadian	2 weeks
Batter, gingerbread	3–4 months
Batter, muffin	2 weeks
Batter, spice	1–2 months
Biscuit, baking powder	1–2 months
Bologna, sliced	2 weeks
Cake, sponge, egg yolk	2 months
Cake, spice	2 months
Dough, roll	1–2 months
Frankfurters	2 weeks
Gravy	2 weeks
Ham, sliced	2 weeks
Poultry giblets	2 months
Poultry livers	2 months
Sauce, white (wheat flour base)	2 weeks
Sausage	2 months

Foods Having Medium Storage Life

Foods which have a storage life of medium length—listing follows (Tressler *et al.* 1968)—will remain in good condition for 6 to 8 months at 0°F (−17.8°C) or lower. Storage stability is predicated on the formulation, methods of preparation, and packaging. The optimum storage life of any food is dependent on many conditions; therefore, the following list is intended merely as a guide. Rotation and good freezer control should be applied to all products.

Chicken, fried	Meat loaf
Crab	Pies, chicken
Fish, fatty	Pies, fruit, unbaked
Fruit, purees	Pies, meat
Ham, baked, whole	Potatoes, French-fried
Lobster	Soups
Meals on a tray	Shrimp
Meatballs	Turkey

Foods Having Long Storage Life

Foods of high storage stability should remain in good condition for 12 months or more at 0°F (-17.8°C). These products are solid-packed stews, bread, rolls, and waffles. A representative list follows (Tressler *et al.* 1968):

Applesauce	Candies	Peanuts
Apples, baked	Cherries	Pecans
Bread	Chicken, creamed	Plums
Bread (rolls)	(waxy rice flour-based)	Stew, beef
Blackberries	Chicken a la king	Stew, veal
Blueberries	Cookies	Waffles
Cake, fruit	Fish, lean	

EFFECTS OF STORAGE ON FOODS

The effects of storage on foods have been briefly discussed in previous sections of this chapter. These include microbiological, physical, and chemical changes resulting from humidity, exposure to air and light, temperature, and length of storage and sanitation. The last factor, sanitation, is fully covered in Chapter 12.

Effects of Humidity

Humidity within all storage areas must be controlled to prevent changes in the quality of food. Some effects of humidity are described below:

(1) Humidity, if not controlled, may increase microbiological contamination. Refrigerators used to store vegetables may contain airborne contaminants like mold spores. Fresh fruits and vegetables with bruised skins then become target areas for the growth of mold. Mold will spread rapidly, resulting in major spoilage problems.

(2) Foul odors caused by the growth of *Pseudomonas* organisms on poultry skins or meats can be transmitted to other foods in the same box, causing off-odors and off-flavors. These organisms are found on most fresh meats.

(3) Controlled humidity of a food storage atmosphere is necessary to prevent spoilage on food surfaces. Microorganisms require adequate moisture to grow and multiply. Each type of organism, yeast, mold, or bacteria, achieves optimum growth in a certain humidity range (see Table 5.1).

(4) The extent of change in flavor and quality of a product is proportional to storage time and temperature. At lower temperatures and humidities there is less bacterial and enzyme action.

(5) Freezing does not inactivate all microorganisms present at the time the food was frozen. If, during the storage stage, increases in temperature occur and humidity is excessive, activation of these organisms will result in their growth.

(6) Dehydration may preserve microorganisms. If dehydrated foods are subjected to conditions favorable to microbial growth, spoilage may result.

(7) Shrinkage in meat, vegetables, or fruits is appreciable at humidities of 75%.

(8) Dried foods that are hygroscopic must be kept hermetically sealed, otherwise they will absorb moisture rapidly. These foods include onion powder, instant coffee, instant tea, chocolate, gelatin, dry milk powder, and foam-dried fruit. Desiccants such as silica gel in moisture-permeable bags are sometimes packed with foods of this

TABLE 5.1. Lowest and RH Values Permitting Growth of Spoilage Organisms[1]

Microorganisms	Minimum a_w	Equilibrium RH[2] (%)	Storage RH (%)	Susceptible Foods
Normal bacteria	0.91	91	Below 90	Meat, fish, poultry, eggs, milk
Normal yeasts	0.88	88	Below 87	Syrups, puddings
Normal molds	0.80	80	Below 79	Fruits, vegetables, meats, cereals, bread
Halophilic bacteria	0.75	75	Below 74	Cured meats
Xerophilic fungi	0.65	65	Below 64	Dried meats
Osmophilic yeasts	0.60	60	Below 59	Jams, jellies, syrups, honey

Source: Smith and Minor (1974).

An a_w of 0.70 inhibits spoilage at room temperature. This is approximated in dry milk at 8% moisture, dried whole egg at 10 to 11%, flour at 13 to 15%, nonfat dry milk at 15%, dehydrated fat-free meat at 15%, seeds of leguminous crops at 15%, dehydrated vegetables at 14 to 20%, dehydrated fruits at 18 to 25%, and starch at 18%.

RH is relative humidity.

a_w is water activity—a ratio of the vapor pressure of a solution to the vapor pressure of pure water at the same temperature.

type to prevent the absorption of moisture. Dry storage areas should be equipped with dehumidifiers to maintain the relative humidity at less than 30%.

(9)   Canned food containers may deteriorate when stored in damp, corrosive atmospheres.

(10)   Dried fruits should be stored below 70°F (21.1°C) and at a relative humidity below 55%. If these conditions cannot be met, the fruit should be refrigerated to prevent the growth of surface molds.

EFFECTS OF LIGHT AND AIR ON FOODS

In addition to microorganisms, light and oxygen play a major role in food decomposition. The oxygen in air is an oxidizing agent. Although other compounds have similar properties, air is the oxidizing agent most frequently encountered in storage. Basically, oxidation is a process whereby substances are converted to oxides. This process is accelerated by high temperature and increased concentrations of oxygen. For instance, the deterioration of fat-containing products is caused by oxidation and enzyme action. Some fats and oils readily oxidize when exposed to air, causing off-flavors or rancidity, and sometimes causing loss of nutritive values, destruction of some vitamins, and deterioration of biological value of proteins as well. Butter and margarine must be completely and securely wrapped when stored to protect them from light and air, both of which accelerate rancidity and absorption of odors. Milk powder loses some of its amino acid content. Vitamins A, B, B_6, C, E, K, and biotin are susceptible to oxidation. Other changes of character and quality due to light and air follow:

(1)   Light and air will cause color changes in many foods. For example, strawberries discolor because of oxygen in cold storage and either turn purple or fade. Cherries darken, whereas blackberries turn brown.

(2)   Light effects on milk fat bring about changes in taste and odor.

(3)   Orange juice undergoes oxidative changes associated with rancidity. The volatile oils contained in the orange skin give a "terpeney" off-flavor.

(4)   Fresh pork sausage often undergoes oxidative rancidity, even though refrigerated. Frozen hamburger meat oxidizes in a few weeks at 0°F (−17.8°C). Turkey fat turns rancid within a few days after freezing. Ice cream may develop an oxidized flavor resembling cardboard or tallow.

(5)   Raw frozen vegetables can develop a "hay" flavor which is partly due to enzymatic oxidation of vitamin C. Dehydrated potatoes undergo oxidation resulting in off-flavor and -odor.

(6) Prolonged exposure to light affects the quality of certain flavoring agents and soft drink syrups. Wines are susceptible to light or photo-chemical oxidative reactions, and must be stored away from light and heat.

STORAGE CONDITIONS FOR FOODS

Fresh Fruits

Fresh fruits should be stored at temperatures of 40° to 45°F (4.4° to 7.2°C) and a relative humidity of about 80% and be shaded from light. Air circulation is necessary to maintain freshness and firmness. During respiration and ripening, fresh fruits give off carbon dioxide and water and may become wilted, dull in appearance, and less flavorful. Lack of ventilation is conducive to spoilage and deterioration. Fruits in storage should be inspected regularly for the removal of any that have begun to spoil.

Bananas require special handling. At temperatures ranging from 56° to 60°F (13.3° to 15.6°C) and a relative humidity of about 90%, ripe bananas may be held for 7 to 10 days. Storage below 60°F (15.6°C) adversely affects the flavor and causes skin discoloration. Bananas which have been bruised or have begun to deteriorate may show indication of excessive softness or a watery exudate. Table 5.2 shows the storage properties of fresh fruits.

Fresh Vegetables

Most fresh vegetables retain top quality for only a few days, even if storage conditions are ideal. In their life processes, vegetables utilize the constituent elements of air; they begin to lose their vitality when these processes are interrupted and slow down, so ripening results. Ripening is the conversion of certain insoluble and indigestible substances into more soluble and digestible food substances. The rate of ripening and loss of moisture are greatly influenced by temperature. At high temperatures they are rapid, whereas at low temperatures they are slow. Consequently, vegetable storage requires low temperatures and high humidity to preserve texture, tenderness, flavor, nutritive content, and attractive fresh color. Vegetables should be stored at 40°–45°F (4.4°–7.2°C) with a relative humidity of 85–95%. If fresh fruits and vegetables come packed in an impermeable film, it should be perforated to allow the contents to ventilate, otherwise off-flavors and -odors will develop.

Green leafy vegetables quickly wilt and change flavor if water evaporates from the tissues. Other vegetables—corn, beans, and peas—lose sweetness within a short time as sugars are converted to starch. Corn can lose up to 40% of its sugar content in 24 hr if not refrigerated properly.

If lettuce, celery, and other leafy vegetables are washed prior to storage, they should be fully drained of moisture to prevent rapid deterioration and browning. Tops should be removed from beets, carrots, and radishes. Always sort vegetables before storing. Discard or use at once any bruised or soft vegetables.

Store lima beans uncovered in pods in refrigerator for up to 2 days.

Store eggplants at 45°F (7.2°C) for 7–10 days at a relative humidity of 80–85%.

Onions keep well from 4 to 6 months at 35°–40°F (1.7°–4.4°C) and a relative humidity near 70%. Onions should be separated from other products since their odor may be absorbed rapidly.

Potatoes should be stored in a dark, dry place with good ventilation and at a temperature of about 45°F (7.2°C). Under these conditions they may be held several months without much change in flavor.

Ripe tomatoes should be stored at 45°F (7.2°C) and a relative humidity

TABLE 5.2. Storage Properties of Fresh Fruits

Fruit	Storage Temperature (°F)	Storage Temperature (°C)	Relative Humidity (%)	Storage Life (Approx.)
Apples, summer	30–32	−1.1–0	85	1–2 months
Apples, winter	30–32	−1.1–0	85	4–6 months
Avocados	40–50	4.4–10.0	85–90	3–4 weeks
Bananas	56	13.3	75–85	7–10 days
Blackberries	31–32	−0.6–0	80–85	7–10 days
Blueberries	32	0	80–85	7–10 days
Cherries, sour	31–32	−0.6–0	80–85	2 weeks
Cherries, sweet	31–32	−0.6–0	80–85	3–4 weeks
Cranberries	36–40	2.2–4.4	85–90	1–4 months
Currants	32	0	80–85	7–10 days
Dates	30–32	−1.1–0	75–80	3–6 months
Gooseberries	32	0	80–85	7–10 days
Grapefruit	32–34	0–1.1	85–90	6–8 weeks
Grapes, European	31–32	−0.6–0	85–90	4–6 months
Grapes, American	31–32	−0.6–0	80–85	3–4 weeks
Lemons	55–58	12.8–14.4	85–90	1–4 months
Limes	45–48	7.2–8.9	85–90	6–8 weeks
Melons				
muskmelon and cantaloupe	32–34	0–1.1	75–76	7–10 days
honeydew and honeyball	36–38	2.2–3.3	75–85	2–4 weeks
casaba and Persian	36–40	2.2–4.4	75–85	4–6 weeks
watermelon	36–40	2.2–4.4	75–85	2–3 weeks
Oranges	32–34	0–1.1	85–90	1–2 months
Peaches	31–32	−0.6–0	80–85	2–4 weeks
Pears, Bartlett	30–31	−1.1 to −0.6	85–90	45–90 days
Pineapples	40–45	4.4–7.2	80–85	2–4 weeks
Plums	31–32	−0.6–0	80–85	7–10 days
Raspberries	31–32	−0.6–0	80–85	7–10 days
Strawberries	31–32	−0.6–0	80–85	7–10 days

Source: Gelman and Tennant (1946).

of 85–90%. Under these conditions they will keep up to 10 days. Mature green tomatoes should be stored at about 55°–60°F (12.8°–15.6°C) and a relative humidity of 85–90%. Under these conditions they will keep up to 6 weeks.

Dried Fruits

Dried fruits may be stored for long periods at temperatures of 34°–38°F (1.11°–3.33°C) and at a relative humidity below 55%. Under these conditions, dried fruits such as apples, apricots, figs, peaches, pears, prunes, and raisins may be stored up to 30 months.

Deterioration may be caused by microoraganisms and insect infestation. If dried fruits are held at high temperatures they will tend to darken, resulting in a loss of palatability.

Meat

Meat and meat products are procured in a number of forms such as fresh, frozen, cured and smoked, dried, and canned. Each form presents a special problem in storage and issuing. Fresh meat can be stored for several weeks at temperatures of 33°–36°F (0.56°–2.22°C) and a relative humidity of between 80 and 90%. These storage conditions must be carefully maintained. At 32°F (0°C) or under, meat will discolor or darken due to a gradual dehydration process. Above 36°F (2.22°C), a slime develops and the meat surface must be trimmed before use.

Meat Spoilage. Fresh, cured, and smoked meats, if in good condition, have individual characteristic aromas, and any deviation from the norm is indicative of deteriorating changes in their chemical makeup. These changes can be attributed almost exclusively to oxidation, microorganisms, and enzymatic action. Microorganisms break down proteins into amino acids and ammonia. Bacteria, molds, and yeasts, which cause surface spoilage, grow in the air on the meat surfaces and thrive in high humidity and temperature. Adequate air circulation in the storage area, although it causes shrinkage if the air is dry, preserves qualities by preventing moisture condensation on meat surfaces. When pieces of meat come in contact with each other, circulation of air is retarded, moisture condenses, and mold growth results.

Sliminess. Sliminess is due to bacterial growth on the surface of meat and is an indication of a lack of proper air circulation, temperature, and moisture control. This condition is usually indicated by moist, smooth, slippery surfaces and an unpleasant odor. Sliminess can be removed by surface trimming.

Souring. The term souring is generally used to cover practically any phase or degree of meat spoilage of an internal nature, as distinguished from sliminess and other forms of surface deterioration.

Skippers. The skipper is an insect that does considerable damage to smoked meats. The skipper is the larva of a small blackfly, which moves by skipping. Although this condition is rarely encountered, if observed the meat must be set aside and separated from uninfected lots. Careful inspection is advised, especially in the crevice of meat near the bone or in the fat.

Ground Meat

Ground meat should not be held for more than 24 hr, unless it is frozen. Deterioration is rapid due to the increased surface area. In addition, during the grinding process, meat may come into contact with bacteria, which will continue to grow and spoil the entire lot; thus, holding temperatures should be as near freezing as possible.

Fish and Fish Products

The storage life of fresh fish is extremely limited and is dependent upon the following factors: species, season of the year, physical condition (whether filleted, dressed, or round), and manner of handling. Fish should be held under refrigeration at a temperature of 30° to 34°F (−1.11° to 1.11°C). Since fish will spoil even under these conditions, they should be used within 24–48 hr.

Shipments of fresh fish should be inspected for signs of spoilage before storing. Frozen fish should be placed directly in the freezer and should be securely wrapped to protect against moisture loss, texture changes, and freezer burns.

Eggs and Egg Products

Fresh eggs may be stored for several months at 32°F (0°C). For short-term storage, temperatures of 33° to 45°F (0.56° to 7.22°C) and a humidity of 75% are ideal for preserving egg quality.

Egg products such as frozen whole eggs, egg whites, and yolks should be stored at 38°–45°F (3.33°–7.22°C) for short-term storage.

Egg crates should be cross-stacked on a slotted platform to allow full circulation of air.

Poultry and Poultry Products

Poultry must be handled carefully and can be stored at 33°–36°F (0.6°–2°C) for short periods of time. The wrappings of chilled, tightly packaged poultry should be loosened prior to storage. If this procedure is not followed, bacterial growth will ensue. Giblets should be spread loosely in covered pans. Frozen poultry and poultry products may be stored at 0°F (−17.8°C) or lower for a period of from 4 to 6 months.

Table 5.3 illustrates storage temperatures and relative humidities of a variety of food products.

TABLE 5.3. Storage Properties of Various Foods

Product	Temperature (°F)	Temperature (°C)		RH (%)
Meat	32–34	0–1.1		88–92
Mild-cured hams	60–65	15.6–18.3		50–60
Poultry	32	0		85
Fish	33–40	0.6–1.1		90–95
Scallops, shucked clams, oysters, lobster meat, crab meat, shrimp	0	0	4–6 months	—
Eggs				
fresh eggs	29–31	−1.7 to −0.6		80–85
frozen whole eggs, yolks, whites	32	0	1 year	Low as possible
dehydrated	35	1.7	6 months	Moisture-proof container
Dairy products				
butter	32–36	0–2.2	2 months	
	−10 to −20	−23.3 to −28.9	1 year	80–85
cheese (hard)	35	1.7		65–70
milk, dry nonfat	40	4.4	6 months	Moisture-proof container
milk, dry whole	32–40	0–4.4		Moisture-proof container
milk, evaporated	35	1.7	1 year	60
Fats and oils				
margarine	32–36	0–2.2	2 months	50
salad dressings	35	1.7	1 month	—
vegetable oils	35	1.7	1 year	—
vegetable shortenings	50	10.0		—
animal fats, lard	32–35	0–1.7	1 month	—
chicken fat	32–35	0–1.7	1 month	—
turkey fat	32–35	0–1.7	2 weeks	—
Fruits and vegetables				
fruits	32–50	0–10.0		80–90
corn (fresh)	31–32	−0.6–0	4–8 days	90–95
mushrooms	32–35	0–1.7	Use at once	80–90
prepeeled potatoes	32–35	0–1.7	5 days	85–90
new potatoes	50–55	10.0–12.8		85–90
mature potatoes	38–50	3.3–10.0		85–90
ripe tomatoes	32	0	7 days	85–90
unripe tomatoes	55–70	12.8–21.1	2–5 weeks	85–90
avocados	40–55	4.4–12.8	4 weeks	85–90

Source: Smith and Minor (1974).

ISSUING

Regardless of the product, the basic issuing procedure revolves around the FIFO system. An issuing or product removal list should be followed.

This list may include foods which will be used within a specific period of time, such as within a 12–24 or 36 hr period. Transfer of foods from storage areas to preparation or satellite coolers, thawers, or freezers should be performed rapidly and uniformly. Transfer points should be ready for the arrival of the required products; the areas should be cleaned and sanitized. Leftovers or other foods should be stored in front, so that enough room is available for the new products.

Frequent trips to main storage coolers or freezers are not advisable. Systematic removal will prevent temperature fluctuations in these units, which might result in product deterioration affecting texture, appearance, and quality.

6

Preparation and Production Equipment

Preparation and production equipment must function at optimum efficiency to maintain the quality of food. Those quality factors affected by inefficiently operating equipment are color, flavor, and texture. To bridge the gap between steps in an effective quality control program requires constant discipline on the part of management. Surveys reveal that this, and proper sanitation procedures, are the most neglected phases of quality control. The latter is fully covered in Chapter 12, Sanitation, but is briefly mentioned in this section as an adjunct discussion along with each item of equipment illustrated in the text.

The purpose of this chapter is to point out the extreme importance of this phase of quality control and to provide the reader with the simplified instructions necessary to evaluate equipment performance. Although numerous categories of equipment are marketed, only those that are in wide use are mentioned.

FACTORS RELATED TO EQUIPMENT PERFORMANCE

Regardless of type or purpose of equipment installed in foodservice establishments, the evaluation of optimum efficiency is covered by the following factors:

(1) Temperature evaluation
(2) Timing measurements and internal timing mechanism checks
(3) Pressure tests
(4) Humidity control
(5) Accessory checks, e.g., signal alarms (buzzers, bells), blowers and exhaust systems, signal lights, and control activating devices
(6) Sanitation procedures
(7) Preventive maintenance
(8) Updating instructional charts and cooking guides

If we review these eight factors related to equipment performance, we find that not every one applies to each piece of equipment. For instance, when efficiency evaluations are performed on microwave ovens, factors 2, 5, 6, 7, and 8 are evaluated; however, for convection ovens, items 1, 2, 4, 5, 6, 7, and 8 require evaluation.

IMPLEMENTS REQUIRED TO PERFORM EVALUATION CHECKS

The tools required to perform accurate evaluations of preparation and production equipment were discussed in Chapter 2. Before proceeding with these evaluations, the tools needed for such tasks must be accurate and calibrated. It will serve no purpose to use inaccurate thermometers and timers that are out of adjustment. The following are essential tools:

(1) Timing Mechanisms—Either a hand stopwatch or electrical timer (equipped with a sweep second hand, and a start, stop, and reset switch) calibrated to read in 0.01 sec. These timers will provide an accurate determination of the cooking timer of a microwave oven, which may range from 15 to 30 sec.

(2) Thermometers—Several types of thermometers are necessary for temperature evaluation: mercury or fluid column thermometers needed to check temperature of fluids; bimetallic metal stem thermometers to check internal temperatures of solid or semisolid foods like meat, poultry, fish, and frozen foods; thermocouples to check interior temperature of ovens; deep-fat fryer thermometers; low-range registering thermometer ($-40°$ to $+15°F$, $-40°$ to $-11°C$) for refrigeration calibration; and surface activated thermometers to measure temperatures of flat surfaces like griddles.

(3) Pressure Testers—One or two of these devices are necessary to check pressure gauges on pressure cookers and steamlines.

(4) Electrical Measuring Meters—Voltage or a combination voltage, amperage, resistance meter that may be used to check current fluctuations.

(5) Leveling Bubble—Glass Device—This device is necessary to ensure that equipment such as grills, griddles, microwave ovens, and coffee brewers is level. Some equipment like a half-gallon coffee brewer will not brew coffee uniformly unless it is at the proper level. One brewer manufacturer recommends that their brewer be tilted five degrees forward to maintain a uniform flow of brew water.

(6) Microwave Energy Radiation Leakage Meter—These meters are required to measure energy leakage from a microwave oven, in compliance with U.S. Dept. of Health and Human Services standards for limiting radiation emission.

PREVENTIVE MAINTENANCE

Preventive maintenance of equipment will solve many problems related to equipment breakdown and will ensure that all units are operating at maximum efficiency. Preventive maintenance programs must be scheduled on a regular basis. The timing of such maintenance depends on type of equipment, frequency of use, age, and manufacturer's guidelines. Some equipment, like a deep fat frying kettle, may require daily evaluations, while others may need only semiweekly or weekly checks. Regardless of time span, exacting records should be kept detailing frequency of inspections, manufacturer's recommendations, and type and kind of checks required. In addition, model and serial numbers, warranties, and guarantees should be filed with the maintenance records, so when parts or service are required a complete history is available for immediate reference.

Preventive Maintenance Program

A preventive maintenance program may include the following:

(1) Electrical checks of switches, controls, fuses, signal lights, alarms (buzzers and bells), voltage line evaluation, wiring, and plugs and receptacles.

(2) Heating element checks to determine if heaters need replacement. This step also includes steamline examination to observe if a specified amount of steam is reaching a unit. Also included is the examination of gas-fired elements to determine flame uniformity. If a blockage is observed, gas jets may require cleaning and reaming to clear out any obstructions.

(3) Leveling of certain equipment must be checked. Items such as microwave and convection ovens will not operate properly if not level. Most equipment that requires leveling has adjustable legs for this purpose.

(4) Cooking surfaces, both interior and exterior, should be examined for accumulations of grease, residues, and other debris which may interfere with uniform heat transfer. If accumulations are heavy, the coefficient of heat transfer may be substantially altered, resulting in a longer cooking time that may affect texture and color.

(5) Doors, locks, latches, and hinges require examination to ensure against heat loss. Loose hinges and latches may also pose a safety hazard.

(6) Gaskets located on pressure cooker doors, ovens, and refrigerators need periodic examination to prevent heat leakage or, in the case of pressure cookers, to prevent pressure drops.

(7) Oiling and greasing of motors should be performed regularly or in accordance with manufacturer's specifications to avoid binding of

bearings and malfunctioning of motors. An early indication of motor failure is the overheating of a unit. Some motors normally may run hot, especially if located near ovens or other units that produce high external temperature. Placing a surface activated thermometer on a motor when it is new can provide temperature data for normal operation. These readings can then be compared with those obtained when maintenance checks are made.

(8) Sanitation is considered an essential part of preventive maintenance. It was previously mentioned that this subject is treated in depth in Chapter 12. Poor sanitation procedures head the list of major quality problems and are directly related to inefficient equipment operations and food spoilage.

SIGNIFICANCE OF TEMPERATURE CONTROL

Temperature is well recognized in cooking as the common denominator for producing the correct degree of doneness. Heat is controllable and is, along with timing, the most important element in the culinary arts and other food processing operations.

Temperature gradations, or the amount of heat necessary for cooking, vary dramatically to assure the desired degree of doneness or palatability for different food categories. This is brought about by physical and chemical changes which occur when food components reach certain temperatures. Physical changes produced when foods are subjected to heat alter a product's state, from solid to liquid or liquid to vapor. Chemical changes are more complex and can best be illustrated by the sequence of events that takes place as meat is heated or cooked. The changes occur in the molecular structure of meat proteins.

At the beginning of cooking, as the temperature starts to rise, the *myofibrillar* proteins in muscle fibers become denatured, resulting in a tightening and stiffening of their structure. Actually, meat first becomes tougher. The tenderness which appears later is due to chemical changes in *collagen* protein of connective tissue. The chemical bonds by which the original structure was maintained are altered. As a higher temperature of cooking is reached, *collagen* is converted into more soluble gelatin, which is partially dissolved in released juice.

The changes brought about by heat in the structure of meat proteins cause a reduction in acidity, i.e., an increase in pH. The reduction of acidity alters the moisture-holding capacity of meat. The rate at which meat loses its capacity to hold moisture as temperature increases is related to changes in pH, and this in turn determines differences in degrees of doneness.

If we equate food preparation to the production of fine chemicals or perfumes, it may help in understanding the importance of precise temperature controls in the art of cooking. Basically, the processes of refrigeration, baking, roasting, frying, and boiling are examples of *heat exchange*. All of these exchanges of heat are either from hot air or steam or, in the case of frying, from hot fat, to the product. Energy in the form of heat can also be transmitted directly on a griddle, in a salamander, or during baking or roasting.

The Thermostat as a Means of Temperature Control

The proper control of temperature is dependent on a device called a thermostat. Thermostats control temperature automatically and precisely. Thermostats in modern heating and refrigeration equipment are usually either preset by the manufacturer or hand operated by turning a dial to the desired temperature. Since thermostats are mechanical, they can malfunction, so some external means is necessary to determine their accuracy. Occasionally thermostats on new equipment may be defective or inaccurate. This may be due to jamming or sticking; presence of corrosion or of protective coating applied to a unit while in storage or in transit; presence of foreign matter derived from protective coatings; or metal filings which may get into valves or switches and thus prevent proper functioning.

Basic Designs. Thermostats are manufactured in two basic designs, for gas and for electrical equipment. The thermostat installed in gas equipment contains a metal bulb filled with liquid. When temperature increases, the liquid expands and activates a bellows. This causes the bellows to open and to push out one end of a lever, making the other end of the lever move inward to gradually close the gas valve, thus reducing the amount of gas flowing to the oven burner. The system is set by a dial to the desired temperature. As the temperature drops, the liquid in the bulb contracts and pulls the lever forward, re-opening the gas valve. Another type of thermostat operates by a metal rod which expands as the temperature rises, and contracts when it falls. Both types can be adapted to electrically heated units. Many other designs exist; however, their operation is based on the same principles just described.

Specifications for Thermostats. (1) They should not be affected by changes in ambient temperatures. (2) They should possess adequate sensitivity to respond quickly to temperature changes, for example, opening of an oven door or adding cold food to the deep fat fryer. (3) They should be designed to operate within a narrow range, permitting the heating to continue until the temperature is near the desired setting, and then shutting off immediately. (4) The "dead zone" should be as small as possible. The "dead zone" is the change in temperature of the sensing element of a thermostat which occurs without causing a change in the setting of the valve controlling the energy flow. (5) They should be strongly constructed, not liable to corrosion, and readily cleaned, serviced, and adjusted. (6) Since overheating of a thermostat valve body may cause problems, the valve body and other parts of the unit should not become too hot. If the temperature of these equipment parts changes radically, the thermostat will lose its accuracy.

Methods of checking thermostats will be found under various equipment headings.

SIGNIFICANCE OF TIMING

The second most important factor in cooking is time. The study of time and its relationship to people and subjects such as cooking and food handling (storage) is called *chronosophy*. Although the study of chronosophy is generally related to man and his habits, it can also explain poor results in food preparation where haphazard timing results in low quality. Haphazard timing practices are those which rely on "guess-work," i.e., without the aid of some type of mechanical timer. Man is governed by two kinds of time: *outertime* and *innertime*. Outertime is mechanically guided, while innertime projects a person's psychological feelings to a particular time span. Unfortunately, the two can be radically different.

Successful cooking depends on outertiming, which in essence means reliance on accurate timing devices. Such devices may be installed as accessories on equipment or may be portable. In either case, the paramount importance of correct timing must prevail.

Time-Temperature Relationship

Time and temperature are related elements in cooking. Solid foods, such as a thick slab of meat, when roasted, require lower temperatures but a longer period of time to reach the desired degree of doneness. Thin pieces of meat, chicken breasts, fish fillets, or hamburger patties can be cooked at higher temperatures in a shorter time. Methods of heat transfer are related to time. These include conduction, radiation, and convection. In order to preserve the nutrient content of vegetables, a short cooking period is recommended. It is well recognized that the time-temperature relationship to produce baked goods successfully is dependent on accurate timing and temperature control.

Timing Accessories

Equipment such as convection ovens, deep fat fryers, coffee brewers, pressure cookers, and microwave ovens contain built-in timing devices. These operate by turning a dial to the desired time period. An alarm is sounded, or a combination alarm and signal light system may be installed where an alarm is activated and a light flashes at the expiration of the heating cycle. Establishments such as large commissaries that are equipped with batteries of cooking devices may have a central control panel that houses a series of signal lights attached to each unit of equipment. As the cooking period ends, a signal light is activated which alerts the attendant manning the control panel.

Microwave ovens come equipped with precise timing devices. Since the only variable control for proper cooking is time, the accuracy of these mechanisms is critical in achieving the desired degree of doneness. Later in this chapter, the quality control relationship between timing and cooking is discussed.

Timer Control

Timing devices, like other electronic and mechanical equipment, require constant maintenance to ensure accuracy. The only available method is the employment of precalibrated reference timers to determine the accuracy of those installed in equipment. The procedure for calibrating timing accessories is simple. Calibrations may be made at various settings like 15, 30, 60, 90, or 120 min. Three determinations should be made at each setting, and the results totaled and divided by three. This average time is a measure of accuracy when compared with a precalibrated check. Generally, timing accessories can be adjusted by loosening a nut in the dial or pointer. If adjustments cannot be made, it is advisable to post a sign on the equipment indicating the degree of inaccuracy for each setting, and a plus or minus differential for the correct time.

Timing devices should be handled with great care. They should be kept free of dust and grease. If they get hot from ambient conditions or from their locations in a unit, extra precautions must be employed to ensure accuracy.

EQUIPMENT REQUIRING PERFORMANCE EVALUATION

The following list includes preparation and production equipment that requires periodic performance evaluation.

Broilers—Charbroiler, unit broiler, rotisseries, combination broiler and griddle, salamander
Egg boilers
Fryers—Deep, pressure, tilting fry pans
Griddles and grills
Holding cabinets—Hot and mobile, refrigerated, heated hand lift, warmers
Kettles—Steam (direct jacketed and flow mounted), tilting, factory charged, and self-contained
Ovens—Bake, convection-fan type, convection-steam type, infrared quartz and radiant, roasting, microwave, rotary, and revolving

Steam cookers—Low and high pressure
Warmers—Infrared
Preparation Equipment—Blenders, mixers, choppers, slicing machines, grinders, tenderizers, cutters, peelers, meat saws, dicers and shredders, can openers

Discussion will center on several types of pre-preparation, preparation, and product equipment. These will serve as examples of the scope of typical performance evaluations, since space limitation does not allow for a complete examination of all the units listed.

CONVECTION OVENS

Regardless of make or model, experimentation should be performed to check manufacturer's cooking guide and to solve special cooking situations. These initial tests will allow the operator to learn about the features and operating characteristics of an oven. For example, Table 6.1 shows the time-temperature relationship and shelf location for satisfactory results with various foods.

Manufacturer's preparation data should be used as a guide, since the time and temperature will vary with oven load, portion size, food texture, initial food temperature, oven insulation, moisture content of food, and other mechanical characteristics of the unit.

Procedures and Performance Evaluation

The following procedures are common to convection ovens:

(1) Never overload an oven or increase heating temperatures to force cooking.

(2) Foods should be uniformly spaced on each shelf, allowing sufficient space between items for good air circulation.

(3) Preheating is essential; never load an oven until preheating temperature has been reached. Preheating temperatures should be set at about 50°F (28°C) higher than final cooking temperature. This method will reduce the temperature drop when the door is opened for loading. When the oven is loaded, the thermostat should then be adjusted to the desired cooking temperature.

(4) If the convection oven is not equipped with automatic steam or water injection, then a bowl of water may have to be placed in the oven to maintain moisture balance. This is advisable for foods such as meat roasts, fish, poultry, and baked goods.

(5) Thermostats and timers should be checked monthly or whenever a problem arises which can be traced directly to oven operation. Use procedures previously outlined for thermostats and timers. Study the manufacturer's guide for calibrating these accessories.

TABLE 6.1. Convection Oven Heating Information

Food Item	Pan Size (in.)	Recommended No. of Shelves[1]	Temperature (°F)	Temperature (C°)	Heating Time (min)
Bread					
rolls, white	18 × 26 × 1	3	350	177	12–15
bread, white	1 lb loaf	3	350	177	23–27
French bread	18 × 26 × 1	4	350	177	20–25
hot-cross buns	18 × 26 × 1	3	350	177	12–15
Desserts					
brownies	18 × 26 × 1	5	350	177	25–30
gingerbread	18 × 26 × 1	5	325	163	20–25
pies, fruit	8	3	400	204	35–40
meringue	8	3	400	204	5–8
cake, yellow	18 × 26 × 1	5	350	177	20–25
chocolate	18 × 26 × 1	5	350	177	18–22
banana	18 × 26 × 1	5	325	163	20–25
coffee cake	18 × 26 × 1	3	400	204	12–15
pastry squares	18 × 26 × 1	3	400	204	35–40
Meat, fish, miscellaneous					
meatloaf	12 × 20 × 2½	3	325	163	60–75
sausages	18 × 26 × 1	5	375	190	30–35
hamburger patties	18 × 26 × 1	9	400	204	9–12
turkey, fresh	12 × 20 × 2½	2	300	149	150–210
roast beef[2]	12 × 20 × 2½	2	300	149	150–210
haddock fillets	18 × 26 × 1	5	350	177	10–15
baked macaroni and cheese	12 × 20 × 2½	3	325	163	25–30
grilled cheese sandwich	18 × 26 × 1	3	400	204	10–12
sirloin steaks	18 × 26 × 1	5	400	204	10–12

Source: Courtesy of Market Forge, Everett, MA.
[1]The information provided by this table is for a Market Forge convection oven Model 2500 and 2600. There are nine tracks on the sidewalls of the oven. Five shelves are standard equipment. The correct location of shelves is important for satisfactory results. The tracks are numbered from the top down.
1 Shelf   Track 9   4 Shelves   Tracks 2, 4, 6, and 8
2 Shelves   Tracks 4 and 9   5 Shelves   Tracks 1, 3, 5, 7, and 9
3 Shelves   Tracks 3, 6, and 9
[2]Special racks are recommended for roast beef.

(6)   If the convection oven has a steam injection pressure system, check recommended steam pressure. Also check steam jets to prevent blockage.

(7)   Check doors for tight fit to avoid heat and moisture loss.

(8)   Check venting to make sure it is free of blockage to prevent back-flow of moisture and localized hot spots.

(9)   Check fan operation and heat circulation to prevent localized hot spots.

(10) Shelf and pan positions are important and vary with the foods being cooked. Shelves are usually numbered, starting at the top of the oven.

Some Results of Improper Oven Operation.

(1) Uneven degree of doneness: oven may be overloaded, oven fan may be faulty, or food items may be placed too closely together, preventing hot air from circulating evenly.
(2) Underdone food may be caused by low heating temperatures.
(3) Excessive shrinkage may be due to low heating temperatures and long time cycle.
(4) Exterior of food done or brown, but interior undercooked: temperature may be too high or the oven crowded. Oven load should be reduced and temperature-time relationship may have to be changed.
(5) Food with gravy or sauce dried out on one side: check level of oven. Liquid may have been concentrated on one side of the pan, because shelf was uneven or tilted.

MICROWAVE OVENS

Timing and Timing Test Procedures

It was pointed out that time is the one factor which must be controlled for quality production. Continuous testing of all products undergoing microwave preparation must become a fixed function of daily operational activities. The following step-by-step procedures are suggested for this testing program:

(1) Set up a timing chart in front of the oven. The chart should be placed at eye level for ease of reading. A slate board or magnetic sign set with removable letters is also suggested, so that changes can be made when required.
(2) Manufacturer's instructions should be read. These usually cite methods for plating and the time necessary for preparation. If instructions are not provided, they should be requested so a basis for comparison is available.
(3) Measure the thickness of the food to determine whether it conforms to optimum height requirements of 0.5 to 1 in. Observe the geometry or configuration of the item. If the shape appears irregular, it may pose a problem of uneven doneness.
(4) Take a temperature reading of the food. The starting temperature of the food prior to heating should always be the same, otherwise the finished food will vary in finished quality. If the product is thawed, the temperature should range between 34° and 38°F (2° and 5°C). Foods heated directly from the freezer should register temperatures of −10° to 0°F (−23° to −18°C). If both heating from the frozen state and heating from the thawed state are used for otherwise identical products, then two sets of heating cycles will be necessary. This practice should not be encouraged; but it may be necessary

during slow periods when single portions are ordered which must be prepared directly from frozen stock.

(5) Before actual testing, an inspection of the oven cavity and door closure is recommended to ensure that they are thoroughly cleaned.

(6) When placing the test product in the cavity, always place it in the center. After the correct cooking time is ascertained, retest by placing the food in another location. This will determine if the oven is working properly and is transmitting the energy uniformly throughout the chamber.

(7) Follow the packer's heating recommendations for the first test. At the completion of the cycle, check the temperature of the item, inserting the stem of the thermometer into the center of the food. Taste the product for palatability, texture, flavor; check for eye appeal. If the packer's recommended time does not meet with approval, another trial must be run. The time and internal temperature of each run should be noted as well as the reason for rejection.

(8) Once the initial optimum heating cycle has been established, further testing should be done on a once-a-day schedule. Tests should be made on all new shipments, regardless of the supplier's reliability. It is important to perform tests at the same time of day, preferably in the morning or during a slow period.

(9) A critical factor that is sometimes overlooked and can lead to erroneous results is the type of package or plating material. For uniform results, these items should have the same properties. If it is customary to remove the product from the original container, this procedure must be followed for each test.

Plating and Primary Preparation

Plating and primary preparation of food before heating are important steps in quality cooking. In actual production these steps encompass defrosting, assembly, heating techniques, and shielding.

Defrosting. It is advisable to defrost foods before microwave heating. This procedure will ensure an even doneness. Less energy is required and heating cycles are shortened. Where microwave cooking is an integral part of the production center, a more smoothly flowing system will result from prior thawing. In this case defrosting is easily accomplished in thawing refrigerators which should be installed between the main freezer storage area and the production center.

If emergencies arise, or in slow demand periods, defrosting can be done successfully in the microwave oven if certain procedures are followed. For immediate thawing of meat, poultry, or fish, each 6 to 10 oz portion should be heated for about 20 sec per side. Set the timer for 20 sec; when the first cycle is completed, remove the product from the oven and turn it over. In order to prevent spilling or spattering, do not turn the food in the oven. Keep a record of the actual time so that a reference will be available for future use. In addition, the temperature of the item before and after defrosting should be noted and compared with the heating time.

After defrosting, the food should be removed from the chamber and allowed to "rest" for 60 to 90 sec, to permit any remaining ice crystals to melt. The product is then ready for cooking.

Microwave ovens are adaptable to production defrosting, where more than one oven is installed or where the final preparation is performed in a broiler or convection oven. Bulk portion packs can be thawed prior to microwave heating, or several portions can be removed from the container and heated. Table 6.2 shows the defrosting time for a variety of foods heated in an oven with a power output of 1¼ kW.

TABLE 6.2. Defrosting Time in Microwave Oven

Item	Procedure	Time for Defrost (sec)
Strip steak (12 oz)	Cover with waxed paper, defrost in microwave by applying 25 sec of time to both sides. Finish off to desired doneness in conventional broiler. Reheating may be done later in microwave.	50
Lobster tails (two 5-oz tails)	Cover with waxed paper, defrost, and cook either in microwave or under broiler.	45
Trout (12 oz)	Cover with waxed paper, defrost, and cook either in microwave or under broiler.	50
Lamb or pork chops (2)	Cover with waxed paper, defrost in microwave, cook under broiler.	50
Doughnuts	Heat uncovered.	5
Cakes	Heat uncovered.	25
Frozen, baked stuffed potato	Depress center before freezing. Cover with waxed paper, defrost. Heat to serving temperature in microwave or else brown under broiler.	45

Source: Litton Industries.

Plating and Food Positioning.   Casserole type dishes, such as Beef Burgundy and Shrimp Creole, will heat evenly if the product is uniformly positioned around the inner rim of the plate and the center is slightly depressed. Reduction in the thickness of the center area allows the energy to penetrate more uniformly, resulting in an even degree of doneness.

When plating combination platters, such as roast beef, potatoes, and buttered Brussels sprouts, excellent results will be obtained if food overhanging in dish is eliminated. Microwaves will tend to heat these overhanging sections more rapidly, producing overcooked, dried out, or charred food. Combination platters also pose problems of uneven cooking if the percentage of each component is not correctly adjusted. Entrees consisting of meat or fish, potatoes, and a vegetable will heat properly if the percentage of each does not exceed the following: fish or meat about 50%; potatoes about 25%; and vegetables about 25%.

Loose-textured foods will absorb more energy and heat faster than those that are firmer. Meat portions should be sliced and placed flat on a plate. Stacking of solid food items will produce uneven cooking. Before heating, a thin gravy or au jus should be applied to the meat in sufficient amounts to just "top" the surface of the product. If too much gravy is used, the excess will probably boil off, spill over, or give the dish an unappealing and unappetizing appearance. Speedier production is possible by covering the food. Dome covers, waxed paper, or inverted unwaxed paper plates can be used for this purpose. Covers should be placed over the dish loosely to allow for venting. Dome sets of various sizes are manufactured. They are designed with side vents to allow steam to escape, preventing moisture buildup and soggy food. Finger grips are molded into the dome for easy removal. Most are disposable and therefore will not add to the sanitation load. For increased eye appeal, shallow entree plates are recommended. Shallow dishes are easier to handle and permit easier positioning of the food.

Foods packaged in plastic cooking pouches can be heated directly. The top side of the pouch must be punctured before heating to allow steam to escape and prevent bursting from an increase in internal pressure. Pouches should be placed in an upright position, preferably in a serving dish, to avoid leakage through the steam-escape holes. Plastic pouch heating should be performed in two stages: stage 1 consists of heating for 1 to 2 min, or until the bag begins to expand; the pouch is removed from the cavity (stage 2) and shaken so that the contents rest on the bottom. Holes are then punctured near the top, and the pouch is again inserted in the oven on a dish in an upright position. Heating is continued for an additional period. When the cycle is completed, the bag is opened by cutting across the top. Place the contents in an appropriate serving dish, garnish, and serve.

Production Assembly Problems.   Production assembly problems may be encountered with items requiring different time cycles or with foods that are similar but vary in size, such as potatoes. If potatoes are of different sizes, they may be separated according to size before cooking; the smaller ones require less preparation time. Another method is to group the potatoes by size in the oven, the smaller ones toward the front, the larger at the rear. The timer is set for the smaller ones which are removed from the oven when cooked. The timer may then be reset for the larger potatoes. However, this may not be necessary; the time cycle can be determined for the larger unit, and at the appropriate time the oven door can be opened and the food removed. When the door is reclosed, the timer will continue until it reaches its final setting. This procedure should be followed when cooking foods that require turning. Items such as turkeys and large roasts may have to be turned 2 or 3 times during a cycle to equalize the degree of cooking.

In cases of volume production, foods requiring similar heating cycles can be assembled and prepared together. It is important to realize that there are no short cuts to quality production. Correct timing in microwave cookery is essential for ultimate success.

Delayed Cooking Procedure.   Delayed cooking procedures or shielding may be necessary when preparing irregular cuts of meat. This method can be compared with the photographic process of enlarging prints, wherein masking or dodging is practiced to increase or highlight a specific area of the picture.

Since metal reflects microwave energy, it is possible to take advantage of this fact by using metal foil to restrict heating of specific areas. When preparing a leg of lamb, the narrow section can be wrapped in foil for a part of the cooking cycle. The same technique can be applied to chicken and turkeys. The wings and legs are wrapped in foil and unwrapped when ¾ of the cooking cycle is completed. In all cases the foil must be smooth and the edges evenly folded. Shielding prior to microwave cooking has many other advantageous applications, although only a few examples have been cited; improvising should be attempted to supplement standard procedures if uneven cooking of irregularly shaped foods becomes a problem.

Browning in Microwave Cooking

A major disadvantage attributed to microwave cooking is the absence of surface browning, especially with meat products. Foods that are not properly browned or lack a crisp texture are considered unappealing and unappetizing by most consumers, who anticipate browned and crisp food surfaces when dining out because this tantalizing texture is seldom duplicated in home cooking.

Browning is a result of a chemical reaction between food sugars and amino acids found in protein products. At low temperatures the reaction proceeds slowly. As temperatures are increased, the process is accelerated. Temperatures above 350°F (177°C) are necessary to produce an acceptable brown color on food surfaces.

In microwave cookery, surface temperature rarely exceeds 212°F (100°C), and in many cases it is lower. Thus browning does not occur, and the food surface appears gray and unappealing. Under certain conditions, however, browning will take place. Beef roasts, chickens, and turkeys, because of their large size, require long cooking cycles. These items and others that contain surface fat will reach temperatures above 212°F (100°C) at the surface so that some browning will result.

There are alternatives that are capable of overcoming this deficiency. Presearing will promote an acceptable browned surface. After searing, the food is ready for final microwave heating. This method is effective with steaks, chops, and small roasts. Another procedure is to remove the food from the microwave oven when 80% cooked and place it in a convection or regular oven or broiler for the remainder of the cooking operation. This method will develop the desired brown, crisp surface.

Dual-purpose ovens are being marketed that combine microwave processing with convection or infrared heating. Shallow metal pans may be used in these combination ovens, because the second-stage heating process (convection or infrared) is sufficient to heat all areas to an even degree of doneness. To ensure uniformity, all food prepared in dual-purpose equipment should be turned after the microwave cycle is completed.

Testing for Oven Efficiency

Periodically, microwave equipment should be tested for operating efficiency and food quality characteristics. Before purchasing new equipment it is advisable to compare efficiency and operating characteristics of all models on the market. Comparisons of cost and production output should also be made. The following factors are pertinent to this survey:

(1) Construction of all new equipment must conform to federal regulations promulgated by the Department of Health and Human Services, Department of Labor, and the FCC. This must be labeled on the oven.

(2) Timing devices should be checked against a reliable stopwatch. This test is extremely important, since the element of time is the guiding factor for quality preparation.

(3) When testing an oven, timer, or magnetron, never operate it empty, as damage will result to the energy-producing component. Place a glass of water in the oven before testing to prevent damage.

(4) Selected food items should be used when tests are made to determine energy distribution. Always employ the same type of food for these tests, so that a pattern of the degree of doneness can be developed and compared. A record of each test should be kept for reference. The following data are necessary: food item, weight, geometry of sample, internal temperature at completion, time cycle, degree of doneness, quality comments.

(5) A quick method to check the energy distribution is to place six equally filled glasses of water in various oven locations. These should always be positioned in a predetermined pattern, equidistant from each other, so that the energy can be checked over the entire area. Check the starting temperatures in each glass and record. Plot the position of each glass on a cardboard template. The dimensions of the plotting board should be the same as the shelf. Save the template for future tests. After each cycle, insert a thermometer into the water and note the temperature of each glass. If the difference between the

final and initial temperature is about the same for all glasses, then the energy distribution is considered satisfactory. If wide temperature variations are noticed, uniform cooking results will be hard to achieve, and a check of the oven's components is necessary. At this point, the mode stirrer may be inoperative and need an adjustment or replacement. The magnetron tube should be checked or replaced.

Extended testing will warrant the employment of different types of food, namely: potatoes; rolls or muffins; chicken parts, preferably legs or wings; or two small whole chickens tied and positioned so that they rest on their backs. Refrigerated biscuits are good test items. Thawed frozen entrees are also useful for testing purposes. These foods should be carefully placed in glass casseroles and distributed evenly to prevent high or low spots. Three portions are sufficient for each test. Spacing and shelf positioning must conform to a fixed pattern following the scheme which was previously discussed.

Oven Sanitation and Maintenance

Sanitation and basic maintenance are necessary to sustain a successful trouble-free microwave heating program. These activities are related and should be scheduled together so that they become part of the daily routine. The following steps are recommended for a daily program.

Make a solution of a mild detergent, using warm water. Immerse a clean lintless cloth in solution, remove excess liquid, and rub the cavity, walls, doors, and shelves until all traces of encrusted food and other foreign matter are removed. If equipment has a glass grease shield, it should be removed for cleaning purposes. Repeat the procedure for all exterior surfaces. Where food has hardened and cannot be removed by the described method, a soft bristle brush should be used. Rinse all surfaces with warm water. Sanitize the exterior surfaces and door with an approved sanitizing solution, rinse, and allow to dry. Wipe spills as they occur.

Never apply steel wool or any other abrasive to metal surfaces. Do not wet any of the exposed electrical components which may be located at the upper section of the cavity. This applies mainly to older models.

Every two weeks, the air filter should be cleaned by washing in a mild detergent solution or with soap and water. After rinsing, the filter should be dried.

Daily inspection of the door, hinges, and lock is recommended. This inspection is important to prevent radiation leakage. The door should swing freely and close securely. Loose hinges require tightening or replacement. If the oven is not level, door closure may be affected. Verify the proper door operating efficiency by using the "1 in. paper test." Partially insert a piece of paper about 1 in. wide by 8 in. long in the oven cavity. While holding the paper, close the door. Attempt to withdraw the paper. If the paper cannot be removed, it can then be assumed that the door is tight and properly fitted. Repeat the test on all sides of the door.

As a further guarantee against energy leakage, meters have been developed which measure microwave radiation. These instruments register the radio frequency emissions (R.F.) directly on the instrument scale. Figure 2.12 shows a picture of a portable meter. A premeasured probe automatically gauges the proper distance of the meter from the oven. The meter is calibrated for 1, 5, and 10 mW/cm^2 in compliance with Dept. of Health and Human Services standards for limiting radiation emission.

Every three months, a light oil should be applied to the hinges, latch, and blower motor. Remove excess oil so it does not contaminate the food.

Timing devices, switches, voltage and current, and inlet plug should be inspected every three months.

Check the level of the oven, especially if installed on a mobile cart. If noticeably off balance, it will not function properly, especially as regards heating of liquid and foods with gravy. Proper door alignment may also be affected by an off-level oven.

Inspection for interior and exterior breaks or ruptures and cracks in the metal seams or walls should be performed periodically.

DEEP FAT FRYERS

Key Factors for Quality Deep Fried Food

The following are the key factors that contribute to high-quality, appetizing, and appealing deep fried foods:

(1) High-quality shortening, fat, or oil that withstands high temperatures and moisture, has a high smoke point, will not emit unpleasant odors, and will not interfere with the delicate and natural flavors of the food
(2) Modern frying equipment that has fast temperature recovery and precise temperature controls
(3) Proper frying procedures developed by concise training methods
(4) Posted and easily read operating instructions
(5) High-quality foods, as the initial starting point for a successful program

Deep Frying Equipment

Deep frying equipment consists of four basic parts: (1) a deep kettle with sufficient capacity for the fat to cover the food adequately so that simultaneous cooking of all surfaces takes place; (2) an accurate thermostatic device to control the cooking temperature; (3) a sturdy long-handled basket to hold the food; and (4) a heat source and uniform heat transfer devices. Many refinements and accessories exist that help to increase production and cooking accuracy.

Efficiency and Capacity Ratings

The fryer's capacity or output is rated according to the pounds of product fried in 1 hr. Most manufacturers base their ratings on the hourly production of raw to finished French fried potatoes (⅜ in. cut).

There are four basic fryer designs: (1) pressure fryers; (2) high production equipment where the food is conveyed through a bed of shortening; (3) nonautomatic fryers ranging in size from a 10 × 10 in. well with a shortening capacity of 15 to 20 lb, to a 24 × 24 in. well that holds 125 to 135 lb of shortening; and (4) automatic units activated by pressing a button that starts the cooking cycle. The basket is lowered into the well by mechanical means. When the cycle is completed, the basket is raised to the drain position. A fryer of this type measuring 18 × 22 in. is capable of producing 48 lb of raw to finished potatoes per hour, or 70 lb of blanched potatoes per hour (Fig. 6.1). High output models that will prepare 125 lb or more of raw to finished potatoes per hour are referred to as superpowered frying equipment.

When new frying equipment is installed, tests should be performed for temperature stability and recovery, rated capacity per hour, and efficiency.

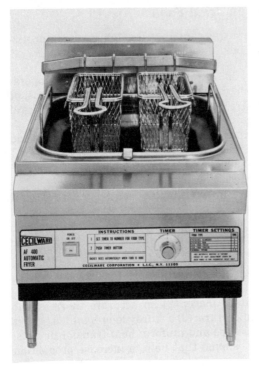

FIG. 6.1.   Automatic fryer.
Courtesy of Cecilware Corp.

Figures obtained from these tests can then be compared with the manufacturer's ratings and will serve as a guide to the true characteristics of the equipment.

The efficiency rating is determined by measuring the ratio of fat capacity to the rated hourly production. For example, if a fryer produces 100 lb per hr of French fried potatoes in 30 lb of fat and another requires 35 lb of fat, the equipment using the lesser quantity of fat is more efficient.

Determining Size and Number of Units per Installation

The question of size and number of units needed for an efficient frying operation may be difficult to answer. There are guidelines that can be followed, e.g., previous experience gained from a similar situation or an established pattern developed from multiunit construction. As a starting point, the following guidelines are suggested:

(1)   A guess may have to be made as to the number of anticipated portions of fried food that will be served in 1 hour. If an establishment specializes in fried foods, this may be 80% of the food output.

(2)   The size of each portion must be established so that the number of portions that fit into a fryer basket can be determined. When ascertaining basket capacity, keep in mind that not more than ⅔ of its capacity is used, and preferably only one-half, to avoid overloading. Overloading may affect product uniformity and degree of doneness. In this regard, the volume of food to be fried is more important than weight. Food should never be packed tightly, but placed loosely in a basket so that all sides of each piece are exposed to the fat. Weigh the number of portions in the basket.

(3)   Use as the average preparation time 5 min for each batch or 12 cycles per hr. Multiply the weight of food per basket by 12. The resulting answer is the capacity of a fryer required for 1 hour of continuous production.

(4)   If production during short peak demand periods warrants a large fryer, it will be wiser to purchase two units equaling the capacity of the larger one. Two fryers will furnish versatility so that two food varieties can be cooked simultaneously and during low demand periods one can be shut down. If uncertainty prevails, the installation of multiple equipment should be given serious consideration. Extra space should be allowed at the fryer station so that additional equipment can be installed if needed. In cases where one fryer is installed, a problem of cooking dissimilar foods at the same time exists. For example, large food portions may need a longer time cycle and frying temperatures will vary according to the type of food being fried.

THE FRYING MEDIUM

Use of the most efficient frying medium is as important to quality fried foods as the equipment used for preparation. Many products of animal and vegetable origin are marketed. Blends of the two are also available. To arrive at a satisfactory solution as to which brand will produce quality fried foods, the following characteristics should be evaluated: cost of the product, flavor transfer, smoke point, frying life, and ease of filtration.

The Smoke Point

The smoke point is the temperature at which a fat heated under specific conditions emits a continuous stream of bluish smoke. The smoke point of an acceptable frying medium should be as high as possible. A high smoke point usually indicates prolonged stability. Excessive smoking may be due to fat deterioration or a product which is not suitable for the equipment.

The following is a list of frying products and their respective smoke points:

	Smoke Point	
Product	(°F)	(°C)
Hydrogenated vegetable oil	440–460	227–238
Standard vegetable shortening	420–440	216–227
Cottonseed oil	410–430	210–221
Chicken fat and corn oil	400–430	204–221
Lard	340–350	171–177
Olive oil	300–315	149–163
Bacon fat	290–300	143–149
Beef suet	235–245	113–119

Rendered beef suet is the lowest-priced frying medium, but it has a low smoke point. Hydrogenated lard is economical and has a relatively high smoke point of 380°F (194°C). If not overheated, it is relatively stable. Vegetable shortenings and oils have the highest smoke point, a long production life, and a lower flavor-transfer factor.

Handling Characteristics of Frying Mediums

Shortenings are more time-consuming to load in the kettle than liquid frying media. Shortening becomes a solid at room temperature (70°F, 22°C), whereas oil is a liquid under the same conditions. Shortening has to be packed around the heating elements and heat cautiously applied to prevent scorching before melting. Filtering must be done in the liquid state. Oils, on the other hand, are relatively unstable, may cause smoke or foam sooner than shortenings, and increase cleaning chores. Opaque, liquid all-vegetable deep-frying fat combines the advantages of both shortening and oil, is highly stable, and pours at room temperature.

Quality vs Economy

The saving of a few cents may result in poor, unappealing fried products as opposed to those that are highly acceptable and of superior quality. The production of specialty frying oils and fats has progressed significantly over the years and many products are available today that possess excellent characteristics. Changing from one frying medium to another usually causes detectable differences in the finished foods. Before such changes are contemplated, tests should be performed to determine the final effect on taste and flavor properties of food.

The following is a summary of desirable characteristics that should be considered when selecting an oil, fat, or shortening.

(1) Bland flavor, so that foreign flavors are not imparted to food
(2) Long frying life, resulting in an economical frying operation
(3) Low absorption properties, reducing incidence of greasy food and assuring lower frying costs
(4) Ability to produce an appetizing, golden brown, nongreasy, crunchy crust
(5) Resistance to smoking
(6) Resistance to gumming: a high gum factor will increase cleaning difficulty
(7) Resistance to transfer of flavor from one food to another, such as a fish flavor to potatoes
(8) Resistance to rancidity under normal care and conditions
(9) Ability to fry uniformly under normal conditions of exacting temperature control and even heating
(10) Easy digestibility

Fat Absorption

Proper and careful handling of the frying medium will assure a more economical operation and products of higher quality. The frying medium becomes an integral part of the food. During frying the fat is being displaced by evaporation of surface moisture. Absorption is slowed down by the formation of a crust but it will continue until the food is removed from the fat. Fat absorption is generally lowest when surface browning or crusting takes place immediately after the food is placed in a kettle. Slow cooking and low temperatures cause a high absorption of fat by delaying crust formation. The amount of fat absorbed varies with the kind and preparation of food being fried, conditions of the frying fat, and frying temperature. Table 6.3 shows the range of fat absorption by various foods.

Absorption depends on surface conditions and characteristics of food, moisture content, and frying temperature. It can be controlled by maintaining the frying medium in satisfactory condition.

Signs of Deterioration

Often one need do no more than step inside a restaurant to detect signs of deteriorated fat. An irritating, unappealing, rancid odor is proof that either

TABLE 6.3. Range of Fat Absorption

Food	Absorption (%)	Food	Absorption (%)
French fries	8–12	Oysters	10–14
Potato chips	32–40	Fish	11–15
Carrots	7–10	Shrimp	12–17
Eggplant	9–14	Chicken	8–18

Source: Anderson Clayton Foods (1971).

the fat must be changed or the temperature checked. The color of the fat is a useful index of deterioration. Usually the color of a fresh frying medium varies from water-white to pale amber. Dark color is a sign of fat deterioration, which will produce darker fried foods. A color test kit is available containing five vials, each with a different-shaded liquid. A sample of fat is drawn from the kettle and matched to a vial of similar color to obtain the score.

A final determination is made by means of a *taste test*. This test should be performed on a daily basis. If the flavor is rated unpleasant, acid, or burnt, or reveals foreign characteristics, the medium needs changing. Other signs of deterioration are foaming, gummy or syrupy condition, and excessive smoking. If the rate of deterioration is abnormally high, an attempt should be made to trace the causes.

Investigation of Excessive Deterioration

The following factors contribute to fat deterioration.

(1) The main causes of fat spoilage arise from chemical changes induced by oxidation, hydrolysis, and polymerization. *Oxidation* is the result of a reaction between oxygen and fat. It begins the moment air comes in contact with the frying medium and is speeded up as the temperature rises. *Hydrolysis* is caused by the presence of water in fat which splits fat molecules, alters the structure, and reduces usefulness. *Polymerization* (two or more molecules joining together to form one large one) results from high temperatures. The formation of gums and resin in a kettle is the result of *polymerization*.

(2) Contamination by foreign materials, such as bread crumbs, potato ends, and other pieces of food debris, contributes to oxidation. It is for this reason that daily filtering is mandatory. Fryers with built-in collection or cold zones reduce the problem of rapid oxidation from this source. Built-in filtering systems or external accessory equipment make the job easier. For expediency, the use of a funnel lined with cheesecloth or filter paper is recommended.

(3) Contamination by metals such as brass and copper will contribute to fat breakdown; these metals should not come into contact with the fat.

(4)   The use of detergents to clean the kettle is recommended; however, complete rinsing is necessary before replenishing the kettle with fat.

(5)   Deterioration is also caused by holding fat at preparation temperatures for prolonged periods when not in use. During low demand or slack periods, the temperature should be reduced to 200°F (94°C).

(6)   A continuously operating fryer will keep the fat in good condition. Fryers that are infrequently used contribute to a faster rate of fat deterioration. Fat is continually removed from the kettle by absorption. To maintain a constant quantity of frying fat in the kettle, fresh fat must be added. The rate at which this is done is designated as "fat turnover." A satisfactory daily measure of fat turnover is 15 to 20%. Rapid fat turnover keeps the frying medium in good condition because deteriorated material is constantly replaced by fresh fat. In a well-balanced frying operation with adequate turnover, it is seldom necessary to discard any used frying fat.

Deep Frying Procedures

Deep frying procedures are simple, especially when using automatic equipment. However, simplicity will not produce quality food unless rigid schedules of operating and sanitation procedures are also followed. The following procedural pointers should be incorporated into a well-defined operational program:

(1)   Determine if cooking time and temperature settings recommended by the manufacturer are adequate. Periodic checks should be made of time and temperature to determine if changes have occurred because of a malfunction of the timer and thermostat. Use an accurate thermometer to check cooking temperatures and a stopwatch to check the timer. Determine the temperature drop when the kettle is loaded; a sharp decrease in temperature may cause prolonged heating so that foods become greasy. Observe the time necessary for the temperature to reach its cooking setting. Reduce food load in the basket until the recovery period is reduced to assure optimum performance. Place a time-temperature chart in front of the equipment for reference.

(2)   Before putting food in a fry kettle, wipe off or shake off all excess moisture, crumbs, and loose breading. All portions or pieces of food should be about the same size. Food having a high moisture content, like fish, oysters, or thawed items, should be drained before frying.

(3)   Always keep the fat content of a kettle at the proper indicated level. Add additional fat when the level drops.

(4)   Fill basket only half full of food and never exceed two-thirds of capacity. Never overload as a means of increasing production. Overloading will delay heat recovery and result in excessive fat

absorption due to improper frying temperatures. A general ratio is 1 lb of raw food to 6 lb of frying fat.

(5) When frying frozen foods, do not thaw, but place in kettles directly from the freezer. Below-counter freezers are ideal for temporary storage. These units should have removable stainless steel drawers. Counter fryers can be installed directly over the freezer box.

(6) Do not salt food over the kettle or use excess salt. Addition of salt to frying oil tends to shorten its usefulness and retards browning of the food.

(7) Turn kettle off or set at 200°F (94°C) during slow periods. Most fryers will recover rapidly.

(8) Allow finished fried food to drain. Where excess fat is observed, blot food on absorbent paper.

(9) If charred pieces of food are floating on the surface of the fat, gather them together with a long-handled mesh scoop and remove.

(10) For foods that are breaded on the premises, the following procedures are suggested. Start breading when food reaches room temperature. Dipping and breading should be done by using both hands—one had for dipping, the other for breading. Heavily breaded foods require additional frying time. Certain wet or moist foods, such as oysters, scallops, fish, or fillets, should be allowed to "set" or "rest" for several minutes before frying, so that the breading and dip mixture can seal. If necessary, redip and bread. When frying breaded foods, place them flat and separated in the basket.

(11) To ensure continuous high-quality production, taste the fat for signs of deterioration. This should be done at the beginning of each shift or at the start of the day's business.

Sanitation

High-quality fried products are dependent on proper and complete sanitation of deep fryer equipment. Procedures recommended for daily and weekly programs follow:

Daily. (1) After power is turned off and fry basket removed, raise heating elements to half position to drain, then move to the upper limit or until they lock in place. (2) Remove fat well (for safety, wear heat-retardant gloves or use a pot holder) and filter the fat. If fryer contains a filtering device, turn it on. (3) Wash baskets and tank and rinse. Remove all traces of soap or detergent. Allow to dry. After drying, replace tank and refill with the filtered fat. Replenish with fresh fat to proper level.

Weekly. (1) Drain and clean kettle. (2) Replace kettle and fill with water mixed with a fry-kettle cleaning agent (2 oz per 1 gal. water). (3) Lower the heating elements into the cleaning solution and turn on the power until the liquid comes to a boil. (4) Turn off power and allow to stand for 10 min or overnight. (5) Rinse and dry the heating elements, fry tank, and baskets. Apply a final rinse of diluted vinegar solution to "sweeten" metal surfaces. (6) After drying, replace filtered fat and add fresh fat to the proper level. (7) Turn unit on and check the thermostat and temperature with a hand thermometer.

CAUSES OF COMMON FRYING PROBLEMS

Fat Darkens Excessively and Prematurely.

(1) Use of inferior or wrong type of fats
(2) Overheating
(3) Faulty thermostat
(4) Inadequate filtering of fat
(5) Improper and inadequate cleaning of equipment
(6) Hot spots in kettle
(7) Food may be improperly prepared; too much moisture
(8) Foreign matter entering fat

Excessive Smoking.

(1) Inadequate filtering of fat
(2) Improperly prepared food
(3) Use of wrong type of fat, smoke point too low
(4) Overheating of fat
(5) Faulty thermostat
(6) Inadequate cleaning
(7) Hot spots in kettle
(8) Poor ventilation

Poor Browning and Undercooked Food.

(1) Excessive foam development
(2) Overloading kettle
(3) Faulty thermostat
(4) Frying temperature too low
(5) Improper preparation of food
(6) Poor or slow recovery of temperature
(7) Check cooking procedures for time and temperature

Excessive and Persistent Foaming.

(1) Use of wrong type of fat
(2) Overheating or faulty thermostat
(3) Hot spots in kettle
(4) Fat being held at frying temperatures for long periods without cooking

(5) Improper sanitation and failure to remove gum from equipment before replenishing fat
(6) Overfilling kettle with fat
(7) Kettle too large for the operation
(8) Salt in fat
(9) Poor or no filtering

Greasy Foods.

(1) Frying temperature too low
(2) Overloading kettle
(3) Frying in foaming fat
(4) Improper preparation of food
(5) Overcooking
(6) Improper draining of food after frying
(7) Slow temperature recovery

Obnoxious Odors from Kettle.

(1) Use of inferior fat
(2) Use of deteriorated or spoiled fat
(3) Use of poor quality food
(4) Excessive debris (crumbs, charred food) in fryer
(5) Foreign matter in kettle

Objectionable Flavor of Fried Foods.

(1) Use of inferior, deteriorated, or spoiled fat
(2) Foreign matter in kettle
(3) Use of poor quality food
(4) Inadequate filtration and presence of debris in fat
(5) Excessive fat absorption
(6) Poor turnover

DAILY RECORD OF DEEP FRYING OPERATION

For economy, continued quality, and troubleshooting, records of the deep frying operation should be maintained. The following data should be recorded:

(1) Date   _____
(2) Time of test   _____
(3) Fryer number, if more than one   _____
(4) Location   _____
(5) Fat capacity of kettle (lb)   _____
(6) Brand of fat   _____
(7) Daily fat replenishment (lb)   _____

(8)   Percentage of fat used for replenishment   _____
(9)   Filtered time, A.M., P.M.   _____
(10)   Fat taste test   _____
(11)   Color comparison test   _____
(12)   Frying temperature   _____
(13)   Type of food fried   _____
(14)   Temperature of food prior to frying   _____
(15)   Appearance of finished food   _____
(16)   Color wheel comparison test   _____
(17)   Odor, taste, texture of finished food
       (greasy, crisp, off-flavor, off-taste)   _____
(18)   Date of last complete cleaning   _____
(19)   Date of last fat change   _____
(20)   Date of last check of thermostat   _____
(21)   Date of last check of timer   _____
(22)   Remarks   _____

STEAM COOKERS

Steam cooking equipment categories are: steam kettle, high-speed compression steam cookers, compartmented steamers, and countertop superheated wet and dry steamers.

Modern steam-cooking equipment is adaptable to many kinds of preparation, e.g., basic cooking, reconstituting, and reheating. It is widely used for vegetable preparation. Vegetables prepared by steam cooking are enhanced in appearance. In addition, meat, poultry, and numerous other products can be cooked speedily, efficiently, and with a minimum of labor. If correctly timed and maintained, steam cooking gives results that are superior to other forms of preparation, since more of the original flavors, colors, and nutritional values are preserved.

General Features of Steam Cookers

Pressurized steam cookers are safe to operate. They have been used in homes for some 30 years and have a proven safety record. Although basic principles of home and commercial equipment are the same, the home cooker is slower and can prepare only one type of food at a time. Controls on home cookers are not as accurate as those made for commercial application. One of the reasons for the high safety record of domestic units is the build-in safety gasket that will rupture should the internal pot pressure exceed safe limits.

Commercial steam cookers are fitted with a number of safety devices. These are of paramount importance and should become a prerequisite when selections are being made. Gaskets must be durable and snug-fitting. Grooves should be provided so that gaskets will not loosen during loading and unloading. Doors should be provided with positive locking devices and interlocks. A safety valve is necessary to limit internal pressure.

Pressure gauges should be fully visible, easily read, and marked with a danger zone. Gauges should be durable and easy to remove. If several pressure cookers are installed, a spare gauge should be available for checking purposes. Pressure readings should be recorded periodically. If a pressure drop is observed when preparing identical foods under similar conditions, then the gauge should be tested. If the gauge proves satisfactory, the pressure drop may be caused by a loose or worn gasket, loose door hinge or lock, insufficient steam, or too low voltage.

Stainless steel construction is advisable for durability and ease of cleaning. Versatile interiors are mandatory in order to accommodate pans of various sizes. A safety thermostat is an excellent feature. If a cooking chamber overheats, the thermostat will activate a switch which will turn off the power. Other important features are a timer, buzzer, signal light, defrost cycle, low water cutoff switches, electric browning elements, simmering controls, and automatic door release.

Steam Cooker Design

Because of the importance of steam cooking and the increasing role this form of preparation equipment is playing in fast food operations, it is essential to understand the basic designs of each category.

Steam-jacketed Kettles. Steam-jacketed kettles have been used for many decades. They are the earliest form of steam equipment specially made for cooking. The double boiler was employed before the steam kettle and is still used for some forms of conventional preparation.

Steam-jacketed equipment consists of an outer and inner vessel welded together. A space is provided between the two kettles for the flow of steam. Cooking temperatures are controlled by regulating the amount of steam. Capacities vary from a 10 qt counter unit to a 200 gal. floor kettle. Variations in basic design have resulted in the development of many useful types of jacketed kettles. Small tilting units have become an integral part of food production.

Most steam-jacketed kettles are easy to keep clean since they are made of stainless steel. If they are installed with sufficient surrounding free space, the burden of exterior sanitation will be reduced. When not in operation, the kettle cover should be removed to keep the interior open for full air circulation. This will reduce off-flavor problems resulting from stale food odors. It is also advisable to fill the kettles with water during shutdown for the same reason. A mild solution of detergent should be used for cleaning. A stiff-bristle, long-handled brush will facilitate removal of food soil and residues. Several freshwater rinses are necessary to remove all traces of cleaning solution. Covers, faucets, and all exterior sections require the same cleaning procedures. The final step is sanitizing by applying a product approved for this purpose. It must be remembered that sanitation consists of two steps, cleaning and sanitizing. The latter will prevent the growth of microorganisms. It is not advisable to use steel wool or any abrasive material that may damage or pit highly polished metal surfaces.

A hot and cold water supply should be located within easy reach of the kettle area. Floor drains should be provided for large stationary kettles. Plastic tubing or hose should be made available for rinsing. Rubber or synthetic rubber hose is not recommended, since these may impart off-flavors to food.

Compartmented Steam Cooker.   Compartmented steam cookers resemble an upright chest of drawers or a cabinet. They are constructed of heavy-gauge metal and contain 1 to 4 compartments which can be controlled individually. Compartmented cookers are available in gas, electric, steam-coil, and direct steam models. Steam pressure varies between 5 and 8 psi (34.5 and 55.2 kPa) at 200°–225°F (94°–108°C). Gas and electric units generate their own steam. Depending on the model and manufacturer, interior designs may be modified for a specific size pan. For example, a 3-compartment model will hold six 2½-in. pans; a 2-compartment unit will accommodate four 4-in. pans. Shelves are either stationary or pull-out type. Automatic, semi-automatic, and manually operated cookers are manufactured. Automatic models feature a self-releasing door at the completion of the cooking cycle plus a steam-release valve. An audible signal sounds when food is ready. Automatic models start the time cycle when the preheat temperature has been reached. Door design is important. Some units feature a wheel mechanism, others a hand lever. Wheel locks should not be overtightened as this practice will destroy the effectiveness of gaskets. If steam pressure falls below the normal cooking range, gaskets should be inspected and replaced if worn or damaged. Figure 6.2 shows a pressureless convection steamer.

High-Pressure Steam Cookers.   High-pressure steam cookers operate at pressures of 12 to 15 psi (82.8 to 103.5 kPa) at 235°–250°F (114°–122°C). These units are the "workhorses" of the food production center. Most are small enough to fit on a counter, so that they form an integral part of a flow system. There are many models and designs to choose from. Some units incorporate several useful features; in addition, there are specialty cookers which are described under a separate heading.

High-pressure steam cookers are manufactured to utilize four forms of heating energy: self-generating gas or electric models, steam-coil, and direct steam-induced units. Cookers that apply steam directly into food encompass several designs: one type sends tiny jets of dry steam onto food; another fills the cooking chambers with a uniform atmosphere of steam. Models can be purchased that offer multiple compartments, each of which can be timed separately, thus affording the opportunity of cooking different foods simultaneously.

FIG. 6.2.   Cleveland
pressureless convection
steamer.
*Courtesy of Cleveland Range
Company.*

High-pressure steam cookers will prepare many varieties of food, from fresh to frozen, such as vegetables, seafood, rice, poultry, eggs, spaghetti, potatoes, and most pouch-packed edibles.

The main advantage of high-pressure steam cookers is speed. During peak periods they will perform efficiently, and if they are located near a service line, preparation can keep up with service load. Pot washing is reduced, since this method of cooking will not burn pans. To facilitate production, these cookers should be installed near a freezer or cooler storage.

Tests must be made on all items prior to production. Even a minor variation in time will make a difference in quality. Once a decision has been reached as to the correct cycle, it should be recorded on a chart and placed next to the control box. Time settings for identical foods require periodic checks, especially where brands have been changed. Where new foods have been introduced, more than one check run is necessary to establish the optimum time.

Browning and Steaming Cookers.   Browning and steaming cookers are specialty models that perform two functions, cooking in steam and browning the surface. A heating element is installed in the cooking chamber that browns food during the steaming cycle. This eliminates the need of transferring the product to another unit for browning.

Countertop Specialty Steam Cookers. Equipment the size of a large battery-type bread toaster is charged with distilled water and operates on electricity from an ordinary 120 volt AC outlet. It generates superheated steam that is capable of poaching eggs, melting cheese on a meat patty, heating a meat sandwich, and reconstituting a single portion of prepared frozen entrees. This cooker can be moved from station to station depending on operating schedules.

Another specialty unit is built into a counter and operates on the same principle. This cooker is fully automatic. It injects steam into the cooking chamber every 15 sec. A pulsating timer controls the steam input. The timer can be programmed for 15 min intervals. The cooker is attached to the water system; however, a deionizer is provided that removes water impurities. The ion-exchange mechanism contains a cartridge filled with an approved resin. When the resin changes color, a replacement is needed.

General Care of Steam Cookers

Steam cookers are reliable and, with a diligent cleaning program, trouble-free service is ensured. Always read and keep available manufacturers' instructions. Salient points should be recorded on an instruction card and hung in front of the unit. Cleaning should be done with all power off.

In all cases, use a mild solution of detergent, followed by rinsing and an application of sanitizer solution. Polish the exterior with a lint-free cloth. Never use an abrasive. When cleaning a chamber, remove all shelves and wash food soil with a brush. Clean strainer and replace. Inspect steam inlet areas and remove any debris that may tend to clog these sections. After cleaning, turn on the cooker and run one cycle to ensure proper operation. During the test run, check pressure relief valve and pressure gauges. Check the door for correct sealing.

Review of Maintenance Procedures

For efficient and optimum performance, a guide follows that encompasses the salient features of a pressure steam cooker maintenance program.

(1) Gaskets, doors, locks, and hinges should be inspected regularly. Never force a door shut as this may cause permanent damage, leakage of steam, and pressure fluctuation. If damage to doors results, they may have to be realigned. Gaskets are an important feature. They prevent leakage and keep doors snug. Frayed and worn gaskets should be replaced. Keep a supply of them in inventory for immediate replacement.

(2) Safety devices should be checked for operational reliability.

(3) Pressure gauges should be checked. These can easily be removed and replaced with a test gauge. Variations in pressure should be noted on a cooking guide chart or the pressure gauge repaired or replaced.

(4) Shelf stability is important. Shelves should be checked for damage or loose fit.

(5) Timers require periodic checking as previously outlined. If a timing device is installed to shut off the cycle automatically, its accuracy should be determined.

(6) Check alarm system and its relationship to the timing mechanism.

(7) Exhaust system and trap must be maintained in top operating condition to ensure a dry steam interior. This is necessary for condensate to drain from the trap. Check for obstructions and proper valve operation.

(8) Flush boiler once or twice a week, depending on water conditions. This step will prevent corrosion and increase the life of equipment.

(9) Preheat cookers to ensure a steady steam flow and accurate cooking results.

(10) Study manufacturer's instructions and cooking guides. Make test runs and compare results with the guide supplied by the manufacturer. Record results as they may be different. Place the chart in front of the cooker. Charts should be reviewed on a regular basis. Conditions change that may alter the original cycle.

TILTING SKILLETS

Tilting skillets are useful cooking devices in food preparation centers. This equipment has a wide range of cooking applications, such as stewing, simmering, pan frying, braising, and sautéing. The operation is rapid and the results uniform. Tilting skillets can perform the work of a range, griddle, small kettle, fry pan, and moist operating oven. Models are available that operate on either gas or electricity. They are easy to clean and sanitize because of easily accessible polished stainless steel cooking surfaces. Skillets are provided with stainless steel balanced lids which give easy accessibility for loading, unloading, and cleaning.

Controls consist of a main power switch, signal light to indicate when power is on, and a thermostat with a temperature range from 100° to 450°F (38° to 233°C).

The skillet pan is capable of tilting 90° under positive control by turning a crank. A removable pan support locks the pan in place when in the tilt position, holding it about 2 in. from the pouring lip, thereby eliminating splashing. Pan supports are available to hold pans of various sizes, such as 12 × 20 in., 12 × 18 in., or 10 × 16 in.

The following cooking temperatures are suggested; preheating is necessary for satisfactory results.

Simmering	200°F (94°C) (maximum to avoid boiling)
Sautéing	225° to 275°F (108° to 136°C)
Searing	300° to 350°F (149° to 177°C)
Frying	325° to 375°F (163° to 191°C)
Grilling	350° to 425°F (177° to 219°C)

Operating Factors

Frozen vegetables can be cooked in a tilting skillet by leaving them undisturbed in the original serving pan and, after heating, transferring them to a holding cabinet or serving station. The loss of moisture is minimized by a cover which reduces evaporation; it has a lip at the back edge which collects and directs condensation into the skillet. Two different products can be prepared at the same time by putting two pans into the skillet and heating simultaneously.

Breakfast foods which can be prepared in volume for mass feeding include sausage, bacon, pancakes, fried eggs, scrambled eggs, and French toast.

It is important to portion meat uniformly, so that all pieces are of equal thickness and have the same weight. Potting meat or corned beef, for example, requires uniformity; otherwise, degree of doneness will vary.

Tilting skillets are excellent for storage or holding. This function is performed by placing water in a skillet, setting the thermostat to 175°–180°F (80°–83°C) and immersing panned food in the hot water.

Labor Savings and Sanitation

Tilting skillets have the advantage of reducing labor. Heavy lifting, transferring of foods from one pan to another and pot washing are greatly reduced. A skillet's interior should be cleaned with a mild detergent solution. If residues are difficult to remove, they should be soaked free with cleaning solution. Wash water, waste, and scraps are easily removed by tilting a skillet and catching the material in a bucket. Several rinses with warm water are necessary, followed by sanitizing with an approved solution. The cover should not be neglected. All crevices, grooves, condensate, and pouring lips must be cleaned. After cleaning, the cover should be left in an upright position so air can circulate freely over all cooking surfaces. The exterior should be wiped with a damp cloth, followed by sanitizing.

Leveling is important. Use a leveling glass bubble to check the position of a pan. Off-balanced pans will have a tendency to draw liquid to the low point, thus producing an uneven degree of doneness.

GRIDDLES

Griddle (Fig. 6.3) maintenance and upkeep are simple. For optimum results that the following procedures should be followed.

(1) Check level of cooking surface. This step is important so that runoff is in proper position to drain fat and other liquids.
(2) Check thermostat.
(3) Check heating elements and uniformity of surface heating by using a metal surface thermometer. Take temperature readings across the back, center and front. At least four readings should be obtained, depending on width of the griddle.
(4) Temperature readings will relate the rate of initial heating and recovery time for uniform and rapid production.
(5) Post operating instructions, which should include food positioning.
(6) Post cleaning and maintenance instructions. Cleaning must be performed daily or more often, depending on production load. A food-release agent, such as lecithin or silicone spray, will help to reduce sticking and hard cleaning.
(7) Cooking surfaces require constant and proper cleaning and preparation to eliminate sticking. This preparation utilizes a partially carbonized fat cooking. The surface temperature is set at 375°–400°F (191°–205°C), and a specially prepared material is poured over the metal and is allowed to heat until it reaches the smoke point. The surface is then wiped clean and the procedure is repeated.
(8) Spatulas that are used to remove carbon residues should be handled carefully to prevent scratching or damage to the smooth metal cooking surface.

FIG. 6.3.   Heavy duty gas broiler-griddle.
Courtesy of Cecilware Corp.

BLENDERS

Blenders can perform a number of diversified operations, such as aerating, liquefying, blending, chopping, crushing, grating, homogenizing, and mixing. These units are both time- and labor-saving devices. They have limitations and cannot be used for grinding uncooked meat. If used for beating egg whites, too much air will be absorbed and they will become too fluffy.

Correct timing of each operation is essential. Changes in texture may occur if the optimum time is exceeded.

Hospitals have developed feeding programs around the use of blenders. They are employed in preparing tube feeding, diet, and infant foods.

Blenders are useful for the following applications.

(1) To blend beverages, and to reduce vegetables to juices and fruits to nectars

(2) To provide a rapid means of blending and mixing soup ingredients: for borscht, fruit, cream bisques, vichyssoise, and tomato vegetable

(3) To prepare omelet mixes and soufflés

(4) To prepare sauces, gravies, and salad dressings

(5) To mix efficiently and quickly certain kinds of desserts and batters, such as waffle, pancake, muffin, and popover

Sanitation

Proper and complete sanitation is necessary at all times to achieve complete success. After each operation, a blender must be cleaned and sanitized. If the bottom portion of the container is inaccessible, a mild detergent should be used to dislodge all food soil. Pour a tepid detergent solution into the container and run the motor for several minutes. Fill the container almost to the brim so that the motion of the swirling water will splash on the lid. Run at low speed. Rinse the container several times and apply an approved sanitizing solution. Rinse again and allow to air dry. During overnight or prolonged storage, the cover or lid should be removed.

Propeller blades should be treated gently to prevent damage or misalignment.

Proper sanitation will minimize off-tastes and off-odors.

OTHER EQUIPMENT

Can openers, slicers, peelers, and shredders all require constant attention for proper operation. Can openers require cleaning and sanitizing daily. These units are breeding places for bacteria and molds. Can openers, slicers, and other devices used for cutting need periodic inspection of blades. If allowed to become encrusted with food, they will not cut accurately. Keep blades sharp. Dull and nicked blades produce metal shavings and should be discarded. Watch for tiny particles of metal from cans when operating a can opener. These may fall into food and create a serious condition.

Dispensing equipment, coffee brewers, and dairy equipment are discussed in Chapter 11. Vending equipment is discussed in Chapter 14.

7

Precooking Quality Control

Precooking includes storage, assembly, thawing, portioning, and other food handling procedures performed prior to heating or other means of preparation.

This category of food handling involves products that require little or no preparation, and/or are served directly to the customer. Items like salads, sandwiches, some desserts, bread, rolls, condiments, juices, eggs, cheese, butter, and cold beverages are included in this phase of an operation.

Improper and careless storage techniques will downgrade quality. Poor stock rotation and prolonged storage in any of the primary storage areas (dry, cooler, or freezer) may lead to spoilage, flavor and texture changes, and loss of nutritive value. Positive storage control procedures will tend to eliminate these problems. These procedures were discussed in Chapter 5.

Haphazard food handling methods, such as piling or stacking food products on top of each other and spillage or mixing of liquids such as sauces and gravies, will destroy the inherent character of the original food. Spices, condiments, and herbs should be carefully labeled to avoid confusion during rushed production periods.

All ingredients should be assembled in an organized fashion until needed for further processing. Sandwich spreads should be kept refrigerated and stored in tight containers during slow periods. Meats, fish, and other food spreads that are utilized for sandwiches and have a tendency to form a crust or hard surface when exposed to air should be mixed in small quantities or kept tightly covered when not in use.

Improper thawing procedures will affect quality, resulting in changes in texture and appearance and loss of nutrients. Items intended for heating in microwave ovens may require special thawing techniques to prevent uneven cooking. Foods to be cooked in deep fat fryers, like French fried potatoes, should not be allowed to thaw, but rather held in a freezer until ready for use.

The preceding examples represent techniques and problems where quality may be downgraded because of improper handling of foods. In this chapter and in Chapters 8 and 9, selected detailed discussions are presented exhibiting the effects on quality when poor control activities prevail during the three stages of processing and production: precooking, cooking, and postcooking.

Some precooking operations are centered in a section of the kitchen known as the pantry. Pantries will be found in many conventional kitchens which prepare and cook products from raw to finished state. Fast-food kitchens usually do not include pantries.

Pantry production comprises a variety of small hand operations. A highly organized system is necessary to enable pantry personnel to perform all required chores. Quality control techniques must be applied. Sanitation must be of the highest magnitude so that food spoilage is reduced to a minimum. Pantry operations include: garnishing, preparation of all types of salads, sandwiches, assembly and plating of appetizers (canapes and hors d'oeuvres), and some desserts like puddings and fresh fruit dishes.

RECIPES

Quality control in the kitchen or preparation area starts with explicit formulations or recipes. It is not the intention of this text to present specific recipes but to create an awareness of their importance in quality control. In a previous section of this book, a comparison of cooking operations was made with commercial processing of foods and food additives. Food processing relies on exacting formulations and physical conditions. The same analogy applies to foodservice.

Recipes must follow a clear, uniform, and simplified format. Figures 7.1 and 7.2 illustrate acceptable formats. Standardization is also important as it ensures a continuity of product. Recipes should be kept in a master looseleaf book. Copies can be made on 5 × 7 in. cards protected from dirt and grease by transparent plastic shields. Suction clamps or clips should be attached so that cards can be hung in the vicinity where they will be used. By employing a looseleaf book and cards, modifications and updating can be readily made.

As shown in Fig. 7.1, a recipe contains vital and exacting information, such as the measurement and weight of ingredients; yield or the number and size of portions; and instructions for applying ingredients. In addition, preparation and cooking instructions are shown. Additional information which may be added under *remarks* includes approved and tested substitutions or modifications to an original recipe. If applicable, information pertaining to holding time and disposition of leftovers may be made a part of the remarks. Many multi-unit operations also include color photographs of finished products for purposes of plating, garnishing, and standardization.

WEIGHTS AND MEASURES

The development of food formulas in a test kitchen or laboratory depends on accurate weights and measures. Accurate scales and portioning devices are employed by food chemists to achieve reproducibility of results. The

RECIPE NAME OR TITLE			
CODE— DISTRIBUTION SCHEDULE 1. 2. 3.			DATE— REVISION— REVISION— REVISION—
YIELD—		PORTION SIZE—	
INGREDIENTS	QUANTITY WEIGHT MEASURE		METHOD OR DIRECTIONS FOR USING INGREDIENTS
SPECIAL NOTES, REMARKS, OR SUBSTITUTIONS			

FIG. 7.1.   Suggested recipe format.

same methodology applies to foodservice preparation, where many chemical changes occur during cooking. In order to obtain consistent results, precise weighing and measuring of ingredients must be followed.

There are many types of measuring devices available to the trade. Quality control involves the correct employment of these tools and an understanding of the kinds of foods (solids and liquids) where they are to be used. The following is a list of measuring devices most commonly employed.

(1) Urn cups—Round-lipped containers with cool handles. Used for measuring hot liquids, such as water for brewing coffee. These containers are usually 1 gal. capacity with indentations showing quart measurements.

(2) Measuring cups—Round, accurately calibrated cups with handles. These hold 1 standard cup (½ pt) when leveled at the top and are graduated in quarters.

(3) Measuring spoons—Accurately calibrated metal spoons, usually linked together in sets of five, including one each of tablespoon, teaspoon, ½ teaspoon, ¼ teaspoon, and ⅛ teaspoon. Edges are parallel for precise leveling.

(4) Measures—Round, lipped, side-handled measuring containers, accurately graduated (usually in quarters). They are used for measuring liquids and certain dry ingredients and are available in gallon, half gallon, quart, pint, and half pint (cup) sizes. When fabricated from glass, they are suitable for measuring all liquids (hot or cold).

(5) Ladles—Metal bowls or cups of known capacity attached to long handles which have hooks at the opposite end to prevent them from

(FRONT)

BEEF STEW

Protein-Rich Food/Vegetable   Main Dishes D-17

Ingredients	100 Portions		For___ Portions	Directions
	Weights	Measures		
Boneless stew beef, cubed	19 lb 4 oz			1. Brown Beef in fat. 2. Add water and simmer 2½ hours or until meat is tender. Add more water if needed.
Oil or fat, melted	1 lb	2 cups		
Water		4½ gal.		
All-purpose flour	2 lb	2 qt		3. Skim off fat and blend with flour and salt. Stir into beef mixture. Cook and stir constantly until thickened.
Salt	4¼ oz	½ cup		
*Onions quartered	1 lb 4 oz	1 qt ¼ cup		4. Boil or steam vegetables until tender (card J-4).
*Potatoes, diced	9 lb	1 gal 2¼ qt		5. Add to meat mixture ; combine carefully.
*Carrots, diced	7 lb	1 gal 1½ qt		
*Celery, cut in 1-inch pieces	4 lb	3½ qt		

PORTION: 1 cup—provides 2 ounces cooked meat and ½ cup vegetable.
Cost per portion_____

VARIATIONS

a. LAMB STEW: Use 19 lb 4 oz boneless stew lamb in place of beef. Portion as in basic recipe.
b. LAMB OR BEEF PIE: Place hot stew mixture in 4 baking pans (about 12 by 20 by 2 inches) about 1¼ gal. per pan. Top with biscuits (card B-1) and bake. One portion provides 2 ounces cooked meat, ½ cup vegetable, and a serving of bread.

*See Marketing Guide on back of card.   (OVER)

(BACK)

BEEF STEW—Continued

MENU SUGGESTIONS

Beef Stew	*Beef Stew*/Dumpling
Jellied Citrus Salad	Orange Slices and Pineapple Chunks
Whole Wheat Bread Butter or Margarine Milk	Bread Butter or Margarine Milk
Coconut Cream Pie	Bulgur Sand Tart

MARKETING GUIDE FOR SELECTED ITEMS

Food As Purchased	For 100 Portion Recipe	For ___ Portion Recipe
Mature onions	1 lb 6½ oz	
Potatoes	11 lb 2 oz	
Carrots, without tops	8 lb 10 oz	
Celery	5 lb 6 oz	

FIG. 7.2.   Sample recipe card.
From U.S. Dep. Agric. (1971).

slipping into containers. They are used to measure liquids for service portion control and for stirring, mixing, and dipping.

(6)   Scoops (ice cream dippers)—Metal bowl-shaped devices fastened to a rigid handle. They have a thumb-operated rotating vane to release semisolids. They are used both to measure and to shape contents in serving and portion control.

Scoop Sizes

Number	Measure, tbsp	Weight, oz
30	2	1 to ½
24	2⅔	1½ to 1¾
20	3	1¾ to 2
16	4	2 to 2¼
12	5	2½ to 3
10	6	4 to 5
6	10	6

(7)   Scales—Discussed in Chapter 2.

THAWING

Methods of thawing frozen foods are as follows: thawing at room temperature; thawing at cooler or refrigerated temperature (Fig. 7.3); direct cooking of the frozen product; forced thawing under cold running water or in ice water bath (if in original watertight containers); and thawing in a warming or microwave oven. Food packers generally label frozen products with explicit instructions for thawing and subsequent heating. It is essential either to follow these directions or to experiment with small quantities of food to find optimum thawing procedures. Improper thawing will result in texture, appearance, and flavor changes. The following is a thawing guide for many widely used foods:

(1)   Fruits—Thaw in cooler or refrigerator, under running water, or in ice water bath.

(2)   Fish—Thaw in cooler or refrigerator. Fillets or steaks may be cooked in the frozen or thawed state. If breading or batter is to be applied, fish should be thawed.

(3)   Juices—May be thawed for immediate use or used frozen.

(4)   Meat—Thaw in refrigerator or at ambient temperatures. Meats should be thawed slowly to avoid texture changes. Some small cuts of meat or hamburger can be cooked in the frozen state.

(5)   Poultry—If large size, thaw in cooler or refrigerator; if small size, thaw at room temperature or cook frozen. If breading or batter is to be applied, poultry parts should be thawed.

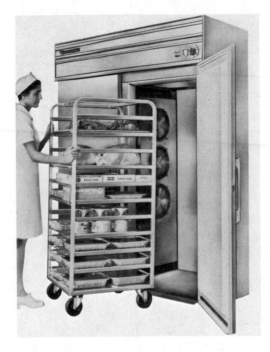

FIG. 7.3. Victory Rapid-Thaw ® self-contained refrigeration system which thaws foods quickly and with a minimum of product waste, spoilage, and texture change.
Courtesy of Victory—A member of Bastian Industries, Inc.

(6) Prepared foods—Follow manufacturer's instructions.
(7) Shellfish—Thaw in refrigerator. Thaw oysters, clams, scallops, and shrimp just enough to separate prior to cooking. If shellfish is to be batter-dipped or breaded, prior thawing is necessary.
(8) Vegetables—May be cooked without thawing.

Foods which have been partially thawed may be refrozen. However, once a food is thawed, it is susceptible to spoilage and refreezing is not recommended, especially if a product has been subjected to temperatures above 40°F (5°C) for an extended period of time. Loss of quality occurs from thawing and refreezing.

Waste and spoilage can be reduced by comprehensive planning. Efficient planning will control the amount of food that should be removed from the freezer for immediate production. If extra food is required, rapid thawing techniques can be followed.

SALADS AND SALAD GREENS

Salads and salad greens are usually prepared in the pantry. Proper handling ensures an appetizing product of high quality. Procedures for quality control are simple, but must be followed for proper results.

Salad greens should be washed and drained of excess water. During washing, leaves should be separated to facilitate removal of all dirt and grit. Excessive handling is not advisable, as this causes brown, rusty leaf discoloration. Always remove greens from wash water carefully so that any sediment is not stirred up or disturbed. Hand-break leaves to bite size; cutting tends to injure the leaves and promotes browning.

If salad greens are prepared in advance, place in a colander or stainless steel wire mesh receptacle, cover with a towel or cheesecloth, and store in a refrigerator. This procedure allows cold air to circulate around the greens and excess moisture to evaporate, resulting in a crisp, cool product for service. Some moisture is absorbed by osmosis, swelling the leaves. A loss of moisture produces limp, unappealing greens.

Dressings and garnishes are added later if the salad greens are to be refrigerated. This procedure prevents soggy and discolored greens. Potato, meat, chicken, and seafood salads can be mixed with dressings prior to short-term refrigerated storage. The flavor of the finished product is enhanced by this method.

To prevent darkening of some fruits and vegetables, such as apples, pears, peaches, and avocados, they can be dipped in an acid fruit juice. Grapefruit, lemon, lime, apple, or orange juice may be used. Flavor is improved and discoloration eliminated. A cool, slightly salted water dip will also produce the same results.

Whole melons should not be stored next to products which will absorb the melon odor. Cut melons are highly susceptible to the absorption of odors and should be segregated.

Salads and salad greens must be stored in stainless steel or crockery utensils. Aluminum will accelerate discoloration. Plastic bags or containers are suitable for this purpose.

CONTROL OF SANDWICH PREPARATION

Sandwiches perhaps are the most widely served items in foodservice establishments. Quality control is essential to produce appealing and tasty sandwiches. All fillings and spreads, garnishes, and breads must be fresh.

Fillings

Fillings should be tender, tasty, and not strongly flavored. They should not be chewy. Downgrading of quality will result if the character of a filling is harsh, bland, too sweet, or too tart. Fillings should spread easily without breaking or tearing bread. They should be uniform in consistency. Soggy fillings will moisten bread and thereby create messy unappetizing products. Dry fillings and dried-out meats and cheese slices have poor appearance and result in an unacceptable chewy tough texture.

Spreads

Spreads like butter or margarine are used for flavor and moistness. If applied in excess, they may create soggy or dripping bread, and their flavor will no longer be subtle.

Breads

Breads used for sandwiches should be fresh and firm (no soft, pasty centers). Because breads absorb odors very readily, they should be stored apart from odor-producing foods and in a dry area at temperatures ranging from 75° to 85°F (24° to 30°C).

Breads with hard crusts should be stored unwrapped while breads with soft crusts should be stored in original wrappings or rewrapped with waxed paper or plastic film. Supplies should be rotated. Use several drawers or storage areas, one for the current supply and another for fresh stock. Breads freeze well, but cooler or refrigerator storage increases staling when they are stored unwrapped.

Storage of Sandwiches

Sandwiches prepared in quantity well in advance of serving or containing fillings susceptible to spoilage should be stored under refrigeration. Wrapping is advisable to prevent loss of moisture and absorption of odors.

QUALITY CONTROL OF EGG COOKERY

Eggs are very important items in any foodservice operation. Every establishment serving food regardless of size or menu utilizes eggs in one form or another. However, this important product is usually taken for granted, in that poor to mediocre quality controls exist. Eggs can be used not only as menu entrees but also for functional purposes, such as clarifying, binding, glazing, thickening, emulsifying, and adhesion. In addition, eggs possess high nutritional value and contain all essential amino acids, making them an excellent source of protein.

Storage

Eggs should be stored under refrigeration at temperatures ranging from 35° to 40°F (2° to 5°C). They must be covered since eggshells are porous and odors can be absorbed. If possible, eggs should be stored with the large end upright. For optimum or peak flavor, eggs should be used within one week of storage.

Due to eggshell porosity, contaminating odors may be absorbed and remain under the shell surface. Thus eggshells should be discarded and never used for purposes for which valid benefits or performance do not exist. Eggs that are cracked or dirty should be set aside and added to foods that are to be fully cooked for an extended time at high temperatures.

Yolks should be covered with cold water and refrigerated in tightly covered containers. When actually used, the water is poured off gently. Follow an identical procedure for whites. Both yolks and whites should be used within 48 hr.

Poaching

Slightly acid water is required to set thin egg whites firmly around the yolk. The addition of 1 tbsp of distilled vinegar plus a pinch of salt to 1 qt of water provides the slightly acid medium. This solution has no effect on egg flavor. Eggs with thick whites poach normally in plain water, while thin whites require poaching in acid water. After the egg white is firmly set, eggs are placed in cool water to stop the cooking action. This procedure is employed for quantity production. Poached eggs can then be reheated as needed in hot salted water.

Frying

The following will affect the quality of fried eggs:

(1) If the eggs are fried at too high temperatures, a burnt tough product results.
(2) If the temperatures are too low, the egg white will be "watery" and runny.
(3) Too much frying medium yields greasy, soggy eggs.
(4) The frying medium should be bland and not affect the flavor of the finished egg.
(5) Clarified butter is recommended to reduce the possibility of burning.

Scrambling

(1) Excess liquid (water, milk, cream) will cause runny and "watery" eggs.
(2) Use a heated, buttered pan so eggs begin to coagulate immediately.
(3) Slightly undercook eggs, as cooking continues after removal from the pan. Overcooked scrambled eggs are dry, hard, and unappetizing.
(4) To extend holding time, light cream can be mixed into the finished scrambled eggs. This procedure quickly lowers the temperature and stops or retards further cooking.
(5) Raw eggs should be placed in a bowl and beaten gently with a fork or wire whip. During beating, water, cream, or milk can be added. Stir the egg mixture in a pan gently with a wooden or Teflon utensil until desired doneness is reached.

Simmering (Boiling)

(1) Whole shell eggs should not be boiled but rather simmered at 185°–195°F (86°–91°C). Cooking at these temperatures produces excellent texture and color and does not destroy any nutrients.

(2) High temperatures and incorrect cooking may yield eggs with a green film around the yolk. Immersing eggs in cold water immediately after cooking will correct this condition. The cold water immersion releases the pressure in the exterior of egg whites by allowing trapped gases to escape. Eggs that are too cold may crack when placed in hot water; hence, bring them to room temperature prior to cooking.

(3) Cooking time and temperature vary with size and quantity of eggs to be prepared. Soft-cooked eggs require a cooking time of 3–5 min; medium 7–8 min; and hard 12–15 min.

(4) Boiled egg immersion cookers require periodic maintenance and timing checks. These utensils consist of perforated metal cups into which eggs are placed. The cup is attached to a chain connected to a timer. The egg and cup are immersed in a hot water bath and held until withdrawn by a mechanism attached to the timer. The water needs changing daily to avoid absorption of off-flavors. Clean and sanitize the water bath, rinse, and fill with clean water. Temperature of the water should be checked periodically.

Omelets

Omelets vary in fillings and shapes. They may be served as an entree for lunch or dinner, or plain for breakfast. The three basic shapes are folded, pancake, and rolled.

(1) Omelets should always be made to order, otherwise the texture becomes hard, tough, and rubbery.

(2) Initially, omelet preparation follows the same steps as for cooking scrambled eggs. However, instead of stirring eggs in a pan while cooking, allow them to spread over the entire pan until coagulated. Tilt the pan to allow any liquid portion to flow to the sides of the pan. When firmly set, the product is folded. The folding is done while the eggs are still moist on top. The omelet is then removed from the pan and folded with the browned side on the top.

(3) Use a minimum of frying medium to avoid greasy and soggy eggs. Place the finished omelets on warm platters or plates.

Convenience Egg Products

Convenience egg products may be purchased in liquid, dried, or frozen forms.

(1) Frozen eggs should be defrosted well in advance of cooking. Defrosting should be slow and never at room temperature. Thawed eggs

cannot be refrozen, but may be stored overnight in a holding refrigerator at a temperature of 38°F (3°C). Hard-cooked eggs are thawed by submerging in boiling water for 7 min or in hot tap water for 15 min. Unused portions can be refrigerated for up to 72 hr.

(2) Manufacturer's instructions must be followed to assure quality. Generally, moderate to low temperatures with proper timing are recommended to produce uniformly tender, appealing dishes. High temperatures and long cooking times cause egg protein to shrink and lose moisture so that the egg becomes rubbery or tough.

CHEESE AND BUTTER

Cheese

Like eggs, cheese and cheese products are universally employed in foodservice. The following quality control procedures are recommended:

(1) Store all cheese under refrigeration at about 40°F (5°C). To prevent dehydration, cheese should be completely covered with waxed paper or plastic film.

(2) Serve all cheese at room temperature with the exception of some soft cheeses like cream, farmer, and cottage cheese. These soft cheeses should be served directly from refrigeration. This procedure preserves natural flavor and texture.

(3) Correct cooking temperatures are important to preserve the natural character of any cheese. High temperatures cause stringiness and a tough rubbery texture.

(4) Grate or dice cheese for quick, uniform melting in cooked dishes such as sauces, soups, or casseroles. Grating is accomplished easily if cheese is cool.

(5) Cheddar is the primary cheese used in cooking and may separate when prepared. To prevent separation, a starchy product or white sauce can be added.

(6) Cheese will keep for about one month without much change when frozen. Creamed cheese can be frozen but may separate when thawed. If separation does occur, it can be reformed by gentle mixing.

Butter

(1) Butter freezes well; however, keep it in the original container and rewrap in moisture-proof material. Wrapping is important since butter absorbs odors readily. At 0°F (−18°C) butter can be stored frozen up to six months.

(2) Refrigerate thawed or unused portions of butter. Place in a covered container to avoid contaminating odors and refrigerate at 32°–35°F (0°–2°C).

OTHER FOODS AND BEVERAGES

Discussions relating to foods such as bread, desserts, and beverages will be found in subsequent chapters.

8

Cooking Quality Control

Cooking applies to all methods of heating or heat application to foods, either partially (warming) or complete (raw to finish). Examples are heating by (1) steam pressure; (2) convection, microwave, or other types of ovens; (3) deep fat frying; (4) broiling; (5) boiling; and (6) griddle preparation. Coffee and tea brewing can also be considered in this category since heat is required for the extraction process.

Although cooking refers to all types of heating, several other pertinent factors, including temperature, timing, formulations (recipes), handling, and equipment maintenance, are involved in sustaining the quality of a food at the highest level. For instance, a faulty timer on a microwave oven will alter degree of doneness; unfiltered fat used for deep frying will produce poor quality fried products; a loose door or a worn gasket on a pressure steam cooker will render unsatisfactory results.

Utilizing the proper utensil size is essential for consistent quality. The use of a 10 gal. container to heat 1 gal. of a product will cause excessive shrinkage, texture changes, and loss of flavor and nutrients.

Forcing or inducing rapid heating by using high temperatures or exposed flames will reduce flavor, decrease tenderness, increase shrinkage, and may also produce a burnt character. Cooking should always be performed within the prescribed time cycle and temperature.

As previously pointed out, formulations or recipes should be concise and clearly presented. All quantity measurements must be explicitly listed together with appropriate size of measuring device, such as ladle or scoop size and number. Heating and timing cycles should be posted adjacent to, or in front of, each working station. Processor's instructions for the heating and handling of pre-prepared frozen foods must be followed to obtain satisfactory quality. Deviations may be made if the directions do not produce expected results. Changes of this sort require intensive testing and discussion with the processor or purveyor.

Proper heating procedures not only add to or increase refreshment and palatability of foods but also are required to deactivate enzymes, reduce spoilage, and alter physical characteristics like flavor, aroma, appearance, and texture. However, uncontrolled heating may reduce the nutritional value of foods, which may include alteration of protein components and destruction of vitamins.

Nutrients and vitamins may be destroyed under unfavorable conditions. Destruction of these food components may also change taste or flavor characteristics. For example, long storage at above-normal temperatures affects the ascorbic acid content in fruits while thiamin and riboflavin in low-acid vegetables are often destroyed. Prolonged freezer or cool storage also will decrease nutritive value. Thawing results in a loss of some nutrients.

Steaming of foods may result in significant nutrient losses. However, this can be prevented by steaming under controlled conditions.

Microwave oven cookery of meat, if not precisely timed, may cause destruction of some essential amino acids.

Effective production is directly related to quality control. An efficient layout and a smoothly flowing system will facilitate the introduction of an efficient and effortless quality control program. Such a production system will result in a steady flow of freshly prepared food, which will increase customer satisfaction. A good way to judge quality acceptance is to monitor customer leftovers or waste, complaints, and menu selections. These factors plus those encountered in the postcooking operation will indicate the effectiveness of quality control procedures.

It is not the intent of this text to provide a detailed study of cooking procedures. Many excellent cookbooks are published that treat this subject effectively and in depth. The reader is directed to the end of this book for selected examples of cookbooks which may be used as references. The intent of this chapter and the subsequent one covering postcooking control is to illustrate the need for quality control for a selected group of food categories. If these examples are understood, then quality control procedures can be applied to other food categories that were not touched upon.

VEGETABLES

Fresh

(1) Thoroughly clean all vegetables prior to cooking. In the case of excessive dirt or insect spray, preboiling is necessary to rid products of these contaminants. Preboiling is a form of blanching and it will retain white vegetables at their peak of color. After preboiling, vegetables should be cooled and drained. Wash leafy vegetables in cold water and rinse several times. Carefully remove leafy vegetables from rinse water so that sand and dirt are not remixed with them.

(2) Prepare small amounts of vegetables. Overproduction may lead to alterations in flavor, color, and texture.

(3) Use a small quantity of water.

(4) Green vegetables—Cook in rolling boiling water until tender.

(5) Root vegetables—Cook in gently boiling water until tender.

(6) Cover cooking utensils to speed cooking and to reduce loss of nutrients and color when preparing red vegetables.

(7) Cook green vegetables uncovered to allow acids to volatilize. This method will maintain good green color, since chlorophyll pigments can be destroyed by acids and alkalis at high temperatures.

(8) Cook white vegetables only until tender and avoid overcooking, which results in a color change from white to gray.

(9) Season or add sauces immediately after removal from heat and serve as quickly as possible.

(10) For uniformity of doneness, cut fresh vegetables into equal-sized pieces.

(11) Salt cooking water slightly to enhance flavor.

(12) All vegetables should be slightly undercooked if they are to be held in a stream table. Heat from this source will be more than ample to finish the cooking process.

Canned

The addition of water may not be necessary as there is usually enough liquid in the can for heating. Bring products to a quick boil and serve immediately.

Dehydrated

Reconstitute dehydrated vegetables in tepid water (90°–100°F, 33°–38°C) prior to cooking. Onions should be presoaked in cold water for 10–15 min and then prepared by normal procedures.

Frozen

If frozen vegetables are to be boiled in pots or steam-jacketed kettles, cook them from the frozen state. If large quantities are frozen, partial thawing may be necessary to separate them into smaller sections. As with fresh vegetables, the use of small quantities of slightly salted water is advisable. After water begins to boil, immerse frozen vegetables and when tender remove them immediately.

Pressure steaming requires a change in the foregoing techniques. Large quantities should be thawed to control the timing cycle more efficiently. Temperatures of frozen vegetables may vary so a constant cooking time under pressurized steam could result in different degrees of doneness. For small quantities, vegetables may be steamed after thawing. Training of personnel, optimum effectiveness of equipment, and prior testing and experience will all serve to produce tasty and appealing cooked vegetables.

Potatoes

Potatoes are a major menu item. Therefore, the procedures required for producing a quality product are important. Potatoes used for baking and deep frying should contain a high starch content. High-moisture potatoes are desirable for boiling or steaming, whereas those containing lower moisture levels are excellent for deep frying and baking.

If time is available, potatoes can be separated into categories by employing a flotation test. This simple test determines age, agricultural growing conditions, and solids content. Inexpensive varieties may be purchased and separated as follows: Dissolve 1 lb of salt in 1 gal. of cold water. Place potatoes gently on the surface of the saline solution. Those that float can be boiled, while those that sink are excellent for baking and frying.

Prior to baking, potatoes should be punctured on both ends to allow moisture to escape and to reduce sogginess. Sizing is important for baking. Those of uniform size will reach the desired degree of doneness at the same time. Baking is done at about 400°F (204°C) in a preheated oven. Usually cooking is complete when piercing indicates a soft textured center.

Baked potatoes should not be held over 1 hr since they will lose their luster and become gray and soggy.

MEAT

General Considerations

Meat is cooked for the following basic reasons: to tenderize, to improve flavor and aroma, and to destroy microorganisms. Cooking procedures depend on cut, type, quality, and grade. The cooking cycle is dependent on factors such as temperature during preparation, temperature of raw product, weight of cut, shape of cut, amount to be cooked, degree of doneness, and amount of fat on the cut.

Tenderness depends on amount and type of connective tissue. Lower grades of meat and meat from older animals contain a larger percentage of connective tissue than do high grades and meats from younger animals.

When meat is cooked, cellular tissue structure and pigmentation are altered, resulting in a color change. As protein in the muscle fibers thickens, the meat gradually firms. Collagen, a component in connective tissue, is changed to gelatin which results in tenderization.

Browning of meat is the result of an interaction between reducing sugars (such as glucose) and amino acids (especially lysine) and is known as the Maillard reaction. An intermediate colorless product is formed (hydroxymethylfurfural), and following a complex series of reactions, brown pigments (melanoidin) are produced.

Meat is cooked by two basic methods, namely *moist* and *dry* heat. The underlying difference between the two procedures is the liquid or the atmosphere (wet or dry) surrounding the product during preparation. Quality, meat category, grade, and cut of meat will determine which method shall be used. Examples of *moist heat* cooking are boiling, steaming, simmering, braising, and other methods where a liquid is employed. *Dry heat* methods include broiling, roasting, sautéing, deep fat frying, grilling, and pan frying. A combination of both is stewing.

Moist Heat

Moist heat is generally applied to less expensive cuts, as this method is better able to tenderize tougher products. Simmering is employed at temperatures below the boiling point of a liquid to prevent stringiness and loss of nutrients and to increase tenderness.

Dry Heat

Dry heat is used for better grades and cuts which are inherently tender and possess lesser amounts of connective tissue. Sautéing, a dry heat process, is done by frying quickly and lightly in a small amount of a fat. Usually thin slices of meat are sautéed. This method requires agility and constant observation to avoid overdoneness. Observing the surface of the meat is paramount. When blood appears on the surface, meat should be quickly turned and heated on the other side for an equal amount of time.

Roasting

Roasting is accomplished in an oven, on a rack in an uncovered shallow pan, with the fat side up. By placing the fat side up, the meat will self-baste while roasting. Controlling heat at a constant temperature, as low as possible, is profitable since shrinkage is reduced, tenderness is increased, and the product becomes more flavorful. Temperatures will vary with type, grade, size, and cut of meat, and oven efficiency. Temperatures range from 250° to 375°F (122° to 191°C). Continuous testing should be performed to assure the accuracy of an oven (thermostat and internal temperatures), and if grade and quality of meat are changed, heating specifications may also require amending.

If a roast is to be salted, it should be done on the fatty side, as the addition of salt to lean meat will tend to reduce surface moisture, creating a dry and tasteless product. In ovens other than the convection type, the position of panned meat needs to be changed periodically to compensate for temperature gradations within the chamber.

Measurements for Degree of Doneness.   Measuring the degree of doneness for roasted products is necessary (Table 8.1). Three methods may be employed: (1) insertion of a meat thermometer into the roast, (2) insertion of a thin stainless steel piercing device, or (3) by determining the time/weight ratio which is based on a time for each pound of meat being roasted.

Meat thermometers are the most accurate means since they make direct measurements of internal temperature. These instruments consist of a bimetallic helix located in a metal stem. Changes in temperature cause a

TABLE 8.1. Internal Temperatures of Large Beef Roasts for Different Degrees of Doneness

Degree of Doneness	Oven Temp (°F)	(°C)	Color of Inside of Roast	Meat Thermometer Reading When Roast Comes from Oven (°F)	(°C)
Rare	300	149	Bright pink	120–125	49–52
Medium	300	149	Pinkish-brown	135–145	57–63
Well done	300	149	Grayish or light brown	150–160	66–71

Source: Courtesy of the National Live Stock and Meat Board.
The temperatures at which color changes take place in beef during cooking are considerably higher than the temperatures above indicate; however, large roasts continue cooking for some time after they are removed from the oven. Therefore, to prevent overcooking, roasts should be removed from the oven when a meat thermometer shows several degrees lower than the temperature at which the actual color change takes place.

rotary action of the helix which moves a shaft on which a pointer is mounted. The dial may show the actual temperatures in degrees F or C or may indicate the various degrees of doneness, such as rare, medium, and well done. Degrees of doneness are also denoted by a 10-point scale. Number 1 indicates rare, while No. 10 means the product is overdone. Proper placement or insertion of the thermometer stem is essential for accurate measurements. The stem should be inserted away from any bone or fat, and into the largest or thickest part of the muscle.

Postroasting must be given consideration when assessing degree of doneness as internal heat continues the cooking process after the roast is removed from the oven. Holding for ½ hr prior to carving is advisable to allow a reduction in internal pressure, which in turn evenly distributes fluid or juice.

Cooking Frozen Meat

Methods of cooking frozen meat depend on type and quantity to be cooked, available equipment, and category of foodservice.

Small cuts of meat such as steaks, chops, and patties can be prepared from the frozen state. Large cuts like roasts are thawed or partially thawed before cooking. When large cuts are cooked frozen, additional time must be allowed. It is not unusual for the time to double when cooking unthawed meat; however, less weight loss occurs when meat is cooked without being thawed.

POULTRY

Poultry is another very important food in the foodservice industry. The same cooking methods apply to poultry that are applicable to meat. Quality control measures are necessary to cook poultry to the correct degree of doneness, i.e., "well done." However, overcooked birds are dry, stringy, and tasteless. The following factors affect the quality of the cooked product:

(1) Broilers or fryers may be broiled, panfried, roasted, simmered, stewed, and braised.

(2) Chicken to be steamed or boiled should be cooked whole to retain proper shape and to reduce shrinkage.

(3) Fowl or mature hens are usually simmered whole since they are less tender and must be processed by moist heat techniques. These birds are used for chicken pie, chicken a la king, salads, fricassee, and as a source of stock for soups and sauces.

(4) Spoilage of poultry is one area that must be scrutinized carefully, as it is extremely perishable and may produce characteristic off-odors and off-flavors. If spoilage is detected, the product should be discarded to avoid incidents of food poisoning.

(5) To produce uniformly cooked poultry in quantity, factors of size and shape must be taken into consideration. These factors should be nearly constant for consistent results.

(6) Cleaning of fowl is essential to remove all traces of blood. Frozen turkeys, after thawing, should be cleaned to remove any blood in the cavity. Cleaning consists of a short soaking period. Agitation of water is advisable to ensure that all traces of blood are removed. A second rinse under cold running water will aid in the removal of blood from crevices. Some fowl or other birds may require a gentle singeing to remove final traces of fine, small feathers or hair-like appendages called filoplumes.

(7) Measuring the degree of doneness is performed with a metal stem thermometer. This method is especially useful for large birds like turkeys. The same techniques apply to poultry as to meat. Hand testing may also prove to be reliable, but experience is necessary to perform this procedure skillfully. If the leg can be easily turned or twisted, a bird has reached the proper degree of doneness. This technique applies to broilers. If, upon pressing the flesh of a leg, the meat exhibits a firm feel but yields easily, the bird is properly cooked.

Fowl must be removed from the cooking vessel to test for degree of doneness. To remove the bird safely and without injury, a range fork is inserted next to the backbone and behind the wing. The lower leg is then pinched or squeezed between the thumb and forefinger. If properly cooked, the flesh will give easily. At this point it is placed under cold running water to prevent additional cooking and browning.

(8) Frozen poultry is generally thawed prior to cooking for easier handling. Turkeys or other large birds should be thawed in a refrigerator. Depending on size and temperature, thawing time may be 48 hr for a turkey weighing 18 lb.

For short notice thawing, place the unwrapped product in cold water. Change water often to hasten thawing. Time required will be about 1 hr for small birds and from 6 to 8 hr for larger ones. Thaw until pliable.

(9) As with all foods, use care and cleanliness in handling fresh-chilled, frozen, or cooked poultry to guard against food poisoning and spoilage. Before cooking poultry, the main concern is avoiding possible cross-contamination with other foods or surfaces in the kitchen. For this reason, after handling raw poultry, hands should be washed before working with other foods. Always clean and sanitize any food-handling equipment, such as knives and cutting boards, after contact with raw meat, poultry, or fish. Do not partially cook poultry one day and complete the cooking the following day, since this practice provides microorganisms an additional opportunity to multiply.

SEAFOOD

Fish and shellfish require different handling and cooking procedures from meat or poultry. Fresh fish and shellfish should be used as soon as possible to reduce spoilage. If storage is necessary, the lower the temperature, the slower the deterioration. A refrigerator temperature of 35°–40°F (2°–5°C) is needed to maintain a quality product. Prepackaged fish and shellfish may be stored in original wrappings. These packages normally are designed for short-term refrigeration. If the original wrappings are not adequate, remove them and rewrap with aluminum foil or plastic sheet. Do not store under normal refrigeration longer than 48 hr prior to cooking.

Frozen fishery products will maintain their quality for longer periods at 0°F (−18°C) or lower. Freezer storage requires that products be wrapped in moisture- and vapor-proof packaging material. Proper packaging prevents cold air from contacting the surface of fish, which may cause dehydration, oxidation, and freezer burn. Label each package with the date, kind, and type of product, as well as weight and number of servings. Frozen seafood will maintain good quality at 0°F (−18°C) or lower for 4–6 months. Cooked or pre-prepared frozen seafood will keep its quality for up to 3 months. The following handling procedures are advisable to produce quality seafood:

(1) Thaw fish and shellfish just before cooking. Refrigerator thawing is best. Allow 24 hr for thawing 1 lb of product. If quick thawing is necessary, place the wrapped package under cold running water. Allow about 1 hr for thawing 1 lb of fish. Do not thaw at room temperature or under warm water.

(2) Frozen breaded fishery products should not be thawed before cooking. Frozen fillets, steaks, and shrimp may be cooked without thawing if additional cooking time is allowed.

(3) Fish and shellfish are cooked to develop flavor and to soften the small amount of connective tissue present. Cooking them at too high a temperature or for too long toughens, dries, and disintegrates the flesh and destroys the fine natural flavor.

(4) Fat content of fish is a factor in determining the proper cooking method. Lean fish requires moist heat cookery, unless some moistening agent is used. Fish with a high fat content may be broiled or baked, which helps to reduce excessive oiliness. Moist heat is used for nearly all types of fish cookery.

(5) Degree of doneness is determined by experience. Raw fishery products have a watery, translucent appearance. During cooking, the watery juices become milky colored, giving the flesh an opaque, whitish tint. This change in color is quite discernible. When the flesh is opaque in the center of the thickest part, the fish is cooked to proper degree of doneness. At this point, the flesh will flake easily when tested with a fork and will separate readily from the bones.

(6) Cooked fish is tender and delicate and should be handled as little and as gently as possible during and after cooking to preserve its appearance. Serving should be done as soon as possible. Holding at serving temperatures will have the same effects as overcooking.

PRE-PREPARED FOODS

Manufacturer's Processing Guidelines

Pre-prepared or convenience foods can be handled and served successfully if the preparation instructions issued by a manufacturer are followed. Figure 8.1 illustrates heating and serving instructions which are comprehensive yet easy to follow because of their simplicity.

It is assumed that all products purchased from reliable suppliers have been properly tested in product development kitchens and instructional guidelines written as a result of such programs. If the instructions are not clear or steps are missing, the manufacturer or his agent should be notified. After their procedures are fully understood, all data should be recorded and displayed according to those directions previously discussed for recipes. Instruction cards, clearly marked, which list each step of a procedure should be drawn up and posted at the appropriate station. However, prior to a full production run, several trials of the processor's instructions should be attempted. Their directions are merely guidelines, and since a number of production variables may be encountered, trials are recommended for quality results.

Quality Checks

Pre-prepared foods need the same quality checks as other foods of a similar nature. These include flavor, texture, appearance, nutritional aspects, ease of handling, secure packaging, and an economic evaluation. Pre-prepared foods should be selected for their natural color and flavor

EXCHANGES: Each serving 6 ounces (by volume) will supply 2 meat exchanges (less 5 grams fat) and 1 bread exchange.		
TABLE OF ANALYSIS	Per 100 grams	Each 6 oz. serving
Carbohydrates (gms)	9.4	15
Protein (gms)	10	16
Fat (gms)	3	5
Available Calories (mg)	108	173
Sodium (mg)	20	32

COOKED MEAT CONTENT = 31%

FROZEN
SAUCE, GROUND
BEEF & MACARONI

FOR MODIFIED DIETS: SODIUM CONTROLLED, FAT CONTROLLED, SOFT, BLAND, DIABETIC DIETS.

INGREDIENTS: Tomato sauce (water, tomato paste, tapioca starch, wheat flour, artificial color), cooked ground beef, macaroni.

NET WT. 5 LBS.

U.S. INSPECTED AND PASSED BY DEPARTMENT OF AGRICULTURE EST.20-L

14 — 6 oz. servings by volume.
14 — 5.6 oz. servings by weight.

HEATING INSTRUCTIONS
Minimum recommended serving temperature 160°F.
Remove label. Pierce center of cover.

CONVENTIONAL OVEN
Preheat oven to 450 F.
Heat 55 to 70 minutes.

CONVECTION OVEN
Heat for 30 to 45 minutes.

INFRA RED OVEN
Preheat oven to 450 F.
Place tray in oven. Heat for 30 to 45 minutes.

PRESSURE STEAMER
Low pressure 4 + to 7+.
55 to 65 minutes.
High pressure 15 +.
30 to 45 minutes.

MEDI-DIET T.M.

DISTRIBUTED BY NATIONAL HOSPITAL FOODS, INC. 540 FRONTAGE RD., NORTHFIELD, ILL. 60093
SPECIALISTS IN PREPARED ENTREES FOR MODIFIED DIETS
A SUBSIDIARY OF WILSON-SINCLAIR CO.

FIG. 8.1.   Heating and serving instructions, properly displayed, are shown at right side of product label. These instructions are concise and meet most heating operations.
Courtesy of National Hospital Foods, Inc.

characteristics, pleasing texture, and appealing balanced flavor. Accompaniments such as gravy and sauces must be smooth and compatible with foods that they are placed on. Existing government standards that regulate the amount of meat and poultry required in pre-prepared dishes may require determination. This may be necessary because usually mention is made neither of the grade and cut of meat or poultry nor of the quality and composition of other ingredients, as long as they are wholesome. The final quality will also depend on the method and type of heating equipment and whether the convenience food and the heating device are compatible.

9

Postcooking
Quality Control

Incorrect and haphazard handling of foods and hot beverages at the postcooking or postheating stage is responsible for more poor quality and unappealing products than any of the other stages previously discussed.

Postcooking handling covers a myriad of techniques and procedures. Included are plating, portioning, holding in steam tables or hot and cold cabinets, storing leftovers, and holding prepared foods in temporary cool storage or under infrared warming lamps. Some desserts such as puddings, fresh fruit, fruit salads, pies, and cakes require special handling to retain their highest palatability.

Holding food in a steam table, hot cabinet, or under infrared warming lamps for extensive periods of time will downgrade its quality by altering factors such as texture, flavor, shrinkage, and nutritional content. Foods will become mealy, mushy, soggy, and dried out. In addition, microbial spoilage may become a problem. Overproduction, as a result of poor planning or incorrect forecasting, is an important cause of low quality at the postcooking stage. Overproduction is not only wasteful, it also has a deleterious effect on the profit structure and causes loss of business.

The period between final preparation and service to the customer must be monitored so that it is held to a minimum. Beverages like brewed coffee should be held at 185°–190°F (86°–88°C) for a maximum of 1 hr. Desserts such as cream or custard pies require refrigerated storage at the service area to prevent spoilage and other forms of deterioration.

Salad dressings should be added to salads just prior to serving. Tossed or mixed salads containing soft-textured components (tomato wedges or slices) require short holding periods to prevent a soggy unappetizing product. Lettuce and other salad vegetables should be kept dry to prevent loss of crispness and enzymatic browning. Tossed or mixed salad ingredients require refrigerated storage until served.

In this chapter, common postcooking problems that lead to poor quality are illustrated as a guide to maintaining the highest degree of quality prior to customer service.

POSTCOOKING MICROBIOLOGICAL CONTAMINATION

An area of wide concern in the postcooking stage is microbiological contamination. Although causes for spoilage have been discussed at length, a brief review of this subject is desirable at this time.

Contamination may arise from a number of sources such as personnel, fresh products like fruits and salad ingredients, and spices; or by tangential contact with foods that have spoiled during holding. Cross-contamination occurs, thereby infecting foods that are free of spoilage. Other sources may be poorly cleaned utensils, cutting tables and boards, and airborne pathogens arising from dirty dusty floors, air filters, and ducts.

Proliferation of bacteria is extremely rapid when suitable growth conditions prevail. If cooked foods are held at kitchen temperatures in pots or other containers, conditions may be favorable for rapid microbial growth. These conditions include temperature and moisture that favor proliferation, and certain categories of foods like poultry, fish, mixed salads, and low-acid products, which are highly conducive to microbiological activity. Inadequate reheating of leftovers may also furnish good growth conditions.

HOLDING AND OVERPRODUCTION

General Methods and Results

A dominant result of prolonged holding of food at elevated temperatures is low quality. Preparation and production systems must contain provisions for monitoring overproduction and to provide for the rapid serving of freshly cooked foods. By utilizing rapid-heating ovens, such as microwave, convection, or infrared, foods that were previously prepared and refrigerated or frozen can be reheated as required. This method reduces the possibility of flavor deterioration, texture changes, loss of nutrients, and unappealing appearance.

Holding foods for short periods may be accomplished by several devices, such as the bain-marie, which is a shallow rectangular open vat containing water. The water is heated by gas, electricity, or steam. Food is placed in containers which are then placed in the hot water bath. Temperatures above 140°F (60°C) must be maintained to avoid continued or overcooking and spoilage. Steam tables are similar to bain-maries, but they are usually installed at the service area and are equipped with slotted metal tops to accommodate various shaped pans. This equipment is adaptable for preparing foods like sauces or to continue the cooking of various menu items like roasts.

Hot cabinets, which are manufactured in a number of styles, include mobile units and built in pass-through wall units equipped with doors on two sides leading from the kitchen into the service area. Hot cabinets are ideally suited for controlled temperature holding.

Infrared lamps (Fig. 9.1) are widely employed to hold heated foods for short periods prior to serving. This is a dry method of heating and therefore it is not suitable for all foods, especially items covered with sauces or thick gravies. Unappetizing crusts will form if these foods are held too long. Infrared lamps are excellent for deep fried foods like potatoes and onion rings since dry heat helps to retain the crisp appetizing character.

Regardless of the method used for holding, careful observation must be maintained to prevent overcooking, which results in major texture and color changes.

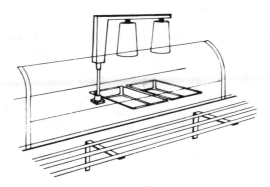

FIG. 9.1.   Infrared Adjust-O-Ray food warmer.
Courtesy of Cresent Metal Products, Inc.

Examples of some recommended holding temperatures are: (1) thick sauces, entrees, fully cooked meats and roasts, 160°–165°F (71°–74°C); (2) thin sauces and gravies, 180°–185°F (82°–85°C); and (3) bread and rolls in vented compartments, 185°–195°F (85°–91°C).

Distribution of Prepared Foods

Distribution of prepared foods to satellite locations requires a rigorously monitored program of rapid movement in insulated carriers that are clean, sanitized, and capable of retaining the original food temperature. If these guidelines are not met, the result will be deterioration and spoilage as well as texture and appearance changes.

Pre-prepared Frozen Foods

(1)   Pre-prepared frozen foods warrant short holding periods. Portion-controlled packages minimize overproduction, as small quantities

may be heated as demanded. Excessive holding rapidly reduces quality, in that appearance, texture, and flavor are altered, affecting customer acceptance.

(2) Pre-prepared frozen foods should not be refrozen after prolonged holding. Food safety and quality deterioration problems can occur due to bacterial growth at elevated temperatures.

(3) Pre-prepared frozen foods may be refrozen if they have not been removed from their original container and exposed to ambient conditions. If a package feels cold and exhibits some hardness, food may be rapidly transferred to a freezer. However, in case of doubt regarding safety, it is wise to discard the package to eliminate any risk of food poisoning.

(4) Refreezing will not correct any damage to food as a result of intermittent thawing or holding at high temperatures. Instead, mild damage to quality may continue at an accelerated pace. The time-temperature relationship determines the amount of food damage which will develop.

(5) The quality of frozen fruits is impaired by storage above 0°F (−18°C). Nutrients like vitamin C are reduced, browning of certain fruits takes place, and losses of natural color and flavor develop. Within 48–72 hr at 30°F (−1°C), rapid changes occur; at 20°F (−6.7°C), such changes take 2–3 weeks; and at 0°F (−18°C) or below, the quality remains unchanged for a year or more.

(6) Frozen juices stored above 0°F (−18°C) will lose flavor and separate rapidly when thawed for reconstitution.

(7) Frozen vegetables when subjected to temperature above 0°F (−18°C) lose flavor and change color. The color of green beans and peas, for example, will change from green to grayish after 3 days storage at 30°F (−1°C).

(8) Cooked poultry loses its fresh-cooked character rapidly and develops a flat insipid flavor. Flavor changes in pre-prepared fried chicken can be detected within two weeks when held at about 20°F (−6.7°C).

(9) Pre-prepared frozen foods which are covered with sauces and gravies are protected against changes during freezer storage for up to 1 year.

(10) Other types of foods not previously mentioned will lose quality at above 0°F (−18°C). Curdling, separation, and loss of smooth textures may develop with gravies, desserts, and puddings when thawed.

(11) When heating and holding periods for convenience foods are not controlled, variations occur in water content and retention of water-soluble and heat-labile nutrients. Prolonged holding slowly destroys nutrients by mechanisms such as oxidation.

SAUCES AND GRAVIES

Functions of Sauces

Sauces are any flavorful soft or liquid dressing, relish, or seasoning served as an accompaniment to food. They are used for moistening, flavor control, and garnishing to make food more appealing. Sauces have a long history. Those with strong flavors were once employed to conceal the character of poor quality meats and other food. As a garnish, sauces provide contrast and enliven appearance. For example, wet-cooked meat which appears gray may be covered with a red sauce; pasta with a green or red sauce; and roasted meat with a clear brown sauce.

Gravies are defined as the juices that drip from cooking meat, poultry, or fish. They are made into sauces by thickening and seasoning, and should complement the flavor of the food with which they are served.

Although one of the functions of sauces is to moisten, the amount placed on a food should be small in relation to the product or entree. Sauces that are thin and "run" so that they do not adhere to a food are of little value. Thin sauces should be served separately as dips.

Sauces should have a smooth, velvety, viscous consistency, with all ingredients in a stable state. To improve the texture of a simple sauce, a stabilizer is added to hold the components together, thus imparting a pleasing mouth feel. To further a sauce's value, various sizes and kinds of solids are added to make it more compatible with food.

Gravies

Gravies are similar to sauces. They are the juices of meats, fish, poultry, and vegetables with the addition of spices and herbs. Gravies are an important part of precooked frozen foods. They enhance the appearance, protect them from loss of moisture during freezing and storage, and protect meat fats from oxidative rancidity during storage.

Gravy is best when served hot. A tepid, thick floury product will downgrade quality.

Effects of Frozen Storage on Sauces, Gravies, and Dressings

Sauces, gravies, and salad dressings all have characteristic structures that may be damaged during freezing, storage, and thawing. The starch in sauces and gravies and the oil and starch in salad dressings are the key ingredients that contribute to structural breakdown. Those that are thickened with common cereal flour and starches appear curdled after freezing and thawing. Although heating to serving temperature improves appearance somewhat, the original character is not entirely restored. Sauces and gravies prepared with waxy rice or other waxy cereals have the greatest stability. So-called "freeze-resistant" starches have proved to be of value for use in sauces and gravies that are frozen. In some products, like frozen meat pot pies, some wheat flour is used to produce the desired flavor, opacity, and texture. Freeze-stability is attained by using a waxy starch or flour in combination with wheat flour at about a 50:50 ratio.

Some sauces such as cocktail and creole sauces will have a high consistency without the use of starchy thickening agents. Stability is excellent and the assortment of sauces available is substantial.

Convenience Sauces and Gravies

Many sauces and gravies are commercially prepared and frozen. These products are quick-frozen and include a wide assortment of popular sauces and gravies. They are easily thawed and heated. The advantages that these products offer are: fresh flavor, elimination of a large and sundry inventory of ingredients, and reduction of labor. These frozen sauces and gravies may require the addition of some spices, herbs, or other ingredients such as wine or cheese to increase their appeal. The following is a partial listing of these frozen products: hollandaise, Béarnaise, Bordelaise, Madeira, smitane, supreme, Eugenie, Hongroise, Mornay, cheese, and mushroom.

An interesting assortment of prepared sauces and gravies are being packed in cans. Many of these require little or no preparation except heating. Some may have to be diluted; others may need the addition of seasoning or a garnish. The following is a partial list of sauces and gravies available in cans: a la king, barbecue, brown, various cheese sauces, chili, hollandaise, Italian, marinara, mushroom, mustard, Newburg, pepper, pizza, various spaghetti sauces, stroganoff, supreme, sweet and sour, white cream sauce (enriched Béchamel), white sauce, and Worcestershire sauce.

Following are a number of canned gravy bases and mixes: beef gravy base and mix, beef au jus mix, Swiss steak gravy mix, chicken gravy base and mix, ham base and mix, onion base and mix, and turkey base and mix.

The items listed at the end of this paragraph are representative examples of dry (dehydrated or freeze-dried) sauce and gravy mixes. These products are usually packaged in air- and moisture-proof film and contain about 8 oz of mix per package. Reconstitution is performed by adding the contents of the package to a specified amount of water, then heating slowly and stirring. If the original recipe calls for wine, it is added to the sauce as a wine concentrate. The items are: a la king, barbecue, Bordelaise, brown gravy mix, various cheese sauces, chicken, ham, hollandaise, Mornay, Newburg, pizza, spaghetti sauces, stroganoff, tomato, turkey, white sauce roux, and white sauce supreme.

Salad dressings and cold sauces are available in a wide selection of items that are packaged in cans, jars, or as dry mixes. These products include the most popular varieties such as: mayonnaise, salad dressing, French, Italian, Thousand Island, Russian, tartar sauce, coleslaw dressing, horserad-ish, blue and Cheddar cheese, and Green Goddess dressings.

It is advisable to read and follow the manufacturer's instructions for reconstituting and heating and other specific recommendations which may help to produce a quality gravy or sauce. When purchasing prepared sauces and gravies, those that exhibit low-to-medium spice flavors and aromas should be selected. It is much easier to enhance and build up seasoning characteristics than to attempt to tone them down. In addition, the extra seasonings that may be required can create a tailored sauce or gravy with an outstanding and distinctive character.

Maintaining the Quality of Sauces

Crust formations are avoided by keeping sauces covered until used. Crusts should be removed by skimming. It is not advisable to stir the crust into the sauce as this will produce lumps.

Lumpy, thin, or thick sauces can be corrected. If they are too thick, heat them or bring them to a simmer and add more liquid, such as stock, milk, or water. They may have to be reseasoned to correct dilution. If too thin, stir a quantity of thickener, such as egg yolk or flour, into the sauce. If the sauce is lumpy, strain to remove the solid particles or lumps, or heat, or put into a blender at low speed.

Store sauces by placing them in covered containers. Prior to storing in the refrigerator, they should be cooled to room temperature.

Reheating can be done in a trunion kettle, bain-marie, or double boiler. During heating, sauces and gravies should be stirred to avoid scorching.

For quality results, prepare only enough sauces and gravies for short periods.

CHEESE AND CHEESE COOKERY

The use of cheese in cooking belongs in the previous chapter; however, the handling of cheese and its subsequent application may be considered as a postcooking function. Successful cheese cookery depends on brief heating at a low temperature. High temperatures and overcooking make cheese tough and stringy and cause fat separation. Hard cheeses are best for cooking since they do not destabilize as quickly as soft cheeses.

Cheese blends more readily with other ingredients and melts more quick-ly if shredded or diced. When preparing cheese sauce, stir in shredded cheese after the white sauce is completely heated or cooked. When making a cheese omelet, add shredded cheese after the omelet is cooked, just before folding. Casserole dishes containing cheese should be baked at low temper-atures. To prevent cheese toppings from toughening or hardening during baking, cover them with crumbs or add cheese just a few minutes before removing food from the oven.

Cheeses keep best when refrigerated. Soft cheeses are highly perishable. Hard cheeses, such as Cheddar or Swiss, will keep several months, if tightly wrapped. Cheeses with strong odors should be stored in tightly covered containers to avoid odor contamination with other foods. Cheese that has dried out and become hard may be grated.

Freezing is not recommended for most cheeses because they become crumbly and mealy when thawed. Small pieces (1 lb or less) of the following varieties can be frozen satisfactorily: brick, Cheddar, Edam, Gouda, Swiss, provolone, mozzarella, and Camembert. Small quantities of blue, Roquefort, and Gorgonzola can be frozen for salads or dressings, or other uses where a crumbly texture is acceptable. Wrap cheese tightly, freeze quickly, at 0°F (−18°C) or below, and store no more than 6 months.

Dehydrated cheeses, such as Cheddar and Parmesan, are available for a number of applications. Rehydration consists of adding water, milk, wines, or other liquids, and the cheeses may be cooked or prepared and used cold.

A large assortment of cheese mixes are available. These are often packed in plastic 1 lb tubes. They include many popular cheeses, such as Cheddar, blue, Swiss, and Gruyere. These are mixed with such products as nuts, caraway, pepper, various wines, bacon bits, smoked items, and herbs.

SALADS

(1) Break into small bite-sized chunks salad ingredients that are difficult to handle or cut with a fork. This procedure will give added consumer satisfaction.

(2) Crisp and cold greens are important for appealing and tasty salads. Proper storage technique will prevent moisture loss. Do not expose lettuce or other greens to room temperature for prolonged periods as evaporation of water is accelerated. If greens become limp, they can be placed in a refrigerator at 35°F (3°C), equilibrated, and sprinkled with water until crisp. Moisture will be reabsorbed by osmosis, thus swelling the leaves.

Evaporation can be retarded by following the simple technique of putting crisp greens in a refrigerator and covering with moist cheesecloth, or placing them in a plastic container. Specially designed containers are available for this purpose. Some refrigerators come equipped with built-in compartments for assuring the quality of salad greens.

(3) Add dressings just prior to serving to minimize the evaporation of moisture. Most dressings contain salt, which removes moisture from leaf cells.

(4) Delicate salad components like certain fresh fruits (pears, peaches) and tomato slices must be handled with care when mixing with firmer ingredients and dressing to prevent bruising and injury to fragile items.

(5) An excess of dressing renders a salad unappetizing and creates a soggy condition at the bottom of a service plate. Too much dressing will also overpower the true taste and flavor character and alter appearance so that quality will be downgraded.

SANDWICH CONTROL

Sandwiches are classified as hot and cold varieties. They have universal appeal and are dominant foodservice items. Cold sandwiches may consist of a filling on one slice of bread (open-faced), between two slices of bread, triple decked, or in a sliced, long roll (frankfurters or salads). Hot sandwiches may consist of one or two slices of bread and are baked, deep fried, or grilled.

Quality controls encompass standard procedures; however, if any of the steps are neglected, problems will arise. These may include soggy or "soaked," pasty, or rubbery texture and off-flavors or -odors. The following procedures will produce tasty, high-quality sandwiches.

(1) All ingredients including bread or rolls must be at the peak of freshness.

(2) Excess spices or flavors will tend to overpower true character of the filling and thus should be avoided. Subtle or delicate applications of spices and flavors will create more appealing and tastier sandwiches.

(3) Fillings that are diced or chopped should be cut uniformly to improve appearance and ease of eating. Crisp, "bitey" items like diced celery, pickle, or cucumbers will add a pleasing texture to soft fillings.

(4) Sandwiches should be served at correct, refreshing temperatures. The fillings of cold sandwiches require temperatures of 45°–55°F (8°–13°C), while 130°–140°F (55°–61°C) is the proper range for hot ones. The latter is essential for grilled items to retain a crisp character.

(5) Ingredients or fillings should spread with ease and uniformity to avoid lumps and dry areas.

(6) If bread or rolls are to be toasted, the toasting should be uniform and the color a golden light brown. Burnt edges and light or unevenly toasted bread will downgrade quality.

(7) If bread is to be cut, hold for 24 hr prior to slicing to prevent tearing the crust or rupturing the crumb. Rolled sandwiches can be made from fresh bread, which is more pliable.

(8) Spreads like butter can be applied easier and more uniformly if soft and "creamy." One slice of bread may be buttered; however, if the filling is moist like tuna or chicken salad, both slices require butter to prevent sopping and soaking. The spread acts like a barrier, thus reducing absorption. Mayonnaise should be evenly spread over butter on one side. Too much mayonnaise masks the filling flavor and leads to a soggy condition.

(9) If sandwiches are to be prepared in advance, storage at 35°–40°F (3°–5°C) is necessary. Before refrigerator storage, sandwiches must be wrapped to eliminate drying. Wrapping materials like aluminum foil, plastic film, or wax paper can be applied. Freezing is applicable if sandwiches are placed in freezer wrapping material. Sandwiches containing tomato, lettuce, or fillings mixed with mayonnaise do not freeze well. Moisture in tomatoes and lettuce will freeze and rupture the cellular structure. Also, the mayonnaise emulsion will break down if frozen.

FRUIT

Fruit must be washed thoroughly to prevent microbiological contamination, to eliminate grit and dirt, and to rid surfaces of residual insecticides or fungicides. A large amount of fresh fruit is utilized for salads or cocktails, served with cheese, or used as garnishes. Berries spoil rapidly, which necessitates washing just before serving. The procedure for cleaning berries is simple: place in a sieve or strainer, rinse with cold water, drain completely, and gently spread on absorbent lint-free paper. Blot the surfaces to remove excess moisture. Most fruits, with the exception of bananas, are more appealing if served chilled. Darkening of some fruits like apples, which is caused by enzymatic action, can be prevented for a short time by covering to protect the fruit from air. This may be accomplished by using a solution of acid fruit juices (compatible with the fruit) or by using an ascorbic acid solution.

Frozen fruit may be defrosted and handled similarly to other types of frozen products. Thawing should be accomplished in the original container, in a refrigerator, at room temperature, or, if necessary, under cold water. To avoid unpalatable fruit, serve immediately after defrosting to eliminate texture changes and poor appearance.

SYNERESIS

Syneresis or "weeping," which is related to the mechanism of coagulation, is the separation of a liquid phase from some solid or semisolid phase of certain foodstuffs. This liquid may not be water, but a dilute solution of the product, such as the whey which separates from curds during cheesemaking. Examples in postcooking are the liquids found on the surface of fruit gelatins, puddings, gravies, and sauces that have been stored under refrigeration for some time, and butter, cream cheese, yogurt, sour cream, custards, margarine, fruit jelly, and cooked meat exudates.

In some cases, retardation of syneresis is accomplished by covering products with aluminum foil or other suitable materials like plastic film.

If custard is baked at temperatures lower than 325°–350°F (163°–177°C), a watery, open-textured product will result. Direct heat will also cause syneresis; thus, it is advisable to place the cup or dish of unbaked custard in a pan of water during baking.

If small quantities of liquid form, often it can be remixed. This procedure does not apply to solid or semisolid foods such as custard, butter, margarine, or cream cheese. A modified form of waxy-maize starch may be employed when preparing gravies and sauces to retard moisture separation.

Hysteresis is a condition that results in the reduction of the waterholding capacity of a food or system. A condition of this type is the formation of a hard crust or film on gravy and sauces. Crust formations are avoided by keeping these products covered until used. Crust should be removed by skimming.

SUMMARY

In the preceding discussions concerning quality control during precooking, cooking, and postcooking, many examples were presented as illustrations of areas that require constant surveillance to assure the highest quality. It was not feasible to illustrate each and every facet and food category encountered in foodservice. The examples which were presented should serve as a guide in tracing poor quality problems and preparation procedures for those products not discussed.

The fundamental steps in maintaining the highest quality standards during precooking, cooking, and postcooking are: (1) Training personnel to follow all directions and instructions as presented on recipes or by the food processor (for convenience foods); (2) developing a strong program for equipment maintenance and operational evaluation; and (3) developing a managerial program of sensory evaluation so that poor quality foods and beverages can be eliminated before they are served to the customer.

10

Desserts and Baked Products Control

Baking and the preparation of desserts from start to finish is rapidly becoming a lost art in foodservice. These types of convenience items are among the most popular foods offered in eating establishments today. Numerous convenience desserts like ice cream and fresh baked products are taken for granted because they have been a part of the American scene for generations.

The growth of the pre-prepared frozen dessert market has been phenomenal. High quality products are readily obtainable. This situation is primarily due to advances made in baking technology, improved freezing techniques, and the development of new equipment for food establishments to simplify heating and serving. In addition, consumer demands have accelerated as a result of wide assortments of interesting and appealing products. Desserts are naturally "mouthwatering" items, and, if they are tasty, attractive, and imaginative, can generate high demand. The profit margin is excellent, far exceeding that for most other menu items. This chapter is devoted to the handling and quality control aspects of prepared and pre-prepared frozen desserts and baked products.

CATEGORIES OF CONVENIENCE DESSERTS

The following are the principal categories of convenience desserts: puddings, fruit, pastry, pies, cakes, pancakes, and frozen combinations that include ice cream, soft-serve, ice milk, sherbet, water or fruit ice, and frozen dairy confections.

Ice Cream

Ice cream and other frozen desserts are defined under U.S. Standards, FDA Title 21, Part 20. Included are ice cream, frozen custard, French ice

165

cream, French custard ice cream, ice milk, fruit sherbet, water ices, non-fruit sherbet, and nonfruit water ices. Ice cream is the most popular frozen dessert.

Quality Scoring.   The scoring system for measuring quality in ice cream as adopted by the American Dairy Science Association emphasizes a 100 point system. The breakdown follows: 45 points for flavor, 30 points for body and texture, 15 points for microbial content, 5 points for melting character, and 5 points for package and color.

The emphasis is on flavor, body, and texture, which are the most critical areas considered by the consumer. The terms most often used to describe texture and body of a high quality ice cream are creamy, smooth, and velvety. Poor quality is associated with a watery, foamy product that is not smooth and lacks body. High quality ice cream has good flavor, is rich and sweet, and does not appear "artificial," nor does it impart an aftertaste.

Flavor Defects.   Flavor defects may result from exposure of a product to intense light or to copper and iron contamination. These defects are characterized as oxidized and metallic off-flavors. Other defects are cooked or scorched flavor, often caused by ingredients of low quality or unsuitable preparation methods.

Handling.   The following techniques will assure the highest quality ice cream:

(1) Check additives or garnishes such as sweet spices, fruits, and nuts for contaminants such as molds. These ingredients should be fresh. Fruits and nuts must be free of stale flavors and aftertaste.

(2) Store at 0° to −10°F (−18° to −23°C); however, prior to service, bring to a higher temperature (10° to 15°F, −8° to −9°C) to enhance flavor.

(3) Short-term or service storage temperatures of 10° to 15°F (−8 to −9°C) are desirable. Avoid refreezing since this will alter the texture.

(4) Scoop the product properly to eliminate texture and appearance changes. Place scoops in cold running water when not in use. Scoops should be free of dents and nicks and should possess sharp edges.

Bakery Products

Available Types.   Baked products include pastry, pie, cake, bread, rolls, buns, and quick breads. These products are obtainable in the following forms: ready-to-serve, partially baked, ready-to-serve frozen, prepared frozen, canned prepared, and prepared mixes.

(1) *Ready-to-serve products* have been baked and are ready to be served. Breads, sweet rolls, doughnuts, pastries, and cookies are examples of these.

(2) *Partially-baked products* are "half baked." Baking must be completed on premises before serving. Available forms are loaves of bread, rolls, and buns.

(3) *Ready-to-serve frozen products* are fully prepared products ready to serve after thawing. If desired, these products can be heated before serving. Cakes, pastries, some pies, rolls, and buns are sold in this manner.

(4) *Prepared frozen products* have not been baked prior to freezing. They require baking before serving. Breads, pies, and rolls are available in this fashion.

(5) *Canned prepared products* must be completely baked before serving. Cookies, biscuits, and rolls are in this group.

(6) *Prepared mixes* are convenient preparations containing basic ingredients like flour, shortening, sugar, and leavening. Ingredients such as water, milk, or eggs may have to be added. Pie crusts, cakes, and roll mixes are obtainable in this form.

Cakes. *Quality Parameters.* A number of factors are responsible for determining the quality of cakes.

(1) The cake should have a uniform shape and be free of cracks and sags.

(2) The color should be uniform. A light-colored cake should have a uniform golden brown hue on all sides.

(3) The crust should be thin and tender.

(4) The bottom should show no evidence of burning.

(5) The crumb should be medium with a fine even grain. It should be moist and smooth but not tacky or soggy.

(6) Unless the type of cake calls for a dominant flavor, the flavor should be balanced with no foreign or off-flavors (oily, starchy).

(7) If icing is present, it should not be separated from the cake and not show any unevenness, nor should it run when thawed or pull apart when cut.

(8) The top of the cake should show no discoloration, which may be caused by moisture as a result of intermittent thawing.

Handling Hints. Unfrosted cakes can be thawed in freezer wrapping. If a cake is frosted, it should be removed from the carton and the wrapping removed to prevent stickiness and injury to the frosting during thawing.

Unused cake should not be refrozen. It can be stored in a refrigerator for a short time.

Handling instructions provided by the processor should be read and followed.

Storage Life. Freezing is an ideal method of prolonging shelf-life of most baked products. Bread, if quick frozen and held at 0°F (−18°C), will remain fresh for many months. When thawed, bread will have a freshness equivalent to a product held for two days at 70°F (22°C). Cakes and cookies will retain their palatability for at least 6 months at 0°F (−18°C) and longer at lower temperatures. Proper thawing conditions, such as a low-moisture atmosphere, are essential to prevent rapid staling. Although almost all kinds of cakes can be frozen and thawed without noticeable change, the following defects may occur as a result of prolonged storage: loss of volume, abnormal softness or compressibility, crumbliness, and tenderness (Tressler *et al.* 1968).

The following are examples of storage life of products held at 0°F (−18°C) (months):

Angel cake, 4   Pound cake, 9
Cheesecake, 12   Sponge cake (egg yolk), 2
Chocolate cake, 6   Sponge cake (whole egg), 6
Cookies, 12   Turnovers, 12
Fruitcake, 12   Yellow cake, 9
Fruit pies, 12

Quick Breads.   Quick breads are what the name implies. They are relatively easy to prepare as well as being quick. Examples of quick breads are muffins, biscuits, waffles, pancakes, and coffee cakes.

There are three types of quick bread mixes:

(1)   Drop batter, such as drop biscuits or muffins.
(2)   Pour batter, as a pancake or waffle batter.
(3)   Dough, such as rolled biscuits or dumplings.

Quick breads should not be overmixed. Overmixing develops the gluten too much, causing tunnels and coarseness in the finished products. Muffins are usually baked at 400°F (204°C) for 20–25 min until browned; biscuits are baked at 450°F (233°C) for 12–15 min or until golden brown.

Pre-prepared frozen waffles, pancakes, and French toast are all available and are widely distributed. Although these products are generally considered breakfast foods, they can be embellished in many novel ways and served as appealing desserts.

Pancakes that are prepared from mixes should be heated on a griddle at 385°F (197°C). Waffles are prepared in the conventional manner using a waffle baker.

Pre-prepared and frozen waffles and pancakes may be heated in an oven or toaster. They may be heated thawed or frozen. If thawing is preferred, allow to thaw 10–15 min. Place in a preheated oven at 350°F (177°C) using standard size sheet pans for 4–5 min. If heated from the frozen state, add another minute to the heating time. When a toaster is used, thaw for 10–15 min at medium setting or toast twice at light setting without thawing. These items may also be heated in a microwave oven. Prior testing is advised to determine the proper timing for the desired degrees of doneness.

Pies. *Characteristics of a Quality Pie.* A pie consists of two main sections and an optional section. The two main sections are the crust and filling. The optional section may be a compatible accompaniment in the form of garnishes, decorations, and toppings.

The ideal crust should be crisp, tender, and fragile, and should not shrink during baking. It should break short and should not be pasty or soggy. Its color should be golden with mottled brown running through it. It should exhibit a clean aroma with a fresh-baked character. The taste should be clean and free from foreign flavors such as oil or burned particles.

The filling must be clear and brilliant but not viscous. It may ooze without being watery. It should not be gelatinous, gummy, or stiff. The flavor of the main ingredient, if fruit, should be true and dominant, without being overpowering. The filling must also be free from foreign flavors and off-tastes.

The percentage of the main ingredient should be sufficient to fill the pie cavity when baked and to provide an adequate quantity for each portion.

Frozen Pies. Frozen pies are available either fully baked or with un-baked crusts. Fully baked pies need no further preparation other than thawing to room temperature before serving.

Frozen pies with unbaked crusts are excellent when prepared according to instructions provided by the processor. The filling and fruit of frozen pies are already cooked. During the baking operation, both the crust and filling have identical time cycles, so that they are finished simultaneously. Dual completion is possible only if pies are baked from the frozen state. Conventional or convection ovens are suited for this type of baking.

The Lloyd J. Harriss Company of Saugatuck, Michigan, bakers of quality frozen pies, has provided the following information for the handling, baking, and serving of these products.

(1) Cut a number of 1½ in. slits or prick the top crust with the tines of a fork. This allows steam to escape while baking. For custard and pumpkin pies, the protective wax sheet should be removed.

(2) An aluminum cookie sheet should be placed on the lowest rack of an oven. Pies are then positioned on the metal sheet. Fruit pies are baked in a preheated oven at 425°F (219°C) from 45 to 55 min until a golden brown color appears on the outer surface of the crust. Custards and pumpkin require 55 to 65 min.

(3) After baking, the pies should be air-cooled to room temperature before serving. For best acceptability, pies should never be served too hot or too cold.

(4) Berry pies will tend to boil quicker than pies made from other fruits. To overcome this problem, such a pie may be baked for a shorter time and at a higher temperature (an additional 25°F or 8.3°C).

(5) Custard and pumpkin pies often require an additional 10 to 15 min baking time. This facilitates moisture reduction and "sets" the pie

filling. If these pies are removed prior to completion of the "setting process," the filling may "run" and have poor flavor.

(6) Ovens should not be overloaded. This may cause a heat loss which may prevent an oven from attaining proper temperature during the baking cycle. Experimentation with any oven is necessary to determine its optimum working capacity.

Pie Defects and Probable Causes. (1) *Raw pie:* May be caused by a pie that is too cold. Frozen pie temperature prior to baking should be 0° to +5°F (−18° to −12°C). Lower temperatures will result in slow heating, unless compensation is made by extending the baking cycle.

(2) *Raw or soggy bottoms:* May be caused by an oven that is too cool, insufficient bottom heat, dirty oven floor, pie bottom dough too rich, or bottom rolled too thin.

(3) *Burned pies:* May be caused by improper temperatures, usually the result of a faulty oven thermostat; or a pie that was partially thawed and cooked too rapidly.

(4) *Burned bottoms:* May be caused by excessive bottom heat or an uneven distribution of heat.

(5) *Blisters on crust:* Crust not stippled or docked and too much egg-wash.

(6) *Filling runs out during baking:* Pies were filled too much, pies were not properly sealed, oven was too cool, too much sugar was used in the filling, and filling was too thin.

(7) *Shrinkage of crust:* Oven too cool.

Pie and Tart Shells. Pie and tart shells are available unbaked and frozen. They are versatile items and may be used for a base for many kinds of novel fillings. Depending on the processor's instructions, shells require about 10 min baking in a preheated oven set at 400°F (204°C). Formation of a golden brown color is usually a good indication that a shell is completely baked. If a filling requires heating, shells should be partially baked to compensate for this condition.

Pie shells are ideal for cream, pecan, cheese, custard, and pumpkin fillings. Graham cracker shells may also be used for cheese fillings.

Many fillings are adaptable for use in tart and pie shells. Tart shells make an excellent and attractive device to hold puddings, berries, and other fruit. Pre-prepared and canned puddings like vanilla, custard, chocolate, or lemon can be presented in a tart shell.

Baked Products from Frozen Dough. Baked products that are produced from frozen dough and are finished on premises have taken a great step forward over the last 15 years. A multitude of bakery items can easily be prepared from frozen dough.

Bread and rolls, over the years, have become highly abused menu items. Among the faults resulting from these improper handling practices are bread and rolls that are unappealing, soggy, doughy, underbaked, stale, and sour. Numerous feeding establishments have built fine reputations by serving interesting and appetizing assortments of baked items. Restaurants located in some American cities, such as San Francisco, Chicago, New York, Miami, New Orleans, and Boston, are expected to provide quality baked products as one way to retain their clientele. Specialty items like brioche, pecan rolls, croissants, popovers, corn sticks, salt sticks, and many kinds of breads are served as part of the daily menu. With the advent of frozen dough on a commercial scale, foodservice establishments were provided with the means of upgrading their bread and roll service. Small bread loaves baked on premises and made in different sizes, shapes, and styles have met with national acceptance. The consumer seems captivated with the idea of slicing his own fragrant, fresh, and hot bread at the table. This concept was introduced over 15 years ago by Bridgeford Foods Corporation, Anaheim, CA.

Standards of Identity for Bakery Products. Standards of Identity have been promulgated by the FDA for bakery products, which are covered in Part 17.

Standards of Identity are provided for the following bakery products:

(1) Bread, white bread, and rolls, white rolls, or buns, and white buns
(2) Enriched bread and milk rolls or buns
(3) Milk bread and milk rolls or buns
(4) Raisin bread and raisin rolls or raisin buns
(5) Whole wheat bread, graham bread, entire wheat bread, and whole wheat rolls, graham rolls, entire wheat rolls, or whole wheat buns, graham buns, and entire wheat buns.

Baking on the Premises. Frozen yeast dough baking is adaptable to all sizes of feeding establishments. Production is suitable for most fast-food preparation systems. Thawing refrigerators or cabinets, convection or conventional ovens, and finished product holding chests will accomodate this form of preparation.

Preparation is not complicated. However, for quality results, handling instructions provided by the processor should be followed. Generally, frozen dough should be thawed well in advance of preparation. The frozen dough is separated into individual loaves before being placed in buttered pans and is then allowed to thaw overnight in a refrigerator. If forced thawing is required, frozen dough may be placed in a warm atmosphere ($85°-140°F$, $30°-60°C$) for a 45 to 90 min period. When thawed, the dough is placed in a proofing area or cabinet until it has risen to the desired size. Some dough may expand 3 to 4 times its original size. Proofed dough does not have to be baked immediately but may be stored in a refrigerator at $38°F$ ($3.3°C$) for up to 12 hr. Depending on type and condition of the oven, baking time will average $20-30$ min at about $350°F$ ($177°C$).

Frozen doughs are available from which a large assortment of baked products may be prepared. The following are selected examples of these products: white, rye, Vienna, pumpernickel, and Italian style bread. Raisin, cinnamon, nut, and date may be prepared from yellow bread dough. In addition, various coffee cake and Danish cake doughs may be purchased. Quick breads may be made easily and quickly from basic frozen dough. Assortments of muffins, including bran, corn, blueberry, and biscuits, are examples of these products.

Mixes. Cake, quick bread, pancake, and waffle mixes are available which require little preparation, other than adding water or milk, stirring or mixing, and following the directions on the package. Improvements in the basic ingredients found in these products during the last 15 years have made it possible to simplify formulations. Notable improvements are starches that are readily soluble, and a variety of interesting flavors which accent taste appeal and produce a highly acceptable product. Development of coldwater swelling starches has led to the successful production of instant puddings. These puddings are pre-prepared, packed in cans, and are excellent for mass feeding.

Cake Mixes. Manufacturers' instructions must be followed. These are explicit, precise, and also include procedures for heating at high altitudes. Instructions are divided into three segments: blending, mixing, and baking. Instructions are included for the addition of optional ingredients like raisins, chocolate bits, fruit, or coconut.

To test cake for doneness, gently touch the center of the top. If the indentation springs back, the cake is done; if the impression remains, additional heating is required. Another test is to insert a toothpick in the center of the cake. If the toothpick comes out clean, the product is done. After baking, remove cake from the oven to prevent dryness. The following are cake imperfections which can be traced to improper heating procedures:

(1) Falling during baking—Temperature too low or pan too small.
(2) Poor holding quality—Temperature too low or baked too long.
(3) Crust too thick—Oven too hot or baked too long at low temperatures.
(4) Unevenly baked—Too much top or bottom heat, or uneven or unlevel shelves in oven.
(5) Hollow spots—Too much heat, moisture in pans, or pans too heavily greased.

11

Nonalcoholic Beverages Control

This chapter is devoted to a comprehensive treatment of the quality control of the many nonalcoholic beverages encountered in foodservice. Each beverage is treated as a separate entity. Those considered to be more important by virtue of their dollar volume are discussed at greater length, namely coffee and soft drinks.

Since World War II, the public feeding industry has witnessed drastic changes in style and methods of foodservice. Nonalcoholic beverage service has for the most part kept pace with these changes. New types of soft drinks, juices, iced tea, and hot chocolate and dairy dispensers were introduced. Coffee brewing techniques were upgraded and automatic brewing equipment developed. New drinks like soft freeze and slush were developed and dispensers devised to make them. Nondairy products covering a wide range of items were formulated and marketed.

Beverages have always been considered high profit items and probably will continue to enjoy this status. The profit structure has been diminishing, however, because of problems related to the introduction of sophisticated dispensing equipment. The reasons underlying this change are basic and can be reversed by an intensive quality control program encompassing preparation, handling, dispensing, sanitation, water quality, and mode of service. Sanitation and water quality are treated as separate subjects (Chapters 12 and 13) because they involve not only beverages but the entire spectrum of foodservice.

This chapter discusses the relationship of quality control for the following products: coffee, soft drinks, dairy beverages (milk and milk products), dairy substitutes, juices, tea, and cocoa beverages. Vended beverages are included in Chapter 14, Quality Control of Vending Equipment.

FACTORS LEADING TO POOR QUALITY BEVERAGES

Many factors within any foodservice establishment contribute to poor quality beverages. Several are interrelated and closely allied to personnel. Two factors that are independent of labor, however, have a marked influence on the outcome of beverages.

Interrelated factors are (1) personnel, (2) sanitation, (3) spoilage of beverages, and (4) maintenance.
Independent factors are (1) water and (2) equipment.

Interrelated Factors

The prime cause of poor quality beverages is mishandling by personnel. During the past 15 years, the shortage of labor required to perform the many basic and menial tasks within a food establishment has become a serious problem and one of concern to the entire industry. Frequent turnover of labor has resulted in a disruption of operational procedures. Poor training and lack of followup supervision have created a wide breach in the fundamentals of basic feeding operations, so substandard beverages and food items have resulted.

Careless cleaning and sanitizing, both of which are related to labor, head the list of factors contributing most to low-quality drinks. Spoilage is also related to faulty handling and lack of thorough sanitation.

Problems such as shoddy repairs, not carrying out good preventive maintenance to forestall breakdowns, and failure to keep equipment in top operating condition are all traceable to the shortage of qualified mechanics.

Independent Factors

Water is the major component of beverages. If not properly treated or purified, water may downgrade quality and produce off-flavors in products. Water is often assumed to be acceptable as long as it is colorless. Until the complexities of water and its effect on beverages are more completely understood by foodservice personnel, this problem will continue to influence quality.

Equipment problems and a need for *standardization* are two other factors affecting drinks. Although foodservice operators look forward to complete automation to overcome personnel shortages, many operational units are too complex and sophisticated for the average operator to appreciate and understand. When a dispenser or coffee brewing unit needs adjustment to improve quality, usually it is left undone for fear of causing a complete breakdown.

COFFEE

Phenomena of Flavor and Aroma

True coffee flavor to the coffee drinking public is a special and delightful phenomenon. The reason for calling it a phenomenon is that coffee flavor has not been fully duplicated by scientific means, and still remains an exclusive product of nature after conversion by the roasting process.

The popularity of coffee as a leading beverage is due to its stimulating and exciting sensory effects on the person. Consumers in their homes or in public eating places rarely experience the true characteristic fragrance and tantalizing effects of this beverage. Since true coffee flavor and aroma are dictated by its delicate character, an inferior blend or mishandling will produce an off-flavored, flat, insipid brew.

Certain food combinations also interfere with taste of the beverage, such as onions, maple syrup, or spices. Artificial creaming agents and synthetic sweeteners also affect the character. Instant coffee and to a large degree vended coffee do not produce the full satisfying effects of the beverage.

Factors Affecting Coffee Character

Superficially, brewing seems relatively simple. Fundamentals of the process include only three steps: (1) heating water in a receptacle to proper temperature, (2) extracting desirable components, and (3) holding the finished beverage in a reservoir.

One of the earliest methods of brewing actually combined these three basic steps into one operation. This method was known as open pot brewing. Advances in techniques and brewing technology led to the development of more elaborate devices. However, these innovations brought about a number of problems which contributed to an unpalatable, unsavory beverage.

Listed are 24 factors which influence aroma, flavor, and taste of the coffee beverage. These factors are related to green coffee quality, processing, packaging, brewing, and serving. Those factors which affect brewing and serving will be developed and related to actual operational problems.

(1)   Size of green coffee beans
(2)   Bulk density of green coffee beans
(3)   Chemical composition of green coffees
(4)   Blend of green coffee
(5)   Roasting technique
(6)   Degree of roast
(7)   Color of roast
(8)   Chemical composition of roasted coffee
(9)   Bulk density of roasted coffee
(10) Particle size distribution of ground coffee
(11) Water composition
(12) Temperature of water
(13) Volume of water
(14) Weight of coffee
(15) Degree of contact between water and coffee
(16) Wettability
(17) Time of contact
(18) Separation of beverage from grounds
(19) Clarity of beverage—freedom from sediment
(20) Length of holding period before drinking

(21) Temperature during holding period
(22) Mixing of finished brew (repouring)
(23) Methods of serving
(24) Cleanliness of brewing and serving equipment

Factors 11 through 24 are all interrelated and are controllable within a foodservice establishment. If a problem arises with the final beverage, then each of these items must be investigated to determine which segment of the process is faulty and requires correction.

Sanitation

Improper, infrequent cleaning and a lack of understanding and training in cleaning techniques head the list of problems which result in substandard coffee. Because of the importance of this subject and its bearing on all beverages, the subject of sanitation is treated in a subsequent chapter.

Temperature

A basic, but major, factor in brewing is temperature. Proper brewing requires that water be heated to and maintained at a temperature that will fully develop the beverage.

Excessive temperatures cause undesirable flavors and bitterness. Low temperatures will result in poor extraction and render a grassy or green flavor.

Roasted coffee contains numerous water-soluble chemical components. The rate at which each of these components dissolves is different and is directly related to temperature of extraction. Those constituents which comprise acceptable flavor, taste, and aroma of a beverage dissolve readily between 195° and 205°F (91° and 97°C). The recommended temperature for optimum results thus is 200°F (94°C). Water temperatures must be checked daily. It is not advisable to rely solely on built-in thermometers since they can be faulty and register erroneous readings. Accuracy can be achieved with precalibrated hand thermometers.

Extraction

Extraction is the focal point of coffee brewing. Regardless of shape or size of any brewing device or its operating principle, the center of the process is within the extraction system. This is where water comes into contact with ground coffee, mingles with it, and is then separated by means of a filtering device.

In the past 15 years, a great amount of research and development has been performed on the subject of extraction, extraction systems, and the design of equipment to function at maximum efficiency.

Dangling urn bags were replaced with gridded risers, so that the coffee bed would be level, thereby assuring a uniform and consistent extraction. Further developments resulted in the use of filter paper with well-designed receptacles. This equipment eliminated the need for urn bags and their inherent problems.

Time of extraction was established and related to particle size of the grind. Measurements were determined for minimum and maximum bed heights. Specifications for brew water temperatures and water treatment were agreed upon.

As work progressed, a theory of extraction was developed, which resulted in working formulas, relating the ratio of brew water to quantity of coffee. Finally a relationship was promulgated, concerning the amount of desirable soluble solids which could be efficiently extracted from ground coffee, thereby setting guidelines for methods to eliminate undesirable brews.

Theory of Extraction.   The results of research conducted by the Coffee Brewing Center established workable standards of extraction.

It was determined that coffee contained a number of chemicals or essences that contributed to flavor, aroma, and taste of the beverage. These were divided into two groups: desirable and undesirable. Undesirable factors are those essences which impart bitterness and astringency. The desirable portion, as the term implies, is the underlying factor which makes coffee a beverage. Desirable essences are readily extractable under controlled conditions, while undesirable or bitter-producing materials require unusual and adverse treatment. The amount of soluble solids which can be extracted from coffee averages about 30%. Sixteen ounces of ground coffee contains about 5 oz of extractable material; however, only 2.9–3.5 oz impart the characteristic and acceptable taste, aroma, and mouth-feel.

To illustrate this important point, at the initial stage of the process, all desirable elements are rapidly removed. Bitter astringent components, however, dissolve at a steady, continuous rate throughout the entire brewing operation. The chemical composition of roasted coffee is shown in Table 11.1.

Overextraction.   Overextraction of undesirable essences that impart bitterness and astringency is the result of a number of faulty conditions of the brewing operation, physical properties of the coffee, and formulation. Improper water temperatures, grind too fine for equipment, incorrect bed height, extending coffee to water ratio, repouring, allowing spent grounds to remain in an urn, contact of grounds with the brew, abnormally long brewing cycle, and irregular wetting of the coffee bed all contribute to overextraction.

The Brewing Cycle

Timing is essential in the culinary arts. Food preparation relies on timing to produce proper results. Coffee brewing falls into this category. To achieve

TABLE 11.1. Chemical Compositions of Soluble and Insoluble Portions of Roast Coffee (Approximate, Dry Basis)

	Solubles %	Insolubles %
Carbohydrates (53%)		
reducing sugars	1–2	—
caramelized sugars	10–17	7–0
hemicellulose (hydrolyzable)	1	14
fiber (not hydrolyzable)	—	22
Oils	—	15
Proteins (N × 6.25); amino acids are soluble	1–2	11
Ash (oxide)	3	1
Acids, nonvolatile		
chlorogenic	4.5	—
caffeic	0.5	—
quinic	0.5	—
oxalic, malic, citric, tartaric	1.0	—
Volatile acids	0.35	—
Trigonelline	1.0	—
Caffeine (arabicas 1.0, robustas 2.0%)	1.2	—
Phenolics (estimated)	2.0	—
Volatiles		
carbon dioxide	trace	2.0
essence of aroma and flavor	0.04	—
total	27–35	73–65

Source: Sivetz and Desrosier (1979).

maximum flavor and body, a brew must be timed within exacting tolerances. Brewing starts the moment water contacts the coffee bed. The cycle is completed when the last traces of water leave a filtering device.

Grind is the determining factor for the cycle period. A *fine grind* requires a brewing period of 3.5–4.5 min, a *drip grind* requires 4–6 min, and a *regular grind* 6–8 min. These cycles are applicable to all types and sizes of brewing equipment. If a cycle is extended beyond the recommended period, chances for a bitter off-flavored beverage are increased. If the timing is shortened, then a brew will be underdeveloped, possessing a greenish, insipid character.

Formula

The quantity of ground coffee used for brewing has a direct relationship to the beverage quality. A formula ranging from 2 gal. of water to not more than 2.5 gal. of water for each pound of coffee is recommended.

One of the evils which leads to substandard coffee is "stretching." Extensive research has substantiated this conclusion. Desirable coffee essences are delicate and their amount is limited, so that extending or stretching by the use of more water or less coffee only dilutes them. Coffee roasters have tried to overcome this dilution by using dark roasts or finer grinds; however, these methods have only led to overextraction and faulty flavors.

Half-gallon brewers (Fig. 11.1) require a quantity of coffee of from 3 to 3.5 oz. This amount will assure full development of body and flavor. Since these devices tend to underextract, it is necessary that this formula be followed.

FIG. 11.1.   Pourver type of half-gallon coffee brewer.
Courtesy of Cecilware Corp.

Effects of Water on Brew Quality

Water plays an important role on the quality of any brew. Throughout the United States water quality differences are drastic. Even within narrow geographical areas marked differences can be found.

Suitable water treatment is an important step toward the achievement of a satisfactory brew. Water must be free of odors, sediment, and discernible impurities. Very hard, artificially softened, or incorrectly treated water will not yield the most acceptable beverage.

Because of the importance of this subject, not only with coffee, but with all beverages, water, water problems, and corrective measures are treated in a separate chapter.

The Coffee Bed

Extraction takes place within a filtering area. The moment water contacts ground coffee, the process begins. In addition to those factors previously mentioned, uniform extraction is another important element which can be accomplished if certain design criteria of the system are met.

Control of bed height is reflected on the diameter of a filtering area. The coffee bed must be level and should measure from 1 to 2 in. in depth. If these conditions are not achieved, under- or overextraction and nonuniformity follow. Beds which are less than 1 in. deep will lead to a light, bitter brew. Those over 2 in. will cause a slowdown of the cycle and channeling, thus creating off-flavors and a bitter taste. Channeling results when the flow of water follows a path of least resistance through a bed and bypasses many sections of coffee, leaving them completely dry. Areas where coffee is mounded will tend to be overextracted, whereas cavities will tend to be underdeveloped.

Evolvement of the gridder riser, which supports the bottom part of a cloth

FIG. 11.2.   Gridder riser.
Courtesy of Cecilware Corp.

bag and creates a more nearly level bed, reduced to a minimum inconsistent and overextracted brews (Fig. 11.2). Previous to the use of gridded risers, cloth bags were hung in urns, forming cone-shaped beds. Overextraction thus occurred in the center portion and underdevelopment around the outer edges. A flat bed also eliminated the possibility of an urn bag's remaining in the finished brew. Under this condition, a continuation of the brew process resulted until either the bag was removed or the coffee consumed.

The gridded riser and filter paper baskets also made it possible to brew coffee in an urn at less than two-thirds of the capacity of the equipment, thereby maintaining correct bed height. Small size adapters and inserts became available which allowed this conversion, so that waste and stale coffee during slack periods were held to a minimum.

Brew Water Feed and Wettability

Improper application of water to the coffee bed is another factor which can contribute to a faulty brew.

An advantage of manually operated urns over their automatic counterparts is the hand control of water feeding. Complete and uniform wetting is assured if water is applied in a slow circular fashion.

Feeding water to ground coffee must be uniform and gradual so that the entire area receives equal treatment. If a section of the bed is wetted with more pressure than other areas, a brew will be totally inconsistent and overextracted.

Wettability is a characteristic which has gained prominence in the search for uniformity. With the advent of single-cup coffee vending machines, which rely on brewing cycles measured in seconds, it became necessary to ensure total wetting for consistency and full extraction. It was found that some particles of the grind accept water more readily than others. This condition may be attributed to factors such as age of green coffee, poor roasting techniques, or an excess of oils surrounding the cellular structure of ground particles. Surges of carbon dioxide gas from freshly ground coffee, which form a protective envelope around each particle, may also contribute to incomplete wetting.

Filtering Systems and Clarity

Filtering systems are responsible for the separation of water from spent grounds. There are a variety of devices available to perform this operation. Many of these are an integral part of a brewer, and once equipment is installed, it may be impossible to substitute a more efficient unit.

Ensuring clarity or freedom from sediment and cloudiness is the main function of any filter. If the finished brew contains appreciable sediment, extraction will continue, thereby increasing the possibility of bitterness. This situation may also lead to customer complaints. Cloth filters, woven wire screens, perforated plates, and metal discs all allow some sedimentation. Paper filters of good quality and free of pinholes will perform a good job of separation.

There are many advantages and disadvantages to the type and design of filtering systems available.

Metal plates, discs, and woven screens, although more expensive to purchase initially, are far less costly over the life of equipment when compared with the cost of filter paper and urn bags. However, these devices require constant attention and frequent cleaning. If not properly maintained, they will become clogged with coffee oils and off-flavor-producing residues. If roughly handled, pores may become damaged, resulting in excessive and localized leakage.

Cloth or muslin urn bags require utmost care to keep them clean and free from foreign materials.

If an urn bag is of poor quality or the stitching stretches, muddiness and excessive sedimentation will be observed. Care and sanitation of urn bags and related filtering systems are discussed in detail in Chapter 12 (Sanitation). One of the major factors contributing to urn bag difficulties is the vegetable origin of the cloth used to manufacture them. Rapid breakdown of fibers is accelerated because of constant high temperatures and the variety of chemicals which are absorbed into the cloth.

Urn bags are manufactured from a number of cloth materials, and in various sizes and shapes. Certain types of urns require specially designed bags. Urn bags are designated according to their diameter and depth. Weave of materials is designated as slow, standard, and rapid extractor. Flannel is also used as an extraction retarder and sediment reducer. In any case, selection of proper type and design of urn bag cannot be made haphazardly. Tests should be run employing bags of various weaves and depths so a determination can be made on the character of the finished brew. Where urn bags are inserted into a gridded riser, the bottom of a bag should fit squarely and evenly, otherwise an unevenly mounded bed will develop.

Paper Filters

Paper filters have a number of advantages, including sanitation, since they are disposable, labor-saving, and eliminate sediment and cloudiness. However, there are a number of disadvantages which may lead to serious beverage defects.

In order for filter paper to give consistent results, the paper must not shed fibers, should be free of pinholes, and should possess an even texture. It must be temperature resistant and have high wet-strength properties. The paper should not leave an aftertaste. Its fluting and shape must be maintained, otherwise the paper will fall away from the sides of a basket, which may result in bypassing the brew water from the coffee bed. Proper storage is necessary. Humid conditions will destroy the shape of paper, and, in addition, mold and mildew may develop. Because of the porosity of paper, foreign odors can be readily absorbed, thereby leading to brew contamination.

Filter paper is manufactured with smooth, medium, and rough texture. A smooth texture is recommended. Papers are also made to give very rapid, medium, slow, and very slow extraction rates. It is advisable that, once a brand of filter paper has been tested and found satisfactory, it not be changed. Grind changes may have to be made to accommodate a change in filter paper so as to avoid under- or overextraction. It is advisable to resist bargains, and if paper is being supplied free of charge by coffee suppliers, periodic checks should be made of quality.

Testing for aftertastes originating from the paper is a simple procedure. Fold a piece of filter paper loosely and put it into a vessel. Pour boiling water over the paper, covering it completely. Allow it to cool to about 120°F (50°C). Sniff water for off-odors, then taste water for off-tastes or foreign flavor when compared with a hot water control.

Mixing and Repouring

Finished beverage uniformity depends upon mixing or agitation. Observe the brew stream of a half gallon brewer. At the beginning of the cycle, the brew is extremely dark. As the cycle continues, the stream becomes lighter, and near the end of the period, it appears colorless. The same principle applies to all gravity feed equipment. The need for mixing, in order to achieve uniformity, is a paramount part of the brewing process.

Mixing can be accomplished by several means: by automatic agitation, by stirring with a paddle, or by removing a portion of the brew from the urn and pouring it back through the top after removal of spent grounds.

Finished coffee should never be repoured through spent grounds. Repouring results in a loss of aroma because of aeration. It renews the brewing cycle and causes extreme bitterness due to overextraction. A loss of desirable essences also occurs due to reabsorption during the second filtration.

When a brew is mixed by pouring a quantity back over an urn, a minimum of 1 gal. of liquid should be drawn off for each pound of coffee used. It should then be poured very rapidly to ensure thorough mixing. Prior to serving, a small amount of brew should be removed from the faucet. This quantity which is lodged in the bottom recesses is not uniform. If the automatic agitator is inadequate for its intended purpose, manual mixing is required. If a brewer is supplied with an adjunct agitator control switch, it should be activated for a short time to ensure sufficient mixing.

One of the first areas which should be investigated if complaints of brew inconsistency are received is the mixing or agitation procedure. In all probability this problem can be solved by immediate remedial action of the mixing operation.

Holding Techniques

Brewed coffee exhibits its best qualities when consumed immediately. Since the accepted characteristics are its aroma and flavor, volatile substances which induce these factors are quickly dissipated. Reheating, once a brew has cooled to room temperature, will yield a flat, insipid, and totally unacceptable beverage.

Prolonged holding has a marked effect on a brew. Chemical reactions within any beverage occur and excessive vaporization develops. Both of these factors alter flavor components. Detectable cloudiness or turbidity also occurs, as well as an increase in bitterness and astringency of a beverage.

Small quantities of coffee remaining in serving bowls, especially during slow periods, become unpalatable because of prolonged heating. These portions should be discarded and not added to or mixed with a fresh batch.

The following suggestions are recommended for proper holding: (1) don't hold coffee over 1 hr; (2) holding temperature range should be maintained at about 185°F (86°C); (3) when coffee is stored in a serving bowl, never hold less than one-third of bowl capacity since small amounts break down more rapidly.

Individual Service

Coffee is served in vessels of many types, shapes, and sizes. Materials of construction cover a wide range, from fine porcelain to paper cups.

Cups of varying wall thicknesses have a marked effect on an individual's sense of mouth feel. Those cups manufactured from fine china produce a satisfying lip feel resulting in a more appealing beverage. Thick-walled mugs, although more durable, tend to give the brew a thin, off-flavored character. Cardboard containers render a "paper" aftertaste, and if the construction material is low grade, a chemical flavor may become apparent. Since the advent of vending machines, "take-out" orders, and office brewing facilities, the amount of coffee consumed in paper or flexible containers has soared. Plastic-coated containers are available in a variety of wall thicknesses. Foam-type plastics are being used successfully to retard cooling.

The cup color has an effect on the consumer. Coffee served in a white background cup makes the beverage appear weak, whereas the use of tan or brown gives more eye appeal.

Cracks, chipped edges, and brown rings are unsightly. Cracked and chipped cups are also unsanitary and should be discarded. Cups that are stained should be bleached and rinsed thoroughly prior to use. Dishwashing procedures should be maintained at their highest level to prevent detergent residues from adhering to the interior of cups. Rinsing agents should be incorporated into a washing operation so that all traces of soap or detergent are eliminated. A quick test for determining a soapless or detergentless surface is the use of alkali-acid indicator paper. If a result is in the alkaline range, then a check of washing procedures is warranted.

Multiple Service

Serving containers which hold more than one cup of coffee are widely used. These are made from a variety of metals or plastic materials. They vary in shape, size, and wall thickness. Most come equipped with a lid to aid in heat retention. Thermos or vacuum bottles are another form of receptacle popularly employed. Their heat-retentive properties are superior to single-walled units so that a beverage will remain hot for at least 1 hr. However, a lack of proper sanitation is a major drawback for all multiple service units. Incorrect cleaning procedures and faulty handling result in beverages that are unsanitary and off-flavored. In the chapter on sanitation, detailed steps will be found to ensure against these possibilities.

Bulk Coffee Carriers

Bulk carriers ranging in size from 1 to 5 gal. are used to transport coffee from the preparation area to the consumer. These units are insulated and airtight. Some are constructed on the same principle as a vacuum bottle. Many are equipped with a snapon lid which is provided with a rubber or plastic gasket. A faucet is provided, which is similar to those installed on urn equipment. Provisions have also been made so that these carriers can be transformed into portable brewers by the use of gridded riser inserts.

Once again, a major drawback is a lack of proper sanitation procedures. These units must be treated and handled like stationary coffee brewers. Of special importance are the carrier cover and gasket. A gasket absorbs residues and other contaminants. These must be removed and cleaned separately. They also have a tendency toward brittleness, so their vapor sealing function may be lost.

Instant Coffee Packets

Caffeine-free instant coffee packets are available in a majority of foodservice establishments. Methods of serving vary and some are contrary to accepted practices of good service.

A pot of boiling water should be provided with each serving. The contents of a packet can then be poured into a cup and boiling water added. This method will ensure an acceptable and palatable temperature and rapid dissolving of the crystals.

Cream and Whitening Agents

The background and use of these products are discussed in detail later in this chapter.

Mishandling of coffee creamers is prevalent in the industry. Improper storage, temperature control, and portion control are just a few types of mishandling which can alter the composition of these agents and produce off-flavored and objectionable tasting beverages.

Curdling is another factor leading to customer dissatisfaction. This condition is caused by chemical alteration of cream and excessive temperature or undue acidity of coffee. The latter causes coagulation of milk protein and frees the milk fat from a stable emulsion. Excessive temperatures act in the same manner; however, if coffee cream is fresh and homogenized, curdling will not occur. Poor methods of homogenization also result in separation and feathering. High acidity results from a blend that contains defective coffees. Although acidic coffees are desirable and are characteristic of a quality blend, excessive acidity will cause curdling. Brews which are held too long will also create conditions leading to curdling.

Storage

Coffee is like a "magnet" in its ability to readily absorb foreign odors. This property applies to both green and roasted coffees. Ships which transport beans from growing areas to the United States must be free of odor-contaminating materials. Storage areas in restaurants must be free of objectionable odors as well as cool, dry, and clean. Products such as spices, onions, garlic, and odors emanating from frying should be far removed from coffee.

Grinding on Location

There are several advantages to grinding coffee on location. The aroma emitted from the grinding process has a favorable effect on customers. Also, whole bean roasted coffee remains fresher than preground and packaged products.

However, the disadvantages far exceed the few advantages. Small, on-location grinders do not produce a crisp cut particle. Grind tolerances are impossible to maintain, so noticeable defects become apparent. Accumulations of rancid oils, chaff, and other undesirable materials offset the fine sparkling flavor expected of freshly ground coffee. As grinding plates wear, the grind becomes even more inconsistent. Large percentages of coarse and fine or pulverized particles are evident, so that a bitter muddy brew develops. Since a large percentage of carbon dioxide is released during and immediately after grinding, the coffee bed may float during brewing. This situation will cause underextraction and a weak brew.

Commercial grinders gradually reduce particle size through a series of corrugated mill rolls. Grind consistency is controlled by varying the bean feed and changing the roller openings. If changes do occur, they are detected by a grind analysis and corrected accordingly.

Roasted Coffee Deterioration

Roasted coffee, whether whole or ground, can undergo changes that lead to deterioration and beverage unacceptability. The main deteriorative effects are loss of freshness, staling, and rancidity.

Loss of freshness involves the volatilization of aromatic components and gases during roasting. These gases consist of 90–95% carbon dioxide and 5–10% carbon monoxide. Gases are liberated very slowly in whole bean coffee but more rapidly in ground coffee. Volatilization of aromatic components is noticeable by the distinct aroma emitted during and immediately after grinding. As coffee starts to stale, the characteristic coffee aroma lessens and finally disappears completely.

Staleness is caused by oxidation of aromatic components which yield nonaromatic oxidation products. Noticeable staleness can be detected in 10 days and is readily apparent after 3 weeks.

Rancidity and off-flavor resulting from reactions between coffee oils and oxygen develop slowly. True rancidity may not be apparent for 7–8 months.

Troubleshooting Brew Problems

Off-Flavors and Odors.   (1) Check filter, brewing basket, and gridded riser for dirt. Smell for off-odor. (2) Check urn bag for off-odor. (3) Check paper filters for off-odor, mildew. (4) Check urn liner, connecting pipe, faucets, and spray head for dirt and residues. Replace seat cup (washer) in faucet if black, brittle, and off-odor (dirty, rubbery). (5) Check cups and serving pots for cleanliness. (6) Check quality of coffee; it may be inconsistent or an inferior grade.

Figure 11.3 shows a sample of a coffee brewing inspection report.

Bitterness.   (1) Check for overextraction. Time brewing cycle; it may be too long. (2) Check holding temperature of brew; it may be held too long at too high a temperature. Don't exceed 190°F (88°C). (3) Check mixing procedures and agitation. Be sure that brewed coffee is not repoured through spent grounds. (4) Check water softening system. Ion exchange systems will produce adverse effects on brew.

Weak, Watery Brew.   (1) Check brewing formula. Don't exceed 2.5 gal. of water per pound of coffee. (2) Check yield of brew from half-gallon brewer.

COFFEE BREWING INSPECTION REPORT

Restaurant address: _____   Store No.:____ Date: _____

Time of inspection: _____   Manager's Name: _____

Brewing device in use: _____   Model: _____

Condition of brewing device: _____   Brewing cycle:____min____sec

Filter medium: _____   Temperature of brew water: _____ °F

Formula: _____

Brew water calibration: _____   Temperature of finished Brew: ____°F

If half-gallon brewer: Liquid level of finished brew in serving bowl: _____

If half-gallon brewer: Was brew stirred prior to serving? Yes____No____Sometimes____

Holding time at inspection:____ Temp. ____°F   Character of holding brew: _____

Brew character: Aroma—Pleasant____   Taste—Flavorful____
                        Some____   Light____
                        None____   Medium____
                        Other____   Heavy____
                                                      Bitter____
                                                      Other____

Customer comments: _____   Store personnel comments: _____

_____   _____

_____   _____

_____   _____

_____   _____

Did brewing device require adjusting?____

Brew character after adjustment: _____

Is stock rotated? _____   Is case coded?___ code___

Are cups warm? _____   Are cups clean?__

Type of cream vehicle used: _____   Temp. of cream: _____°F

Water conditions: _____   Quantity per portion: _____

Filter installed: _____   Type: _____

REMARKS:

FIG. 11.3.   Coffee brewing inspection report form.

Yield should be 54 to 58 oz. (3) Check mixing procedures. If not mixed, top portion of brew will be watery. (4) Check brewing cycle. It may be too short due to coarse grind, water line may be blocked, or solenoid or timer may need replacement.

Staleness or Rancidity. (1) Check stock rotation. (2) Check storage temperature; if too high, coffee will stale quickly. Store in cool dry area; refrigerate in dry atmosphere.

Excessive Sediment. (1) Check filter. It may be worn or torn. (2) Check grind. It may be too fine for type of filter used. (3) Check filter paper. It may have pinholes. (4) Check water feed. Too much pressure or localized pressure will wash grounds up and over extractor.

Table 11.2 is a coffee evaluation form for a quick check of quality.

TABLE 11.2. Coffee Evaluation Form

Instructions
  (1) Evaluations should be performed with brew sample at about 140°F and must be tested black.
  (2) If sugar, cream, or both are used, two evaluations should be made. Take the average of the two scores.
  (3) If a foreign flavor or aroma or bitterness is detected, inspect the coffee brewing procedure for correct extraction, temperature, and sanitation. If the same defect (off-flavor) occurs again, score sample accordingly.
  (4) Brew color with cream vehicle added will depend largely on the butterfat content and quantity of the cream vehicle or the nondairy additive used.
  (5) Cup quality scoring depends upon your past experience and customer performance. For example, if you have been serving a strong heavy cup of coffee and the sample equals this character, your scoring will be the full percentage mark under cup qualities.

	Score (%)	
Aroma—Total score 25%		
(1) Good coffee character (no harshness)	25	[ ]
(2) Some aroma	15	[ ]
(3) No aroma	5	[ ]
(4) Foreign or objectionable odor	0	[ ]
(fermented) (medicinal) (musty) (rubbery) (other)		
Cup Qualities—Total score 50%		
(1) Good character, smooth, and flavorful	50	[ ]
(2) Medium body, some flavor	40	[ ]
(3) Light body (recheck coffee:water ratio)	20	[ ]
(4) Heavy body [see Instructions No. (5)]	20	[ ]
(If okay, score 50%; if objectionable, score 20%)		
(5) Flat (no flavor, insipid taste)	15	[ ]
(6) Bitter (recheck brewing procedures)	10	[ ]
(7) Foreign or objectionable taste[1]	0	[ ]
(medicinal) (fermented) (sour)		
(musty) (dirty) (rubbery) (other)		
Color of Brew with Cream Vehicle—Total score 10%		
(1) Good straw color	10	[ ]
(2) Dark-brownish color	5	[ ]
(3) Grayish color	0	[ ]
Preparation of Ground Coffee—Total score 15%		
(1) Uniform grind (is it correct for your brewer?)	5	[ ]
(2) Roast color (dark, medium, light)	5	[ ]
(3) Uniformity of weights, soundness of package, and coding	5	[ ]
Your total score		[ ]

[1] See Instructions, paragraph (3) above.

SOFT DRINKS

Soft drinks are defined as any nonalcoholic beverage containing syrup, essences, or fruit concentrates that are mixed with water or carbonated water.

Fundamentally, a quality soft drink should conform to the following specifications:

(1) A balanced blend of flavor at the proper intensity, leaving a clean mouth taste with no lingering flavor or unpleasant aftertaste.
(2) Clear, clean water so that it is free of obnoxious and overpowering aftertastes which affect the delicate syrup balance.
(3) Chilled to correct temperature, a major factor of acceptability.
(4) Ice, if used, at the proper solidity and firmness, so as not to dilute the drink.
(5) Correct carbonation to impart zest and sparkle to the drink.
(6) Clean glassware, and good shape and glass capacity.

Soft Drink Classification

The most popular soft drinks sold throughout the United States today are colas, orange, root beer, ginger ale, lemon, and lime. These beverages are divided into three categories: carbonated, still, and sparkling or soda water.

Carbonated beverages consist basically of sugar syrup, natural or synthetic acids, flavoring agents, carbonated water, and colors. Still beverages consist primarily of sugar syrup, colors, fruit flavors (citrus or synthetic), and water. Sparkling or soda water beverages are colorless, contain minerals or various salt components, or are carbonated water specially treated at high pressures.

The primary categories are further subdivided as follows:

(1) Carbonated:
    Acidulated (containing acids such as citric): Ginger ale, fruit-flavored, quinine, cola, cream, celery, coffee
    Nonacid: Root beer, birch beer, sarsaparilla
(2) Still (with pulp or essences): Fruit-flavored (citrus, berry) natural and artificial fruit juices
(3) Sparkling water: Soda water, carbonated water, seltzer.

Control of Dispensing Components

Regardless of the numerous methods of dispensing soft drinks, fundamental operation and control of the basic elements involved in the preparation of quality beverages are identical. The only difference that exists is whether a soft drink is carbonated or still.

The following are the basic elements involved: (1) syrup handling and storage, (2) water purification and precooling, (3) carbonation, (4) refrigeration, (5) ice, and (6) quality control.

Syrup Handling and Storage

Syrups are generally delivered in 1 gal. glass containers or in waxed or plastic containers similar to those used for milk. Under normal conditions, syrups will not spoil; however, methods of inventory control should be adopted to avoid aging, which will affect delicate flavor balance. Prior to use, a syrup should be examined for separation and presence of sediment.

Excessive heat will accelerate aging, hence it is important that inventories be stored in moderately cool areas not exceeding 65°F (22°C). Syrups should not be stored in direct sunlight. Partly used containers should be resealed tightly and stored under refrigeration.

Syrups readily absorb foreign odors which can seriously affect the finished beverage. Caution is advised when root beer is stored in an adjacent tank. Root beer has a strong and penetrating odor that will be absorbed by other syrups if they are not covered tightly.

All surfaces coming into contact with a syrup, such as tanks, reservoirs, tubing, and nozzles, can become encrusted with syrup residues after prolonged use and can therefore interfere with dispensing. If this situation develops, it is impossible to dispense a quality drink, and syrup tanks (plastic), tubing, and other accessories will require replacement. When changing flavors, the entire system requires sanitizing, to lessen the likelihood of contamination. If flavors are constantly changed to maintain consumer interest, polyethylene bags can be used as inserts to hold syrup and facilitate cleaning. This method is particularly feasible for vending machines. Lid gaskets used to seal syrup pressure tanks are susceptible to contamination and should be changed periodically.

Water Purification and Precooling

Water, the major component of a soft drink, requires critical examination so that it does not become a source for poor quality. The role of water in beverages is treated in detail in Chapter 13. It is a general opinion among foodservice personnel that water used from municipal systems is free of contaminants and will produce quality beverages. Most water consumed in the United States is treated with chlorine to eliminate harmful microorganisms. During certain times of the year, such as summer, chlorine content is increased. This results in a destruction of true flavor and imparts an off-flavor similar to bleach. Many public water systems contain particulate matter which interferes with carbonation. Slime and scum which have accumulated in old water pipes may also enter the dispensing system, thus affecting carbonation and flavor. Equipment is available to remove waterborne impurities so that water is acceptable and compatible with beverages.

This equipment is manufactured in many sizes and capacities adaptable to vending machines, in-store dispensers, and ice makers. Hard water will also affect beverage quality by neutralizing the acid content of flavors.

Precooling water supplies may be necessary, especially during warm weather, if refrigeration capacity of a dispenser or maker is not great enough to contend with warmer than normal water temperatures.

Carbonation

Carbonated water is a mixture of plain water and carbon dioxide. High-quality carbonated beverages contain the correct amount of carbonation, which enhances the flavor and aroma of the syrup.

Of prime importance for proper and sustained carbonation are water temperature and dispensing temperature. Finished carbonated beverages will not retain required volumes of carbonation if dispensing temperature exceeds 36°F (3°C). A temperature of 40°F (5°C) is considered the upper limit since higher temperatures result in a rapid deterioration of quality. Table 11.3 demonstrates the effect of temperature versus loss of carbonation.

The addition of ice to a beverage will reduce temperature but cannot restore carbonation lost at high dispensing temperatures.

Carbonation is reduced during the glass filling operation. The reason for this is agitation of liquid at a faucet spout and splattering as liquid falls into a glass, exposing the beverage to warm air. To reduce aeration, direct the liquid stream toward inner top wall of a glass by slanting it inward. Poorly cleaned or rinsed glasses will allow bubbles to form on the walls of a receptacle and increase foaming. Foreign matter suspended in a liquid will also drive carbon dioxide out of beverages. Clean nozzles are a necessity. Accumulation of dried syrups around a nozzle will become a contact point for bacterial growth. Pipe cleaners dipped in cleaning solution can be used for freeing surfaces of contaminating residues.

Weather has an influence on carbonation. In many areas, water temperature varies considerably from winter to summer. Since cool water absorbs CO_2 gas more readily, summer operations may necessitate higher pressure settings on a gas pressure regulator. Figure 11.4 shows an exterior view of a carbonator.

TABLE 11.3. Effect of Temperature on Carbonation

Temperature of Drink		Carbonation	Loss of Carbonation	Temperature of Drink		Carbonation	Loss of Carbonation
(°F)	(°C)	(%)	(%)	(°F)	(°C)	(%)	(%)
36	2.2	100	0	46	7.8	81	19
38	3.3	96	4	48	8.9	78	22
40	4.4	92	8	50	10.0	75	25
42	5.5	88	12	52	11.1	72	28
44	6.7	84	16	54	12.2	69	31

Source: Courtesy of the Coca Cola Co.

FIG. 11.4.   Exterior view
of a carbonator.
*Courtesy of Bastian-Blessing
Co.*

Occasional "bleeding" of the gas vent of a carbonator to eliminate air lodged in the mixing tank is advisable. Uneven carbonation will result from this condition due to water pressure fluctuation and improper venting of a newly installed carbonator. Changes in water pressure also affect the efficiency of a carbonator. If water pressure exceeds that of the CO_2, normal flow will be obstructed, resulting in decreased carbonation. Pressure regulators adjusted to reduce the force of incoming water will correct this condition. Traces of oil in a water supply may hinder carbonation and create off-tastes in beverages.

Excessive carbonation rarely creates a serious problem other than increased foaming. Charged water will not hold more than 4.5 volumes of gas and will become unstable at dispensing temperature when exposed to the atmosphere. If a dispenser is not used for several hours, cold water may absorb an excessive amount of gas; however, this is a temporary situation that disappears after the first several drinks are served.

Periodic checks should be made for gas leaks within a system. This can be done by allowing the pressure to become balanced and by noticing whether the needle on the pressure regulator dial is steady. The valve on the CO_2 cylinder should then be closed. If pressure reading on a gauge decreases after a 5 min period, then a leak in the gas system exists. All connections including the cylinder valve should be coated with a high concentration of soap suds. Leaks can then be traced by the appearance of bubbles. New gaskets should always be installed in the regulator valve when a CO_2 tank is replaced.

Refrigeration

Although it is not within the scope of this book to discuss the details of refrigeration, there are segments of this subject which have an important bearing on the outcome of a quality beverage.

Refrigeration is the heart of a dispensing system. Adequate cooling facilities, whether by mechanical or ice-cooled means, must be capable of reducing beverage temperature to 35°–40°F (2°–5°C). Sanitation of refrigerating equipment is necessary to maintain top cooling efficiency. Exposed tubing in water baths should be freed of slime and other matter so that efficient heat exchange will not be impaired. Dust, dirt, paper, boxes, and other debris should be removed from areas surrounding compressors to ensure a free air flow.

Tubing and lines for remote control systems should be carefully routed so as to bypass hot water pipes, stoves, and other sources of heat. Temperatures of syrups require control so that syrup viscosity will remain constant. Warm syrups will be less viscous and tend to flow more rapidly, resulting in waste and inconsistent drinks. If syrup is colder than carbonated water, it will settle to the bottom of a glass. This situation can be corrected by the installation of a diffusion faucet cover.

Ice

The addition of ice to a soft drink provides two important factors. It adds to the customer's enjoyment and it keeps the beverage cold and more palatable. Unfortunately, the mishandling of ice leads to a serious downgrading of soft drinks. The primary problems contributing to drink defects caused by ice are poor sanitation procedures within ice making equipment and haphazard addition of ice to a drink. The former results in off-tastes, whereas the latter leads to inconsistency and to watery drinks.

The study of ice and its formation is called cryology. Cryology is the science of the physical characteristics of solid forms of water produced by temperatures below 32°F (0°C).

Ice exists in several forms. These are numbered from Ice-I, the ordinary variety, to Ice-VI. The change from one category to another is caused by increasing the pressure on water during the transitional stage. The bursting of pipes is an example of a change from Ice-I to Ice-II. This change is the result of internal pressures created by freezing within a confined area. Ordinary ice, Ice-I, melts at 32°F (0°C) at 1 atm (101.3 kPa) pressure. It is the only variety that is lighter than water under identical conditions. Ordinary ice is the common ice generally encountered and the one used for beverages.

Ice used in the foodservice industry is manufactured in many shapes and sizes. Cubed ice ranges in size from ¼ to 1 in.^{2} and may be hollow, rounded, square, or rectangular. One manufacturer has named its cubes super, compact, and miniature. Shaved, snowy, and chipped varieties are the particle types commonly used. The question often arises as to which form is best for a particular application. There is no definitive answer to this question. The only guideline applicable to beverages is that ice should be slow-melting to avoid dilution.

The use of ice as a substitute for refrigeration with the anticipation that it will resolve faulty carbonation is not feasible. Poor carbonation can be corrected only by using water at 35°F (2°C) within the carbonator.

The quality of ice added to a glass or cup is important to the quality of any beverage. The haphazard use of ice is a major source of poor quality. Ice should constitute at least $\frac{1}{7}$ and not more than $\frac{1}{6}$ of the total volume of a receptacle. Although consumers favor ice, too much is frowned upon as poor value and cheating or cheapening a beverage. Cold, clear, bite-size portions of ice are more readily acceptable by the consumer than shaved, snowy and soft ice, which often contains a large percentage of water and leads to dilution.

The Water Cap

Ordinary ice will float in water. As ice melts, a layer of cold water accumulates on the top of a beverage. This layer or "water cap" is neither carbonated nor adequately flavored with syrup. The water cap will tend to remain separated from the beverage it covers unless the drink is vigorously stirred.

Depth and size of a water cap are dependent upon the amount of ice added to a beverage, its temperature, and physical state. In addition, the lapse of time involved in serving a drink is another factor toward partial elimination of water cap. Formation of water caps is unavoidable; however, good dispensing and serving techniques will minimize the problem.

Ice Making Equipment

Care in the operation and sanitization of ice making equipment will reduce contamination and maintain a steady flow of acceptable ice. Regardless of the make of equipment, certain fundamentals must be considered so that ice will be suitable for consumption.

Water used for this purpose requires treatment if it contains impurities and minerals affecting the freezing point and reducing the equipment's capacity to function efficiently. Periodic ice temperature readings should be taken to determine operating efficiency of a unit. The product should be palmed and squeezed as a test for firmness. Ice should be put in a glass to determine its water ratio. Frequent cleaning must be made to rid interior sections of accumulated impurities, scum, and slime, since these materials will impart off-tastes. Cleaning compounds and solutions are available for this purpose. Frequent sanitation will also freshen the interior and remove stale odors. Periodic sanitization will minimize the growth of microorganisms that thrive in slimy, cold areas.

Wet ice may result from the following: (1) surrounding air temperature too high, (2) refrigerant under- or overcharged, (3) inlet strainer partially plugged, (4) water level in reservoir too low, (5) defective thermostat, and (6) temperature of water supply too high. Figure 11.5 illustrates the effects of water and ambient temperatures on ice maker output.

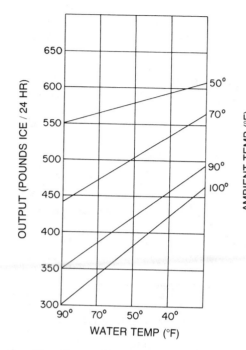

FIG. 11.5.   Effects of water and ambient temperatures on ice maker output.
Courtesy of Scotman Ice Machines.

Quality Control Procedures

Quality control should be performed on a regularly scheduled basis. The results of each test should be recorded and used as a guide to evaluate profit or loss structure of beverage operations and equipment efficiency.

Quality control for this purpose can be broken down into the categories of *system* and *product* controls.

System Quality Control.

(1)   Detection of foreign objects in a system
(2)   Determination of efficiency of glasswashing facilities
(3)   Determination of efficiency of ice making equipment
(4)   Determination of water impurities

Product Quality Control.

(1)   Determination of syrup-water ratio
(2)   Determination of volumes of carbonation
(3)   Determination of product spoilage
(4)   Sensory evaluations by taste-testing techniques

System Quality Control. Detection of foreign objects in a system can be performed by visual observation. Excessive foaming may be due to sediment or particles of foreign matter. Observations of syrup and water, by holding samples in the light, will give an indication of suspended matter and clarity. Water strainers, nozzles, tubing, pipes, and storage tanks should be inspected for residues that may have entered the system.

Determination of the efficiency of glasswashing facilities can be made by use of indicator paper or an indicator solution. These tests will reveal the presence of detergent films. If indicator paper is used, the intensity of the color change can be compared with a color chart. Phenolphthalein solution (2 or 3 drops), available at most drugstores, will turn pink or red if detergent residues are present. This indicator cannot be used where water is naturally alkaline; however, thymolphthalein can be used and turns blue if traces of cleaning agent exist.

Determination of the efficiency of ice making equipment was previously described.

Determination of water impurities, including efficiency of water treatment equipment, can be accomplished by a simplified water testing kit described in Chapter 13.

The following water problems show their respective effects on soft drinks and dispenser equipment.

Water Problem	Effect on Drink and Equipment
Iron	Imparts metallic taste
Dirt, cloudiness	Excessive foaming, reduces carbonation
Chlorine, mustiness, fishy tastes and odors	Destroys flavor
Hard water (lime scale)	Plugs valves, reduces cooling efficiency, plugs lines, affects flavor
Acid	Corrosive to pipes, causes metallic tastes
Sulfur water	Imparts rotten egg odor

Product Quality Control. Determination of *syrup-water ratio* can be accomplished by three methods. The first method employs a metal separator that is attached to a nozzle or delivery head. The separator consists of two orifices, one for syrup and the other for carbonated water. A dual purpose plastic graduate calibrated in ounces catches syrup in a small tube, while carbonated water flows into the large tube (Fig. 11.6). The amount of syrup is then compared with the volume of carbonated water. Dispenser adjustments can then be made, if necessary, to correct the syrup ratio. If a nozzle does not accommodate a separator, a second method of evaluation is available using a Brix hydrometer. The third method employs a refractometer calibrated in °Brix.

FIG. 11.6. Determination of syrup-water ratio. A—Syrup-carbonated water separator. B—Syrup flow adjusting stem screw. C—Carbonated water adjusting screw. D—Measuring cup.
Courtesy of the Purlick Co.

Determination of *volumes of carbonation* can be made by a pressure tester especially designed for this purpose. Carbonated water or a finished beverage is poured into a metal cylinder and allowed to settle for 5 min. The top of the tester which includes a gauge is fastened into place. The unit is shaken until maximum pressure is recorded on a dial. After the reading is recorded, the temperature is taken and the volumes of carbonation are read from a conversion chart. The apparatus for this test is distributed by The Bastian-Blessing Co. and is called an Excelall carbonation tester.

Determination of *product spoilage* is performed by sensory evaluation. Under normal operating conditions, proper storage, and stock rotation, spoilage of syrups due to microorganisms is negligible. However, if spoilage does occur, certain superficial characteristics can be detected by visual observation and taste testing.

Changes in drink appearance, such as loss of cloud stability, appearance of haze and sediment, and color fading are traceable to syrup spoilage. Excessive and prolonged foaming is another condition resulting from syrup spoilage. It may be difficult to distinguish between foaming caused from sediment, overcarbonation, and dirty glasses, and foaming as a result of spoilage. In the case of "still" drinks, determination is an easy matter, since spoilage foaming is prolonged, not as intense, and will resemble the head on a glass of beer. Off-odors and -flavors due to syrup spoilage may show up as mustiness, sourness, or resembling the odor of buttermilk.

Sensory evaluations by taste-testing techniques are discussed at length in Chapter 2; however, every operator should become totally familiar with all the characteristics of his beverages. Tests should be performed daily, at the same time of day, and under identical conditions. For accurate results, at least 1 hour should elapse after eating before taste tests are performed. Strong odors from foods such as onions can mask delicate flavors of soft drinks. Tests should not be performed while smoking or in an area where strong odors permeate the air. Fluctuations in quality can be quickly detected, and remedial actions can be taken after pinpointing the problem by following the test procedures previously described. Figure 11.7 shows a carbonated drink poster employed by a major restaurant chain.

Serving Better

COLD DRINKS

the White Tower Way . . .

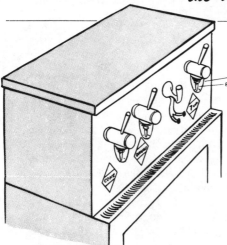

Top quality cold drinks make your customers happy and your work easier and more pleasant. Just a few minutes of your time each day will do it. Please read and follow these simple rules carefully.

Thank You   WHITE TOWER

DISPENSER FAUCETS
Remove spouts or caps (A) and wash and clean them thoroughly EVERY DAY! Also unclog holes in faucet nozzles (B) every day.

SYRUP TANK
Before refilling, check inside for sediment floating in syrup. If sediment exists, do not refill but call office immediately. If no sediment is visible, rinse and clean tank lid and gasket thoroughly before replacing. **Make sure lid is back on tight!**

SYRUP and ICE
Keep replacement supply of syrup in refrigerator at all times so that it is COLD when put into tank! Keep ice compartment 2/3 full (no more) at all times. If slushy water accumulates in ice compartment, reach in and unclog drain at bottom.

CO_2 TANK
Check gauges regularly for pressure and gas supply in tank. If left hand gauge is in red zone supply is nearly gone and tank should be changed: On double installations, switch knob from A to B (or B to A) and order replacement tank immediately. On single tank installations, shut off tank valve by turning clockwise, remove gauge nut with wrench and detach from assembly pipe. Install full tank . . . attach to assembly pipe with gauge nut and **turn tank valve back on!** If pressure gauge (right) reads less than 90, call office immediately!

SERVING DRINKS
First . . . be sure glass is clean! To fill, hold and tilt glass as shown with inside surface next to spout. Good drinks depend on this!

COMPRESSOR
Requires free flow of air all around. **Do not smother by storing goods on or close to compressor!** If screen gets dusty, dirty or cobwebby, report to office immediately.

QUALITY CHECKS

✓ **DRINKS TOO WEAK** . . .
Check syrup. If low, replenish immediately! Check for kinked or twisted syrup tank hose which could diminish or stop flow. If neither of these steps correct drink strength, call office at once!

✓ **DRINKS TOO STRONG** . . .
Check CO_2 tank gauge per instructions on right. Check syrup tank and ice compartment. Syrup may be too warm.

✓ **EXCESSIVE FOAMING** . . .
Check syrup tank lid and tighten if loose. Check your method of filling glass . . . you may not be holding glass close enough to spout. See opposite paragraph on serving. If this does not correct problem, call office immediately!

✓ **DRINKS OFF TASTE** . . .
Report matter to office immediately and ask for maintenance check-up of cold drink system.

FIG. 11.7.   Carbonated drink instruction sheet.
Courtesy of White Tower Management Corp.

Soft Drink Spoilage

The determination of spoilage characteristics in soft drinks will in some cases be obvious, while in others a defect may not be apparent. In addition, off-tastes as a result of poor sanitation should not be confused with those caused by spoilage. The following is a list of those characteristics indicating spoilage: (1) extreme changes in taste and flavor, e.g., musty, sour, putrid; (2) formation of sediment, cloud, or turbidity; (3) formation of slime; (4) change in color; and (5) excessive foaming or constant bubbling.

Microbiological Spoilage. Microbiological spoilage in soft drinks can be caused by yeasts, molds, and bacteria. Of the three, yeasts are the major cause of deterioration, whereas contamination with molds and bacteria is less common. Algae are not very common, but may contribute to off-tastes and off-odors. Algae can be eliminated by activated carbon water purifiers.

Yeasts. Yeasts can grow in syrups. Once syrup is contaminated, yeasts multiply rapidly. Yeasts travel through the air and consequently can contaminate syrups in a number of ways that are all directly related to poor sanitation.

When replenishment of the syrup tank is necessary, a product should be inspected for evidence of fermentation, such as a sour odor or bubbles. In addition, presence of yeasts can be recognized by the following changes: (1) formation of an opalescence or cloudiness, (2) formation of a ring (usually of a brownish-white color) on the surface of a drink, (3) formation of floc, especially in tonics or colas, (4) formation of sediment, (5) formation of excessive gas or bubbling, and (6) changes in color, either partial or complete.

Molds. Properly carbonated drinks do not contain enough air to support the growth of molds, as molds are dependent on oxygen for their development. Molds, however, can grow in still drinks, fruit juice, and syrup. Molds will produce a musty taste and odor. Floc and sediment will also appear. Nozzles and mixing heads, if not sanitized regularly, will enhance the growth of molds, since these areas are exposed to the atmosphere.

Bacteria. Bacteria are responsible for haze or cloudiness, excessive gas formation and slimy sediment. The primary defects are off-odors and off-tastes. Their development in a fruit drink produces an odor and taste resembling that of buttermilk which is caused by lactic acid bacteria.

Microbial Growth and pH Value. It was previously explained that pH is an internationally accepted method of expressing acidity or alkalinity of a product. The scale runs from 0 to 14. Distilled water has a pH of 7.0 and is neutral. A highly acid product such as 50% citric acid solution has a pH of 1.8–2.0. An alkaline detergent in a dishwasher may give a pH reading of 10 or more.

Soft drinks are acidic products and thus have a pH of less than 7. Colas have a pH of about 2.5 and orange and other citrus drinks are between 2.5 and 3.5.

Microorganisms develop rapidly at pH values of 6.5–7.0. The point at which most microorganisms cease to grow is between 4.5 and 5.0. Fortunately, the acid-sensitive group includes all bacteria harmful to human health. With the exception of lactic acid bacteria, which thrive in an acid medium, soft drinks having a pH value of 4.0 are considered safe from a public health point of view. Figure 11.8 shows the effects of pH on the growth of bacteria.

Table 11.4 summarizes the effects of contamination considered microbiological in origin.

Physical Spoilage.   Physical spoilage of soft drinks is primarily due to the effects of light and temperature.

Excessive exposure to light will produce undesirable flavor changes. Off-flavors such as sour, oily, or terpene-like can develop. Terpene and oily tastes are found principally in citrus-flavored drinks. Even drinks with light-fast colors can fade when exposed to strong light. To prevent spoilage from light, soft drinks and syrups should be stored away from direct sunlight.

Extreme temperature changes may cause undesirable flavor defects in the finished product and a reduction in carbonation. Carbon dioxide is more soluble in water at 35°–38°F (2°–4°C) than at higher temperatures. Table 11.3 illustrates the effects of an increase in temperature on the reduction of carbonation. Care must be taken not to overcool a product to the point of

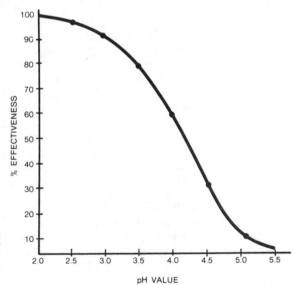

FIG. 11.8.   Effect of pH on the preservation of soft drinks.
Courtesy of Naarden-Flavorex, Inc.

LE 11.4. Symptoms of Microbial Spoilage of Soft Drinks

Symptom	Type		Causative Organism
hanges in appearance			
Haze or cloud	For consumption *without dilution*	Not containing fruit juice	In high-acid drinks: yeasts In low-acid drinks: yeasts and/or bacteria
		Containing fruit juice	Yeasts and/or bacteria (especially lactic acid bacteria)
	For consumption *after dilution* (syrups)	Not containing fruit juice	Mostly osmotolerant yeasts
		Containing fruit juice	Osmotolerant yeasts *Leuconostoc* in medium-acid medium-Brix syrups
Ringing	All drinks—however, typical for fruit juice syrups		Yeasts, especially osmotolerant species
Floating particles	Still drinks		Yeasts and/or molds
	Carbonated drinks		Yeasts
Sediment	In all drinks intended for consumption without dilution		Yeasts
Ropiness	Medium-acid drinks		*Leuconostoc* or *Lactobacillus*
	Low-acid drinks		*Bacillus*
Loss of cloud stability	Drinks containing fruit pulp		Pectolytic organisms
Color fading	Drinks containing natural color only		Yeasts Bacteria (in low-acid drinks)
Gas formation			
Foaming	All types		Yeasts
Blowing (cans)			Heterofermentative lactic acid bacteria
Leakage			
"Going off"			
Off-odors and off-tastes			
1. "Brewed" taste	All types		Yeasts
2. "Sour" taste	Especially drinks containing fruit juice		*Lactobacillus, Acetobacter*
3. "Buttery" off-flavor	Especially drinks containing fruit juice		Lactic acid bacteria
4. "Musty" off-flavor	All types		Molds

ırce: Courtesy of Naarden-Flavorex, Inc.

freezing. Some colors and flavorings are much less soluble at low temperatures. Precipitates can occur that may not redissolve during subsequent
temperature rises, and if they do redissolve, the shade of color or the flavor
may be altered. Flavor emulsions should not be exposed to freezing temperatures. If the emulsions are exposed to low temperatures, the product will
separate, producing a heavy cloud in a beverage.

Chemical Spoilage. Chemical spoilage of soft drinks may result from
reactions with oxygen of the air or from substances contained in the water
source. Light and high temperatures will tend to accelerate chemical spoilage problems.

If too much air is introduced in a system, oxidation may occur, affecting
several components of syrups, such as aldehydes or terpenes. Rancidity can
develop in flavors containing vegetable oils. Stock rotation and storage of

syrups in a cool area are recommended as steps toward the elimination of this problem.

Chemical reactions can also develop from too much iron or copper in the feed water. Excessive chlorine and high alkalinity of water will contribute to extreme flavor changes.

Dirty glasses, or those that are poorly rinsed so that traces of detergent remain on surfaces, will present a problem of excessive foaming and a loss of carbonation.

Biochemical Spoilage.   Biochemical spoilage as a result of natural food enzymes can be prevented by employing consistent stock rotation. Syrups containing fruit or citrus concentrates are susceptible to this type of deterioration. Enzymes present may react to alter viscosity of a syrup.

DAIRY BEVERAGES

Milk

Milk is perhaps the most perishable of foods. It would be superfluous to expand on the extensive care given to maintaining a healthy herd of cows, but healthy cows give "good" milk. With the numerous safeguards and regulations imposed on the dairy industry, we can assume milk processed for human consumption starts out as "good" milk from healthy cows. But from this point on, even the best milk can be ruined by improper handling on the farm or in transit to processing facilities, by inadequate processing and storage, poor inventory rotation, abuse at the final distribution point, or any combination of these critical points.

The following flavor defects in milk and cream will particularly concern a foodservice manager.

(1) Barny, feed—Absorbed initially at the source from the cow and her surroundings. The processor should be able to control this problem.

(2) Metallic, cardboardy (oxidized), tallowy—Copper and iron in processing equipment could cause this. Again the processor must be notified. The action of sunlight may also be the cause. If this is the problem, the delivery vehicle, your unloading area, and storage areas should be checked for excessive exposure to sunlight.

(3) Burnt or cooked taste—Overheating by the supplier.

(4) Sour—Improper handling, inadequate refrigeration, or old product can be the cause; all areas must be checked. The importance of proper coding by the processor and accurate records of product received are essential.

Dispensing of Milk

It is important to consider how a dairy product should be properly packaged and dispensed and what should be done by foodservice personnel to control the quality of these perishable products at their respective distribution levels. The dairy industry is well aware that no matter how good the quality of their product, the consumer, whether in the home or restaurant, can damage it. Milk and milk products are delicate and cannot stand harsh treatment.

The following rules are simple.

(1) Milk should always be kept cold. Milk should immediately be placed under refrigeration (40°F or 5°C average) after delivery. The very nature of the dairy business dictates an early start by delivery route men; however, the foodservice industry must not take for granted that early "drops" on a rear platform will suffice because it is dark, or semidark, and cooler than in daylight. An attendant must place milk deliveries under refrigeration immediately unless access to a walkin refrigerated box is available to the delivery man. The restaurant or catering service should not accept delivery under any other conditions. Milk that is warm cools slowly when finally placed under proper refrigeration and is subject to an increase in bacterial growth affecting either directly or indirectly the development of "off-flavors" and spoilage. Modern dispensing units, which are seen frequently today, have undergone extensive improvement. Multigallon plastic lined milk cartons are enclosed in a refrigerated unit that is practical, clean looking, and generally made of eye pleasing stainless steel. (It is advised that state or local agencies be checked for information on restrictions regulating types of acceptable dispensing equipment prior to installation of units.)

Most milk dispensers contain temperature gauges indicating "safe" and "danger" zones rather than thermometers showing actual temperature. Although these gauges are fairly reliable, accurate daily temperature checks using a standard dial type or dairy thermometer is suggested. This can be easily accomplished by cooling a glass in a refrigerator for 15 to 20 min, drawing off a portion of milk from a dispenser, and taking a temperature reading. It is also recommended that the actual readings and dates be kept in a record book.

In the case of individual cartons, a container of water can be kept in the same refrigerated storage area as the milk. A thermometer can be placed into this container daily and a reading taken and recorded. The advantage of such a permanent container is that it will reflect changes in refrigerator temperature.

Since tasting is the simplest quality criterion, it is also suggested that milk be tasted upon receipt and the temperature taken. Again, all results should be recorded. The supplier should be made aware that records are being kept. It will serve to alert the supplier to your concern and position on quality.

(2) Milk should be kept away from direct sunlight. Whether on a receiving platform or on a table, exposure to direct sunlight can cause change in flavor within as little as 15 min and also a loss of riboflavin (vitamin B_2).

(3) Keep milk covered. An open container of milk in a refrigerator will soon absorb odors and flavors of other foods. Closed containers will prevent contamination from drippings from the shelf above and will ensure cleanliness.

(4) Do not return poured milk to its original container. It is illegal as well as unsanitary.

(5) Rotate inventory properly. Some areas of the country still cling to outdated theories that coding is not necessary. This is foolish thinking. Fresh foods are better if consumed as soon as possible and milk is no exception. If incoming milk is not coded and dated, it is suggested that the foodservice establishment control order of use by separating by shipment date of supplies, or, in the case of dispensers, writing the date of receipt on cartons. Care should be given not to order in excess of anticipated usage plus a reasonable safety factor.

(6) Do not freeze milk or cream. Although milk can be thawed, it is difficult to do so properly and almost impossible to maintain consistent quality. Milk that has been frozen changes in consistency and tastes watery.

(7) Keep dispensing equipment clean and sanitized. Nozzles, hoses, and units themselves should be cleaned daily. Milk deposits will build up in these areas and cause an increase in bacterial count, thus contributing to spoilage and off-flavor problems. Extreme care should be given to keeping hands and fingers from contacting surfaces over or through which milk will flow. In the case of disposable milk dispensing units, special attention should be given to the dispensing nozzle. A good practice is to discard that portion of milk which remained in a nozzle overnight prior to selling the first glass each morning.

It is wise to remember that the foodservice business is dependent upon repeat sales. If the customer is not pleased, he or she will not return. Therefore, the time required for proper care of dairy products should not be considered a nuisance or an expense but rather an investment in good business relations.

Microbiological Spoilage of Milk

Microbiological contamination is a major contributor to product spoilage resulting in financial loss. Bacteria can be introduced into milk or any other dairy beverage from a number of sources, including: (1) the cow's udder, (2) exterior of the cow, (3) atmosphere, (4) milker or handler, (5) various processing and packaging equipment, (6) added ingredients, (7) poor storage and distribution practices, and (8) poor handling prior to consumption.

Since the dairy industry is more highly regulated than any other food industry, more attention is given to its products. Spoilage due to mishandling through inadequately cleaned dispensing equipment or poor temperature control during storage has been the principal cause of spoilage.

Sour milk is so unpleasant that many customers have become nauseated when exposed to its pungent, putrid odor and taste. Although most soured products do not contain "food poisoning" organisms, complaints arising from serving a soured product can be damaging to the reputation of a food-service establishment.

Chemical Spoilage of Milk

Oxidative deterioration of milk products contributes to a number of flavor defects, such as cardboardy, metallic, oily, rancid, and tallowy.

Oxidation is brought about by exposure to (1) oxygen in the air, (2) sunlight and artificial light, and (3) excessive and prolonged high temperatures.

Exposure to certain metals, e.g., copper, has in the past been a contributing factor to oxidation; however, regulations limiting use of copper have eliminated this metal from processing equipment.

Exposure to sunlight or artificial light is another factor. The degree of off-flavor is dependent upon length of exposure, intensity of light, properties of milk, and type of container used. Although it is unlikely that milk will be exposed to sunlight, exposure to fluorescent or incandescent light sources will cause similar defects. In many restaurants, cream is stored in glass containers and left on the table or counter for the customer's use. In this case, cream will become unacceptable more quickly than usual due to prolonged exposure to room temperature and artificial light.

Exposure to sustained or high temperatures is perhaps a major cause of oxidation in food establishments. It is recommended that storage temperatures be maintained at 38°–40°F (4°–5°C). This range will provide safe short-time storage so that spoilage from microorganisms and oxidation are held to a minimum.

It is interesting to note that phospholipids, components of milk fat, are one of the factors contributing to oxidation. The products most susceptible to oxidation are cream and buttermilk, which contain a high percentage of phospholipids.

Milk Dispenser Contamination

Dispensing nozzles and hoses are usually not kept under refrigeration overnight and therefore any milk or cream remaining within a nozzle is susceptible to bacterial growth. The first portion drawn through a dispenser the following day could contain a bacterial count far in excess of legal standards and it may also be sour. Subsequent dispensing would contain contamination less than, but in direct proportion to, the amount of original contamination. Portion packages of coffee cream cannot be left on a serving counter indefinitely. A general practice is to stack them near a coffee urn with the result that excessive heat will sour them within several hours.

Dairy spoilage can be prevented by following routine procedures.

(1)   Clean and sanitize all dispenser parts daily. It is important to note that milk spilled inside a dispenser should be cleaned quickly, since it will form milkstone and harbor bacterial growth which will eventually lead to off-odors.

(2)   Try to schedule usage of milk dispenser containers so as not to have any milk left at the end of the day. If small quantities remain, draw them off into a cleaned and sanitized container and place them in the refrigerator. This milk should be used only for cooking. Under no circumstances should it be used for direct consumption.

(3)   If substantial amounts of milk are left over, the nozzle hose should be pinched off as close to the container as possible and drained. The partially filled container should then be removed from the refrigerated dispenser and stored in the refrigerated chest overnight. The same precautions apply to cream and cream dispensers. Portion-packed cream should be stored in a refrigerator until used. During peak serving periods, several dozen can be stored on the counter in a chest or tray of ice water.

Milk Spoilage from Poor Temperature Control

Higher than recommended storage temperatures are by far the greatest cause of bacterial spoilage. Most dairy products have a limited shelf-life and must be handled correctly from the outset. At room temperature (68°–72°F or 20°–23°C), bacterial count can double in approximately 1 hr. If storage temperatures either in a cold chest or dispensing unit are inadequate, the product in question could have unacceptable bacterial counts that would within a short period of time cause spoilage.

CREAM DISPENSING

There are three methods of foodservice cream dispensing. The first and most common is the individual portion control package. The stainless steel manually operated dispenser is the second method. These are used in many foodservice establishments primarily for economic advantages. The third and least used method today is cream served in small pitchers. This method of dispensing cream is not recommended. Although still legally acceptable in some areas of the country, it has several public health ramifications. These include difficulty in maintaining proper temperature control and controlling microbial contamination, and therefore such practice is considered unsatisfactory by many regulatory agencies.

Portion Control Cream Dispensing.   Coupled with growth of the portion control creamer has been the trend toward increased production of sterilized, aseptically packaged cream which has prolonged shelf-life without refrigeration. It is not uncommon for sterile cream to be held at room temperature for several weeks before flavor deterioration takes place. An extended shelf-life and adaptability to room temperature storage have been found to be advantageous where logistics prevent desired delivery scheduling or where adequate refrigeration is not available. The sterile pack can also be stored on the shelf, leaving premium refrigerator storage space for other uses. Whether or not it is practical for a restaurant to use a sterile product and whether this type of product would be necessary depends upon individual circumstances.

Recent years have seen the sale of portion control creamers make remarkable progress. Such packets as the Dixie Cup, Tetra Pak, Ultra Pak Form Seal, and others can be found in many restaurants today. The more expensive cup type packet has been streamlined to include a variety of plastic containers with an equal variety of sanitary and leakproof closures.

When determining cost of a portion control creamer, a restaurant manager would be well advised to carefully calculate the labor of cleaning dispenser equipment as well as direct product cost. He should also consider the quality control aspects of this type of dispensing packet. It is a fact that the more times a product is handled from processing to consumer, the more the chances are for external contamination, eventual spoilage, and financial loss.

Plunger Type Cream Dispenser.   The stainless steel cream dispenser continues to maintain a price advantage over the portion control creamer due to bulk purchasing.

We shall again stress the point that increased handling requires proper attention in order to minimize points of possible contamination. Cooling must be done with ice, cold water, or some other adequate coolant. Regardless of which coolant is used, extreme caution must be given to ensure that cream inside a dispenser does not come in contact with the cooling agent.

The manager must locate dispensers in an area accessible to coffee makers, and yet not so close that the entire cream supply is heated to temperatures in excess of 40°F (5°C).

A dispenser requires more than just washing if bacterial contamination is to be avoided. Basically, cream dispensers should be disassembled to their smallest component parts, rinsed, washed with an appropriate detergent, and sanitized. A recommended procedure is detailed in Chapter 12.

Handling Soft-Serve Products

Since the ingredients used in formulating soft-serve mixes are highly perishable, they require careful handling and storage. Buying from reputable firms is essential as soft-serve thick drinks, being primarily warm weather sales items, may have to be stored longer than desired if there are sudden weather changes. Inventory control becomes increasingly important as do adequate storage temperatures. Most suppliers ask that their products be kept at 40°F (5°C) or lower until use. Product report data sheets, similar to those described previously in this chapter, should be maintained, with particular attention given to product codes and delivery temperature.

The operator of soft-serve equipment must share the responsibility of quality control with regard to maintaining proper sanitation of equipment as well as proper storage or holding temperatures. Modern packaging of plastic bags with outer cardboard containers affords good insulation and protection against heat; conversely, however, warmed prefrozen mix will cool slowly when finally placed under proper refrigeration. This high temperature period may allow ample time for bacteria to multiply and thus decrease shelf-life.

It should be noted that the temperature at which an end product is drawn from a freezer will depend on ingredients used in the mix and the consistency desired. The stiffer the body the lower the temperature. The usual draw-off range is 25° to 27°F (−3° to −2°C).

Slush

The newest and most profitable items to appear in recent years are carbonated or noncarbonated "slush" beverages. Unlike thick dairy shakes, slush beverages are nothing more than sweetener, flavoring, stabilizer, and water. Processing is almost fully automatic with very little concern given to material handling, inventory, and loss due to spoilage. Slush is primarily a seasonal item.

Curdling in Ice Cream Soda

The reaction of a jet stream of carbonated water with mixtures of high acid syrups and dairy or nondairy milk or cream substitutes items can result in a soda with a curdled effect. The soda has not soured but has undergone a chemical change altering the pH balance. Although this problem comes under the heading of chemical spoilage, it is a very common occurrence and therefore deserves special mention.

This condition can be avoided if high acid syrups, such as strawberry, are processed using disodium phosphate as a buffer to neutralize acidity. This approved additive has no detectable taste. The label of a syrup container will indicate the presence of this ingredient. However, if syrups with this additive are not available, the following alternative method of preventing curdling can be used.

An operator can mix syrup with cream, milk, or dairy substitute in a soda glass, then add carbonated water, initially reducing the jet spray and thereby minimizing the acidity effect upon the mixture. This can also be accomplished by running carbonated water down the side of a soda glass instead of directly into the syrup-milk blend.

Although no spoilage is involved, there could be a loss of time and ingredients since the curdled appearance is unattractive and therefore unacceptable to the consumer.

NONDAIRY PRODUCTS

Simulated cream and other milk product substitutes are widely used in the foodservice industry. A steady growth has been registered over the past 15 years. Foodservice personnel are being attracted to these items and many are faced with various problems related to this changeover. A number of considerations must be weighed before a final choice is made. When a comparison is made between two products, the following parameters must be considered:

(1) Does an equal amount of nondairy whitener enrich and lighten coffee in the same manner as Half-and-Half?

(2) Does a nondairy product produce an off-flavor and lingering after-taste? These are major defects of nondairy whiteners and must be carefully determined.

(3) Will a customer readily accept a change? Signs may have to be posted or a statement made in the menu to indicate use of substitutes.

(4) Will a product be uniform or will quality change with each shipment?

It should also be noted that sales efforts on behalf of nondairy manufacturers have misinformed foodservice operators on claims for extended shelf-life and storage stability of these products. This has led to mishandling and resulted in spoilage and product deterioration. Nondairy products must be handled, stored, and refrigerated with the same precautions as dairy items, otherwise, serious defects in beverage quality will result.

Definitions

Prior to further discussion relative to quality control of these products, two basic terms must be defined.

Filled Milk or Filled Milk Products. Filled milk or filled milk products are those products in which some milk solids are used with dairy substitute formulations. The most widely used dairy ingredient is nonfat dry milk to build up the solids content of a product. Filled milk, therefore, consists of nondairy fats and oils combined with skim milk solids.

Nondairy Substitutes. Nondairy substitutes, as the name implies, are products containing no milk solids in the formulation. All fats, oils, and other ingredients in the product are of food origins other than milk, except that sodium caseinate, a milk protein component, is a common ingredient in most coffee whiteners. Whey is also used in some brands.

Spoilage

The composition of nondairy or filled milk items lends itself to a variety of spoilage possibilities. A product combining emulsifiers and stabilizers with fats and sweetening agents creates an emulsion that is extremely delicate and highly sensitive to external changes.

Physical Spoilage.   Perhaps the greatest problem facing processors of liquid or liquid frozen imitation milks or coffee whiteners is the treatment their product will receive after it leaves the processing plant. Assuming that a product purchased is of good quality meeting all regulatory requirements, a shelf-life of 1 to 2 weeks can be expected. This period should be more than ample to meet the needs of any foodservice establishment. However, holding and thawing temperatures must be such that extremes are avoided. The emulsion created during processing can easily be broken by mishandling and result in product "separation" or "oiling off." Frozen products should be thawed under refrigerated temperatures. Quick thawing can be accomplished with careful attention; however, the rush and confusion of peak periods often create a situation of unintentional forgetfulness. If improperly handled, cream substitutes will show an oil film on coffee surfaces.

Powdered nondairy or filled products should be covered at all times and kept tightly sealed to prevent moisture absorption resulting in clumping and, in turn, dispensing difficulty.

Chemical Spoilage.   Chemical spoilage due to flavor deterioration is the most common defect found in liquid or frozen products. Exposure to light for excessive periods of time will cause a reaction in nondairy and filled milk similar to dairy products. Oxidized off-flavors resulting from this exposure will leave the same cardboardy or oily taste, especially in filled products containing milk solids. To avoid flavor deterioration, the same precautions should be followed as given for milk products.

Microbiological Spoilage.   The combination of sugar, fat, and other solids makes nondairy and filled milk products susceptible to spoilage discussed under milk products. Mishandling and excessive heat can result in proliferation of microorganisms and cause souring. Improperly cleaned and sanitized dispensers will contaminate nondairy products. Even sterile nondairy products, once opened, are subject to contamination.

The same precautions discussed for milk products also apply to nondairy and filled milk products.

Characteristics of Nondairy Coffee Whiteners

(1) The nondairy product should readily dissolve.
(2) There should be no feathering.
(3) There should be no chalking.
(4) There should be no dominant aftertaste.
(5) The body or consistency of a simulated product should be equal to the consistency of the dairy product.
(6) The coloring action should be equal to the dairy product.
(7) The nondairy product should be completely homogeneous at all times.

Simplified Methods for Testing Nondairy Creaming Agents

Maintain at the same temperature as cream.

Testing procedures: (1) Open the carton and smell for rancidity; check discoloration, such as green mold, if detected, set shipment aside. (2) Separation—Insert a knife or fork into container; withdraw slowly. If products adheres uniformly, with no evidence of stringing, product is homogeneous. Pour some into a glass; observe uniformity of shade. (3) Feathering—Pour a cup of brewed coffee (5 oz) into a glass; add the usual measure of nondairy product. Stir gently; look for feathering, oiling off, or lumps. If present, set shipment aside. (4) Whitening—Whitening should be comparable to an equal amount of Half-and-Half. Test as follows: Pour a cup of brewed coffee into a glass (5 oz); add a standard measure of nondairy product; stir. Repeat in another glass with Half-and-Half. Hold both glasses to the light. They should be the same. If the shade of nondairy product is darker, add an additional quantity until shades are equal. Make a notation, for the record, of the additional amount required.

JUICES

Juices are highly perishable food items. Haphazard handling, poor storage techniques, and improper sanitation of dispensing equipment have contributed to serving substandard juices in many foodservice establishments. Although dairy products are more prone to spoilage, extensive educational programs, municipal regulations, and assistance from the dairy industry have almost eliminated them from the "perishable" category.

Juices, compared with other beverages, are simple to serve, since little or no preparation is required by the consumer. Probably this simplicity is why correct handling procedures are overlooked. For example, long holding periods after juice is opened and removed to serving areas or dispensing equipment result in undesirable flavor changes. Holding pasteurized concentrated fruit juice above 35°F (2°C) for extended periods, or storing canned juices at 68°F (20°C) or above for several months creates off-flavors and unpalatable products. Fresh orange juice, if squeezed too far in advance, will develop a cloudy appearance and flat taste. Frozen juices when allowed to thaw and refreeze during transportation and storage exhibit structure, appearance, and flavor defects.

As spoilage becomes evident, a product not only loses consumer appeal, but is a financial loss to an establishment both in business and in waste. However, a foodservice operation can minimize damage caused by improper handling and storage through the application of quality control procedures.

Spoilage of Fruit and Vegetable Juices

The technology of fruit and vegetable juices is extensive. There are so many different juices that it would be impossible to cover each one individually. This section will be devoted to the basic types of spoilage common to most juices. Specific examples will be given where necessary.

Elimination of spoilage within any operation can be controlled by proper handling of juices and performing thorough sanitary practices. Chapter 12 deals with spoilage problems in conjunction with sanitation as a means to eliminate them.

Microbial Spoilage of Juices

Bacteria.   There are several types of bacteria found in fruit and vegetable juices that deserve special mention because of their frequent occurrence. These include lactic acid and butyric acid bacteria.

Lactic acid-forming bacteria are the most frequent cause of spoilage in apple, pear, grape, and citrus juices. These bacteria are important because of their rapid multiplication in the absence of air, and their ability to survive in a carbon dioxide environment. Thus, they can grow in sealed cans. Lactic acid bacteria are more acid tolerant than other bacteria and can grow in juices with pH values as low as 2.5. These organisms are destroyed by pasteurization. Careful consideration should be given to juices that are hot packed or pasteurized. Cold pack products are acceptable, but must be of quality grade and held under proper refrigerated storage (38°–40°F or 4°–5°C) at every level of distribution to prevent multiplication of bacteria. The most common defects resulting from lactic acid bacteria are off-flavors and slimy or stringy conditions.

Butyric acid-producing bacteria are significant because they can develop in products whose pH is around 4.0. Butyric acid bacterial spoilage is easy to detect due to the objectionable odor. These organisms are also destroyed by pasteurization.

Acetic acid bacteria are quite acid tolerant, but require oxygen to grow and therefore are not usually a spoilage problem. These organisms may cause spoilage of orange juice concentrate.

Coliform bacteria of *Salmonella* are not usually found in juice of high acidity values. However, these organisms (which are of public health significance) may multiply if present in tomato juices. Other food poisoning types of organisms such as *Staphylococcus* may be found on occasion in juices, but cannot multiply in acid conditions of pH 4.5 or lower.

The following precautions should be taken to protect previously opened containers from possible outside contamination during storage. Canned juices should be transferred to a previously sanitized glass or stainless steel container if juice is left over. Drain carefully and dry these storage containers since excessive water can dilute juice and thereby raise the pH, thus making a stored product more susceptible to bacterial growth. The temperature of a refrigerator should be 38°–40°F (4°–5°C) and it should be free of foreign odors. The container should be equipped with a tight-fitting lid. Figure 11.9 gives the approximate pH ranges of various fruit juices.

Yeasts. Yeasts are present in air, creating a problem in juices left exposed and at room temperature for any prolonged period of time. The significance of some yeasts is that they ferment sugar, producing ethyl alcohol and carbon dioxide, whereas others produce organic acid. The ultimate result is development of off-odors and off-flavors resulting in a completely unacceptable product. Yeasts usually do not grow at low temperatures, but are acid tolerant. It is important to store juices in closed containers at refrigerated temperatures, especially after original container

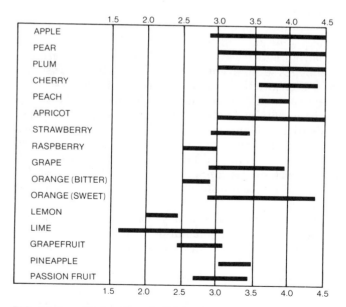

FIG. 11.9. pH of various fruit juices.
From Tressler and Nelson (1980).

has been opened. Yeasts can be detected by taste, by bulging can ends (which may or may not be due to yeast entirely), by a change in viscosity, or in some cases by a filamentous growth on the surface of the juice.

Molds.   Molds are directly related to fruit spoilage and may be found in juices. Like bacteria, some mold spores are heat resistant and survive pasteurization temperatures. Fortunately, mold growth is slow at temperatures below 40°F (5°C), thus affording protection for longer periods once the original container is opened. Molds need oxygen, therefore juices packed with carbon dioxide under pressure usually have no mold present. Molds can be detected by surface growth on the juice, off-odors, and off-flavors. Dispensing nozzles and slop trays generally are breeding areas for molds.

Chemical Spoilage of Juices

Flavor Deterioration.   Flavor deterioration is of prime concern to the foodservice operator. Canned citrus juices develop off-flavors after storage periods of just a few months. Just how quickly a flavor change takes place depends on the temperature at which juices are stored. It is advisable to store juices in the coolest available area. The temperature should not exceed 68°F (20°C). The lower the temperature the slower the flavor deterioration. It should be noted, however, that, regardless of storage temperature, off-flavor will eventually develop. Absence of oxygen cannot retard this off-flavor formation.

Since refrigerated storage space is at a premium and not always available, careful purchasing and proper inventorying can be a successful alternative to cold storage. Packing codes or dates should be carefully noted on incoming supplies so an inventory rotation system can be established. This procedure will ensure that the oldest product is used first.

In addition, a detailed data sheet should be used so that a permanent record can be maintained for checking purposes. In the event of spoilage, such records are invaluable in determining the responsibility of a supplier.

Defects in the tinning of cans will accelerate changes in peel oil constituents which cause citrus juice off-flavor development. The action of acidity on the untreated surface of a can, most commonly located along seams, will cause a chemical reaction resulting in flavor deterioration.

Color Changes.   Color changes may also occur in juices during storage. Juices which possess high pigmentation such as grape, cherry, raspberry, and strawberry are especially susceptible to color changes.

Brown particles found in juice are the result of prolonged storage of canned juices at room temperatures. This condition might not readily be observed in such juices as orange or tomato, but it can be present. In light-colored juices, such as grapefruit and pineapple, this browning effect can easily be detected.

Oxidative Rancidity. Oxidative rancidity has an undesirable effect on juices containing oils, such as orange. This condition will result in a change of color and flavor and a reduction of nutritive value. When oxidation has occurred, it can readily be detected by an intense objectionable odor. Although this situation can be prevented by antioxidants when the juice is manufactured or by deaeration, oxidation can develop in fresh-pack and reconstituted concentrates if exposed to air for a period of time.

A second type of rancidity may develop in the absence of oxygen. This type is called *hydrolytic rancidity* and is favored by moisture, high temperatures, and natural enzymes.

Cloud Formation. Cloud formation in juices such as orange can sometimes be misleading. Fine particles within juice solids produce a layered effect; one layer is clear and the other precipitated solids. Before discarding what might be considered a spoiled product, vigorously shake juice and taste it. The clear layer should not be treated separately. It is the precipitated layer that contributes the flavor, and just tasting the clear portion could lead to discarding what might be a salable item.

Frozen Concentrates

Frozen concentrates present different problems from those mentioned previously. Storage temperatures in excess of 0°F (−18°C) can adversely change the flavor of frozen juices. The cloud layer diminishes in quantity as temperatures rise. The higher the temperature the greater the flavor loss. The foodservice purchasing agent should know both the reputation of a supplier and the storage conditions in his warehouse.

Storage of Unfrozen Juice

Cold storage of unfrozen juice is not sufficient to delay growth of microorganisms over two weeks. Cold storage at 0° to 10°F (−18° to −12°C) for frozen juices is ample for extended protection, providing thawing does not occur during shipping. Temperatures of 10°F (−12°C) or above induce slow changes in flavor and a gradual loss of vitamin C. Other factors influencing storage changes are: fluctuating storage temperatures, oxygen content, and permeability of a container.

When canned juices are opened and partially used, the remainder must be stored in stainless steel or glass containers equipped with airtight lids. Containers employed for this purpose should meet the following specifications. They should: (1) be impervious to air and moisture, (2) be able to be readily opened and sealed, (3) not be manufactured from materials that contaminate contents, (4) be capable of being completely cleaned and sanitized, (5) be equipped with a wide, dripless pouring spout, and (6) be free of crevices or indentations which create pockets for the growth of microorganisms.

Ideal storage temperatures should be from 35° to 40°F (3° to 5°C).

Squeezing Fresh Oranges

Some food establishments continue to serve freshly squeezed orange juice since consumer appeal is high for this product. The shortage of restaurant personnel has relegated this item to the food processor. Several drawbacks exist in the method of squeezing fresh juice. Overextraction may result in a bitter beverage or lack of proper sanitation of a squeezer may produce objectionable flavors. Squeezers require daily cleaning and sanitizing to minimize contamination from surfaces coming into direct contact with oranges.

To produce high-quality, refreshing, and palatable freshly squeezed orange juice requires that oranges be chilled to about 40°F (5°C) and rinsed under cold tap water prior to squeezing. If a hand press is used, limited pressure should be applied to avoid bitterness. The same technique applies to electrically powered juicers. A firm, but gentle application of an orange half to the reamer is all that is necessary for proper extraction.

Dispensing

Dispensing of fruit and vegetable juices consists of two basic methods, premix and postmix. Premix methods are those that involve serving juice directly from a container, or reconstitution of concentrates or powders into batches.

Postmix methods involve automatic mixing of concentrates, powders, or syrups with water upon activation of dispensing equipment as a drink is drawn. This method has the advantage of speed and uniformity, provided the elements of sanitation and preventive maintenance are followed.

Classification.   The premix method of dispensing pertains to the following products: (1) chilled juices packaged in waxed containers of bottles, (2) juices packed in cans, (3) juices reconstituted from concentrates and stored in dispensers until served, (4) powdered juices reconstituted and stored in dispensers until served, (5) portion packed cans (5.5 oz) sold by vending machines, and (6) portion packed 4 oz plastic cups.

The postmix method includes refrigerated dispensers that automatically discharge a quantity of juice concentrate and water upon activation of the machine.

Premixed Juices.   Chilled juices, packaged in bottles or waxed containers and generally delivered with milk from dairies, require special stock rotation and storage temperatures. If these products are delivered daily, then spoilage due to prolonged storage will be eliminated provided old stock is moved aside and consumed first. If delivery is infrequent, storage temperatures should not exceed 35°F (3°C). Prior to serving, containers must be agitated or shaken to ensure uniformity of juice.

Juices packed in cans other than the 5.5 oz portion pack should be transferred to stainless steel or some other suitable container as previously described. This procedure is not necessary if the entire contents are consumed within several hours after being opened. During that period, a can should be immersed in an ice bath.

Portion packed 4 oz plastic cups are delivered in ready-to-serve plastic containers. Orange, tomato, prune, and apple juices are available in these disposable receptacles. It is claimed that waste is reduced by avoiding pouring, measuring, and serving spillage. They are often delivered with dairy products.

Juices (either concentrated or powdered) that are reconstituted with water can be served from self-contained refrigerator dispensers, quart or gallon containers, and glass or stainless steel receptacles. The most popular method is by a mechanically refrigerated visual merchandiser. These units keep juice, ade, or punch in constant motion within a clear plastic reservoir. They are designed to minimize aeration. Excessive aeration can result in off-tasting, flat beverages. Capacities range from 3 to 10 gal.

Postmixed Juices. Postmix dispensers if properly cleaned, sanitized, and adjusted to deliver the correct ratio of concentrate to water will serve juices in a fresh, flavorful state.

These units are manufactured to dispense one or two varieties of juice. If a concentrate is uniform and metering devices are operating within specifications, variations in hydrometer readings will be minimized. Hand mixing is eliminated and waste from spillage is reduced. Contamination from airborne microorganisms is less apt to occur; however, spoilage within any machine will develop unless strict sanitizing procedures are followed. These units also provide excellent portion control and positive cost accounting.

If brands of juice concentrate are changed, a dispensing or portion control mechanism may have to be reevaluated so the correct water to concentrate ratio is maintained.

Thawing Frozen Concentrates. Thawing frozen concentrates must be performed properly in order to retain the original quality of a juice. Of prime importance is to thaw juice quickly and maintain the finished product as 40°F (5°C) or lower after thawing. Small watertight cartons, jars, or cans of juice can best be thawed by placing them in running cold water, and shaking from time to time. About 15 min are required to thaw a small container.

Probably the simplest procedure is to place frozen concentrate in a refrigerator from 8 to 24 hr prior to mixing. However some experimentation is needed, as thawing time will depend on size of container, temperature of juice, and temperature and amount of air circulation in a refrigerator. Experience is the best guide to this method and to knowing the quantity of juice required for the next day's operation. Under no circumstances should more juice be thawed than is needed.

Still another procedure is to place a container in warm water just long enough to permit removal of the contents. The cake should be crushed to a slush, added to water, and stirred rigorously to ensure complete uniformity.

Addition of Ice.   Regardless of the methods employed to dispense juices, ice should not be added to restore them to a palatable refreshing temperature range. Ice dilutes drinks and destroys their natural characteristics. Juices should be properly chilled prior to serving. If juices are stored at 30°–40°F (3°–5°C), ice is not required. Glasses should be clean, free of detergent film, and dry.

Quality Testing of Juices

Product uniformity and quality can be determined by several quick and simple testing procedures.

(1)   Government standards, as previously described, can be followed to achieve a full understanding of grading methods. Unless a testing laboratory is available, it is impossible to perform all tests necessary to arrive at a grading score. However, tests for consistency, defects, and flavor of juices can and should be made.

Standards as promulgated by the United States Department of Agriculture and the Food and Drug Administration are explicit and detailed. Various samples of known standards as expressed on labels should be compared with present inventory. This procedure will serve as a guide so future appraisals will then become routine.

(2)   The concentration of soluble solids in juices can be estimated with a refractometer or a hydrometer (see Chapter 2). These instruments determine percentage of soluble solids, largely sugars, expressed in degrees Brix. This term relates specific gravity of a test solution to an equivalent concentration of pure sucrose. When a description is given of a juice's taste or tartness, the terms sugar-to-acid ratio or Brix-to-acid ratio are used. The higher the Brix, the greater the sugar concentration in a juice. In addition, the higher the Brix-to-acid ratio, the sweeter or less tart the juice.

These methods will be helpful in determining operating efficiency of postmix dispensers and uniformity of single strength juices and reconstituted drinks from concentrates.

(3)   The easiest, most readily available, and direct method of quality control is sensory evaluation as described in Chapter 2. Color comparisons can be performed, and tastes and odors differentiated. Spoilage resulting from yeast or mold formations can be ascertained, since these defects are discernible by the senses of sight and smell.

TEA

Tea drinking is considered a culmination of culinary satisfaction. Tea is an extremely profitable beverage and one of the simplest items to serve. Yet, as with many other beverages, the consumer rarely receives the full benefit of its flavor because of careless handling.

Spoilage of Tea Leaves and Powdered Tea

Bulk tea leaves and tea packed into tea bags are not susceptible to spoilage under normal conditions. Bulk tea if stored under extreme dryness will have a tendency to dry out, lose its flavor, and give a flat, insipid brew. On the other hand, if the tea is stored in an atmosphere of high humidity, chances for the growth of mold are increased. The fine aromatic flavor of tea will be impaired by mold.

Instant tea powder requires absolutely dry conditions. If ambient surroundings are such as to cause moisture uptake, powdered tea will tend to absorb water readily. This will result in liquefaction, forming a sticky and gummy appearance. If tea powder is dispensed from a machine, this gumminess will reduce measuring efficiency so brew inconsistency will be noticeable. In addition, mold formation will develop on surfaces exposed to moisture, imparting off-flavors in the brew.

Brewing Preparation and Serving

One out of 10 customers drinks tea when dining out, while 1 out of 4 people drinks tea at home. The reason for the overall lack of popularity in restaurants is partly due to improper preparation and handling, resulting in a substandard brew. Care in selecting the component parts of tea and blending is often lost through careless service.

Optimum preparation of this beverage should extract a maximum amount of caffeine, and about one-third of its tannins, while conserving the full benefit of its essential oils that add aroma and flavor. The process of tea extraction is referred to as an "infusion." This term is commonly used in the tea industry to describe an extract resulting from steeping leaves in hot water without boiling.

Under normal conditions, most of the caffeine dissolves within 2 min after boiling water has been poured on leaves. Within 5 min about one-third of the tannins is extracted from the leaves. This amount is considered ideal for the pungent effect of tea. When milk is added, tannins combine with casein in milk, thereby removing the astringency. For this reason, milk is added to very strong brews, as it allows the true flavor of the tea to come through. Lemon is often preferred instead of milk and acts as a flavor intensifier.

Teas infuse more readily in soft than in hard water. Teas are sometimes blended for water conditions. Small, thick, full teas are required for soft water, while brisk, full flavor teas are used for hard water.

Hot Tea.   Tea is probably the simplest beverage to prepare properly. The following steps are recommended for hot tea.

(1)   Use a teapot and preheat by rinsing it out with hot water. This step prevents a temperature drop if a pot is cold. The same applies to a cup. Cups and pots must be clean and free of contaminating odors. Pots should be examined for residues as these will induce off-flavors in tea. Lids should also be carefully examined for soil accumulations.

(2) Bring fresh cold tap water to a full rolling boil. Water that has been reheated gives tea a flat taste. Only boiling water can perform the ideal extraction. Don't use water from coffee urns or half-gallon brewers unless it is fresh and boiling. Instantaneous water heaters should be checked for correct temperatures if used for tea service.

(3) Use 1 tsp of loose tea or 1 tea bag per cup (about 5.5 oz) of water and pour boiling water over tea.

(4) Optimum brewing time is 3–5 min. Don't judge tea strength by its color. It takes time for an infusion to take place. Some weak teas produce a dark brew, whereas strong teas and those of fine quality produce a light brew. The color may also be affected by differences in water conditions. If tea is preferred less strong, hot water should be added after brewing.

Bulk Preparation of Hot Tea. The following method is recommended for preparation of large batches of hot tea. This procedure is ideally suited for mass servings of hot tea where it is not practical to handle large quantities of boiling water.

Bring 1 qt of freshly drawn water to a full rolling boil. Pour water over ⅔ cup of loose tea. Cover contents and allow to stand 5 min. Stir and strain into a quart teapot or other container. This concentrate will make 25 cups of tea. It can be held for 4 hr at room temperature, and should not be refrigerated. When ready to serve, pour 2 tbsp of tea concentrate into a cup and fill with hot water.

Iced Tea. Iced tea requires 50% more tea to allow for melting ice (Table 11.5). When ice is used, it should be firm and solid. Only about one-half the capacity of a glass should be filled with ice, otherwise a beverage will be light and watery. Hot tea should never be poured over a glass full of ice. This method will result in a light-drinking, inconsistent beverage.

Clouding of the finished concentrate is a common condition. It is caused by precipitation when iced tea reaches a certain coldness. Flavor or quality is not impaired by cloudiness. It can easily be removed by adding a small quantity of boiling water. It is not necessary to refrigerate the brew since the flavor will hold for 3–4 hr after preparation.

For best results iced tea should be prepared like hot tea, then diluted to the volume required. The following steps should be followed for the preparation of 1 gal. of iced tea.

TABLE 11.5. Quantity Formulas for Iced Tea Preparation

Gal. Iced Tea	Qt Boiling Water	Oz of Tea	Qt Cold Tap Water
2	2	4	6
3	3	6	9
4	4	8	12
5	5	10	15
10	10	20	30

Source: Tea Council of the United States.

(1)   Pour 1 qt of boiling water over a 2 oz tea bag, or ⅔ measuring cup of loose tea.
(2)   Cover the crock or pot and allow to stand 5 min.
(3)   If loose tea is used, strain contents, otherwise pour concentrate into 3 qt of cold water and stir. Pour the contents into a clean, dry, iced tea dispenser.

FIG. 11.10.   TeaJet® Model LT1 instant liquid iced tea dispenser.
Courtesy of Jet Spray Corp.

Instant Iced Tea

The premix method of preparing instant iced tea uses a ¾ oz packet for 1 gal. of finished product. If a 12 oz glass is used, half filled with ice, the yield will be about 20 glasses. Stir contents of a packet into 1 gal. of freshly drawn cold water and pour into a dispenser for serving.

Postmix instant iced tea is prepared from automatic dispensers (Fig. 11.10). A jar of instant tea is turned top side down and set into position in a dispenser. These units are easily adjusted to allow for various quantities of powder and water, depending on glass size and product strength desired.

Sanitation procedures must be followed so that a dispenser will operate properly at all times. Daily cleaning is recommended of dispenser mixing and delivery areas. Humidity will tend to solidify instant powder at the orifice, so that inconsistent throws will develop. Density and particle size of instant tea will affect the amount measured. If a brand is changed, a test for quality and strength should be made to ensure continued consistency. If the new product proves too strong or weak, the machine must be adjusted accordingly.

COCOA BEVERAGES

Cocoa beverages, of which hot chocolate is one of many varieties, have increased in popularity and are looked upon by foodservice personnel as important items because of their high profit yield. Drive-in establishments, fast food outlets, drugstores, and luncheonettes are the major foodservice operations with the greatest sales of these beverages.

Hot chocolate is the major cocoa beverage sold. The term hot chocolate is actually a misnomer, as the basic ingredient in the mixture is cocoa. Cocoa and cocoa product beverages are healthful, nutritious, filling, and mildly stimulating. For these reasons they are primarily considered to be drinks for children and teenagers. Unlike coffee and tea, which derive their full stimulating effects from caffeine, cocoa's effect is obtained mainly from the alkaloid theobromine.

The term cocoa has taken on many meanings. Actually there are three basic groups:

(1) Cacao is the term designating the raw or semiraw product, such as beans, tree, pod, flower, seed-shell, and butter.

(2) Cocoa is the term designating the product used as an ingredient in beverages.

(3) Chocolate signifies those products which are solidified and are used for candy, such as sweet chocolate, milk chocolate, baking chocolate, and bitter chocolate.

Prepared Cocoa Products

Prepared cocoa products are bases for cocoa or "chocolate" beverages. These cocoa products are prepared for home, soda fountain, restaurant, dairy, vending machine, and bottled or canned consumption. Powder and syrup are the two principal forms used. Basically, their composition consists of various sweetening agents (dextrose, maltose, sucrose), nonfat dry milk, and stabilizers. Additional items such as malt extract, preservatives, flavoring agents, and acidulants also may be included, according to specifications of the finished product.

Chocolate Milk Beverages

These beverages are manufactured by dairies and carbonated beverage bottlers. Methods of processing are different. Dairies use cocoa syrup and skim milk. Bottlers employ cocoa powder, nonfat milk, and simple syrup. If a product is homogenized, stabilizers may not be required. Stabilizers, such as various starches or Irish moss, are used to increase liquid viscosity, thus preventing the separation of cocoa solids from the liquid phase.

Hot Chocolate Beverages

Chocolate or cocoa powdered mixes for beverages are used in foodservice establishments and vending machines and are retailed in supermarkets for home consumption.

These items are winter or cold weather drinks. The North Central, Northwest, and North Atlantic regions of the United States are the areas where these beverages are most popular.

Dispensing and Serving

Classification and Dispensing Methods. Premix dispensing is used for the following: (1) bottled, (2) canned, (3) container, and (4) batch.

Premix. Premix methods of dispensing involve preparation of a mix and subsequent bottling, canning, or containerization, at either dairies or bottling plants. These beverages are served chilled. Chocolate milk packaged in individual containers is generally sold by dairies along with milk and cream. Canned products are handled by wholesalers and dispensed in vending machines.

Batch preparation methods for volume feeding establishments, such as schools and camps, require proper formulation of water or milk with cocoa, mixing, holding at a temperature, agitation, and sanitation. Depending on the quantity needed, a coffee urn is a suitable device to hold or serve this beverage, and temperature can be controlled when holding is necessary. Depending on taste requirements, 16 oz of cocoa mix normally will yield 1 gal. of finished beverage. The mix should be slowly poured into 1 qt of hot water at a temperature of about 200°F (94°C). Stir in liquid while cocoa mix is being poured. After powder is dispersed, the liquid concentrate is poured into the remaining water to make 1 gal. Further stirring is advisable for beverage uniformity. Holding temperature should be maintained at 175°–180°F (80°–83°C). If a beverage is to be held for any length of time, it should be periodically mixed by paddling or withdrawing a portion and pouring back into an urn. Boiling milk or water should not be used because alteration of milk and cocoa may result.

Postmix. The most popular method of dispensing hot chocolate beverages is automatically by counter dispensing machines (Fig. 11.11) or by vending machines. Powder has wider application, since syrups tend to congeal and deteriorate faster.

Operating principles of both machines are the same. Syrup is held in a reservoir while powder is stored in a hopper. When a cup is positioned under the finished product spout, a switch is activated that starts machine operation. A quantity of powdered products, measured by auger feed, is mixed

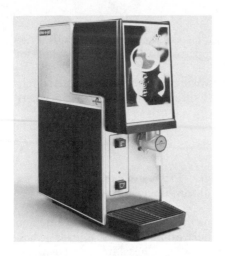

FIG. 11.11.   Choc-O-Jet® Model PHC1
portable hot chocolate dispenser.
Courtesy of Jet Spray Corp.

with hot water. Water enters the system in a swirling flow and meets the cocoa mix in a whipping chamber. The whipping action develops viscosity so a drink becomes creamy. This step is a major reason for the wide popularity of this beverage. After whipping, the liquid is discharged into a cup.

For best results, water temperature should be maintained at 185°–190°F (86°–88°C) so that a drink reaches the customer at a refreshing palatability range of 140°–145°F (60°–63°C).

The quantity of powdered chocolate (throw) should weigh 1 oz per 5 oz water. This volume will be ample for the usual 7 oz cup.

Hot chocolate dispensers are available either fully automatic or semiautomatic. The former is equipped with a timer. When the unit is activated, water and powder are measured according to preset volumes and delivered to a cup. The semiautomatic dispenser requires constant activation of the switch until a cup is filled.

If proper maintenance procedures are followed, quality beverages will be provided. Periodic checks of water volume, temperature, and product throw are necessary along with frequent sanitation.

Although cleaning is fully discussed in Chapter 12 on Sanitation, problems of inconsistency, if they occur, can be traced to solidification of powder around hopper discharge or within the mixing chamber. The mixing area should be flushed daily by operating the "water only" switch to assure thorough rinsing. If a hopper is overloaded, or powder becomes caked, incorrect measurements through the auger feed will result.

Hot chocolate also can be prepared manually from portion controlled mixes packaged in envelopes. Each envelope usually contains 1 to 1¼ oz of powder that will yield 5.5 to 6 oz of finished beverage. Water temperatures should be close to the boiling point, because of heat loss due to agitation and the transferring of liquid from the blender to a cup. The powder is poured into a blending receptacle and hot water added. The receptacle is then set on a blender or mixed for 1 min or until a creamy texture is achieved.

Chilled chocolate beverages served at soda fountains are prepared from syrups and milk. The components are mixed in an electric blender and served. Carbonated water, milk, and syrup combinations require no external agitation. These drinks are prepared in a glass and stirred with a spoon. The syrup used for chilled drinks is metered from a chocolate syrup pump, which fits into a porcelain, stainless steel, or plastic reservoir. When the pump handle or plunger is pressed, about 1 oz of syrup will be delivered to 5–6 oz of liquid. These pumps can be calibrated and should be checked periodically for accuracy.

Spoilage of Hot Chocolate Powder

Biological Spoilage.   Hot chocolate powder products do not generally support microbiological growth because moisture content is too low to support growth of microorganisms. However, condensation of moisture on the surface can permit growth of bacteria and mold. Ambient conditions in and around hot chocolate dispensers of high humidity can condense moisture on dispensing nozzles, in mixing chambers, and in hoppers if lids are not securely fastened.

Hot chocolate concentrates have a milk and sugar base and are susceptible to mold growth. Mold contamination can alter the flavor of the entire drink. It is impossible to remove surface mold and have the remainder of a product free of contamination and palatable. Milk components are subject to bacterial spoilage. Susceptibility varies depending on whether whole milk, sweetened condensed milk, or milk solids are used in manufacturing a concentrate. Milk components also introduce bacteria into finished products, and, if not properly processed, microbiological spoilage may result.

Chocolate syrups can also undergo bacterial spoilage from contaminated cocoa if the syrup is not heated sufficiently during manufacture.

Physical Spoilage.   Hot chocolate powders are hygroscopic and readily absorb moisture. Absorption of moisture causes powders to clump, thus reducing the accuracy of portion control settings on various dispensing machines. This situation will lead to inconsistent drinks. Powdered mixes should be stored in dry areas where the temperature does not exceed 68°F (20°C). Liquid concentrates also require cool storage areas.

Portion control packages of hot chocolate powder can become contaminated with insects. Periodic inspection of package seals and contents should be made to determine presence of insects, which tend to accumulate in and around the paste sealant of a package. Heat-sealed packages or those formed from plastic film will prevent entry of insects unless a powder was contaminated at the time of filling.

Chemical Spoilage. If a high-heat milk powder is used or the water employed for blending is excessively high in temperature, milk solids may curdle, giving a beverage a soured appearance, much the same as using sour cream in coffee. If blending is not adequate, the customer may receive a weak drink and find excessive cocoa residue at the bottom of a cup.

Stock rotation and storage in cool, dry areas are recommended for optimum performance.

12

Food Spoilage and Sanitation Control

Microbial growth which may result in contamination and food spoilage is directly related to two factors: (1) poor sanitary practices, and (2) improper food handling. The latter may be traced to incorrect dry or refrigerated storage or to exposure of food to elevated temperatures for extended periods of time.

External sources may also contribute to food spoilage. Foods that are prepared elsewhere and not examined thoroughly when received may have been contaminated during processing, public storage, or in transit. It is difficult to determine the extent of contamination from appearance, odor, and taste since food may seem acceptable in all these respects when compared with other noncontaminated products. In cases where foods are moldy, discolored, or exhibit other distinct alterations in appearance, spoilage becomes evident. Off-odors and off-tastes may also be clues to contaminated products.

It was previously pointed out that a number of basic factors are responsible for significant quality changes. Spoilage due to microbiological, biochemical, physical, or chemical factors and poor sanitation practices head the list. This chapter examines the reasons underlying these common problems and describes simple remedies and solutions to correct and eliminate them. It is of paramount importance that foodservice personnel at all levels understand food spoilage problems and maintain positive preventive control procedures.

FOOD SPOILAGE AND CONTAMINATION

It is unfortunate that the process and results of food and beverage spoilage cannot be readily observed. The adage "what you don't know won't hurt you" applies to the thinking of a majority of foodservice personnel. If the wording were changed to "what you don't know *can* hurt you," a greater awareness of food and beverage deterioration, its problems and solutions might be achieved.

All foods will deteriorate, some more rapidly than others. Measures must be taken and procedures instituted to ensure correct handling and storage of foods, otherwise spoilage will result, profits will diminish, and customer dissatisfaction will occur.

The importance of preventing spoilage cannot be minimized. The customer demands and has every reason to expect that the food and beverage served to him will be safe, wholesome, and possess all quality attributes. The customer has been well informed through various news media as to restrictions and safeguards enacted by federal, state, and local governments and supposes that all items served are free of contamination, infestation, and adulteration.

It is the purpose of this discussion to show how to prevent spoilage and what can occur if the basic rules of good housekeeping, sanitation, and product handling are neglected.

The study of microbiology is a broad, complex subject. Without at least an elementary knowledge of its scope, one cannot comprehend the significance, importance, and effect of microorganisms on food spoilage. Since this book is limited in coverage, only brief mention can be made of this subject, but an attempt will be made to couple the underlying reasons for spoilage of foods to their corrective measures.

The following list designates the major types of spoilage of foods and beverages: (1) microbiological spoilage, (2) biochemical spoilage, (3) physical spoilage, and (4) chemical spoilage.

Microbiological Spoilage

There are thousands of known species of microorganisms. Not all of these are harmful. Many are valuable and useful in the preservation of food, the production of alcohol, or the development of special flavors. Those used in food production are specially cultured and are employed under controlled conditions. Microbial activity is considered to be a primary cause of food and beverage spoilage. Microorganisms are found everywhere: in the soil, air, and water, and on fruits and vegetables. All food processing equipment, as well as the human body and clothing, is contaminated with various spoilage organisms. The main factors that initiate the growth of microorganisms are suitable temperature, moisture, and a substrate to live on, such as foods and beverages. There are three common forms of microorganisms: (1) bacteria, (2) molds, and (3) yeast.

Bacteria. Bacteria are microscopic unicellular organisms of varying shape and size. The three shapes most commonly encountered are spherical, rod, and spiral. A number of bacterial produce spores which are resistant to heat and chemicals. Commercial sterilization temperatures normally will deactivate these highly resistant spores, however. Bacteria are measured in units called microns. One micron (μ) is equivalent to 1/25,000 in. Most common bacteria range from 1 to 10 or more μ in length and are about 0.5 μ in diameter.

Molds. Molds are larger than bacteria and are more complex in structure. They are members of the plant family, are composed of many cells, usually cylindrical or tubular-shaped. They grow in a network of hairlike fibers called mycelia and send up fruiting bodies that yield spores. These organisms can penetrate the smallest opening, are tenacious, and become anchored to a substance by their hairlike fibers. Molds are probably the most common type of spoilage organism that can be identified by the naked eye. They are recognized by most foodservice personnel. Examples are bread mold and the mold that forms on the surface of meats and cheese products. An outgrowth of mold contamination that is generally readily identifiable is the odor referred to as *mildewy*.

Yeasts. Yeast cells are larger than either molds or bacteria, measuring about 20 μ in length. Yeasts are unicellular plants, are spherical or ellipsoidal in shape, and play an important role in the food industry. They produce enzymes that have a favorable effect on certain chemical reactions, such as leavening of bread and the production of alcohol and glycerol. Yeasts can induce undesirable reactions in such items as citrus juices and fruit-flavored drinks. The result of uncontrolled fermentation is generally identifiable by a sour or vinegary taste.

Biochemical Spoilage

Biochemical spoilage, probably the second greatest source of food deterioration, is caused by natural food enzymes. These are complex catalysts that initiate many complicated reactions. If enzymatic reactions are uncontrolled, then off-flavors, off-odors, and off-colors may develop in foods and beverages. Many foods contain natural enzymes, which under certain conditions produce significant changes, such as enzymatic browning in apples. When the fruit is peeled and exposed to air, apples turn brown due to enzymes activated by oxygen. Natural tenderizing or aging of meat is a desirable result of enzymes. However, conditions favoring these reactions can sometimes cause deterioration due to the undesirable growth of microorganisms.

Microorganisms that proliferate in various foods and beverages produce enzymes that induce significant changes. An example is the production of alcohol by enzymes derived from yeast. Enzyme formation can be controlled in much the same manner as microorganisms. Heat, cold, drying, the addition of certain inhibiting chemicals, and radiation are the principal means used to control and inactivate natural food enzymes.

Physical Spoilage

Physical spoilage can be brought on by temperature changes, moisture, and dryness. Excessive heat destroys emulsions, dehydrates food, and destroys vitamins. Extreme cold can also cause deterioration. A common example is the freezing of milk, which break the emulsion, causing fat to separate. Some sauces exhibit a like tendency.

Excessive moisture in powdered beverage concentrates, such as instant tea or hot chocolate, can support the growth of molds or bacteria. Such moisture levels need not extend throughout the entire product to allow growth. Surface moisture will cause lumping, caking, stickiness, and crystallization in a product. These conditions are prevalent in vending machines and counter-served iced tea or hot chocolate dispensers. Entrapped moisture in protective film packages can damage the contents, creating conditions suitable to support the growth of microorganisms.

Chemical Spoilage

Chemical spoilage may be caused by the interaction of certain ingredients contained in a food or beverage with oxygen (air), by light, or by time (extended storage). Temperature changes can accelerate reactions, producing undesirable chemical changes. In addition, the reaction of incompatible substances in a food or beverage can lead to chemical spoilage. Examples of this are the effects of certain metals on the brewing of coffee and in deep fat frying; and the effect of iron, copper, or other impurities, such as high alkalinity in water used for carbonated beverages.

Algae

Algae are plants that live in fresh and salt water, and on moist surfaces. They are not parasitic and synthesize their nutrients by photosynthesis. Although algae are not important food spoilage organisms, they play an important role in food processing. Irish moss, a form of algae, is used in chocolate milk to hold the chocolate in suspension. In some parts of the world, algae are used as a food (kelp). Certain varieties of algae contain iodine, bromine, and potassium and are used as fertilizer. However, algae can produce undesirable side effects on foods and beverages by influencing water sources.

If they grow in large masses and die, their residues will impart putrid odors and tastes to water. If this water is used for cooking, coffee brewing, or soft drinks, off-flavors and off-odors will be noticeable. Old city water systems may contain large quantities of algae. Steps must be taken to treat water containing algae residues.

FACTORS CAUSING BACTERIAL SPOILAGE

Critical Factors

Three factors are critical to bacterial growth in foods: moisture, temperature, and pH.

The acidity of foods is directly related to the growth of microorganisms. A food that exhibits a pH near neutral (pH 7) favors the growth of organisms, while at a pH of 4.5 or lower, growth of many organisms is inhibited. The following are categories of foods based on their pH:

(1) Low-acid foods—(pH above 5.3) peas, corn, lima beans, meats, fish, poultry, meat pies, dressings, sandwich spreads, and salad mixes, cream-filled and custard-filled pastries.

(2) Medium-acid foods—(pH between 5.3 and 4.5) spinach, asparagus, beets, and pumpkin.

(3) Acid foods—(pH between 4.5 and 3.7) tomatoes, pears, red cabbage, mayonnaise. Due to the number of varieties and hybrids of tomatoes which have relatively high pH's, they should be handled as a medium acid food.

(4) High acid foods—(pH below 3.7) sauerkraut and berries.

Food Frequently Contaminated

To simplify this presentation, a summary follows of those foods, or food mixtures, that must be observed for contamination:

(1) Poultry, meat, and meat products such as meat pies, pressed beef, sausages, cold cooked meats, reheated meats and gravies, salads, casseroles, croquettes

(2) Eggs and egg products such as dried egg powder, egg albumen, frozen egg, synthetic cream

(3) Milk and milk products such as ice cream, cream, sour cream, custards, cream-filled pastries, eggnogs

(4) Fish, prepared fish dishes, and shellfish

INTRODUCTION OF FOOD CONTAMINANTS

There are three areas where foods and beverages can be subjected to contamination.

(1) At the source, e.g., the processor, canner, or manufacturer

(2) In storage, in a freezer, in transit, or in a food establishment's refrigerators.

(3) In preparation in a commissary, kitchen, or counter.

Methods of Prevention

Health habits of personnel involved in food preparation should reflect a number of basic rules of hygiene including: washing hands in hot water, using plenty of soap; drying hands on a clean cloth or paper towel; keeping fingernails short and clean; using hair net or cap; remaining away from food when a person has an infected cut, boil, or other infection of the exposed skin; using transfer tools that are properly cleaned and sanitized; covering sneezes and coughs by means of a tissue or handkerchief; and reporting to management cases of diarrhea, fever, or other serious symptoms so that a job replacement can be made. In addition, all foodservice personnel should receive periodic medical checkups and all new personnel should be given medical examinations to determine freedom from tuberculosis and other infectious diseases or whether he or she is a typhoid carrier.

Insects and rodents such as flies, roaches, rats, and mice are carriers of disease and spoilage-producing organisms. Provisions must be made to eliminate them. Vermin control is necessary as a precautionary measure and should be performed by specialists. Entry points, like loose-fitting doors, pipes, tiles, and broken screens, should be repaired, patched, or replaced.

Overhead and airborne sources of contamination are areas generally neglected. These become breeding grounds for contaminants. Overhead pipes, stairwells and casing, fans, blower blades, stove hoods, window frames, and skylights are areas requiring periodic and systematic cleaning and sanitizing.

Preparation equipment (items used for preparing foods and beverages) include grinders, slicers, choppers, dicers, blenders, mixers, and can openers. An item such as a can opener is rarely sanitized, yet it is one piece of equipment that is in constant use. It is a prime spawning area for microorganisms.

Work surfaces require constant attention, especially if made of wood. Usually a damp cloth is used to wipe the surface, and little thought is given to its sanitary condition. Tables, sandwich boards, meat blocks, breadboards, and other items upon which food is prepared comprise this type of equipment.

Transfer containers and utensils (items which come in intimate contact with foods and beverages for long periods of time) include pots, pans, beaters, scoops, spoons, knives, ladles, and liquid-measuring vessels. All may harbor bacteria and unless completely sanitized become potential sources of food-spoilage organisms.

Table 12.1 is a reference chart of foodborne illnesses and their causes, sources, and effects. This chart was compiled by the National Restaurant Association as a quick guide to the causes of these illnesses, with the intent to help eliminate the sources of contamination.

CAUSES OF FOODBORNE ILLNESSES

The three most common causes of foodborne illnesses in the United States are related to the ingestion of:

(1) *Staphylococcus aureus*
(2) *Salmonella*
(3) *Clostridium perfringens*

TABLE 12.1. Foodborne Illnesses: Their Causes, Sources, and Effects

Illnesses of Frequent Occurrence

Name of Illness	Causative Agent	Foods Usually Involved	How Introduced into Food	Preventative or Corrective Procedures
Staphylococcus food poisoning	Staphylococcus enterotoxin—a poison developed by *Staphylococcus* when it grows in food	Cooked ham or other meat, chopped or comminuted food, cream-filled or custard pastries, other dairy products, Hollandaise sauce, bread pudding, potato salad, chicken, fish, and other meat salads, "warmed-over" food	Usually food handlers through nasal discharges or purulent local skin infections (acne, pimples, boils, scratches, and cuts)	Refrigerate moist foods during storage periods; minimize use of hands in preparation; exclude unhealthly food handlers (having pimples, boils, and other obvious infections)
Perfringens food poisoning	*Clostridium perfringens*	Meat which has been boiled, steamed, braised, or partially roasted, allowed to cool several hours and subsequently served either cooled or reheated	Natural contaminant of meat	Rapidly refrigerate meat between cooking and use
Salmonellosis	Over 800 types of *Salmonella* bacteria, capable of producing gastrointestinal illness.	Meat and poultry, comminuted foods, egg products, custards, shellfish, soups, gravies, sauces, "warmed-over" foods	Fecal contamination by food handlers; raw contaminated meat and poultry, liquid eggs, and unpasteurized milk	By good personal habits of food handlers; sufficient cooking and refrigeration of perishable foods; eliminate rodents and flies
Salmonellosis (a) typhoid fever (b) paratyphoid A	*Salmonella typhosa* S. *paratyphi* A	Moist foods, dairy products, shellfish, raw vegetables, and water	By food handlers and other carriers	Prohibit carriers from handling food; require strict personal cleanliness in food preparation; eliminate flies

(continued)

TABLE 12.1. *(Continued)*

Illnesses of Less Frequent or Rare Occurrence

Name of Illness	Causative Agent	Foods Usually Involved	How Introduced into Food	Preventative or Corrective Procedures
Streptococcus food infection (beta-type), scarlet fever, and strep throat	Beta-hemolytic streptococci	Foods contaminated with nasal or oral discharges from case or carrier	Coughing, sneezing, or handling	Exclude food handlers with known strep infections
Streptococcus infection (alpha-type) (intestinal)	Enterococcus group; pyogenic group	Foods contaminated with excreta on unclean hands	By unsanitary food handling	Same as above; thorough cooking of food and refrigeration of moist food during storage periods
Botulism	Toxins of *Clostridium botulinum*	Improperly processed or unrefrigerated foods of low acidity	Soil and dirt; spores not killed in inadequately heated foods	Pressure cook canned foods with pH over 4.0; home-canned foods boil 20 minutes after removal from can or jars; cook foods thoroughly after removing before serving; discard all foods in swollen unopened cans
Bacillary dysentery (shigellosis)	*Shigella* bacteria	Foods contaminated with excreta on unclean hands	By unsanitary food handling	Strict personal cleanliness in food preparation; refrigeration of moist foods; exclude carriers
Amebic dysentery	*Endamoeba histolytica*	Foods contaminated with excreta on unclean hands	By unsanitary food handlers	Protect water supplies; ensure strict personal cleanliness with food handlers; exclude carriers
Trichinosis	Larvae of *Trichinella spiralis*	Raw or insufficiently cooked pork or pork products (also whale, seal, bear, or walrus meat)	Raw pork from hogs fed uncooked infected garbage	Thoroughly cook pork and pork products over 150°F (66°C), preferably to 160°F (71°C)

234

Fish tapeworm	Parasitic larvae	Raw or insufficiently cooked fish containing live larvae	Fish infested from contaminated water	Cook fish thoroughly; avoid serving raw fish
Arsenic, fluoride, lead poisoning (insecticides, rodenticides)		Any foods accidentally contaminated	Either during growing period or by accident in kitchen	Thoroughly wash all fresh fruits and vegetables when received; store insecticides and pesticides away from food; properly label containers; follow use instructions; *use carefully*; guard food from chemical contamination
Copper poisoning	Copper food contact surfaces	Acid foods and carbonated liquids	Contact between metal and acid food or carbonated beverages	Prevent acid foods or carbonated liquids from coming into contact with exposed copper
Cadmium and zinc poisoning	Metal plating on food containers	Fruit juices, fruit gelatin, and other acid foods stored in metal-plated containers	Acid foods dissolve cadmium and zinc from containers in which stored	Discontinue use of cadmium-plated utensils as food containers; prohibit use of zinc-coated utensils for preparation, storage, and serving of acid fruits and other foods or beverages
Cyanide	Silver polish		Failure to thoroughly wash and rinse polished silverware	Discontinue use of cyanide based silver polish, or wash and rinse silverware *thoroughly*

Source: The National Restaurant Association.

The previous methods of prevention in general are applicable to all three of these organisms. However, each pathogen is unique, and an understanding of the differences in growth patterns, disease symptoms, etc., is important for adequate quality control.

Staphylococcus Food Intoxication

Organism. *Staphylococcus aureus* microscopically appears like clusters of grapes or in pairs and short chains. Some are very salt-tolerant (10–20% NaCl) and also fairly nitrite-tolerant. Some are fermentative and proteolytic but usually do not produce obnoxious odors in foods or make them appear unattractive. Other food bacteria, competing with "staph," may repress growth, but this varies with the kind and number of competitors, type of food, time, and temperature. Ordinarily, "staph" in foods are in low numbers and are outnumbered by competitors, but this competition may not occur in foods that have been heated, so unrestricted growth of "staph" may ensue. Primary sources of "staph" are the upper respiratory tract (especially the nose), skin of humans, skin of poultry, and mammary glands of cows. Investigations have shown many humans who are nasal carriers of "staph."

Enterotoxin. Appreciable toxin is produced only after considerable growth of organisms (10^6–10^9/g or ml). Appreciable amounts are usually produced between 60° and 115°F (16° and 46°C), with production best at 104°F (40°C). Type of food apparently affects the amount of toxin produced, with starchy and protein foods encouraging toxin production. Little toxin is produced in salmon, but much in meat products and custard. The toxin is very heat-stable and is not inactivated by normal cooking processes. Heat processing most likely would kill "staph" bacteria so that no "staph" could be detected in food products examined by laboratory methods.

Disease. Individuals differ in susceptibility to "staph" toxin, so that a group eating contaminated food will contain some who become very ill, more, moderately ill, and possibly some who are affected little or not at all. The incubation period usually is short, usually 2–4 hr (ranging from 1 to 8 hr). Symptoms include nausea, vomiting, retching, abdominal pain of varying severity, diarrhea (all more or less violent), headache, sweating, and chills. Prostration and weakness may also occur. Body temperature usually is subnormal and duration is brief, 1–2 days.

Conditions Necessary for Outbreak. At least four conditions must occur to implicate "staph" food intoxication:

(1) Food must contain toxin-producing "staph."
(2) Food must be a good medium for growth and toxin production by the "staph."
(3) Temperature must be favorable to growth and enough time must be allowed for production of toxin.
(4) Toxin-bearing food must be eaten.

Foodborne Salmonellosis

Organism. Salmonellosis may result following the ingestion of living cells of the genus *Salmonella*, which are Gram-negative, nonsporeforming rods that grow between 44° and 114°F (7° and 46°C), with the optimum being 98.6°F (37°C) but that also may grow well at room temperature. The pH range for growth is 4–9. Depending upon food and serotype, *Salmonella* differ in heat resistance due to various environmental factors. The likelihood of infections depends on number of organisms consumed with food (usually 10^5–10^9/g), resistance of the consumer (age and general health), and virulence of the serotype. The more organisms in the food eaten, the shorter the incubation period.

Disease. Individuals differ in susceptibility to infection. The incubation period ranges from 6 to 72 hr, usually 12–36 hr. The symptoms include acute gastroenteritis, with inflammation in the small intestine (resulting in sudden onset of abdominal pain), diarrhea, nausea, vomiting, and a moderate fever. Headache and chills may precede these. Usually the symptoms persist for 2–3 days (range 1–7) followed by uncomplicated recovery. Laboratory studies of any leftover incriminated foods and the patient's stools should be done to isolate a *Salmonella* serotype. Cases should be reported to public health authorities.

Clostridium perfringens Gastroenteritis

Organism. *Clostridium perfringens* type A is a Gram-positive, anaerobic (not using atmospheric oxygen), sporeforming rod with a pH growth range of 5–9. Growth can occur between 60° and about 125°F (16° and 52°C), with the optimum between 110° and 117°F (43° and 47°C). This organism has exacting nutritional requirements, requiring 13 to 14 amino acids and 5 to 6 vitamins. Under good conditions, a generation time is only 10–12 min. Spores can survive cooking, so long, slow cooling and nonrefrigerated storage encourage multiplication. Counts of 10^6/g or higher in food are usually associated with illness. The organism is found in soil, dust, and the intestinal tracts of animals and humans.

Disease. Symptoms normally appear in 8–22 hr (mean = 10 hr) after consuming food. Sudden acute inflammation of stomach and intestine occurs causing abdominal pain and diarrhea. Vomiting and fever are usually absent. This is a relatively mild disease of short duration, one day or less.

Conditions Necessary for Outbreak. At least four conditions must occur to implicate gastroenteritis:

(1)   Food must contain or become contaminated with *C. perfringens*.

(2)   Food must be cooked and oxygen eliminated resulting in the anaerobic conditions necessary for bacterial growth (food usually cooked the previous day or several hours in advance of serving, giving bacteria chance to multiply).

(3)   Food must be held at an inadequate temperature (neither hot enough nor cold enough) to give bacteria a favorable environment for appreciable growth.

(4)   Food must be consumed without reheating so a large number of bacteria are consumed (over 10^6/g of food).

SANITATION PROCEDURES

Poor sanitation heads the list of all contributing factors responsible for low quality beverages and becomes a dominating element in the reduction of food quality. In many instances, incomplete sanitation leaves behind enough contaminants on equipment to cause definite off-tastes and off-flavors. A lack of understanding of the need for sanitation, improper procedures on automated equipment, along with little or no personnel training are the three basic reasons for this widespread problem.

Sanitation consists of two parts: (1) cleaning and (2) sanitizing.

Cleaning means the removal of residues of food, dirt, dust, foreign material, or other soiling ingredients or materials.

Sanitizing means the effective bactericidal treatment of clean surfaces of equipment and utensils. Effective treatment is defined as equivalent to that of a solution containing 50 ppm of available chlorine.

Sanitation within foodservice establishments can best be understood if it is separated into the following four divisions, each requiring a different approach and procedure: (1) warewashing and sanitizing, (2) equipment cleaning and sanitizing, (3) interior cleaning (tables, counters, floors, toilets, and storage areas), and (4) exterior cleaning (sidewalks, parking areas, trash storage areas, and windows).

Detergents

Detergents are classified as cleaning agents and include soaps, synthetic powders, liquids, solvents, or abrasives such as sand. Generally, detergents that are packaged for laundering, dishwashing, and surface scouring are referred to as cleaners. They are products which have soapy characteristics without having the disadvantages commonly found when soap is used in hard water.

Soap is the product formed by saponification of fats, oils, waxes, resins, or their acids, with organic or inorganic bases (alkalies). Under acid conditions or in hard water, the detergent properties of soap are destroyed. Soap forms a precipitate with the hard salts of water, resulting in undesirable films and a considerable waste of soap. For example, 1.5 lb of pure soap is destroyed per 100 gal. of water per grain of hardness.

Detergents are formulated from a number of different compounds, and include the following:

(1) *Alkalies*, which help soften water by precipitating hard ions and saponify fats. Alkalies used are caustic soda, sodium metasilicate, soda ash, or trisodium phosphate.

(2) *Complex phosphates*, which emulsify, disperse, and suspend fats and oils, soften water by sequestering, and provide rinsability characteristics without being corrosive. Sodium tetraphosphate, sodium tripolyphosphate, sodium pyrophosphate, or sodium hexametaphosphate is used for this purpose.

(3) *Organic and inorganic compounds*, which act as chelating and wetting agents, include mineral or organic acids. Chelating agents soften water, prevent mineral deposits, and peptize proteins without being corrosive. Wetting agents emulsify and disperse fats, help water to wet solids, form suds, and are rinsable without being corrosive. Organic acids (citric, gluconic, or hydroxyacetic acid) prevent material deposits and soften water without being corrosive. Inorganic acids prevent mineral deposits and soften water; hydrochloric, sulfuric, nitric, and phosphoric acids are used for this purpose.

Detergents are grouped according to the kinds of work they perform. There are three types: (1) neutral, (2) alkaline, and (3) acid. Neutral types are used for cleaning floors, similar structures, and walls. Alkaline types are used for routine and heavy-duty cleaning. Most food deposits are slightly acid and require an alkaline detergent to neutralize and dissolve them. This type is employed on beverage dispensers, glasses and most preparation equipment. Acid types are used to remove lime deposits and to neutralize or dissolve deposit accumulation. Deposits in coffee urn jackets, heaters, and inside washing machines are best removed by acid detergents.

Germicides or Sanitizers

Germicides and sanitizers are chemicals that destroy or inactivate bacteria on dishes, pots, pans, tables, floors, and all equipment surfaces contacting food or beverages. For products to meet this classification they must be registered with the U.S. Department of Agriculture. Sometimes a sanitizer is combined with a detergent: the product is then called a "detergent-sanitizer."

Sanitizing agents must be used correctly to be effective. Too little will not do the job and too much is wasteful. Instructions should be written and posted for proper formulation with water and subsequent use. These agents, if properly used, are a prime safeguard against the growth of microorganisms. In addition to those areas already listed, germicidal agents should be used when cleaning storage rooms and all refrigerating equipment.

Hot Water

Requirements. Hot water in sufficient quantities and at correct temperatures is essential for sanitation of equipment and warewashing.

Foodservice establishments need large volumes of 140°–195°F (61°–91°C) water so that all peak demands can be met. Capacity and recovery are essential to an efficient hot water system. When the selection of a hot water system is made, several basic criteria should be considered.

(1) The system should be oversized to allow for business growth and unforeseen demands.

(2) Domestic heaters should not be considered, as they will not produce hot water in sufficient quantity or in the temperature range necessary for commercial application.

(3) A two-temperature system should be installed, one for general-purpose water at 140°F (61°C) and the other at 180°–195°F (83°–91°C) for sanitizing; the latter is called high-temperature water.

Hot Water Systems. Three hot water heating systems are available, including: automatic, instantaneous, and circulating tank equipment.

Automatic storage water heaters are self-contained, thermostatically controlled units which supply hot water for immediate use upon demand at a rated flow, and require no separate external tank.

Circulating tank water heaters are units requiring a separate external storage tank; these units heat water as it passes through a heater and is being returned to a storage tank. The water temperature in a storage tank is thermostatically controlled.

High-Temperature Water. An adequate dependable supply of high-temperature water (180°–195°F, 83°–91°C) is essential for final rinse operation of dishwashing machines. The high temperatures required for effective sanitization make it uneconomical and unsafe to maintain general-purpose water at such temperatures. Therefore, a separate hot water generating system is normally required; this should be properly sized, installed, and operated to deliver a water volume at the flow pressure and temperatures required as specified (Section 6, NSF Standard No. 5, Commercial Gas Fired and Electrically Heated Hot Water Generating Equipment for food establishments using dishwashing machines).

Hot Water for Beverages. Coffee brewing equipment such as urns and semiautomatic or fully automatic half-gallon brewers have water heaters built into each unit. This water, however, is not hot enough for tea service. An auxiliary source is needed to deliver water at 212°F (100°C) for this purpose. If counter-type instantaneous water heaters are installed, periodic temperature checks should be made of this equipment. These temperature checks are necessary where hard water conditions exist because of liming and scaling that will affect thermostat relays.

Strict Cleaning Schedules Are Important

Cleaning chores are usually very difficult to maintain on a strict schedule. Regardless of the size of an operation, a sanitation schedule must be evolved that will include every area, machine, and all preparation equipment within the premises. A schedule should include the following information: (1) area or name of equipment to be cleaned, (2) steps necessary for daily sanitation, (3) steps necessary for weekly or monthly cleaning, (4) names of employees assigned to each task, (5) period of the day or shift when chores should be performed. One employee should be assigned the task of caring for all cleaning equipment, such as rags, sponges, mops, and brushes. When not in use, these should be stored in a utility closet, with a sink provided. Cleaning equipment should be rinsed and cleaned before storage. Cleaning fluids and powders must be handled in a careful manner and kept far removed from the food preparation area. They should be mixed in a utility closet and dispensed from there when needed. Rags should be lint-free, enough being available so that each job can begin with clean cloths. Good rags are expensive and should be laundered and stored in the same manner as tablecloths and napkins. Sponges should be rinsed in a sanitizer and allowed to dry. Greasy, sour, or dirty sponges, if used, will only increase the sanitation washload.

It should be remembered that faulty sanitation will downgrade food quality. Grease, soap, or detergent residues that adhere to dishes, glasses, pots, or other equipment will contaminate food in varying degrees. This can result in a flavor or taste defect.

CLEANING AND CARE OF FOOD PREPARATION EQUIPMENT

Equipment sanitation is based on simple cleaning procedures. Ranges, ovens, broilers, steamers, kettles, and other production equipment require simple but consistent programs. Beverage dispensers like coffee brewers, soft drink units, milk, and cream devices require a more complete program of cleaning and sanitizing.

Each employee should be instructed and shown how to clean the equipment he or she works with. Schedules and lists of procedures should be posted in the vicinity of each unit. Some equipment may require twice-daily, daily, weekly, or monthly cleaning. The following discussions are examples of cleaning and sanitizing procedures required as an important segment of quality control.

Range

(1) Remove all burnt sediment and wipe grease from top of range after each operation.

(2) Scrape grease from cracks, openings, and hinges. A wire brush may be used for this procedure.

(3) When cool, wash top of range.

(4) Run oiled cloth over top of range.

(5) Clean oven by removing grates, scrape off food deposits, wash with a mild detergent solution and dry.

(6) Keep burners clean. If removable, soak, boil, and scrub with a stiff brush, rinse and dry. This procedure is for gas-fired ranges. Clean with brush only if electrically heated.

(7) Before replacing burner, rub with oiled lint-free cloth.

Bake Oven

(1) Clean outside of an oven when cool. Use a soft wire brush to remove debris and then wipe with a mild detergent solution.

(2) Clean steel shelves. Brush with wire brush and wipe with detergent solution. Rinse with moist cloth and dry.

(3) Wipe heat controls with damp cloth. Don't rub dials too hard as this may loosen them.

(4) Clean thermometers and heat sensing devices. Rub lightly to avoid damage to these parts.

Broiler

(1) Remove grid and drain pan. Clean, wash, rinse thoroughly, and dry after each use.

(2) Wash outside, rinse and dry.

(3) Wipe with lint-free oiled cloth.

(4) Clean grease pan. Wash with detergent solution and dry.

Deep Fat Fryer

(1) Drain off fat and filter out sediment. See Chapter 6 for additional procedure.

(2) Fill with water and detergent and boil. Drain completely.

(3) Fill with water, add 1 cup of vinegar, and boil. Drain and flush several times.

(4) After several rinsings, dry interior with lint-free cloth, and wipe exterior of fryer.

Steamers

(1) Remove racks or shelves and clean drains.
(2) Wash interior cavity daily.
(3) Wash exterior and doors. Remove food soil with lint-free cloth or soft brush.
(4) Check gaskets and clean food soil from gaskets. Check for debris which may have lodged behind gasket. Such conditions may distort or tear gasket.
(5) Clean strainers, pressure relief valves, and other accessories referring to manufacturer's instructions.

Toasters

(1) Wipe off all crumbs and burnt debris after each use.
(2) Clean crumb tray after each use.
(3) Soft brush operating parts gently. Do not use paper or cloth toweling for this step.
(4) Wipe exterior with a damp lintless cloth.

Waffle Iron

(1) Wipe baking surfaces frequently.
(2) Brush out grids.
(3) Place a damp cloth between grids overnight (weekly if iron is used daily).
(4) Reseason by brushing waffle iron with an edible oil, closing, and heating for 5 min.
(5) Food release agents can be effective when sprayed on heating surfaces such as waffle irons, griddles, saucepans, cutters, fry-pans, and other surfaces where food sticking may be a problem. These agents usually contain a lecithin base with a propellant.

Mixers

(1) Use rubber scraper if necessary and wash bowl and beaters immediately after using.
(2) If a mixer is used for mashing potatoes, egg mixtures, or flour batters, rinse bowl and whips with cold water before washing with warm water. The use of a sanitizing solution is advisable followed by rinsing.
(3) After drying, the bowls and beaters should be hung in a dry area.
(4) Wipe exterior parts of the machine with a lint-free cloth.

Grinders and Attachments

(1) Remove disk and nut and withdraw grinding or cutting parts.
(2) Remove food particles by holding under warm water. Dip into a sanitizing solution. Rinse and dry.
(3) Interior of a grinder should be flushed with a sanitizing solution after removal of food particles. Rinse and allow to air dry.

Slicers

(1) Clean immediately after using, especially after slicing vegetables and fruits.
(2) Disassemble all parts for ease of cleaning.
(3) Clean cutting blade with a damp cloth, followed by a sanitizing solution. Rinse and allow to dry, then wipe with an edible oil.
(4) Wash carriage slides thoroughly. Sanitize, rinse, and allow to dry.
(5) Wipe exterior with a lint-free cloth.
(6) Lift slicer and remove any food particles lodged under slicer and around legs. Sanitize stand or pedestal.
(7) Wash, sanitize, rinse, and dry slicer guards.

Can Openers

(1) Remove shank from base and scrub in hot detergent solution.
(2) Use a wire brush to remove deposits and then rinse in hot water. Remove and dip into a sanitizing solution; allow to drain and wipe blade with a paper towel to prevent rust.
(3) Wipe base of a can opener with a cloth dampened in hot water to which a sanitizer has been added.
(4) Inspect cutting blades and sharpen if necessary. Nicked blades should be discarded. Watch for tiny particles of metal shreds from cans, which may fall into foods and are very dangerous.

CLEANING AND CARE OF COFFEE PREPARATION AND SERVING EQUIPMENT

Urns

Daily Procedures.   Always rinse an urn immediately after each use. First, rinse with a small amount of water to remove sediment and old coffee from the bottom of an urn and the drainage lines. Put 1 gal. or more of hot water in urn and brush inside carefully; drain and rerinse with hot water until it runs clean. The urn is now ready for the next batch.

If coffee is being served during peak periods, and time is short, brushing may have to be omitted, but be sure that the urn is at least flushed with 1 gal. of hot water between uses. If the urn has an automatic brew water system, activate it so that rinse water can be obtained from this source.

Where restaurants have a single urn, a standby half-gallon decanter can be used into which the final portion of coffee can be drawn to permit a rinse between each batch. Where single urns prevail, brewing coffee on top of coffee is not recommended.

At the end of each day, further cleaning is necessary. Pour 1 or 2 gal. of hot water into the liner and scrub it thoroughly, then rinse until clean and shiny.

Of prime importance are faucets. These must be cleaned thoroughly. Obviously an urn liner is only touched by a comparatively small amount of coffee beverage; however, all of the brew that is drawn passes through a faucet line and faucet. To ensure proper maintenance, use faucets that are easily cleaned (Fig. 12.1). Some older types, though they operate satisfactorily, are extremely difficult to clean. As a result they are often ignored and consequently become coated with deposit and frequently freeze into position and cannot be taken apart and cleaned. Remove cleanout cap at the end of a faucet and scrub pipe leading to the center of urn. Make use of a gauge brush for this step. At the same time, the gauge glass should be brushed and rinsed.

After cleaning is completed, put 1 or 2 gal. of freshwater into an urn and leave until the next use. Remove cover and clean. When replacing a lid, leave it slightly ajar to permit free circulation of air in the interior.

FIG. 12.1.   Urn faucet designed for easy cleaning.
Courtesy of Coffee Brewing Center.

Semiweekly Procedures.   Although it would be desirable to have urns cleaned daily with urn cleaner, it is extremely difficult to reach this standard. Therefore, a compromise has been reached and foodservice establishments are encouraged to clean their urns thoroughly twice a week with urn cleaner.

Most urn cleaners contain trisodium phosphate or oxygenated compounds. Care must be exercised when using either type to be sure that water is placed in an urn before adding the contents of a detergent package. These cleaners should not be used on aluminum as they will corrode the metal. If conventional urn detergent is not available, baking soda can be used successfully, and it has no corrosive effects on aluminum.

Never use an abrasive on an urn or filtering device. There are two reasons for this. First, there is the possibility of causing flakes which may not be rinsed out and can pass into the consumer's cup, and second, the probability of scratching the metal surface, which in turn will lead to pitting, corrosion, and deposits.

Prior to cleaning, be sure that the outer jacket is three-fourths full of water. Follow the directions on the urn cleaner package when possible, otherwise add 1 tbsp of cleaner to each gallon of water. Draw off 1 gal. of detergent solution and pour it back into the urn liner. This is done to permit the urn cleaner to get down into the faucet. The repouring also serves to fully mix the urn cleaner and water. Allow the solution to remain in the urn for 30 min.

Scrub the urn liner thoroughly with a long-handled brush (Fig. 12.2) and follow by scouring the gauge glass and faucet pipeline (Fig. 12.3). Be sure the entire faucet is disassembled (Fig. 12.4) so that all components can be cleaned. Inspect seat cup and replace if worn or brittle (Fig. 12.5). Rinse urn

FIG. 12.2.   Cleaning the urn liner.
Courtesy of Coffee Brewing Center.

FIG. 12.3.   Cleaning the gauge glass.
Courtesy of Coffee Brewing Center.

FIG. 12.4.   Replacement of faucet seat cup.
Courtesy of Leo Perell.

INSPECTION REPORT
FOOD SERVICE ESTABLISHMENTS

Permit No. _____
Type _____ NSD

CITY, COUNTY OR DISTRICT	NAME OF ESTABLISHMENT	ADDRESS	OWNER OR OPERATOR

Sir: Based on an inspection this day, the items marked below identify the violation in operation or facilities which must be corrected by the next routine inspection or such shorter period of time as may be specified in writing by the health authority. Failure to comply with this notice may result in immediate suspension of your permit (or down-grading of the establishment).* An opportunity for an appeal will be provided if a written request for a hearing is filed with the health authority within the period of time established in this notice for the correction of violations.

SECTION B. FOOD
1. FOOD SUPPLIES

Item		Demerit points	Bakery products	Poultry and poultry products	Meat and meat products	Frozen desserts	Shellfish	Milk and milk products	Specify:
1	Approved source	6							
2	Wholesome - not adulterated	6							
3	Not misbranded	2							
4	Original container; properly identified	2							
5	Approved dispenser								
6	Fluid milk and fluid milk products pasteurized	6							
7	Low-acid and non-acid foods commercially canned	6							

2. FOOD PROTECTION

Item		Demerit points	Preparation	Storage	Display	Service	Transportation
8	Protected from contamination	4					
9	Adequate facilities for maintaining food at hot or cold temperatures	2					

SECTION D. FOOD EQUIPMENT AND UTENSILS
1. SANITARY DESIGN, CONSTRUCTION AND INSTALLATION OF EQUIPMENT AND UTENSILS

Item		Good repair; no cracks	No chips, pits or open seams	Cleanable; smooth	Approved material	No corrosion	Proper construction	Accessible for cleaning and inspection	Demerit points
31	Food-contact surfaces of equipment								2
32	Utensils								2
33	Non-food-contact surfaces of equipment								2
34	Single-service articles of non-toxic materials								2
35	Equipment properly installed								2
36	Existing equipment capable of being cleaned, non-toxic, properly installed, and in good repair								2

2. CLEANLINESS OF EQUIPMENT AND UTENSILS

Item			Demerit points
37	Tableware clean to sight and touch		4
38	Kitchenware and food-contact surfaces of equipment clean to sight and touch		
39	Grills and similar cooking devices cleaned daily		
40	Non-food-contact surfaces of equipment kept clean		2
41	Detergents and abrasives rinsed off food-contact surfaces		2

No.	Item	Points
11	Perishable food at proper temperature	2
12	Potentially hazardous food at 45°F. or below, or 140°F. or above as required	6
13	Frozen food kept frozen; properly thawed	2
14	Handling of food minimized by use of suitable utensils	4
15	Hollandaise sauce of fresh ingredients; discarded after three hours	6
16	Food cooked to proper temperature	6
17	Fruits and vegetables washed thoroughly	2
18	Containers of food stored off floor on clean surfaces	2
19	No wet storage of packaged food	2
20	Display cases, counter protector devices or cabinets of approved type	2
21	Frozen dessert dippers properly stored	2
22	Sugar in closed dispensers or individual packages	2
23	Unwrapped and potentially hazardous food not re-served	4
24	Poisonous and toxic materials properly identified, colored, stored and used; poisonous polishes not present	
25	Bactericides, cleaning and other compounds properly stored and non-toxic in use dilutions	6

SECTION C. PERSONNEL
1. HEALTH AND DISEASE CONTROL

No.	Item	Points
26	Persons with boils, infected wounds, respiratory infections or other communicable disease properly restricted	6
27	Known or suspected communicable disease cases reported to health authority	6

2. CLEANLINESS

No.	Item	Points
28	Hands washed and clean	6
29	Clean outer garments; proper hair restraints used	2
30	Good hygienic practices	4

No.	Item	Points
43	Utensils and equipment pre-flushed, scraped or soaked	2
44	Tableware sanitized	2
45	Kitchenware and food-contact surfaces of equipment used for potentially hazardous food sanitized	4
46	Facilities for washing and sanitizing equipment and utensils approved, adequate, properly constructed, maintained and operated	4
47	Wash and sanitizing water clean	2
48	Wash water at proper temperature	2
49	Dish tables and drain boards provided, properly located and constructed	2
50	Adequate and suitable detergents used	2
51	Approved thermometers provided and used	2
52	Suitable dish baskets provided	
53	Proper gauge cocks provided	
54	Cleaned and sanitized utensils and equipment properly stored and handled; utensils air-dried	2
55	Suitable facilities and areas provided for storing utensils and equipment	
56	Single-service articles properly stored, dispensed and handled	2
57	Single-service articles used only once	2
58	Single-service articles used when approved washing and sanitizing facilities are not provided	6

SECTION E. SANITARY FACILITIES AND CONTROLS
1. WATER SUPPLY

No.	Item	Points
59	From approved source; adequate; safe quality	6
60	Hot and cold running water provided	4
61	Transported water handled, stored; dispensed in a sanitary manner	6
62	Ice from approved source; made from potable water	6
63	Ice machines and facilities properly located, installed and maintained	2
64	Ice and ice handling utensils properly handled and stored; block ice rinsed	6 / 2
65	Ice-contact surfaces approved; proper material and construction	2

FIG. 12.5. Sanitation inspection report for foodservice establishments.
From Food Service Sanitation Manual, U.S. Public Health.

Item		Demerit Points
	2. SEWAGE DISPOSAL	
66	Into public sewer, or approved private facilities	6
	3. PLUMBING	
67	Properly sized, installed and maintained	2
68	Non-potable water piping identified	1
69	No cross connections	6
70	No back siphonage possible	
71	Equipment properly drained	2
	4. TOILET FACILITIES	
72	Adequate, conveniently located, and accessible; properly designed and installed	6
73	Toilet rooms completely enclosed, and equipped with self-closing, tight-fitting doors; doors kept closed	2
74	Toilet rooms, fixtures and vestibules kept clean, in good repair, and free from odors	2
75	Toilet tissue and proper waste receptacles provided; waste receptacles emptied as necessary	2
	5. HAND-WASHING FACILITIES	
76	Lavatories provided, adequate, properly located and installed	6
77	Provided with hot and cold or tempered running water through proper fixtures	4
78	Suitable hand cleanser and sanitary towels or approved hand-drying devices provided	2
79	Waste receptacles provided for disposable towels	2
80	Lavatory facilities clean and in good repair	2

Item		Demerit Points
	SECTION F. OTHER FACILITIES	
	1. FLOORS, WALLS AND CEILINGS	
91	Floors kept clean; no sawdust used	2
92	Floors easily cleanable construction, in good repair, smooth, non-absorbent; carpeting in good repair	1
93	Floor graded and floor drains, as required	2
94	Exterior walking and driving surfaces clean; drained	2
95	Exterior walking and driving surfaces properly surfaced	1
96	Mats and duck boards cleanable, removable and clean	2
97	Floors and wall junctures properly constructed	2
98	Walls, ceilings and attached equipment clean	2
99	Walls and ceilings properly constructed and in good repair; coverings properly attached	1
100	Walls of light color; washable to level of splash	2
	2. LIGHTING	
101	20 foot-candles of light on working surfaces	
102	10 foot-candles of light on food equipment, utensil-washing, hand-washing areas and toilet rooms	2
103	5 foot-candles of light 30" from floor in all other areas	
104	Artificial light sources as required	2
	3. VENTILATION	
105	Rooms reasonably free from steam, condensation, smoke, etc.	2
106	Rooms and equipment vented to outside as required	2
107	Hoods properly designed; filters removable	2

6. GARBAGE AND RUBBISH DISPOSAL

No.	Item	Value
81	Stored in approved containers; adequate in number	2
82	Containers cleaned when empty; brushes provided	2
83	When not in continuous use, covered with tight fitting lids, or in protective storage inaccessible to vermin	2
84	Storage areas adequate; clean; no nuisances; proper facilities provided	2
85	Disposed of in an approved manner, at an approved frequency	2
86	Garbage rooms or enclosures properly constructed; outside storage at proper height above ground or on concrete slab	2

7. VERMIN CONTROL

No.	Item	Value
87	Food waste grinders and incinerators properly installed, constructed and operated; incinerators areas clean	2
88	Presence of rodents, flies, roaches and vermin minimized	4
89	Outer openings protected against flying insects as required; rodent-proofed	2
90	Harborage and feeding of vermin prevented	2

No.	Item	Value
108	Intake air ducts properly designed and maintained	1
109	Systems comply with fire prevention requirements; no nuisance created	2

4. DRESSING ROOMS AND LOCKERS

No.	Item	Value
110	Dressing rooms or areas as required; properly located	1
111	Adequate lockers or other suitable facilities	1
112	Dressing rooms, areas and lockers kept clean	2

5. HOUSEKEEPING

No.	Item	Value
113	Establishment and property clean, and free of litter	2
114	No operations in living or sleeping quarters	2
115	Floors and walls cleaned after closing or between meals by dustless methods	2
116	Laundered clothes and napkins stored in clean place	4
117	Soiled linen and clothing stored in proper containers	2
118	No live birds or animals other than guide dogs	2

DEMERIT SCORE OF THE ESTABLISHMENT _____

REMARKS _____

Date _____   Health Authority _____

FIG. 12.5. (Continued).

liner 3 or 4 times with hot water. Repeat this procedure until all traces of foreign odors and cleaning solution are removed. This step is extremely difficult, however, and rinsing must be continued until equipment is entirely clean and fresh.

Make sure urn cover is cleaned. Since it has to be removed before cleaning can start, it is usually placed to one side and completely ignored. It is essential that a lid be cleaned. A lid of an urn full of coffee will be coated with water droplets. Hot coffee gives off vapor which rises and condenses on the underside of a cover. Any off-flavor or off-odors on a lid will be passed into the finished beverage.

Sprayheads

Sprayheads should be disassembled and cleaned of residue. Make sure that all holes are open and functioning properly. If clogged, open them with a stiff wire. Sprayhead arms should also be wiped with detergent solution and rinsed.

Gridded Risers and Urn Baskets

These accessories may be cleaned by immersing in an urn cleaner solution and scrubbing with a stiff brush. Rinse thoroughly and allow to dry. If residues are apparent, allow to soak in detergent solution until the residues loosen and then remove them by brushing or wiping them off with a cloth.

Urn Bags and Filter Cloths

A new urn bag or cloth filter should be cleaned and rinsed in very hot water to remove sizing (starch) or any foreign odors and materials. Failure to remove sizing will produce a cloudy beverage and unpalatable taste.

Rinse thoroughly in hot water after each brew. Hot water removes more old deposits than cold water. Do not attempt to wash bags in soap, bleach, or detergent, as these will affect the flavor of a brew.

Store in cold water when not in use. This procedure prevents them from becoming sour and rancid, or picking up foreign odors.

Replace urn bags and cloth filters when necessary. They have no specific wearout period. They should be replaced when signs of wear or tearing develop, and the removal of unpleasant odors becomes impossible. Discoloration does not harm them. Urn rings should be cleaned by following the procedure for gridded risers.

Filter Paper

Filter paper should be checked for signs of mildew or other foreign odors, and discarded if off-odors are apparent. Filter paper should be stored in dry areas, never next to or on top of brewers. When stored, make sure side walls are supported, as any deformity will reduce filtration efficiency.

Urn and Gauge Brushes

These accessories, if not washed or properly cared for, will become sources of contamination because bristles attract coffee resins and other foreign matter. Brushes should be soaked in hot detergent solution and rinsed. If a stale or foreign odor persists, the cleaning procedure should be repeated. When brushes start shedding their bristles, they should be discarded.

Gallon Measures

Gallon measures and other similar accessories used for coffee brewing require thorough and frequent cleaning with urn cleaner. Unfortunately, it is a practice in many restaurants to use these measures as a means of transporting other foods. In addition, they become repositories for odd pieces of cleaning equipment and dirty rags. These units should be cleaned as frequently as a coffee urn.

Water Jackets

Water jackets should be cleaned weekly if located in hard or alkaline water areas, otherwise monthly maintenance is advisable. A water jacket is filled to the scale line and a stripper or deliming agent is added. The temperature is brought to 160°F (72°C), the heat turned off, and it is allowed to stand for 3–4 hr. A warning tag should be hung on the water faucet to prevent use for tea or other drinks. The solution is drained and the jacket rinsed several times until clear.

Water Tanks

Periodic examination of a water tank for lime deposits should be made. A deliming agent can be added and the machine activated for one cycle. The solution should remain in a tank for several hours or overnight. During this period the heat should be left on. When the soaking period is completed, the solution is drained and tanks rinsed several times. Run through two cycles without coffee to rinse out valves and water lines.

Portable Thermal Dispensers

These units should be treated as urns and the same procedures applied. If mineral deposits are observed, they should be removed by applying a descaling or deliming agent. When not in use, fill with several gallons of water and leave the cover ajar to permit free circulation of air in the interior.

Water Strainers

These should be removed from the water line and reversed so the water pressure will dislodge any accumulations of dirt or sediment. Observation should be made of corroded conditions so strainer or wire mesh can be replaced.

Vacuum Brewing Equipment

An effective method for cleaning vacuum brewing equipment is to replace the coffee with a quantity of detergent and then follow the regular brewing procedure. For example, fill the lower bowl with water and add urn cleaner. Bring to a boil and allow solution to rise to the upper bowl. Remove from the heat so the solution returns to the lower bowl. Rinse upper and lower bowls to remove all traces of urn cleaner.

If a bag is used as a filter device, be sure to discard after cleaning, otherwise traces of cleaning compound will adhere and affect the flavor of subsequent brews.

There are two particular trouble spots in vacuum equipment. First, the stem is difficult to clean and becomes coated with deposit. A long-handled brush, such as a gauge brush, can be used effectively for cleaning. Second, the strainer unit must be cleaned thoroughly. If it is a spring type, be sure the coils contain no traces of deposit.

Half-Gallon Brewers

There are many types of half-gallon brewers, so it is difficult to cover these with specific cleaning instructions. Common to many units are the sprayhead, funnel chamber, and serving bowl.

Wipe all stainless steel or metal surfaces of a coffee maker with a damp cloth. If the equipment is stained or streaked, a mild metal cleaning compound may be used. However, these compounds should never be used on surfaces that come in contact with brewing water or brewed coffee.

Metal brewing cartridges should be cleaned with urn cleaner and then rinsed until all traces of detergent are removed.

The sprayhead and surrounding area should be wiped with a cloth dipped in urn cleaner solution. Remove all traces of cleaner with a moist cloth, followed by repeated wiping with clean damp cloths. If sprayhead is designed for easy removal, take it off the machine and dip in cleaner solution, remove, and rinse. Sprayhead holes should be inspected to be sure they are not clogged. If any holes are clogged, remove material with a fine wire or pipe cleaner.

Inspect funnels for residue buildup, especially around spouts. Immerse funnel in cleaner solution until residues soften and then scrub with a brush to remove accumulations. Rinse until free of all traces of detergent. If funnel is equipped with wire screen or metal disc, these should be removed, cleaned, and rinsed.

After equipment has been cleaned, ream out spray water tube and syphon tube. Replace sprayhead and run at least one cycle without coffee in the chamber or funnel to remove all traces of cleaning material. Notice color of brew water. If yellow to dark brown, continue to flush out tank by repeated cycling until water clears. If water does not clear, the water heater may need cleaning or the water inlet line should be checked for contamination.

Serving Decanters and Pots

Decanters and pots (metal, china, thermal) are generally neglected accessories. These units must be cleaned daily, otherwise they will be a source of contamination. Do not rely on dishwashing machines to produce efficient results. This holds true for serving pots which may have inaccessible areas requiring hand wiping. Serving bowls can be cleaned with a curved brush especially constructed for these decanters.

Pour a solution of detergent into a bowl or pot and hand scrub with a brush or cloth until all traces of coffee deposits are removed. Neck areas, where spouts join decanter body, should be given extra care. These areas are most susceptible to residue buildup. Rinse decanters and pots with hot water followed by cold water. If pots have lids, these should not be replaced when stored.

Due to water conditions, interiors of glass bowls may become etched and pitted. If this condition exists, bowls should be discarded as they cannot be cleaned properly and will continue to rapidly build deposits.

CARBONATED DRINK DISPENSERS

High-quality carbonated drinks are dependent on proper cleaning and sanitizing of the dispenser and its accessories. Serving glasses must be given utmost care and scrutiny. Glasses must be cleaned and sanitized thoroughly, otherwise they will become a source of trouble which has nothing to do with the dispensing equipment. Detergent residue and grease will cause excessive foaming and a sloppy overflowing glass.

The following instructions are general; for specific procedures refer to the manufacturer's manual.

Each day flush all waste drains with warm water to prevent clogging with syrup. Inspect faucet nozzles, remove plastic covers, and rinse in warm water. Inspect nozzles every week, using a fine wire or pipe cleaner to remove accumulated dirt and syrup. Wash plastic covers in warm water. Inspect syrup tanks for sediment. Clean exterior of dispenser with damp cloth and dry. Each month, brush radiator grill on the refrigeration unit to remove dirt and dust. Remove and wash syrup tank covers in mild detergent, and rinse in warm water. Dip into approved sanitizing solution, rinse in warm water, and dry completely. Disconnect syrup tanks, empty contents, and drain fully. Pour a quart of mild detergent into tank and swirl with a hand mop. Remove and rinse with warm water. Add a quantity of sanitizing solution and rotate tank so that solution touches all surfaces. Remove and flush with warm water and allow to dry. After prolonged usage and at least once each quarter, the syrup tank and feeder lines must be cleaned and sanitized. This is done by filling a tank with a solution of cleaner and replacing tank cover. Carbon dioxide pressure is applied which will force cleaning solution through the system. Faucets are opened until syrup tanks are empty. This procedure is repeated with a sanitizing solution, followed by rinsing and drying the interior of a tank. Gaskets and tubing connections should be checked for wear and replaced if necessary.

Carbonators should be cleaned monthly. After shutting off the water supply and power, empty carbonator by drawing water out of the faucet. When all the water is removed, CO_2 gas supply is turned off and any remaining gas is purged by opening the faucet and removing the relief valve. Baking soda should be used as a "detergent" by mixing 4 oz of the sodium bicarbonate into 1 qt of warm water. Pour baking soda solution into carbonator, replace relief valve, and allow the solution to remain as long as possible preferably overnight. The CO_2 pressure is built up to about 60 psi (414 kPa) and the cleaning solution removed by opening each faucet. The water supply and power are turned on and when carbonator is filled, a few glasses are drawn off and checked for proper taste and absence of foreign flavors. If evidence of foreign flavor is found, continue to flush until it becomes clear.

BULK MILK DISPENSERS

Bulk milk dispensers are mechanically refrigerated cabinets fitted with dispensing mechanisms which are designed to refrigerate and dispense servings of milk either manually or by mechanical actuation.

Two contact zones of a dispenser require daily cleaning and sanitizing, namely, the milk contact zone and splash zone. Milk surface zones are those surfaces which normally contact milk, and include those surfaces that drain back into areas normally in contact with milk. Splash zones are those surfaces which are subjected to routine splash, spillage, and contamination during normal use.

Inside areas must be emptied every day. When all traces of milk are removed, the interior is scrubbed with a cleaning and sanitizing solution dissolved in hot water (120°F, 49°C). After application of a sanitizer-cleaner solution, follow with a thorough rinsing. Nozzles and dispensing arms are disassembled and dipped in the same solution used for the interior, followed by rinsing and drying. Outside surfaces are sprayed or wiped with an appropriate cleaner and dried.

In addition to the daily routine, twice a week a solution of delimer or stripper is used to rid all surfaces of milk films or milk stone which may have formed.

CREAM DISPENSERS

Cleaning

A cream dispenser should be disassembled to its smallest component parts, dispensing spouts, "O" rings, springs, etc. All parts should be rinsed with warm water (100°F, 39°C) and then washed with hot water (120°F, 49°C) and an appropriate detergent. A stiff-bristled brush should be used to loosen butterfat during the cleaning operation. Once cleaned, all parts should be rinsed with warm water (100°F, 39°C) until all traces of detergent have been removed. At this time, dispenser and dispenser parts can be examined for wear. Careful attention should be given to smaller parts of a dispenser, and especially dispensing spouts, whether flexible or stainless steel.

Sanitizing

Once cleaned, this equipment can be sanitized in a number of ways depending on the physical facilities available.

Heat is the most reliable agent if both temperature and time are controlled. Dispenser parts that come in direct contact with cream can be boiled in water for a minimum period of 10 min since lower temperatures and/or shorter times will be unsatisfactory for proper sanitizing.

Chemical agents are also effective. Hypochlorites have a rapid action but lose strength easily and are more corrosive to equipment than other common sanitizers. Chlorine is the active agent, and a minimum of 15 sec surface contact is required.

Chloramines, like hypochlorites, have chlorine as the active agent, but are less rapid in action, lose strength less rapidly, and are less corrosive than the hypochlorites. The chloramines should be exposed to equipment surfaces for a minimum of 1 min to be effective.

Quaternary ammonium compounds have the advantage of being active if added to wash water containing a detergent. Although these compounds have the advantages of being less corrosive, remaining stable at high temperatures, and having less loss of efficiency over a longer period of time, the problem of afterrinse to remove the detergent, as well as the theory of thorough cleaning and rinsing prior to santizing, is contradicted by this method.

Dishwashing facilities can be utilized for cleaning these units. If this method is used, it is strongly recommended that movable parts of a dispenser be disassembled, rinsed, and washed separately prior to exposure in a dishwasher. The increased possibility of product buildup and bacterial growth within these smaller parts dictates extra attention.

Many food establishments resort to two cleaning operations daily. This procedure is prevalent where locations are open more than 12 hr per day.

DISPENSING FREEZERS

General

Dispensing freezers are dispensers which, by batch or continuous feed operation, process and serve soft ice cream, malts, custards, and similar frozen products directly into containers for immediate consumption.

These dispensers must be cleaned and sanitized daily and should be handled in the same manner as milk and cream equipment. Five basic steps must be followed to maintain these dispensers at the highest degree of sanitation.

Daily

(1) Disassemble all machine parts in contact with a food product and properly wash and sanitize.
(2) Always thoroughly rinse machines just before starting operations with an approved sanitizing solution.
(3) Never permit intermixing of old and fresh mix supply. This is one of the most important sanitary practices.
(4) At all times keep mix supply covered and under refrigeration.
(5) Never allow unsanitized objects to contact the mix.

Weekly

Once a week, clean syrup pumps and lines by first closing syrup lines, using pinchoff clamps provided, and disconnecting lines at pump heads. Remove entire syrup cabinet to a cleaning area. Disassemble pumps and wash all parts in warm detergent, rinse, and reassemble parts. Wash syrup cabinet and exposed edge of machine base. Reinstall syrup cabinet and flush syrup lines, follow with sanitizing solution, and rinse with clear water.

JUICE AND STILL BEVERAGE DISPENSERS

General

Juice dispensers such as Lykes-Pasco or Minute Maid require daily cleaning and sanitizing. Still dispensers such as the Jet Spray equipment require daily and weekly attention. Juices are highly perishable foods, and thus dispensers must be cleaned and sanitized regularly to prevent growth of microorganisms and off-flavors. After cleaning and sanitizing, never intermix old and fresh juice. Replenishment is advisable during a normal working day, but should be discouraged after 12 hr of operation.

Daily

Handles, faucets, spouts, drip trays, and delivery tubing must be removed and immersed in a mild warm detergent solution, rinsed, and immersed in an approved sanitizer. After removal from sanitizing solution, rinse and allow to dry. Tubing should be reamed with a brush containing detergent, rinsed, sanitized, and rerinsed. Exteriors should be wiped with a damp cloth.

Bowls, covers, gaskets, and juice storage tanks should be emptied and immersed in mild warm detergent solution, rinsed, and sanitized. A brush should be used when these parts are in the detergent to remove solidified syrup or juice. After sanitizing, rinsing follows with clear warm water. Dry completely before reinstalling. Plastic construction is used for the majority of the dispensers. It is advisable to use only mild detergents and warm water, not over 100°F (39°C), to reduce damage to these parts.

Equipment supplied with impeller blades and pumps that contact the beverage must be cleaned and sanitized following the procedure outlined above.

Weekly

Still drink dispensers require the same cleaning and sanitizing procedures as discussed above. Sanitation should be performed weekly or before replenishing fresh beverage. Plastic storage bowls should be removed after all refrigeration and spray mechanisms are turned off. This procedure applies to all dispensing equipment. If convenient, remove bowl to a sink for cleaning, otherwise a large bucket may be used. In any event, all parts must be removed from the chassis for sanitation.

Ventilation is necessary for efficient operation of any refrigeration system. Lint, dust, and other debris will result in poor refrigeration. Condensers should be brushed, and if the machine is supplied with an air filter, remove it and clean under a stream of hot water. Dry before replacing on machine.

ICED TEA DISPENSERS

Iced tea dispensers require daily cleaning so that their operating efficiency will not be impaired.

(1) Wipe exterior components with a clean soft damp cloth.
(2) Empty and wash drip pan and grill with a mild detergent dissolved in warm water. Hot water (120°F, 49°C) should not be used on plastic parts, nor should they be washed in dishwashing equipment.
(3) Open front jacket, remove mixing trough, and wash in mild detergent dissolved in warm water.

(4) All parts and surfaces must be fully dried before reassembly. Moisture will cake tea powder and impair dispensing accuracy. The jar-dispenser assembly, when properly seated, will seal the product and make it airtight. If powder has solidified, remove jar, carefully remove caked particles, and reassemble as quickly as possible.

(5) After all parts are reassembled, the machine should be tested for accuracy, and the beverage checked for strength.

TEAPOTS AND SERVERS

Teapots may be used to hold boiling water or as a receptacle for tea essences. These decanters contain lids, either hinged or removable, and are made from metal or china.

If lid is removable and the mouth wide, a dishwasher can be used for cleaning purposes. Accumulation of residues in the form of rust-colored stains must be removed. Pots should be filled with a hot detergent solution and allowed to stand 15 min. After standing, a soft-bristle brush can be used to loosen the residues. Attention should be paid to the spout and inaccessible crevices. If stains cannot be removed in this manner, a mild bleach can be employed. Complete rinsing is necessary followed by air drying. These units should be stored with lids open or off.

HOT CHOCOLATE DISPENSERS

Efficient operation of hot chocolate dispensers depends on regularly scheduled cleaning procedures.

Jet whippers should be flushed each day by allowing hot water from the system to rinse all surfaces. A hot water system is activated by operating the "water only" switch on such dispensers as the Jet Spray. Jet whippers require monthly service, especially during the summer season. After a whipper is disassembled, immerse parts in a mild detergent solution. Use a cloth to remove encrusted solids. Remove and rinse in warm water. Allow parts to dry completely before reassembly is attempted.

The hot water system requires periodic attention to avoid buildup of contaminants. In hard water areas, apply deliming solution twice monthly. Filters, screens, and water purifiers also require monthly inspection to prevent buildup of sediment which may interfere with water flow.

Powder commodity hoppers should be inspected monthly for mold and moisture. If either is present, empty hopper and wipe with a hot damp cloth which has been immersed in a mild detergent solution. Rinse with a damp cloth and wipe all surfaces with a sanitizing solution. Remove all traces of solution by wiping with clean damp cloths, followed by complete drying.

ICE MAKING MACHINES

General

Ice intended for human consumption is classified as a food and must be handled like other perishable food items. It is not uncommon for ice to be contaminated with a variety of substances such as dirt, insect parts, bacteria, mold, and metal particles. Health agencies throughout the United States are taking drastic measures to provide the public with ice free from contamination. Many open bin ice machines installed in motels and some foodservice establishments are being outlawed because of potential health hazards.

In addition, problems related to off-tasting soft drinks, ice water, and any foods which come into contact with ice can be traced directly to poor maintenance, sanitizing, and cleaning of ice making machines.

The United States Public Health Service has included in its foodservice sanitation ordinance and code for foodservice establishments guidelines for reducing contaminants in ice. A section of this code follows:

(1) Ice shall be made from water that is of safe quality and from an approved public or private water supply system.

(2) Ice shall be handled, transported, and stored in such a manner as to be protected against contamination. If block ice is used, outer surfaces shall be thoroughly rinsed so as to remove any soil prior to use for any purpose.

(3) If ice crushers are used, they shall be maintained in a clean condition and shall be covered when not in use.

(4) If ice is used, approved containers and utensils shall be provided for storing and serving in a sanitary manner. These containers or utensils shall be of a smooth, impervious material and designed to facilitate cleaning.

Cleaning and Sanitizing Procedures

Once each month, or more often if required, defrost ice making equipment and dismantle. Special cleaning and sanitizing agents are manufactured for this purpose. Brush wash all parts of a machine with the solution, inside and out, using a strong, well-constructed nylon-bristled brush.

Make sure holes in water control are completely cleaned so as to give an even flow of water down over freezing board.

Rinse thoroughly, inspect flow line, and reassemble machine for operation.

When brush washing, remember to scrub all corners and areas which may be hidden. Run a finger over the surfaces to ensure complete removal of slime.

To ensure that complete cleaning has been accomplished, ice should be tasted for off-flavors. In addition, allow some ice to melt in a glass and observe for clarity and presence of sediment in the resulting liquid.

Ice tubs and remote storage receptacles require similar cleaning procedures. These units are sometimes forgotten and become a major source of contamination.

Figure 12.5 is an inspection report used by the U.S. Public Health Service for foodservice establishments.

CONTROL OF KITCHEN AIR POLLUTION

The control of air pollution within the confines of kitchens and/or food production areas is one segment of sanitation that is often neglected. The interior control of air pollution requires a stringent program of sanitation consisting of cleaning and maintenance of such items as duct work, ventilation, and exhaust systems. Heavy accumulations of air pollutants can be absorbed in foods and beverages resulting in off-odors and tastes, as well as safety and health hazards. The buildup of grease in air ducts and ventilation systems is a major fire hazard. Hood fires spread rapidly and may cause extensive damage. Obnoxious fumes emanating from a kitchen can also flow into dining areas, resulting in customer annoyance, and may have a psychological and physiological effect on customer attitudes toward the food and service.

If an air exchange system is inadequate and does not meet local regulatory codes, alterations are necessary which should be planned by experts in this field.

Sophisticated equipment is available to prevent interior air pollution. Two systems are fundamental to most foodservice installations. These are the canopy and back-shelf devices. The former is erected over large clusters of equipment which exhaust heat, fumes, odors, and airborne particles. The latter is situated behind deep fryers, griddles, and broilers. Systems vary with the manufacturer; however, the basic principles are to collect airborne grease and fumes on metal mesh-type filters and to air- or water-scrub pollutants prior to removal through exhaust ducts. Other features include fire prevention units, particle precipitators and afterburners to completely rid the atmosphere of pollutants.

Sanitation and maintenance consist of daily cleaning of filters with a solvent or cleaning solution. Grease collectors and drainage areas must be wiped free of residues daily or more often, depending on the amount of material accumulated. Fire control systems must be checked periodically and kept in optimum operating condition. Thermostats which are part of a fire control support system must also be checked periodically for operating efficiency or in accordance with manufacturer's recommendations. Automatic timers which are included as an adjunct accessory should also be checked for accuracy.

OSHA

Although the Williams-Steiger Occupational Safety and Health Act (OSHA) of 1970 does not encompass sanitation, its provisions are indirectly tied to good sanitation practices. The purpose of this act is "to assure so far as possible, every working man and woman in the Nation safe and healthful working conditions and to preserve our human resources." The provisions of the law apply to every employer engaged in a business affecting commerce who has employees.

The administration and enforcement of this Act falls under the Occupational Safety and Health Administration of the U.S. Department of Labor. This Act covers all aspects of safety, noise, and working conditions, and requires detailed record keeping.

OSHA inspections of foodservice establishments have actually aided employers to establish firm sanitation and safety programs. The following are examples: defects in kitchen canopies and ducts, inoperative automatic fire extinguishing system in canopies and ducts, inadequate aisle space, inadequate and blocked exits, slippery floors, excessive noise, cutting and slicing machines without safety guards, hot liquid utensils with loose handles, improper storage of production knives, excessive air pollution, inadequate low temperature clothing for personnel working in freezer areas, ovens and other equipment with loose doors or handles which could result in injuries to personnel.

VENDING

Sanitation and maintenance of vending equipment is treated as a separate subject and is covered in Chapter 14, Quality Control of Vending Equipment.

13

Water Quality and
Warewashing Control

Water can be a complex chemical solution and in nature is rarely encountered in the pure state. It is one of the main ingredients for sustenance and a highly prized natural resource. There is much yet to be learned about water, and scientists continue to research and study the properties surrounding many of its unique characteristics.

To the general public water is water and any variation in its composition does not become apparent until problems arise. Current consumption of water for industrial purposes in the United States is estimated at about 130 billion gallons per day. Less than $1/10$ of this quantity is supplied by municipalities. Surface sources account for 91% and groundwater furnishes 9%.

Water has a direct and major influence on the quality of foods and beverages that are prepared, served, and vended by the foodservice industry. Water treatment, if required, is an important segment of any foodservice quality control program.

Water is the major component in beverages. It lends its properties to those substances for which it is a solvent and has a direct influence on all foodstuffs. The chemical structure of water in its pure state is represented as H_2O. This formula is a simple combination of two familiar gases, hydrogen and oxygen. Unfortunately, water that is universally consumed contains many chemical substances in an infinite variety of combinations, states, and amounts. These materials, if present in relatively large quantities, will cause unusual tastes, odors, and discolorations. These substances are called dissolved or soluble materials because they form an intimate and complete mixture with the water. Water also contains undissolved or insoluble matter (often suspended colloids) in a range of shapes and sizes, including organic compounds, microorganisms, and inorganic forms of fine clay, silt, and sand. For practically every use of water, an attempt is made to remove all undissolved or suspended particles by means of filters or fine screens. Water containing dissolved materials must be treated chemically so that it will perform its specific function more easily and efficiently.

The chemical composition of water can change dramatically from one locality to another. In fact, water changes may occur within relatively short distances. Day-to-day and seasonal variations in both organic and inor-

265

ganic components, turbidity, and temperature have an added effect on water quality. Table 13.1 shows chemical analyses of water supplies, as furnished by the U.S. Department of the Interior.

PROPERTIES AND SOURCES OF WATER

Water has a number of unique properties that enhance its usefulness but also add to its complexities.

(1) Only water occurs on earth in three forms simultaneously: liquid, gas (steam), and solid (ice).
(2) It expands when it freezes, whereas most substances contract.
(3) It is lighter as a solid than a liquid.
(4) It has a high heat capacity, in that it absorbs a great amount of heat without much rise in temperature.
(5) It has a higher surface tension than any other common liquid except mercury. This property becomes apparent with dishwashing, when rinsing or wetting agents are required to reduce surface tension.
(6) It is the prime solvent, universally employed or connected with near-ly every aspect of human existence and life support.

The source of all water is precipitation in the form of rain or snow. Rain is practically pure water but collects airborne contaminants as it falls. These include solids (dust), atmospheric gases (air pollutants), and microorgan-

TABLE 13.1. Analyses of Water Table Supplies Used by Large Cities in the United States[1]

Component	Boston	New York	Chicago	Los Angeles	San Francisco	India-napolis
Iron	0.10	0.03	0.09	0.04	0.02	0.11
Calcium	4.0	13.0	39.0	25.0	1.1	67.0
Magnesium	0.4	4.3	10.0	5.0	1.4	20.0
Sodium	1.8	3.0	3.3	34.0	0.4	6.2
Potassium	0.7	1.4	0.7	4.0	—	1.6
Carbonate	0.0	0.0	0.0	2.0	0.0	0.0
Bicarbonate	7.0	36.0	132.0	138.0	7.0	206.0
Sulfate	5.6	20.0	23.0	23.0	1.6	67.0
Chloride	3.4	5.8	7.2	17.0	1.0	10.0

Component	Cleveland	St. Louis	Kansas City, KS	Galveston	Sarasota	Pitts-burgh
Iron	0.12	0.01	0.01	0.0	0.56	0.3
Calcium	39.0	23.0	75.0	30.0	14.0	60.0
Magnesium	7.3	9.7	22.0	9.7	0.3	18.0
Sodium	8.7	} 33.0	59.0	} 351.0	530.0	} 49.0
Potassium	1.3		5.6		16.0	
Carbonate	0.0	13.0	0.0	0.0	0.0	0.0
Bicarbonate	103.0	20.0	237.0	336.0	161.0	17.0
Sulfate	30.0	109.0	172.0	1.0	817.0	248.0
Chloride	20.0	17.0	29.0	422.0	168.0	58.0

Source: Thorner and Herzberg (1979).
[1]All data given in ppm.

isms. After reaching the earth surfaces, rain runs either over or into the ground. During this process, it dissolves any soluble and many sparingly soluble materials.

Among those materials dissolved in water are common table salt (NaCl), sodium sulfate, and calcium, magnesium, iron, and manganese salts, carbonates, and silicates. All soluble substances dissolved in water are termed "solids," "total solids," or "minerals."

HARD AND BRACKISH WATER

Hard Water

Two types of hardness are encountered: (1) carbonate (formerly called temporary hardness) which includes calcium and magnesium bicarbonates and carbonates, and (2) noncarbonate (formerly called permanent hardness) which includes calcium and magnesium sulfates, chlorides, and nitrates.

Quantitative Classification of Hardness
(Based on Calcium Carbonate)

Classification	ppm	gpg
Soft water	0–60	0–4
Moderately hard water	61–120	4–8
Hard water	121–180	8–12
Very hard water	Over 180	Over 12

Several terms are used in reporting analytical results, and their definitions are listed below:

(1) *Parts per million (ppm)*—A unit (usually mass) of material per million units of solvent, carrier, etc., here water.

(2) *Milligrams per liter (mg/liter)*—The same as ppm, also expressed as grams per cubic meter and μg/ml.

(3) *Equivalents per million (epm)*—A unit chemical equivalent weight of material per million weight units of water.

(4) *Grains per gallon (gpg)*—The number of grains of solute per 1 U.S. gal. of water.

1 grain = 1/7000 lb
1 U.S. gal. = 8.33 lb
1 gpg = 17.1 ppm

Brackish or Saline Water

Water that contains large amounts of dissolved minerals but is less salty than seawater is termed brackish or saline water. Such water occurs in many inland localities. The following is a list showing the concentrations of dissolved solids in saline water.

Description of Water	Concentration of Dissolved Solids, ppm
Brackish	1,000–3,000
Saline	3,000–10,000
Seawater	33,000–36,000
Brine	36,000 and up

An American Water Works Association report on the extent of brackish and saline water in the United States and Canada indicated that of 20,215 municipal water utilities surveyed, 1066 had raw water with a total dissolved solids content of 1000–3000 ppm, and 31 had water with a total dissolved solids content of 3000–10,000 ppm.

The drinking water standards of the U.S. Public Health Service recommend that water containing more than 250 ppm of chloride or sulfate salts or 500 ppm of dissolved solids is not fit for human consumption.

Highly mineralized water is usually unsuitable for general use due to its high hardness, its corrosiveness, its bitter and saline taste, its laxative action, and its adverse effect on the flavor of coffee and other beverages. Treatment of these conditions is explained in detail later on in this chapter.

IMPURITIES IN WATER

The following is a list of impurities, which, if present in sufficient amounts, will have a direct influence on the quality of foods and beverages and on the performance of dispensing or brewing equipment: (1) dissolved minerals, (2) dissolved gases, (3) free mineral acid acidity, (4) oils and greases, (5) turbidity and sediment, (6) color-producing substances, (7) organic matter, (8) tastes and odors, and (9) microorganisms.

Dissolved Minerals

Calcium (Ca^{2+}) and magnesium (Mg^{2+}) are the most common constituents of natural water causing hardness. These ingredients are responsible for scale, excessive soap consumption, formation of undesirable films such as scums and curds, plugging of valves and lines, heater tank burnout, and failure of thermostat relays.

Calcium carbonate ($CaCO_3$) is a hardness salt found in scale and may be deposited at temperatures less than 150°F (66°C). At every temperature, an equilibrium exists between free carbon dioxide (CO_2) in water and the amount of calcium bicarbonate [$Ca(HCO_3)_2$] which can be held in solution.

The conversion of calcium bicarbonate or magnesium bicarbonate [Mg $(HCO_3)_2$] to form scale occurs as follows:

$$Ca(HCO_3)_2 \xrightarrow{\text{heat}} CaCO_3 \downarrow + H_2O + CO_2 \uparrow \text{gas}$$

$$Mg(HCO_3)_2 \xrightarrow{\text{heat}} MgCO_3 + H_2O + CO_2 \uparrow \text{gas}$$
$$\downarrow$$
$$Mg(OH)_2 + CO_2 \uparrow \text{gas}$$

Iron (Fe^{2+} and Fe^{3+}) and manganese (Mn^{2+} and Mn^{3+}) are usually present in rocks and soil in the oxidized form. When rainwater percolates through soil, decaying matter consumes dissolved oxygen. Iron and manganese deposits are then reduced to a soluble form and dissolved. These minerals are likely to be found in water drawn from the lower reaches of reservoirs, where dissolved oxygen is expected to be absent. The presence of iron will lead to metallic tastes. As little as 0.1 ppm of iron will cause staining of dishes. It can also be detected in coffee, particularly if cream is added. Manganese will show up as a gray to black deposit on dishes and glasses.

Sodium (Na^+) is found in nearly all natural waters. At high concentrations and at elevated temperatures, it may cause foaming. It can be removed by hydrogen iron exchange, demineralization, or distillation.

Alkalinity is generally considered to be due to bicarbonates, carbonates, phosphates, and silicates. Alkalinity will cause scaling (Fig. 13.1) and foaming. Its effect on coffee is pronounced, as it destroys its acid character

FIG. 13.1.   Left—View of interior of line fitting showing scale build-up as a result of alkalinity in water. Right—Fitting as a result of water treatment.
Courtesy of Everpure, Inc.

and results in a flat insipid brew. Alkalinity affects soft drinks by reducing the flavor and tang, neutralizing the antispoilage potential of acids, and creating off-tastes.

Chlorides may cause corrosion and destroy flavor. They are found in domestic and industrial wastes and oilfields brines.

Sulfates enter water from the soil or industrial wastes. They combine with calcium to form calcium sulfate scale. Demineralization will remove this scale from the water, or it can be retained in solution by treatment with surface active agents.

Dissolved Gases

Oxygen is picked up by rainwater as it falls through the atmosphere. Carbon dioxide and nitrogen are absorbed in the same manner. Oxygen is also contributed by photosynthesis. At low pH values, oxygen causes iron, steel, galvanized iron, and brass to corrode. The highest rate of corrosion occurs at 160°–180°F (72°–83°C). At high pH values it encourages scale formation. Mechanical or chemical deaeration techniques can be used to remove oxygen from water.

Carbon dioxide is absorbed into water from decaying matter, rocks, soil, or the atmosphere. CO_2 is a factor in corrosion. Its removal can be brought about by aeration, deaeration, neutralization, and lime-soda softening.

Hydrogen sulfide may enter water from the atmosphere, sulfur bacteria, or from oil or gas deposits. It causes corrosion and has a "rotten egg" odor, and, if iron is present, combines with it to precipitate black ferrous sulfide. It can be removed from water by aeration at low pH, by chlorination, or by a highly basic anion exchanger. It becomes evident in beverages at very low levels, 0.05–0.12 ppm.

Ammonia is present in water as a result of the decomposition of organic matter. It corrodes copper, zinc, and their alloys. Removal is accomplished by hydrogen ion exchange or by "breakpoint" chlorination.

Free Mineral Acids

Free mineral acids may be present in water due to the discharge of industrial wastes, particularly acid mine drainage or waste pickle liquor. They are a direct cause of corrosion and produce metallic and sour tastes in beverages.

Oils and Greases

Oils and greases if present in minute quantities will cause foaming and formation of sludges. Films will also be deposited on the surfaces of dispensers and brewing equipment. Oily deposits will become apparent in beverages and will interfere with carbonation. Domestic and industrial wastes and newly installed pipes contribute these contaminants to a water supply.

Turbidity and Suspended Solids

The problems of turbidity and suspended solids in water are the result of domestic and industrial wastes, old water systems and land erosion. Sedimentation and foaming are caused by this situation. Coagulation is the process employed to remove these conditions. Finely divided particles are agglomerated into larger masses to effect rapid settling. Aluminum sulfate (alum) is the coagulant most commonly used in water conditioning. Other agents include ferrous sulfate, ferric sulfate, and ferric chloride. Polyelectrolytes are now more widely used as coagulants. These products are high molecular weight, water-soluble polymers which dissociate to form highly charged, large molecular weight ions.

Color and Organic Matter

Color and organic matter are caused by farm runoff, domestic and industrial wastes, and flooding of swamps and riverbeds. Color of natural waters range from very light yellow to dark brown. Iron in excess of about 0.3 to 0.5 ppm will cause water to appear rusty. These conditions can also be attributed to old water systems and rusting pipes. Color and organic material will affect all beverages by imparting off-tastes, color changes, and foaming and staining of utensils. Activated carbon filters, chlorination, and coagulation act to remove these conditions.

Tastes and Odors

Tastes and odors are caused by many of the impurities previously discussed. Domestic and industrial wastes, and living microorganisms will also contribute to this problem.

Microorganisms

Microorganisms are the result of domestic wastes, farm runoff, flooding, and their growth in reservoirs and old water systems. These organisms may be algae, diatoms, or protozoa. Floral odors emanating from water can be caused by diatoms or protozoa. Fishy, earthy, and grassy odors may be traced to microorganisms. Slime and scum will cause fouling of equipment and corrosion.

WATER TREATMENT

General Considerations

Considering the many impurities in water, treatment is a necessity. When water is used for drinking purposes, it should be safe; it should not carry disease; it should be palatable, free of undesirable tastes and odors; and it should be clean, free of color, dirt, and other unsightly material.

Every industry has its own water problem. A careful study of each aspect of an operation must be made to determine whether impurities or results of a treatment will affect the product.

The food service industry, which includes restaurants, hotels, vending machines, industrial caterers, airline feeding, and steamships, uses water for many different purposes. Two important areas for water in relation to public feeding are in the preparation and serving of beverages and in maintenance and cleaning operations. Hard water must be softened to protect equipment and make cleaning easy. Large volumes of hard water in all parts of the United States are softened during the course of a year. The water softening industry is providing excellent methods and equipment for this program. However, serious problems can result with incorrect treatment since water that is suited to one application may not be equally suited to other applications. A good example of this is the brewing of coffee, which will be discussed in a subsequent section of this chapter.

Treating Hard Water

Two methods are commonly employed for water softening. For waters containing 100–150 ppm hardness as $CaCO_3$, the lime-soda softening process provides the most suitable and economical treatment.

The second method is called an ion exchange process. This procedure will treat water of low hardness from 50 to 100 ppm. The lime-soda operation is not efficient with raw waters of low hardness. The ion exchange process is in wide application for both home and industry.

An ion is defined as an electrically charged atom or group of atoms. Positively charged ions are called cations because they migrate to the negative electrode, or cathode, when a current of electricity is passed through the solution. Negatively charged ions are called anions because they migrate to the anode, or positive electrode.

In water softening where an ion exchange system is employed, a cationic process makes use of small particles of ion exchange resins contained in a tank. These particles are initially charged with replaceable sodium ions. As hard water passes through a bed of resin particles, calcium and magnesium ions come into contact with them. Since calcium and magnesium ions have a greater affinity for the ion exchange resin than do sodium ions, hardness ions are held by resin particles, and a chemically equivalent number of sodium ions are exchanged into water.

$$Ca^{2+} + Na_2R \longrightarrow 2Na^+ + CaR$$
$$Mg^{2+} + Na_2R \longrightarrow 2Na^+ + MgR$$

Hardness ions +	Resin or	→ Sodium	+ Exhausted
in water	Zeolite	ions	resin
		in water	in softener

Although only calcium and magnesium are shown in these equations, iron, manganese, and other polyvalent and heavy metal cations will be removed in the same manner.

This exchange process continues automatically until the supply of sodium ions in a resin is depleted. When this occurs, increasing amounts of hardness ions pass unremoved through the bed and a softener is termed exhausted. To restore a bed of ion exchange material to its original condition, a strong solution of common salt is passed through the bed. Because of the high concentration of sodium ions in a salt brine, the affinity of hardness ions for a resin is overcome, and calcium and magnesium ions are massed away or forced off the resin and rinsed to waste. Sodium ions from salt brine are held by the resin, and, after rinsing, the resin is ready for another softening cycle.

The following basic steps are necessary in any water softener regeneration process: (1) backwash, (2) addition of salt solution, (3) rinse, and (4) return to service. Figure 13.2 shows the interior of a Culligan Mark 5 Aqua Sensor automatic water softener. This unit is designed to soften hard water of up to 75 grains per gallon, reducing it to less than 1 grain per gallon. It will also remove up to 2 ppm of iron. This system is classified as a five-cycle unit. Other classifications are: manual, semiautomatic, and fully automatic (2 and 5 cycles).

Polyphosphate systems will chelate hardness salts in soluble forms so they do not precipitate out of solution as insoluble solids. This material can be added to water in solid or liquid form. The solid is simpler. Figure 13.3 shows a container filled with polyphosphate crystals. This unit is inserted in a coldwater feed line so water must pass over the crystals. These crystals dissolve slowly; however, heat will increase their action, so a container

FIG. 13.2.   Interior of an automatic water softener.
1—Recharge controller.
2—Five-cycle recharge valve.
3—Backwash freeboard.
4—Ion exchange resin.
5—Electronic sensing device.
6—Underbedding material.
7—Collector for treated water.
8—Brine collecting valve.
9—Dry salt storage.
Courtesy of Culligan, Inc.

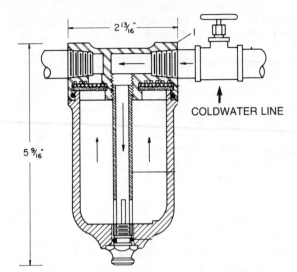

COLDWATER LINE

FIG. 13.3. Polyphosphate water softener inserted in a coldwater line.
Courtesy of Calgon Corp.

should be installed away from high temperatures. The crystals should not be allowed to disappear completely but be replenished as needed. The liquid form in a concentrated solution is fed into the water by a proportional feeder set to provide a water concentration of about 10 ppm. The advantage of liquid is that the concentration may be adjusted to take care of special situations that require added treatment.

Water Purifiers

Water purifiers that operate by absorption and the filtration principle perform an important function by removing off-tastes, off-odors, and other variations in local water supplies. They absorb chlorine that chemically attacks delicate syrup flavors, remove dirt that causes carbonation loss, and reduce maintenance problems of pumps, solenoids, and screens which may be affected by sediment settling on these surfaces.

These water purifiers perform two functions: namely, chemical and physical removal of impurities. The medium used for chemical elimination is usually activated charcoal. This method absorbs off-tastes and off-odors by collecting impurities on the outside surface area of activated charcoal. The ability to filter turbidity or colloids from water is a physical removal function. The pore size of a filter determines the amount of impurity which will pass through. The filter should be of sufficient size to allow fast and thorough cleaning of water. Filters require periodic changing as pores become clogged, resulting in a reduction of water flow. Figure 13.4 shows the exterior of an Everpure C3 purifier. Figure 13.5 shows a purifier connected to a postmix fountain dispenser. Figure 13.6 illustrates its use in conjunction with a coffee urn, and Fig. 13.7 shows a unit installed in a vending machine.

FIG. 13.4.   Exterior view of water purifier.
Courtesy of Everpure, Inc.

Water Strainers

Water strainers are used as an extra precautionary measure to ensure removal of sediment that may enter a system causing damage to moving parts, to solenoids, or line plugging. Figure 13.8 shows a water strainer employed on a half-gallon coffee brewer. The need for cleaning or replacing water strainers varies according to water quality. Strainers are cleaned by reversing water flow. They are disconnected from a unit and reassembled in reverse, so that the force of water will dislodge any accumulations of sediment.

Chlorination

Chlorination is the one universally accepted method for disinfection of water. Chlorine is effective in killing disease-causing bacteria, slime, and algae, and aids in precipitating minerals. Chlorine is supplied as a com-

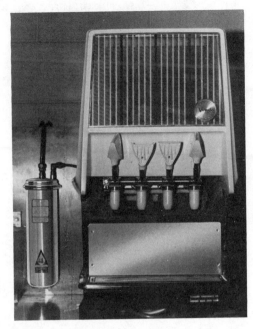

FIG. 13.5. Water purifier connected to a postmix soda dispenser.
Courtesy of Everpure, Inc.

FIG. 13.6. Water purifier connected to a coffee urn.
Courtesy of Everpure, Inc.

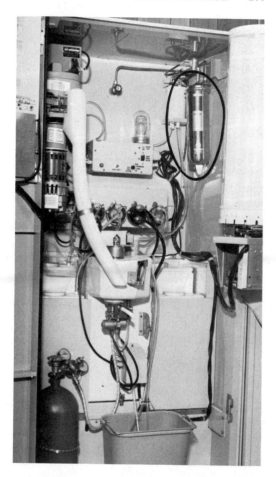

FIG. 13.7. Water purifier installed in a vending machine.
Courtesy of Everpure, Inc.

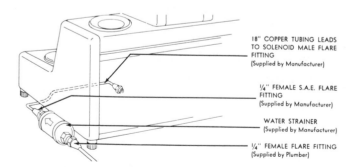

18" COPPER TUBING LEADS
TO SOLENOID MALE FLARE
FITTING
(Supplied by Manufacturer)

1/4" FEMALE S.A.E. FLARE
FITTING
(Supplied by Manufacturer)

WATER STRAINER
(Supplied by Manufacturer)

1/4" FEMALE FLARE FITTING
(Supplied by Plumber)

FIG. 13.8.   Water strainer installed on a half-gallon coffee brewer.
Courtesy of Bunn-O-Matic Corp.

pressed gas in steel cylinders. Powdered or liquid hypochlorite may also be used for the same purpose; however, chlorine gas is safer when applied under controlled conditions. The amount of chlorine required depends on quality and temperature of the water. The measurement unit is in parts per million. Removal of bacteria (iron or manganese), which are responsible for color, taste, and odor problems, requires 0.5–1.0 ppm of chlorine.

Reverse Osmosis

Reverse osmosis is a relatively new method used to correct highly mineralized or "brackish" water. The process involved is a simple one as it requires no moving parts, no regeneration, and uses a minimum of energy. Osmosis is the familiar process whereby trees and plants acquire water and nutrients from the soil and translocate these solutions throughout their structures. When two aqueous solutions of different ionic concentrations are separated by a semipermeable membrane, water passes through the membrane from the less concentrated solution to the more concentrated one. The osmotic pressure developed by this liquid movement can raise the more concentrated solution a considerable distance.

Reverse osmosis is the opposite of this action. Pressure is applied to "brackish" water to force it through a special membrane. The membrane is permeable to water but less permeable to water impurities. This process results in a separation of water from its impurities, both soluble and suspended. Although this process may sound complex, reverse osmosis involves only three steps: water to be treated, membrane, and water pressure.

Membranes contain no pore openings, so they not only remove living organisms and colloidal or other nondissolved solids but also reject practically all dissolved minerals in water.

Figure 13.9 is a numbered cutaway of a Culligan Aqua 1 reverse osmosis water purifier. The following describes the principal parts.

(1) Prefilter holds back turbidity or suspended matter which tends to clog the membrane module.
(2) Reverse osmosis membrane module: This module contains a special semipermeable membrane spirally wound on a central tube to provide 5 ft^2 of surface area. It has the ability to reject dissolved minerals and organic matter from water and purifies while operating on normal water pressure.
(3) Postfilter of activated charcoal.
(4) Waste water tube.
(5) Product water tube.
(6) Plastic housing which also functions as a water reservoir.

The development of reverse osmosis has greatly improved the quality of beverages in many areas of the western part of the United States.

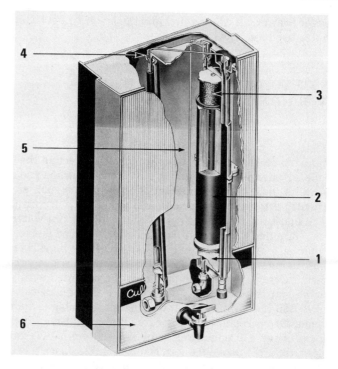

FIG. 13.9.   Reverse osmosis purifier (cutaway). 1—Prefilter to prevent turbidity or suspended matter from clogging the membrane module. 2—Reverse osmosis membrane module— Contains a special semipermeable membrane, spirally wound on a central tube, to provide 5 ft^2 of surface area; it has the ability to reject dissolved minerals and organic matter from water, while allowing purified water to pass through; operates on normal water pressure. 3—Postfilter. 4—Waste water tube. 5—Product water tube. 6—Plastic housing which also functions as a water reservoir.
Courtesy of Culligan, Inc.

Determining Water Treatment Capacity

Determination of the size of a water softener or purifier is based on the number of grains of hardness and other impurities which must be removed in a given period of time. If an ion exchange system is being considered, the regeneration period must also be considered. The total water consumption over a given period compared with peak usage must be evaluated.

If a single-unit purifier is contemplated to treat a piece of equipment, such as a coffee brewer, all water going into the brewer must be totaled, not only the water used for brewing purposes.

EFFECTS OF WATER QUALITY ON FOODS AND BEVERAGES

Coffee

Many impurities found in water supplies have an effect on the taste and aroma of coffee. Hydrogen sulfide imparts a rotten egg aroma and excessive chlorine exhibits unfavorable characteristics. Minerals such as common salt (NaCl) will flatten the flavor peak and produce a salty insipid taste. However, the masking effect of coffee will cover up certain water impurities. The taste of coffee will be significantly altered by 658 ppm of common salt, 1377 ppm of sodium bicarbonate, 221 ppm of sodium carbonate, and 1000 ppm of magnesium sulfate according to statistics gathered by the Coffee Brewing Center. A water supply must be regarded with suspicion and a possible source of difficulty if it has: (1) a total dissolved solids content above 300 ppm, (2) a combined calcium and magnesium content above 100 ppm, (3) a carbonate-bicarbonate alkalinity above 100 ppm, (4) a total hardness above 150 ppm, (5) a combined sodium-potassium content above 50 ppm, (6) a pH above 9.0, or (7) a detectable odor.

Water treatment is looked upon as the "cure-all" for correcting adverse conditions. Unfortunately, this does not apply to coffee. The area of water treatment that cannot be accomplished by conventional means is reduction in hardness. The use of an ion exchange system will create unfavorable conditions in a brewing process so a finished brew will be totally unacceptable. The precipitation of sodium salts, such as sodium carbonate or bicarbonate into treated water will form a cohesive gel in a coffee bed. The result is a dramatic increase in the brewing cycle causing undue overextraction and an extremely bitter beverage. The color of the brew is also affected by the production of a darker coffee.

If water must be softened for another purpose such as warewashing, a separate line of unsoftened water should be installed, bypassing the softener and connected directly to coffee making equipment. Although water containing a total hardness of less than 150 ppm should have little or no adverse effect on coffee quality, it may still give some trouble with brewing equipment. Scaling or lime deposits will occur in heating jackets, piping, and faucets. This condition will also prevent efficient heating of water, cause failure of thermostat relay operation, block inlet feed pipes, and cause seam failures (Fig. 13.10). These conditions can be prevented by treating water with a polyphosphate softener (previously described) that will not affect brewing or the beverage.

FIG. 13.10.   Interior views of water tanks, untreated (left) and treated (right).
Courtesy of Everpure, Inc.

Odor-producing and other impurities may be removed by conventional methods. Brackish water can also be treated by reverse osmosis.

The following lists the effects of various water qualities on brewed coffee.

(1) Untreated water makes the best coffee, providing it is free of undesirable odors and tastes.

(2) Hard water after being treated produced the poorest coffee.

(3) The hardest of all waters made the best coffee.

(4) Distilled water, containing no hardness or dissolved solids, produced coffee that was less desirable than that prepared from very hard, untreated water but more desirable than that prepared with treated water.

Soft Drinks

Water, the major component of a soft drink, requires critical examination so that it is not responsible for poor quality. High chlorine content needed for microbial control alters or destroys flavorings and imparts an off-flavor similar to bleach. Many public water systems contain particulate matter which interferes with carbonation. Slime and scum which have accumulated in old water pipes may also enter a dispensing system, affecting carbonation and flavor. Hard water will affect beverage quality by reducing the acid content.

Food Preparation

Numerous problems may result when poor quality water is employed for cooking. To illustrate the importance of high-quality water in food preparation, selected examples follow which stress this segment of quality control.

Vegetables that are relatively high in protein and carbohydrates, such as pulses (beans, peas), when cooked in hard water become tough and rubbery, causing an increase in cooking time. The surface of beets will take on a white coating when cooked in hard water and become very firm. Hard water results in a cloudy and unappealing tea brew.

Excessive hardness can retard the fermentation of yeasts used in bread and other doughs. High mineral content may produce problems of off-tastes and other undesirable reactions with food components. Sugar used in candy making can be hydrolyzed by some waters, producing discoloration, a change in flavor, a bitter taste, and a strong pungent acid aftertaste. This problem applies to the addition of sugar to water in any food recipe.

Iron, manganese, and off-colored water will result in unappetizing discolorations. Water containing a high iron content will impart a metallic off-tasting character to foods and beverages. Hydrogen sulfide gives off a "rotten egg" odor that will downgrade food quality.

Alkalinity in water also has adverse affects in that it reacts with and neutralizes desirable food acidulants. This factor is significant if acidity preserves food from microbiological spoilage. The acid content of mayonnaise and salad dressings will be reduced or neutralized if dabbed on wet lettuce washed in alkaline water, thus accelerating microbial growth.

Water Testing

Water testing was once considered an art for the experienced chemist. Although the role of a chemist is still regarded as important for more sophisticated examinations, there are analysis kits available that provide for fast, simplified testing of water.

A variety of test kits, packaged in plastic cases and covering a complete range of analyses, are manufactured. Each test is devised for simplicity. Bottles of solutions are numbered. By following an instruction sheet, the numbered bottles of solution are selected and used for a specific test.

The high and low range total hardness test kit employs three reagents, a buffer solution, a stable indicator, and a titrating solution which is added drop by drop until the color changes. Water hardness is determined by counting the number of drops required to bring about the color change: 1 drop equals 1 ppm of hardness.

Water testing should be performed on a quarterly basis, so that seasonal determinations can thus be compared and steps taken to eliminate or forestall problems. Figure 13.11 is an analysis reporting form.

Date_____

CUSTOMER WATER ANALYSIS

NAME_____

STREET_____ _____

CITY_____

WATER SOURCE:_____
Water Treating Equipment Now Being Used:

WATER TEST RESULTS

IRON BACTERIA		ANY COLOR:
IRON	ppm*	CLEAR OR CLOUDY:
SULPHUR	ppm*	ANY TASTE: ODOR:
ACIDITY	pH	Recent Health Dept. Test:
HARDNESS	gpg**	Not a Substitute for Continuous Chlorination

*ppm = Parts Per Million   **gpg = Grains Per Gallon (each gpg = 17.1 ppm)

COMMENT AND RECOMMENDATIONS

ANALYSIS BY:_____

FIG. 13.11.   Water analysis reporting form.
Courtesy of Everpure, Inc.

WAREWASHING

The development and invention of dishwashing machines started in the United States about 1880. The popular appeal of good eating establishments, the multitude of dishes resulting from mass feeding, and the difficulty in securing labor to perform these menial and laborious tasks served to stimulate the development of mechanical devices.

Early dishwashing machines were cumbersome units driven by steam or gasoline engines. Dishes in baskets were raised and lowered into tubs or

TABLE 13.2.   Summary of Factors Which Can Cause Dishwashing
and Equipment Cleaning Problems

Symptom	Possible Cause	Suggested Cure
Films	Water hardness	Use an external softening process. Use more detergent to provide internal conditioning. Use a chlorinated cleaner. Check temperature of wash and rinse water. Overheated water may be precipitating film.
	Detergent carryover	Maintain adequate pressure and volume of rinse water.
	Improperly cleaned or rinsed equipment	Prevent scale buildup in equipment by adopting frequent and adequate cleaning practices. Maintain adequate pressure and volume of rinse water.
Greasy films	Low pH Insufficient detergent Low water temperature Improperly cleaned equipment	Maintain adequate alkalinity to saponify greases. Unclog all wash sprays and rinse nozzles to keep any greases carried in the steam from depositing on dishes. Clogged rinse nozzles will also interfere with wash tank overflow, allowing surface scums to remain in the machine.
Streaking	Alkalinity in the water	Use an external treatment method to reduce alkalinity.
	Improperly cleaned or rinsed equipment	Maintain adequate pressure and volume of rinse water. Alkaline cleaners used for washing must be thoroughly rinsed from dishes.
Spotting	Rinse water hardness Rinse water temperature too high or too low	Provide external or internal softening. Check rinse water temperature. Dishes may be flash drying, or water may be drying on dishes rather than draining off.
	Inadequate time between rinsing and storage	Allow sufficient time for air drying.
Staining	Iron in water	Check for corrosion. Retain iron in solution with surface active agents.
	Color in water	Provide external treatment for iron or color removal.
Foaming	Detergent Dissolved or suspended solids in water	Change to a low sudsing product. Use an appropriate treatment method to reduce the solids content of the water.
	Food soil	Adequately remove gross soil before washing. The decomposition of carbohydrates, proteins, or fats may cause foaming during the wash cycle.
	Alkalinity, oils, or color in water supply Improperly cleaned equipment	Use an appropriate treatment method to reduce or remove these factors. Keep all wash sprays and rinse nozzles open.

TABLE 13.2. *(Continued)*

Symptom	Possible Cause	Suggested Cure
		Keep equipment free from deposits or films of materials which could cause foam buildup in future wash cycles.
Dirty dishes	Insufficient detergents	Use enough detergent in wash water to ensure complete soil suspension.
	Wash water temperature too low	Keep water temperature high enough to dissolve food residues.
	Inadequate wash and rinse times	Allow sufficient time for wash and rinse operations to be effective.
	Improperly cleaned equipment	Unclog wash sprays and rinse nozzles to maintain proper pressure and flow conditions.
		Overflows must be open. Keep wash water as clean as possible.

Source: National Sanitation Foundation.

tanks by means of hand-operated cranks. The water varied in temperature and did not meet present-day standards.

Warewashing machines available today are highly mechanized, sophisticated equipment as compared with those used at the turn of the century. The National Sanitation Foundation sponsored by equipment manufacturers blazed a path to standardization. Uniformity was developed for such factors as time, temperature, volume of water, pressure, spray pattern, size of equipment, and necessity for making an operation as easy and foolproof as possible.

Although progress has been made in the warewashing field, equipment sanitation has lagged behind. This is mainly due to the need for labor to perform these tasks and lack of mechanical equipment to carry them out.

Table 13.2 is a summary of factors which lead to dishwashing and equipment cleaning problems.

Maintenance and cleaning procedures for warewashing equipment should include: (1) Remove strainer pans, wash, and stack outside machine until next use. (2) Add compound to clean water in empty machine, run for 1 min, and rinse. A hose is convenient to flush corners and inaccessible areas. (3) Scrub interior frequently with a stiff brush. (4) Remove and clean the wash and rinse arms and jets daily to remove foreign particles. (5) Wash table dishracks with sanitizing solution, rinse, and dry. (6) Clean all nozzles. (7) Test operation of detergent feed and rinse solution. (8) Use pH test paper to determine if machine is rinsing properly. If pH test indicates excess alkalinity, recheck rinse solution for optimum operation. (9) Check thermostatic controls, thermometers, and timing devices for accuracy. (10) Refer to National Sanitation Foundation Standard Number 3, *Commercial Spray-Type Dishwashing Machines*, for complete information concerning dishwashing machine operation. Also follow manufacturer's instructions for specific guidelines of equipment maintenance and cleaning procedures.

Quality Control of Vending Equipment

Vending is a prime example of fast and automated foodservice operations, combined to form a unique facility that utilizes machine techniques, convenience foods, and a highly organized and efficient commissary program. These elements achieve the ultimate goal of lower labor costs, mobility, and quick service to the customer.

Vending is defined as self-service mechanical distribution, metering, or portioning of service, merchandise, food, and beverages by the insertion of a coin or coins into a slot. The vending industry covers a wide range of products and services. During and after World War II, a major industry built entirely around vendable food products and beverages emerged. Industrial and in-plant feeding formed the focal point for this method of mechanical foodservice. Advances in electronics, refrigeration, and heating units were responsible for the development and design of sophisticated services and complete cafeterias, fully contained and automatic. The industry expanded over the years, so that vending installations are now found in many and varied types of public operations, such as schools, hospitals, office complexes, nursing homes, sports arenas, supermarkets, and entertainment facilities.

CLASSIFICATION OF VENDABLE SERVICES

The vending industry, because of its diverse application and complex operation, can best be understood when divided into three service categories: (1) hiring or leasing of services by mechanical means, (2) dispensing of edible or personal services, and (3) dispensing of sundry items and nonedible services, packaged foods, and bottled beverages.

(1) The hiring or leasing of services by mechanical means includes telephone pay stations, jukeboxes, public toilets, radio and television for hotel and home, auto parking meters, luggage storage lockers, and laundry washing machines.

(2) The dispensing of edible or personal services includes shoe shiners, foot and hotel bed massage machines, soap and towel dispensers,

electric and gas meters, perfume and toilet water dispensers, weight scales, ice machines, and all vending machines that dispense portioned food or beverages, e.g., hot and cold drink dispensers, hot and cold food units, and ice cream dispensers.

(3) The dispensing of sundry items, nonedible services, packaged foods, and drinks includes stamps; subway and bus tokens; coin and dollar bill changers; miscellaneous items, e.g., newspapers, paperback books, magazines, combs, cosmetics, handkerchiefs, postcards, stockings, and contraceptives; flight insurance policies; cigarette and cigar machines; bulk confectionery dispensers; and retail packaged food dispensers, e.g., bread, milk, canned goods.

OPERATING PRINCIPLES OF VENDING MACHINES

Basically, the operating principles of vending machines or dispensing services are identical regardless of the product or service sold. A coin is the medium of payment, acting as the key to unlock a mechanism setting a dispenser in operation. Unlocking mechanisms that activate vending equipment are divided into two categories: (1) mechanical or hand-operated, and (2) electrical.

Mechanical or manual operation uses a coin to bridge the lever or button to interior controls, allowing a product to be released. By moving an exterior lever or push button after a coin is inserted into the machine and accepted by it, pressure exerted by the customer acts as the power source to set a dispenser in operation. When external pressure is released, the coin drops into a money storage box and the machine cannot be operated again until a new coin is inserted in the slot. This type of vending equipment can be placed in any location, as no external power is required for its operation. Early dispensing equipment employed these principles. Bulk vending units dispensing nuts, chewing gum, candy bars, sundry items, and cigarettes employ the mechanical system.

Electrically activated dispensers were made possible during and after World War II from the development of electronic components necessary to create operating systems that were fully automated. Machines were built containing a labyrinth of electrical circuits, encompassing microswitches, timers, fractional HP motors, and solenoids. Depending on the product dispensed, interior designs vary. Generally, the design of a coin acceptor, coin counter, and change dispenser follows the same basic design. After the coin is deposited in a slot by the customer and the selection of an item is made, a master switch is activated that sets interior components in operation.

VENDING MACHINE DESIGN

Modern vending machines must meet certain basic design criteria to satisfy the demands of the consumer, vendor, and, if they are used to dispense food or beverages, government sanitation codes. Depending on the product or service rendered, the following items No. 1 through 6 apply to all vending machines; items 7 to 10 apply to those dispensers serving food and beverages.

(1) Compactness.

(2) Attractive and appealing exterior design and decoration.

(3) Attractive and presentable display of merchandise.

(4) Mechanical reliability and efficient operation.

(5) Ease of loading.

(6) Ease of repairs and servicing, so a semiskilled employee can perform minor repairs and adjustments on location.

(7) Ease of sanitation and full accessibility to all interior parts for cleaning purposes.

(8) If the vending unit dispenses perishable products or ingredients, it must be capable of maintaining a temperature of 45°F (8°C) or below with necessary temperature controls and shutoff controls should the temperature rise above 45°F (8°C).

(9) If the vending unit dispenses hot or heated food, it must be capable of maintaining products at or above 140°F (60°C) with necessary temperature controls and shutoff controls should the temperature drop below 140°F (60°C).

(10) If vending machines are designed to dispense food or beverages, they must comply with regulations set forth by the U.S. Public Health Service 1965 sanitation ordinance and code under the title "The Vending of Foods and Beverages." This code was developed in cooperation with the National Automatic Merchandising Association (NAMA) in 1957 and revised in 1965. In addition, the National Sanitation Foundation (NSF) has also promulgated basic and specific criteria for the evaluation of vending machines for food and beverages.

COIN-OPERATED VENDING MACHINES

There are three classifications of coin-operated vending machines: (1) for beverages, (2) for confections and foods, and (3) for sundry and miscellaneous products.

Vending Machines for Beverages

Coffee.

Instant, freeze-dried, or liquid concentrates
Fresh brew (batch)
Fresh brew (single cup)

The preceding are manufactured in combination with hot chocolate, soup, and tea.

Soft Drinks.

Bottle or canned
Cup service (postmix)
Cup service (premix)

Milk.

Packaged (indoors and outdoors)
Bulk or cup service

Vending Machines for Confections and Food

Bulk
Candy bar
Hot canned foods and soups
Cold foods, sandwiches, salads
Fresh fruit
Pastry, crackers, cookies, and popcorn
Chewing gum
Ice cream

Vending Machines for Sundry and Miscellaneous Products

Cigarettes and cigars
Postage stamps
Coin and dollar bill changers
Ice
Cosmetics, toiletries, novelties, detergents, newspapers, and books

Selected Examples and Their Operational Aspects

Solid Pack Vending Machines.   Solid pack vending machines are manufactured in a variety of shapes and designs and are adapted for many products, both edible and nonedible. They handle confections, solid food, sundries, and miscellaneous products.

Column and Drawer Dispensers.   These machines store products in stacks. Each stack is set above a drawer. When a machine is filled, the bottom package falls into a drawer. Upon activation, the machine mechanisms allows a drawer to be opened. After the product is withdrawn and the drawer is pushed back into place, a subsequent package falls into it. These units dispense cigarettes and candy bars.

Drop Flap Machines.   As in column and drawer equipment, packages are stored in columns. Instead of resting one on the other, each package rests on a hinged drop flap or leaf. When a machine is filled, all leaves or flaps are extended so each package has its own shelf. When a machine is activated, the lowest shelf drops on its hinge and allows a package to fall by gravity onto a vending chute. These machines are adaptable to cigarettes, candy, and packaged sundries.

Cupboard Machines.   Cupboard dispensers consist of a number of small rectangular receptacles or storage spaces covered with a hinged glass door. When a unit is activated, a customer can observe an item desired, open a door, and withdraw the merchandise. Only one door is allowed to open at a time, and once an item is withdrawn the storage space remains empty until reloaded.

Rotary turntable dispensers are available that increase the capacity of a machine. Where a turntable is provided, each shelf, which is divided into segments, can hold up to eight selections. After a sale is completed, the closing of a vend door causes the turntable to move one segment.

There are many variations of cupboard machines. Some have conveyors fitted with slots or pockets. A customer presses a button which activates a conveyor. As the conveyor moves, each item is brought into view for selection.

These vending machines are available with refrigeration systems for dispensing of cold foods or with heating units for hot or perishable foods.

Cigarette Vending Machines.   Cigarette dispensers cover a wide capacity range. Some hold up to 1200 packs of varying sizes. The cigarettes are loaded into columns, up to 36 columns per machine. Horizontal conveyor type units are available in which a package is laid flat. When the machine is activated, a conveyor moves one package length, releasing the merchandise into a chute. Because of the differences in price range of a king, 100, or regular size package, these dispensers require a flexible pricing capability.

Canned Food and Beverage Machines.   These dispensers consist of a series of runways or chutes. When the machine is activated, a can is released and rolls or drops to a takeout shelf. Machines of this type can be adapted to heat-canned food or to cool, canned beverages. Packaged ice cube dispensers operate on the same principle.

Ice Cream Dispensers.   Dispensers that vend ice cream bricks or pops are completely refrigerated and insulated cabinets, constructed to maintain products at proper consistency. In addition, safety controls are incorporated that shut off a machine in the event of refrigeration failure.

Generally, packages are stored in column-type magazines which revolve within a cabinet. When the dispenser is set in motion and the selection is made by a customer, an ice cream package is released from the bottom of a column and drops through a double door—an added precaution to ensure that the inner cabinet is never exposed to the atmosphere.

The Automated Cafeteria

The automated cafeteria and snack service account for the major dollar volume of the vending industry. A typical automated cafeteria may contain the following equipment.

Product Dispensers.

(1) Pastry dispenser[1] (doughnuts, cakes, cookies, pie)
(2) Dessert dispenser (puddings, fruit salad, fresh fruit)
(3) Soft drink dispenser[1] (postmix, premix, bottles, or cans)
(4) Hot food dispenser (stews, prepared dishes)
(5) Soup and canned food dispenser
(6) Sandwich dispenser
(7) Cold food dispenser (salads)
(8) Ice cream dispenser[1]
(9) Milk and chocolate milk dispenser[1]
(10) Coffee, tea, hot chocolate, soup combination vendor[1]
(11) Cigarette and cigar dispenser[1]
(12) Candy dispenser[1]

Auxiliary Equipment.

(1) Change maker
(2) Microwave oven
(3) Condiment table
(4) Can opener
(5) Stirrers, plastic spoons, forks, knives, and napkins
(6) Trash receptacle
(7) Water fountain
(8) Utility and storage closets, slop sink, mops, and buckets
(9) Water treatment system if required
(10) Tables and chairs

QUALITY CONTROL AREAS

The major need for quality control of food and beverage vending equipment is sanitation. The second need is a rigid program of time and temperature control of perishable foods and beverages. The third segment pertains to commissary facilities that prepare foods such as sandwiches, salads, stews, and casseroles; and performs the role of a storage and distribution center. Although the National Automatic Merchandising Association in conjunction with the U.S. Public Health Service and state and local agencies have rendered a valuable service in eliminating many potential haz-

---

[1] Basic needs for a snack service.

ards associated with vended food, problems exist which are continually plaguing the customer with poor quality foods and merchandise.

The operation and quality control procedures for a commissary are identical to those required of any other foodservice facility. Differences are apparent and include wrapping of sandwiches and pastries, containerization of salads and other prepared foods, and transporting these items to vending installations.

For example, sandwiches prepared for vending must be securely wrapped. Machines are manufactured that automatically wrap sandwiches and other foods, such as pie portions, rolls, muffins, and pastries. Wrapping must be rapid so exposure to airborne contaminants is reduced to a minimum and traces of spoilage organisms on products are not given an opportunity to multiply. Labels should be affixed to each item for identification as well as time and date of wrapping. This type of identification will pinpoint the elapsed time, so items can be withdrawn from a vending machine and discarded. Wrapping materials should be moisture-proof and heat sealable. If a product is to be subjected to freezing or heating, the packaging material must be adaptable to these applications.

There are several important parameters of quality control at the vending site. Beverage machines form the focal point of exacting quality control procedures. Water and water-treatment methods discussed in Chapter 13 also apply to beverage vending equipment.

Sanitation of Vending Equipment

General Procedure.   The following sanitation procedures are general. For detailed procedures, check the manufacturer's manual for specific instructions. Local health departments should be consulted for applicable sanitation laws and for information regarding strength of sanitizing solutions.

Vending machines are foodservice equipment and must be treated as such. Food contact parts of a machine cannot be properly cleaned with a rag and a dash of water. This equipment is complex and requires the utmost attention, cleaning, and inspection. Poor quality beverages and complaints can usually be traced to improper cleaning.

The Sanitation Kit.   A professional job cannot be accomplished without sanitation equipment. The exact items depend on type of machine, company procedures, and machine location. The following items are recommended for the kit: (1) three buckets; (2) cleaning cloths and paper and cloth toweling which are lint-free and have high wet strength properties; (3) brushes of various sizes; (4) hand mops and sponges; (5) detergents, approved sanitizers, urn cleaner, and cleaner spray in bomb or bottle; (6) insecticide spray; (7) hand scrapers and soft wire brushes; (8) spare tubing for replacement purposes; (9) spare polyethylene waste bags; (10) spare water strainer and filter cartridge; and (11) flashlight.

Three buckets are necessary: for the detergent solution, sanitizing solution, and hot water rinse.

Definitions. The Public Health Department of the National Automatic Merchandising Association has established certain definitions to easily identify various facets within vending equipment pertaining to food, temperature, and spoilage. These include:

Food—Solid foods, commodities, beverages, ice, and water.

Food contact part—Any part or surface that touches unwrapped food. These surfaces include float tanks, mixes, troughs, tubing, canisters, and brewers.

Safe temperatures—45°F (8°C) or lower for cold food and 140°F (60°C) or higher for hot food.

Potentially hazardous or readily perishable—Foods that can cause food poisoning and require "safe temperatures."

Coffee Vending Machines (General Procedures). Commodity canisters contain sugar, powdered cream, powdered tea, and soup. Remove and shake dry commodity canisters every 10–14 days. Brush canister spout to remove any solidified material. Dump remaining dry cream every 30 days to prevent spoilage. Dust canister lids. Exchange soiled canisters for clean, sanitized ones.

Coffee brewing systems should be flushed with hot water from a service hose at each visit. Remove accumulations of coffee dust and wipe brewer surfaces. Urn cleaner should be used weekly or more frequently. Flush urn cleaner solution through the system after removing, and hand clean filters, heads, and brew chamber. Do not use urn cleaner in aluminum brewers. Inspect filter paper for soil, mildew, and flaws, and replace if necessary.

Pinch tubing or shut off power for several minutes to allow cleaning solution to penetrate deposits. Flush cleaning solution with several hot water cycles. Taste water to determine if off-tastes exist. Brewing chambers which are replaceable should be installed prior to cleaning operation.

Mixing bowls, troughs, and whippers should be exchanged for clean sanitized units. For daily maintenance, flush with a hot water cycle. If exchange units are not accessible, clean and dip into sanitizing solution weekly. Flush with hot water cycle after reinstallation.

Tubes and hoses should be cleaned along with bowls and troughs. Hand clean short lengths of tubing with tube brush dipped into detergent solution. Flush with hot water. Tubing requires replacement at intervals depending on the amount of deposit buildup that cannot be removed by normal means.

Interiors should be wiped or cleaned with a damp cloth, starting at the top and proceeding to the bottom. Use "dry wiping" methods for dust and commodity spillage. Use "wet methods" for splashed and caked-on material.

Rinse drain tubing with detergent, followed by a deodorizer. Flush out air exhaust tubing and clean screening on air vents.

Remove cup well and clean in detergent solution. Dust inside of door and cup storage area. Examine cups for dirt and traces of mildew.

Remove waste and grounds buckets upon completion of each cleaning operation. Wipe splash area around buckets. Check waste and replace with a clean polyethylene bag. Place 0.5 in. (1.3 cm) of clean water into bottom of waste buckets and add deodorizer for odor control.

Water filters and strainers should be checked regularly. Clean water strainer and replace filter cartridge if necessary.

Machines equipped with self-cleaning systems should be cleaned at each service by activating the self-cleaning unit. This procedure maintains all liquid contact points at optimum cleanliness without any "down-time" for a complete cleaning and sanitizing operation.

Soft Drink Vending Machines (General Procedures).   Sanitation procedures follow two approaches. The first is determined by the number of drinks served, such as 1000, 5000, 15,000, or 30,000 drinks. The second method is to set up cleaning and sanitizing schedules on daily, weekly, monthly, quarterly, and semiannual bases. The latter schedule is widely used as it is less complicated and easier for record keeping.

The same sanitation kit used for coffee equipment applies to soft drink machines. Disposable paper towels should be used instead of cloths and should be lint-free and possess high wet strength properties.

Daily Service.   The cup well or delivery compartment is removed and cleaned in a mild detergent solution, followed by an approved sanitizing solution. The waste bucket should be treated in the same manner.

Wash cabinet door, inside and out, with a clean hot damp paper towel and dry thoroughly.

Wipe top of water bath, ice maker, ice hopper, syrup tanks, and tubing, and base of the vendor with a hot damp paper towel followed by complete drying.

Deodorizer or detergent powder is then sprinkled in the waste bucket to prevent and control odors.

Weekly Service.   In addition to daily procedures, brush refrigeration compartment screen to maintain constant airflow and compressor efficiency. Depending on the location of a machine, this step may have to be done daily.

Remove water and syrup dispensing spigots, and wash in mild detergent solution and sanitize. Wipe with paper toweling and rinse thoroughly with clean hot water and dry.

Remove cup turret and its mechanism. Clean with a hot damp paper towel and dry.

Monthly Service.   Follow both daily and weekly procedures. Drain and refill water bath and sanitize ice maker. Remove ice from maker after opening ice hopper dispensing door. Depending on type of ice maker, disassemble unit. Pour 1 qt (1 liter) of ice maker cleaning solution into hopper. Activate the unit and allow to run for at least 5 min. Normal accumulation of slime or algae growth should now be removed. Drain solution and refill with clean clear water; drain and repeat this step several times until assured of complete removal of cleaning solution.

It is advisable to schedule cleaning and sanitizing of syrup tanks and component system monthly. Remove tanks after disconnecting syrup hose. Replace with a sanitized unit. Ends of tubing should be immersed in flushing solution. Cycling will remove all traces of syrup. Inspect tubing and replace if worn. If a sanitized replacement tank is not available, empty syrup tanks and add 1 qt (1 liter) of sanitizing solution to each tank. Pump the solution through pumps and syrup lines and flush out each of the systems with clean water.

Water system maintenance is accomplished by emptying feed cup. A mild solution of citric acid is added which will clean all surfaces without leaving an aftertaste. The acid solution consists of 1 oz (30 ml) of citric acid crystals added to 1 qt (1 liter) of water.

Hot and Cold Food Vending Machines.   *Daily Service.*

(1)   Check pack date codes. Withdraw and destroy items stored beyond scheduled time limit.

(2)   Check accuracy of built-in thermometers with calibrated hand instruments. Foods requiring refrigeration must be maintained at a temperature of 45°F (8°C) or below (preferably at 35°F) and 140°F (60°C) or above for hot foods. Built-in thermometers must be accurate to ±2°F (1°C). Temperature checks should be made in the warmest part of a refrigerated food storage compartment, or the coldest section of a heated food storage compartment.

(3)   All containers or parts of vending machines which directly contact potentially hazardous food shall be removed from a machine daily and shall be thoroughly cleaned and effectively sanitized in the commissary or other approved facility.

(4)   Hot or cold foods that are securely wrapped or in original containers shall be handled in a sanitary manner and loaded into machines rapidly. During unloading and prior to restacking, shelves, chutes, and interior of the door and glass should be wiped with a damp cloth previously dipped into a sanitizing solution.

(5)   Refrigerated vending machines may keep sandwiches for several days at 35°F (2°C); however, bread should be visually examined for any evidence of mold growth.

(6)   A record of all cleaning operations should be kept in each machine, and should exhibit extent of procedures and date performed during each 30-day period.

Weekly and Monthly Service.

(1) Depending on machine workload and operating efficiency, complete interior sanitation and cleaning may be required weekly or monthly. This procedure may involve removal of all food from cabinets so that extensive cleaning and sanitizing can be performed. Food removed prior to this type of service should be stored at safe temperatures during service. Before reloading a newly serviced machine, check that temperatures have reached the safe limit.

(2) Heaters, condensers, fans, and other appurtenances should be inspected and freed of dust and other foreign matter.

(3) Wipe the exterior of a machine with a lint-free cloth.

Coffee Vending Machines. Fresh brew vending machines are completely automatic, with the exception of total cleaning and maintenance. Many machines are manufactured which contain self-cleaning systems. However, additional cleaning is required periodically, depending on manufacturer's instructions. The most widely used coffee brewers are single-cup units. These brew one cup at a time, thus eliminating the problem of holding for extended periods. Batch brewers are still employed but their popularity has waned because of a constant need for detailed sanitary procedures. These machines, if in top operating condition, produce a beverage with characteristics similar to a half-gallon brewer.

Machines for dispensing freeze-dried soluble coffee are gaining support from the industry. These are similar to the old direct soluble powder equipment. This turnabout is due to the development of freeze-dried instant coffee, which possesses more of the character of a fresh-brewed beverage. The process of freeze concentration, in combination with freeze-drying, results in a minimum loss of volatile aroma and flavor components of coffee. In addition, freeze-dried dispensers are not as complicated, hence require less maintenance and cleaning. Staling and product waste are reduced; however, these advantages rely on a completely dry atmosphere within a machine.

One of the major disadvantages of vended coffee is a lack of proper sanitation. One reason for this is a shortage of trained personnel needed to perform these functions. Brewing chambers and their components contain numerous parts and in many cases are inaccessible. Adequate cleaning can be accomplished by the simple removal of an entire chamber in some equipment. Self-cleaning machines, a recent innovation, are available and reduce cleaning to a minimum.

Brewing Principles. For the purpose of this section, discussion will be limited to single cup equipment.

Ground coffee is stored in hoppers which hold from 8 to 12 lb. A volumetric measuring feed is built into the lower section of a hopper. When the unit is activated, a screw type mechanism or worm gear pushes coffee out into the brewing chamber. The amount of coffee, measured in grams, is regulated by setting controls on a hopper or on a cam. Since the quantity or throw of coffee is metered on a volume basis, its bulk density has an important bearing on unit weight. Heavy coffee requires less space, while a light or fluffy product will take up more area. If bulk density varies, then the outcome will be inconsistent. Another factor affecting any brew is grind or particle size. Single cup brewing uses an extremely fine grind. The short cycle, timed in seconds, makes this property mandatory for full extraction. Although many essential brewing techniques apply to vending machines, those most critical are extra fine particle size, short brew cycles, and blend components which ensure complete wettability.

After coffee is placed in the brewing chamber, about 6 oz of hot water are added. Depending on the manufacturer, brewing chambers may operate on an upward thrust of a piston, forcing the brew through a filtering medium into delivery tubes, and then into a cup. Another method employs a downward moving piston, while still another makes use of a rotating brew cup. Brewing chambers are generally rinsed after each brew to rid the interior of residual grounds. Water is heated in open or closed tanks. Regardless of the method, a constant source of hot water is necessary. During peak periods, temperature gradients must remain fairly constant to maintain a brewing temperature of 200°F ± 5° (94°C ± 3°). A drawback for the consumer is handling of the coffee cup at these high temperatures. One machine manufacturer has overcome this problem by the addition of a small quantity of cold water with each serving. Another uses a heat exchanger in the coffee delivery line just before the cup delivery nozzle.

The Key to Quality. Quality vended coffee depends on proper machine adjustments, maintenance, and a coffee blended from choice ingredients and possessing all physical properties required for optimum extraction.

(1)   Cleanliness is the prime requisite for a palatable brew. One area which is generally neglected is delivery tubing. The interior of flexible tubing becomes pitted and scored after prolonged usage. These channels fill up with coffee residues which have an adverse effect on beverage flavor. Slow machines require more attention than busy ones, as a liquid may evaporate and form deposits on brewing surfaces.

A quick test for clean tubing is to take a paper napkin, wrap it around a pencil or screwdriver, and push it into the tube. If the napkin is clean when withdrawn, then tubing is in good condition.

Exhaust fan blades, exhaust screens, and air vent ducts must be dusted weekly, so air circulation is at a maximum. High internal humidity will cause product "hangup," resulting in short weights and inconsistency.

(2)   Water temperature must be maintained at 200°F ± 5° (94°C ± 3°). Industrywide surveys reveal that low brewing temperatures are the

second reason for poor-tasting coffee. Many machines have built-in temperature gauges; however, it is best to use an accurate hand thermometer to check these readings. Depending on the manufacturer, readings can be checked by inserting a thermometer stem into the hot water tank, water from the flush hose, or the hot chocolate or tea water. Another method is to check the temperature of the finished brew. If a machine has been standing idle, it should be activated so that the brewer and delivery line are warmed. A check can then be made on the second or third run. The temperature should read about 170°F (77°C).

(3) Coffee measurement (throw) is very important in producing good coffee. It is impossible to produce a quality, palatable beverage by stretching a pound of coffee to yield 65 to 80 cups. There are no coffees that will give this quantity, nor are there machines available that will brew a good beverage of this high yield. Measurements of coffee throws should be made regularly using an accurate gram scale. Average at least three weight measurements for a good analysis. The normal throw range for 6 oz (177 ml) of brew water is 8.5 to 10.5 g.

(4) Brew water volume is another factor which warrants careful scrutiny so that a correct coffee-to-water ratio is maintained. The 7 oz (207 ml) cup is the size in general use. Yield should be 5.5 oz (163 ml) of finished brew. A quick check can be made by observing the height of liquid in a cup, which for 5.5 oz (163 ml) should measure about ⅜ in. (0.95 cm) below the lip. This will allow ample room for sugar, whitener, and easy handling by the consumer without spillage.

(5) Brew cycle can be accurately timed with a stopwatch. Maintenance manuals should be checked for the correct time cycle setting, as machines vary with manufacturers. Pressure and filter mediums will have an effect on the cycle. Particle size also influences the cycle, hence short cups and inconsistency may result.

(6) Filter mediums are taken for granted and are the last area of investigation should something go wrong. This observation applies mainly to filter paper. If short cups, inconsistency, bitterness, or foreign flavor develops, it is possible that the filter paper may be faulty. The paper may have an inconsistent weave or have pinholes. If a brew has an off-flavor or off-taste, this problem may be poor quality paper. In any case, the roll should be removed, examined, and checked for defects. Sniffing the paper and immersing some in water will also help to detect foreign tastes. Metallic mesh filters should be inspected for flaws and residue buildup. If problems exist with short or erratic cup fill, the filter requires a change.

(7) Water conditions, both external and internal, can result in a poor beverage. Water heaters should be purged periodically. If a machine does not have a water strainer, one should be installed. If water contains sediment, chlorine, or other contaminants, install an activated carbon filter.

Growth of Mold and Bacteria. Coffee vending machines can become a focal point of mold and bacteria contamination if proper and complete sanitation is not maintained. High humidity within a machine will create an ideal atmosphere for the growth of microorganisms. Powdered products, which are a part of most coffee vending equipment such as soup, tea, sugar, nondairy whitener, and coffee are susceptible to contamination. Schedules must be maintained to forestall these conditions, which include provisions for rotating the ingredients and inspecting for off-odors and mold. Hoppers and tubing must undergo regular and frequent sanitation.

Vending of Hot Chocolate. Vending of hot chocolate beverages is an integral part of a fresh brew coffee machine. In addition to coffee and hot chocolate, these units usually dispense tea and soup (Fig. 14.1).

Operation of the chocolate dispenser mechanism within a vending machine is almost identical to counter dispensers. When the hot chocolate selector switch is activated, water and powder are simultaneously discharged into a blender funnel. The combined ingredients are whipped and are then passed into a cup.

Water temperatures are maintained at about 200°F (94°C). Machines are available that contain a mixing valve that allows a small quantity of cold water to mix with hot water to reduce beverage temperature.

Vending machines have provisions to change cup sizes, such as 7 oz (207

FIG.14.1.   Exterior view of a vending machine that dispenses coffee, hot chocolate, soup, and tea.
Courtesy of Coffee-Mat Corp.

ml) to a 9 oz (266 ml) size. The following powder-to-water ratios are recommended for each size cup:

Cup Size, oz	Powder Throw, g	Volume of Water, oz
7	25	5
9	34	7

It should be remembered that the whipping action of a dispenser will increase the liquid volume of a finished drink, so that sufficient head room in a cup is necessary.

The following points are important in the quality control of vended hot chocolate:

(1) Water temperature is identical to that required for coffee. The water source is drawn from the same tank and will be adequate for hot chocolate.

(2) Product quantity or throw requires a weekly check. Hangup or bridging will occur at the spout of a hopper discharge area if chocolate powder solidifies due to high internal humidity. Product inconsistency can be traced to this problem.

(3) The mixing chamber should be flushed each time a machine is serviced. Many units are equipped with a water switch which can be activated to flush the mixing chamber and delivery tubes.

(4) Don't overload the hopper. This practice will cake the powder, hence incorrect measurements via auger discharge feed will result.

(5) To prevent growth of surface mold and bacteria, the hopper cover should be checked to ensure snug, moisture-free fit. The powder should be inspected weekly to determine if it is freeflowing and not contaminated. If contamination is suspected, the entire hopper contents must be discarded and the hopper sanitized, washed, and fully dried before refilling with fresh chocolate powder.

Soft Drink Vending Machines. Postmix vending machines are completely automatic and contain all components including ice making equipment necessary to produce a finished beverage of high quality. These machines are sophisticated automated equipment.

Postmix cup machines dispense a finished carbonated or still soft drink in a cup with or without ice from a choice of flavored syrups. Postmix powder dispensers vend a juice type beverage produced from a powder base, such as orange, lemon, and grapefruit. The Moyer Diebel Powder machine has accommodations for four flavors and holds 460 cups and 8.5 lb (3.8 kg) of powdered ingredients per selection. This type of dispenser has proved successful on commercial, institutional, and recreational locations.

Cup vending machines are available in a number of sizes and capacities, varying from 500 to 1500 seven, nine, or ten-ounce cups. Carbonation may be set for high, low, or none, depending on syrup requirements. Flavor selections range from 4 to 8.

VENDING COFFEE INSPECTION

Client—   Date—   Time of Inspection—
Location—   Busy Location—   Supervisor—
Type Machine—   Model—

Preliminary Tests — prior to adjustments — (black only).
Kind of Cup —   Capacity of Cup —
Brand of Cream Vehicle —   After-taste: Yes _____ No _____
Temperature of Brew at spout —   °   Ounces of Brew —
Throw of Coffee — _____ grams;   equal to _____ cups per lb.
Brew Character: Aroma — Pleasant _____ ; None _____ .
                Taste — Flavorful _____ ; Light _____ .
                Heavy _____ ; Bitter _____ .
                Foreign Flavor _____ .
Sediment: None _____   Some _____   Excessive _____
Test with Cream —

Tests after Adjustments (black only).
Temperature of brew at spout _____ °F.   Ounces of brew _____ .
Throw of Coffee: _____ grams; equal to _____ cups per lb.
Brew Character: Aroma — Pleasant _____ ; None _____ .
                Taste — Flavorful _____ ; Light _____ .
                Heavy _____ ; Bitter _____ ; Foreign Flavor _____ .
Sediment: None _____   Some _____   Excessive _____

Water Conditions —
Is machine clean ? —
Type Sugar —

REMARKS:

FIG.14.2.   Coffee vending machine inspection form.

Depending on design, flavor selections can be made before or after a coin is accepted by the machine. Most dispensers are equipped with coin changers to return change from a quarter. After selection is made and the unit activated, a finished beverage is ready for the consumer in less than 10 sec. Activation starts a chain of events. As a cup falls into place from its storage rack, syrup, carbonated water, and ice are metered and delivered to the cup. The amount of each ingredient is controlled by a cam or electrical sensing device.

Premix Vending Machines.   Premix vending machines dispense individual cup size servings. Their use is limited to locations that do not have a water supply or where temporary installations are required. Portable tanks are filled with syrup and water and the mixture carbonated. These prefilled tanks are then installed in a machine and hooked into a refrigeration system. Carbonation can also be performed within the machine by units provided with CO_2 injection equipment. Greater uniformity is achieved with these dispensers as the filling operation is controlled more carefully; however, a major drawback is limited capacity.

Can and Bottle Vending Machines.   Vending machines are also manufactured to handle cans or bottles. These units have refrigeration facilities to precool about 15% of machine (bottle or can storage) capacity. The can dispenser is in wider use since cans are disposable and pose no empty container storage or breakage problems. Canned beverage vending machines have made rapid progress in recent years. Although the profit structure is lower than postmix vending dispensers, machine maintenance is lower, drinks are more uniform, and customer satisfaction greater.

Quality Control.   Quality control factors for soft drink vending machines parallel those required for foodservice dispensers. Chapter 11, Nonalcoholic Beverages Control, should be referred to for these procedures. The following quality control areas are repeated for continuity.

(1)   Detection of foreign objects in the system
(2)   Determination of efficiency of ice making equipment
(3)   Determination of water conditions
(4)   Determination of effectiveness of water conditioning devices
(5)   Determination of syrup-water ratio if a vending machine is the postmix type
(6)   Determination of carbonation volumes and working efficiency of carbonator
(7)   Determination of syrup spoilage in storage tanks
(8)   An effective and regularly scheduled sanitation program
(9)   Sensory evaluation by taste-testing techniques
(10)   Elimination of possible causes of copper contamination by following maintenance procedures established by the National Automatic Merchandising Association

Various inspection forms are employed to monitor the operating efficiency of vending machines. Figure 14.2 shows a coffee inspection form, and Fig. 14.3 is used for the overall vending installation.

304

(Location & Type Machine)

1. _____

2. _____

3. _____

4. _____

5. _____

Vending Company _____

_____ Address _____

MACHINE AND LOCATION
INSPECTION FORM
FOR THE VENDING OPERATOR

(Supervisor's Code)

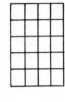 OK

 Not Satisfactory

 Corrected at inspection

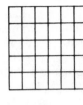 Does not apply

CONDITION OF LOCATION

Machine
1 2 3 4 5

1. General Conditions

a. Floors, platforms cleanable?
b. Floors, platforms clean?
c. Insects, rodents under control?
d. Light adequate for servicing?

2. Machine Placement

a. No overhead sewer pipes?
b. Shielded from rain, dust, etc.?

3. Service Utensils and Equipment

a. Cups, bowls inverted?
b. Spoons wrapped, or in dispenser?
c. Warmers, ovens, etc. clean?
d. Can openers protected, clean?

4. Condiments (if offered)

a. Clean dispensers, or packeted?
b. Protected from flies, dirt?

CONDITION OF MACHINE

Machine
1 2 3 4 5

8. Cabinet Outside

a. Front, sides, top clean?
b. Delivery door, good repair?
c. Utility, bolt holes closed?
d. Vent openings screened?

9. Cabinet Inside

a. Splash, spillage, removed?
b. Waste pail emptied, cleaned?
c. No insects, rodents?

10. Product Containers and Piping

a. Product surfaces, good repair, cleanable?
b. Canisters, reservoirs, pots, tanks, troughs, bowls, chutes, tubes, brewers, valves, pipes, etc., clean?

11. Cleaning Methods

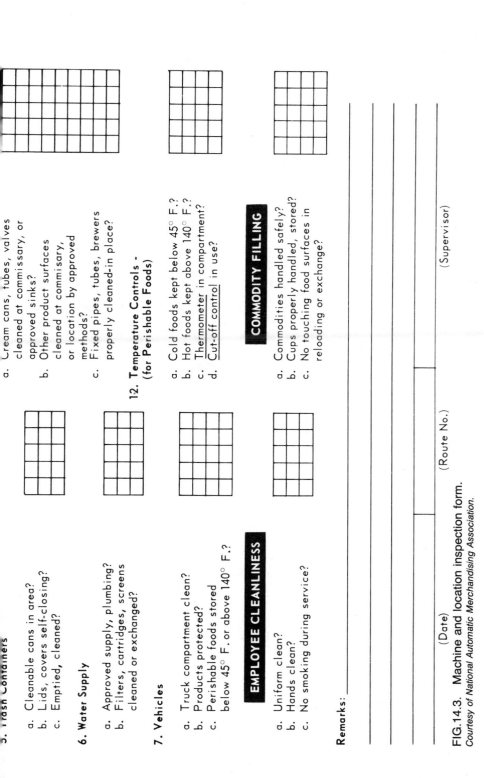

5. Trash Containers

a. Cleanable cans in area?
b. Lids, covers self-closing?
c. Emptied, cleaned?

6. Water Supply

a. Approved supply, plumbing?
b. Filters, cartridges, screens cleaned or exchanged?

7. Vehicles

a. Truck compartment clean?
b. Products protected?
c. Perishable foods stored below 45° F. or above 140° F.?

EMPLOYEE CLEANLINESS

a. Uniform clean?
b. Hands clean?
c. No smoking during service?

a. Cream cans, tubes, valves cleaned at commissary, or approved sinks?
b. Other product surfaces cleaned at commisary, or location by approved methods?
c. Fixed pipes, tubes, brewers properly cleaned-in place?

12. Temperature Controls - (for Perishable Foods)

a. Cold foods kept below 45° F.?
b. Hot foods kept above 140° F.?
c. Thermometer in compartment?
d. Cut-off control in use?

COMMODITY FILLING

a. Commodities handled safely?
b. Cups properly handled, stored?
c. No touching food surfaces in reloading or exchange?

Remarks:

(Date)   (Route No.)   (Supervisor)

FIG.14.3. Machine and location inspection form.
Courtesy of National Automatic Merchandising Association.

15

Energy Management

One of the most profound issues facing both the individual *and* the food-service business is energy and all of its ramifications. In the retailing and service industries, because of their relatively high "energy intensity," this impact of rapidly increasing energy costs is especially hard felt. In fact, energy costs currently are rising at a faster rate than *any other* cost on the typical balance sheet. Management is in a squeeze-play: on the one hand, how to continue to satisfy customer demands, and on the other hand, how to hold the line and reduce energy consumption.

It is tempting to avoid the energy issue as well as to shift the blame for our dilemma to others. Society in general tends to come up with easy answers, such as:

(1) "There are plenty of reserves—we just haven't found them yet."
(2) "The major oil companies are making excess profits, which are energy 'rip-offs.' "
(3) "We went to the moon. . . we'll get out of this one, too."

There are numerous suggestions for solving our energy problems, but in reality there are no simple answers. Rather, three relevant questions must be addressed and discussed:

(1) Are fossil fuels *running out*?
(2) Are energy prices going to continue to *increase*?
(3) Why should citizens and industry *conserve*?

These questions obviously are interrelated, but each is best answered separately.

ENERGY SUPPLY AND DEMAND

As a nation, the United States has (or had) an abundance of energy resources. However, as it prospered and demanded ever-increasing amounts of cheap energy, consumption greatly exceeded the domestic supply, thus necessitating the present reliance on imported supplies, particularly crude oil.

This reliance has led to the much-publicized "OPEC squeeze": in 1970, a barrel of crude oil cost a little more than $1, and by the end of 1980, the cost had risen to about $35 per barrel (OPEC = Organization of Petroleum Exporting Countries). The supply for assorted energy demands is shown in Table 15.1.

Obviously, oil sources constitute almost half of the supply system. Also note that about three-fourths of the demands are supplied by oil plus natural gas—both of which are "fossil fuels" and therefore nonrenewable resources. The past, present, and future United States oil supplies (domestic, foreign, and maybe "synfuels") are shown in Table 15.2.

For comparative purposes, note the changing reliance on imported oil. Economically and politically, it is in the national interest to reduce oil imports, as shown in the estimates for the year 2000. The natural gas situation is somewhat better, but note in Table 15.3 that by the year 2000 there will be an everincreasing reliance on imports, which will gradually push up the cost of natural gas.

On the demand side, the past, present, and future situation—by major demand sectors—is shown in Table 15.4. Except for a slight shift away from transportation needs, these sectors remain fairly constant.

The previous tables only describe "percentage share," or the relative differences in supply and demand. In an absolute sense, however, the total demand ultimately must be reduced. Therein lies the problem, but, more importantly, also the solution. The quickest, easiest, and least expensive mechanism for solving the energy consumption dilemma is *conservation*, by developing and maintaining good energy management.

TABLE 15.1.   United States Energy Supply

	% Share		
Sources	1960	1980	2000
Oil	45	46	32
Gas	30	26	17
Coal	22	19	33
Nuclear	—	5	13
Miscellaneous	3	4	5

Source: U.S. Dept. of Energy.

TABLE 15.2.   United States Oil Supply

	% Share			
Sources	1960	1980		2000
Domestic	82	55		39
old[1]			14	
new[2]			25	
Foreign	18	45		33
"Synfuels"	—	—		28

Source: U.S. Dept. of Energy.
[1] Known reserves.
[2] Discoveries since 1980—estimated.

TABLE 15.3. United States Natural Gas Supply

	% Share		
Sources	1960	1980	2000
Domestic	99	90	66
old[1]		34	
new[2]		32	
Foreign	1	8	26
"Synfuels"	—	2	8

Source: U.S. Dept. of Energy.
[1] Known reserves.
[2] Discoveries since 1980—estimated.

TABLE 15.4. United States Energy Demand

	% Share		
Sector	1960	1980	2000
Residential	18	20	18
Commercial	12	14	17
Industrial	36	32	37
Transportation	25	26	20
Nonenergy	9	8	8

Source: U.S. Dept. of Energy.

ENERGY COSTS

The cost of energy, especially refined oil products, continues and will continue to rise. There will never again be inexpensive gasoline prices. The nation is now witnessing a "redoubling effect"—the cost of energy doubles about every 4 years, as illustrated in Table 15.5. The primary reason for such an extreme rate of increase is the major reliance on imported crude oil and the rapid OPEC price increases.

In addition to the redoubling of electricity costs (Table 15.5), similar increases are also occurring in the case of natural gas, as shown in Table 15.6.

ENERGY CONTROL AND CONSERVATION

Why is it so difficult to get foodservice operations to conserve energy? Since conservation saves money and effectively increases profit, why are they not all for it? There are a number of reasons. First, compared with labor and food costs, energy costs are relatively minor, usually less than 5% of gross sales. In most businesses, management simply has not given a very high priority to reducing energy usage. Second, the foodservice industry continues to opt for the "pass along" principle: as costs go up, so too do menu prices—rather than reducing costs by more efficient management practices. Third, most managers concede that as long as their profit margins are maintained at a forecasted level, they are not too concerned about energy costs.

TABLE 15.5. Redoubling of
Electricity Costs

Year	Cents/kWh[1]
1976	4
1980	8
1984	12

Source: U.S. Dept. of Energy.
[1] National average.

TABLE 15.6. Increased
Natural Gas Costs

Year	Cents/Therm[1]
1971	12.5
1979	27.5
1980	45
1981	55
1985	100

Source: U.S. Dept. of Energy.
[1] 1 Therm = 100 cubic feet
(CCF).

NRA GUIDELINES

The National Restaurant Association in conjunction with the Midwest Research Institute has formulated guidelines and energy management techniques. These are representative of the current effort being expended by the foodservice industry to reduce energy consumption.

The National Restaurant Association has granted permission to reproduce these important and timely guidelines, and they are given in the following sections. Many of the points listed in the guidelines are actually coupled to foodservice quality control procedures discussed in this book.

Figures 15.1 and 15.2 are examples of charts which can be used to record the use of energy. These charts may be modified to better fit a particular operation.

ENERGY SURVEY

Restaurant: _____
Date: _____

Location	Fuel Leaks	Steam Leaks	Water Leaks	Poor or No Insulation	Excess Lighting	Equipment Running and Not Needed	Excess Exhaust Volume	Excess Heating & Cooling	Other	Recommended Action
1										
2										
3										
4										
5										
6										
7										
8										
9										
10										
11										
12										
13										
14										
15										
16										
17										
18										
19										
20										

FIG. 15.1. Energy survey chart.
Courtesy of the National Restaurant Association.

ENERGY SURVEY - EQUIPMENT
(For Test Restaurants Having Meters)

Restaurant: _____
Month: _____

Equipment Item	Electric Load, Rated Input Complete as Applicable				Actual Electric Use	Natural Gas, Rated Input		Actual Gas Use
	Volts	Amps	kWh	Horsepower	kWh/Month	Btu/Hr	cu ft/Hr	cu ft/Month
Fryer								
Range								
Kettle, Steam Jacketed								
Oven								
Broiler								
Mixer								
Refrigerator								
Freezer								
Coffee Maker								
Toaster								
Water Heater								
Air Conditioner								
Heating Unit								
Afterburner								
Electrostatic Precipitator								
Exhaust Fans								
Grill								
Griddle								
Water Cooler								
Food Warmer								
Dishwasher								
Booster Heater-Dishwasher								
Heat Lamp								
Other								

FIG. 15.2.   Energy survey equipment chart.
Courtesy of the National Restaurant Association.

Food Preparation

_____ 1. Determine a schedule of preheating times for ovens, steam tables, grills, broilers, fry vats, etc. Generally, 10 to 30 min (depending on appliance) is adequate.

_____ 2. Stagger turn-on times for heavy duty electrical equipment so that 30 min intervals can be achieved. This should reduce the demand load.

_____ 3. Use a second fry unit, broiler, oven, etc., only for peak business hours. Develop a schedule showing the hours and day where second units are required.

_____ 4. When preheating ovens, set the thermostat at the desired temperature; it will preheat no faster and waste energy if you dial higher.

_____ 5. Calibrate oven thermostats to assure correct cooking temperature and maximum efficiency.

_____ 6. Determine the cooking capacity of ovens. Use the smaller or more energy-efficient oven when possible.

7. Load and unload ovens quickly to avoid unnecessary heat loss. Every second an oven is open, it loses about 1% of its heat.

8. Use correct size oven vent hoods.

9. Use proper blend of makeup air in exhaust hoods.

10. Install twist-on timers or individual switches on food warming infrared heat lamps.

11. Turn off cooking and heating units that are not needed.

12. Check the fuel-air ratio on all gas burners and adjust to the most efficient mixture.

13. Consult your local gas utility company about the use of pilot lights. Adjustments made by persons not thoroughly familiar with the equipment could be dangerous.

14. Begin cooking food while oven is warming up (the exception being for food which will dry out or overcook).

15. Cook meat slowly at low temperatures. Cooking a roast for 5 hr at 250°F (121°C) could save 25 to 50% of the energy that would be used in cooking for 3 hr at 350°F (177°C).

16. Schedule baking or roasting so that oven capacity can be fully utilized, thereby reducing operating hours.

17. Aluminum foil retards the baking of a potato. If foil is necessary, wrap after potato is baked.

18. Oven should not be opened during operation. Food will cook faster and lose less moisture if door is opened at scheduled times.

19. Whenever possible, huddle food on griddle close together and heat only that portion of griddle being cooked on.

20. Placing weight on bacon and sausage quickens their cooking time but may alter the characteristics of the product.

21. Frozen food should be thawed in refrigerator. Food will thaw easily and help reduce power demand for refrigerator. Thaw all foods before cooking, unless product characteristics prohibit.

22. Use only the size of oven that is needed for the job. Extra space heating results in wasted energy.

23. Always turn char-broiler heat to medium after briquets are hot. Keep briquets clean.

24. When using a gas range for full heat conditions, the tip of the flame should just touch the bottom of the pan or kettle.

25. Foods will cook faster when covered with lids.

26. Placing foil under range burners and griddles will improve the operation efficiency and make equipment easier to clean.

27. Griddles should be cleaned every shift. Remove deposits, being careful to prevent loose deposits from falling on hot area and forming air pollution by thermal degradation.

28. Fryers need to be cleaned and the oil filtered at least once a day.

29. Heating equipment should be clustered together and away from cooling equipment.

____30. Develop a schedule for equipment use. Equipment should be turned on at a specific time, to a specific temperature, and turned off at the designated time.

____31. Installation of an in-the-meat thermometer, with gauge outside the oven, will reduce heat loss from opening the oven to check roasting progress.

____32. Install timers for kitchen equipment to automatically control cooking time.

____33. Electric range burners should always be smaller than the kettle or pot placed on them.

____34. Place kettles and pots close together on range tops to decrease heat loss.

____35. Check gas pressure to appliances to assure that adequate pressure is available from supplier.

____36. Turn on food warmers and hot plates only as needed; don't let them run when not in use. Also, run at the lowest temperature permissible for safe food handling.

Heating, Ventilation, and Air Conditioning

____ 1. When heating is required, set the thermostat to 68°F (20°C). For cooling, set thermostat at 78°F (26°C). After closing time, the thermostat can be set for 55° to 60°F (13° to 16°C) during the winter and 80° to 82°F (27° to 28°C) during the summer.

When cooling, each degree the thermostat is raised will result in about 5% reduction in electrical consumption. When heating, each degree lower will result in about 3% reduction in energy consumption. If you anticipate a room to be vacant for more than 2 days during the summer months, cut the air conditioning off. In some areas of the country, high humidity would prevent this practice.

____ 2. Stagger startup times of equipment to avoid heavy electrical demand at one time.

This could save money on the electric bill. Most utility companies charge according to peak demand for each hour, and total power usage.

____ 3. Balance registers properly for best heat distribution between kitchen and dining room.

____ 4. Inspect and clean all HVAC (Heat., Vent., and Air Cond.) system filters at least monthly (remember makeup air units).

The National Bureau of Standards estimates that a general energy reduction of 10% could be realized if a cooling system is kept clean and in good operating condition.

____ 5. Inspect all heating and cooling air ducts for cleanliness, proper insulation, and leaks.

_____ 6. Keep all doors and windows closed.
Perhaps in parts of the country, ambient air can be used instead of conditioned air. In these cases, windows can be opened and air movement accomplished with exhaust fans.

_____ 7. Vestibules should be installed at entrance doorways. Delivery doors should have adequate weather stripping.

_____ 8. All pipes and vents whose thermal control is important (hot water, steam, air conditioning, etc.) should have adequate insulation.

_____ 9. Check the accuracy of HVAC system thermostats.

_____10. Compressors should not be located near heating units.

_____11. Check size and speed of exhaust fans and limit to actual needs.

_____12. Check doors, windows, openings, and walls for tightness. Caulk all fixed openings.

_____13. Ceiling and walls should have adequate insulation. Concrete block walls should be covered with insulation board.

_____14. Attic areas should be ventilated during hot weather.

_____15. Fresh air dampers installed in HVAC return air duct could eliminate the operation of the air conditioning (except fan) during off-peak seasons.

_____16. Fresh air makeup units should be designed so that the damper is closed when the unit is shut down.

_____17. Drop-panel screening should be installed to reduce solar heat gain through glass windows and walls.

_____18. Operations heating with fuel oil should check size of oil nozzle in use.

_____19. Close the damper on unused fireplaces to prevent room heat loss.

_____20. Maintain adequate humidity to eliminate the extra heat needed to ensure customer comfort.

_____21. Install water treatment system on hot water and steam systems if needed. Chemical deposits reduce heating or cooking efficiency.

_____22. Balance ventilation and exhaust systems to maintain the rate of air turnover at the lowest number consistent with adequate ventilation and safety.

_____23. Close off dining areas not in use and turn off their heating or cooling systems (high humidity areas may require some air treatment).

_____24. During cold weather, draperies should be open during daylight hours to allow increased light and absorption of heat. They should be closed during the night hours to conserve heat.

Sanitation

_____ 1. Turn water heater down to 75°F (24°C) on closing, and turn to 140°F (60°C) 2 hr before opening. (Adjust warmup time to fit the particular units.)

_____ 2. Drain water heater every 6 months.

_____ 3. Shut off electric booster heaters on dishwashers when the kitchen is closed.

_____ 4. Use hot water only when necessary.

_____ 5. Do not use dishwashing machine for a small number of soiled dishes. Wait until a full load is available before running.

_____ 6. Keep heater coils free from lime accumulations.

_____ 7. When the main dishwashing rush is over, turn off equipment booster heaters and accumulate dishes until the next rush period.

_____ 8. Dripping water faucets are costly in water and energy use. All leaky faucets should have washers replaced immediately.

_____ 9. Obtain water pressure regulators for hot water line to dishwasher to reduce wasted hot water. Set regulator to the operating pressure required by the machine.

_____10. Make sure power rinse on dishwasher is turning off automatically when tray has gone through machine.

_____11. Insulate hot water lines.

_____12. Limit general use hot water to 140°F (60°C). Some taps can use 110°F (43°C) water.

_____13. Cleaning should be done during daylight hours if possible.

_____14. Mop from bucket to conserve hot water.

_____15. Accumulate trash for full load burning frequencies, when incinerators are used.

Lighting

_____ 1. Standard life lamps save energy when compared with extended life lamps.

_____ 2. PAR floodlights give the same lighting as reflector floodlights but use about one-half the wattage.

_____ 3. High efficiency fluorescent lights will use about 14% less energy than older models.

_____ 4. Incandescent lamps, high-intensity discharge lamps, and some types of fluorescents can be switched off and on as needed without serious loss of lamp life or performance.

_____ 5. Relamp to lower wattage where possible.

_____ 6. For lighting design, use the ESI (equivalent spherical illumination) concept in selecting equipment and layout.

_____ 7. Metallic additive lamps and high-pressure sodium lamps are two of the most efficient lamps.

_____ 8. The energy requirements for office lighting can be reduced around 30% by turning off lights in vacant offices, reducing lighting during noon hours, and using minimum lighting for after-hours cleanup.

_____ 9. The lumens per watt available from various lamps are:

Lamp	Lumens per Watt
Incandescent	17 to 22
Mercury	56 to 63
Fluorescent	67 to 83
Multivapor	85 to 100
Sodium	105 to 130

_____10. Obtain a computer analysis of lighting cost for planned and established restaurants. The analysis will provide information on lamp types, operating hours, and costs.

_____11. Consider time clocks or photocells that automatically turn off power after closing hours for:

(a) Signs
(b) Exterior lights, fountains, waterfalls, etc., on grounds
(c) Exterior lights on buildings

_____12. Replace resistance-type dimmers with transformer type.

_____13. Investigate the feasibility of short-time (twist-on) timers controlling lights in storerooms and walk-in boxes or other time-use areas where light is apt to be left on indefinitely.

_____14. Have local contractor measure lighting output in your kitchen. FEA's lighting guidelines generally call for 50 foot-candles at desks, 30 foot-candles in rooms and work areas, and 10 foot-candles in halls, corridors, etc. However, employees should be consulted about what is sufficient since the light requirements of each person will vary with his age and physical condition.

_____15. Turn off individual office lights when leaving for the day.

_____16. Install individual electric switches to improve control of lighting in specific areas.

_____17. Apply light-colored finishes to walls, ceilings, floors, and furnishings to reduce lighting requirements.

Refrigeration

_____ 1. Close doors immediately after items have been removed from refrigerator. Do not use cooler to store individual portions of products which require opening the door every time a customer is served, such as salads, beer glasses, etc.

_____ 2. Keep all gaskets and seals in good condition.

_____ 3. Keep blower coil free of ice buildup.

_____ 4. Do not store products in front of coils in a manner that would restrict air flow.

_____ 5. Replace refrigerator compressor belts that are worn or damaged.

_____ 6. Inspect and service all electric motors.

_____ 7. Plan ahead so that when a worker enters the walk-in, he can fill many needs at one time. Prepare a schedule for use.

_____ 8. Turn off lights in walk-in cooler when leaving. Units should have pilot lights on light switches to warn if lights were left on.

_____ 9. Food which is hot should not be placed directly in refrigerator but be allowed to cool for a few minutes.

_____10. Check refrigerators for short cycling and loss of temperature control. Check refrigerant level if abnormal operation exists.

_____11. Compressors need to have open space to give off the heat removed from the unit. Keep coils free of dust and do not store anything within 4 ft of the compressor.

_____12. Compressors should be placed in cool areas rather than located near heating units.

_____13. Freezer fan cleaning and compressor checkup should be scheduled as a regular maintenance item.

_____14. Consolidate refrigeration and freezer space where possible.

_____15. Schedule food deliveries, where possible, to avoid overloading refrigeration facilities or under-capacity utilization.

_____16. Expedite receiving and prompt refrigeration of frozen and perishable foods.

_____17. Defrost freezers frequently. Ice should not be allowed to build up more than ⅛ in. (0.3. cm) on the walls and shelves.

Transportation

_____ 1. Drivers should not exceed a speed of 50 mi per hr (80 km per hr). In most cases, speeds from 45 to 50 mph (72 to 80 kph) are the most efficient.

_____ 2. Maintain steady speeds whenever possible. One speed change per mile can increase fuel consumption up to 25%.

_____ 3. Avoid fast starts. Conservative driving in city traffic can save 10 to 20% in fuel consumption.

_____ 4. Slowing down on grades is recommended. It takes 55% more fuel to maintain 50 mph (80 kph) on a 17° grade than on a flat road. A 17° grade is the steepest allowed on any of our interstate road systems.

_____ 5. Keep the vehicle in good operating condition. A tuned engine can save from 6 to 20% in fuel.

_____ 6. Keep tires inflated on the high side recommended by the manufacturer. Vehicles with radial ply tires use 3% less fuel than if equipped with conventional bias ply tires.

_____ 7. Eliminate all engine idling time. A rule of thumb cost figure is $1.50 for every hour a vehicle engine is idling.

_____ 8. Curtail use of company vehicles, especially for employees taking a vehicle home at night. Investigate a possibility of car pools in this type of situation.

_____ 9. Investigate possibility of obtaining in-plant storage, thus reducing the need for vehicles primarily used as storage units.

_____10. Reduce loads carried in vehicles. Even 400 lb (180 kg) added to the vehicle weight can cut mileage by 10%.

_____11. Change oil filter according to manufacturer's suggestion. A dirty filter can reduce mileage by 10%.

_____12. Encourage employee car pools.

_____13. Use the telephone rather than a car when possible.

_____14. Consolidate food delivery schedules.

_____15. Avoid engine warmup. Simply drive slowly for a few minutes until engine is warm.

_____16. Consider exchanging full size cars for economy cars. The fuel savings will amount to at least 35% with compacts and more with subcompacts.

_____17. Use air conditioning only when necessary. A full size V-8 will lose about 2 mi per gal. (0.84 km per liter) and a compact 6-cylinder will lose 2.6 mpg (1.1 km/l) with the air conditioner running.

_____18. Tests using gas catalysts have resulted in about 23% better mileage when used with compact size cars.

_____19. Buy slightly less than a full tank of fuel. This will eliminate wasteful overflow, allowing room for fuel expansion, especially in hot weather.

_____20. If you have a sudden drop in gasoline mileage, you may have mechanical trouble. Repair as soon as possible to save fuel consumption.

_____21. Check and adjust the wheel alignment to the manufactuer's specifications so the car's rolling resistance will be minimized.

_____22. Travel during off-peak traffic whenever possible and use routes with a minimum number of traffic lights and stop signs.

Miscellaneous (Heat Recovery, Pollution Control, General Observation)

Pollution control in the restaurant industry is becoming important for operations which use char-broilers. Local ordinances generally require that the vent gas be no more than 20% opaque or register no higher than No. 1 on the Ringleman scale. In a recent survey conducted by pollution control officials in Kansas City, ordinances which limit visible emissions in restaurant vent gases are common throughout the United States. Most of the cities also enforce the ordinance.

Visual emission codes can generally be met by the following alternatives.

_____ 1. Install an afterburner to reduce visible emissions. Most restaurants will have an average natural gas bill of $75 per month [based on cost of gas at $0.80 per 1000 ft^3 ($0.28 per 10 m^3)] for operation of the unit. The average cost is $0.50 to $0.60 per hr of operation. The cost for the equipment and installation will be approximately $3500 to $8000. The blower fan is generally rated at 3 to 5 hp (2238 to 3730 W) and exhausts 3000 to 6000 ft^3 of air per min (1.4 to 2.4 m^3/s). The efficiency is usually greater than 98%. The total energy requirement for 1 hr of use will be around 1.7 million Btu (498 kJ/s) (charging 1 kWh with 11,100 Btu and 1 ft^3 of gas with 1090 Btu).

_____ 2. Install an Electrostatic Precipitator to trap the grease and smoke particles. The power consumption of a typical unit is 2.6 kWh (0.1 for ESP unit and 2.5 for fan) for 3000 to 6000 cfm (1.4 to 2.4 m^3/s) of exhaust volume. The efficiency of the units is generally 90 to 95%. The units would need an automatic detergent rinse cycle for best operation. Several companies now have many ESP units in operation across the country. The cost of equipment plus installation can run from around $8000 to around $30,000. Many companies are still in the developmental stage of producing a satisfactory unit for a reasonable price.

_____ 3. The char-broiler could be replaced with units which do not have the problem of grease dripping on open flames. Some suggestions are:

(a) *Serrated grill*: A steel plate installed with a 15° slant that allows the grease to run off into reservoirs.

(b) *Overfired broiler*: The flame is above the meat, preventing grease from falling into it.

(c) *Sealed cabinet*: Unit which allows no smoke to escape during cooking.

Restaurants which must meet local ordinances within a short time period will have a difficult choice to make regarding whether to choose an afterburner, an electrostatic precipitator, or to change methods of cooking. Natural gas supplies are limited. In some areas of the country, new services are not being granted. The afterburner would probably use between 1500 and 5000 ft^3 (42 and 141 m^3) of gas per day, with costs varying between $30 and $120 per month [at $0.80 per 1000 ft^3 ($0.28 per 10 m^3) of gas]. The electrostatic precipitator would cost less than $0.05 per day for electricity (to operate 12 hr per day at 0.1 kWh); however, the capital costs could vary from $8000 to $30,000 for equipment which has had only a few years to establish a record for reliability. Switching from char-broil to other cooking methods would reduce business volume for many restaurants.

_____ 4. Heat recovery units are not in general use at the present time. The units could be applied to afterburner exhaust, water heater exhausts, and possibly other equipment if the heat loss is sufficiently high. The efficiency of the recovery units would probably be around 50%.

TABLE 15.7. Energy Use Breakdown and Potential Savings

Categories	Percentage of Total Energy	Million Btu at 68% Gas and 32% Electric	Million Btu Saved with 20% Reduction in Energy Use
Food preparation	45.1	44.87	8.97
HVAC	32.1	31.92	6.38
Sanitation	12.6	12.48	2.50
Lighting	8.2	8.18	1.64
Refrigeration	2.0	1.96	0.39
Totals	100.0	99.41	19.88

General Comments

A. **Administrative Responsibility.**

(1) Obtain management commitment to energy conservation.
(2) Establish an Energy Management Committee.
(3) Determine energy use patterns.
(4) Evaluate energy use patterns and adopt a set of energy conservation guidelines.
(5) Implement the energy conservation guidelines.
(6) Evaluate, analyze, and control energy conservation efforts.
(7) Record baseline energy data.
(8) Establish ongoing energy management plans.

B. **Energy Breakdown Analysis.** Table 15.7 shows energy data which would be typical of a general menu restaurant. The breakdown of where the energy is used would be representative of many restaurants. The purpose of the table is to demonstrate the magnitude of energy savings for various use categories.

Preventive and Corrective Maintenance

The purpose of this chapter is to describe the role of preventive and corrective maintenance of foodservice equipment as an ancillary function of quality control and energy management. The inclusion of this subject matter is intended to make the reader aware that such a program contributes greatly to sustaining food quality at the highest level.

This function when adopted in its entirety will not only meet the many parameters of quality assurance but also reduce energy consumption. Maintenance of equipment has been superficially discussed in several other sections of the text. It is not the intent of this chapter to be redundant but to reinforce and stress the importance of the theme in a unified and clarified manner. In many instances, preventive and corrective maintenance of foodservice equipment has been overlooked in the curriculum and training of personnel at all levels of hospitality education.

DEVELOPING THE PROGRAM

To develop or initiate a comprehensive preventive and corrective maintenance plan, begin by listing all foodservice equipment utilized in a facility. This list must include every item, no matter how insignificant it may appear to the overall back-of-the-house operation. Can openers, heat-holding lamps, dollies, conveyors, and water filters are examples of equipment that require regularly scheduled maintenance checks, which may have been omitted. The dining area also should be maintained, including such areas as coffee-holding stations and salad bars.

When the list is completed, a card file should be compiled. List each item on a separate 3 × 4 or 5 × 7 in. card. If two or more units of identical equipment are listed, a separate card is required for each. For example, if a facility has two coffee urns, a card should be set up for each, denoting location and identification. Figures 16.1 and 16.2 show required information for each card. Figures 16.3 and 16.4 are additional examples of record-keeping.

(FRONT)

TYPE EQUIPMENT—	MODEL—	LOCATION—
MANUFACTURER—	SERIAL NO.—	DATE INSTALLED—
ADDRESS—	TEL. NO.—	LOCAL REP.—
INSTALLER (CONTRACTOR)—		
GUARANTEE OR WARRANTY—	FROM—	TO—
FULL—		
PARTIAL—	(LABOR)	(PARTS)

MAINTENANCE REQUIRED & FREQUENCY
DAILY—   WEEKLY—   MONTHLY—   OTHER—   (over)

FIG. 16.1.   Front of file card for equipment maintenance.

(BACK)

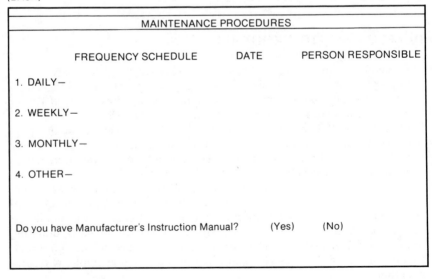

MAINTENANCE PROCEDURES
FREQUENCY SCHEDULE   DATE   PERSON RESPONSIBLE
1. DAILY—
2. WEEKLY—
3. MONTHLY—
4. OTHER—
Do you have Manufacturer's Instruction Manual?   (Yes)   (No)

FIG. 16.2.   Back of file card for equipment maintenance.

MAINTENANCE RECORDS

Form # _____

All equipment information should be filled in on top lines.
Serial numbers, when applicable, should be entered on lower corner of form.

RECORD OF MAINTENANCE

FOR _Electric Sandwich Grill_____ SHOP_____
Date Installed ___1/20/___ New ___X___ Used _____ Installed by _(Contractors name)_
Maintenance should be recorded as soon as it is accomplished.

MAINTENANCE RECORD (Date & Initial)

Year	Jan	Feb	Mar	April	May	June	July	Aug	Sept	Oct	Nov	Dec
	B 1/22 J.D.	B 2/22 J.D.	B 3/22 J.D.	B 4/22 J.D.	B 5/22 J.D.	C 6/12 B 6/22 J.D.						

Under section: Equipment Data and Preventive Maintenance Required:

All maintenance jobs relating to the piece of equipment should be entered in this section. A code letter should be given to each time period of maintenance. The codes are as follows:

CODE	TIME PERIOD
A	Weekly Maintenance
B	Monthly Maintenance
C	Quarterly Maintenance
D	Semiannual Maintenance
E	Annual Maintenance

Any special procedures or precautions pertaining to the maintenance of the equipment should also be listed in this section.

Serial No. _____

FIG. 16.3.   Maintenance record form.

Two duplicate sets of cards for each unit of equipment are suggested. One set of cards should be inserted in clear plastic envelopes and hung next to or on the equipment. The duplicate set is then filed in the Manager's office,

RECORD OF REPAIR AND SERVICE

All information regarding any repair and service should be entered in the appropriate section. Repair and service where there wasn't any charge should also be entered so as to have a record of the problem and corrective action taken in case the equipment breaks down again.

Date	Representative	Time	Cost	Description of Problem and Corrective Action
6/12/	Ace Dust Cleaners	8 hr.	$45.00	Semiannual Cleaning
7/1/	Local Elec. Co.	1/2 hr.	-0-	Loose wire on thermostat right-hand side

SERIAL NO. _____

FIG. 16.4.   Repair and service record form.

WARRANTY

_____ maintains the highest standards of quality control in manufacture. We use the finest components and materials, and employ quality engineering standards and tests on all products.

Within 120 days of shipment, should any _____ product show defect in material or workmanship, repair or replacement will be made, NOT INCLUDING FIELD LABOR CHARGES.

The 120 day warranty period is extended to ONE YEAR on the following listed components of all Urns and Remote Dispensing Automatic Urns only:

Electric Heaters, Thermostats and Switches and Power Contactors, Water Solenoid Valves, All Gas Controls, Thermometers, Liquid Level Relay, Electrode Assembly.

All components or equipment must be shipped to factory prepaid for acceptance. NO FIELD LABOR CHARGES PAID. We regret we cannot be held responsible for any repairs not made in our factory. EXCEPTIONS — The above Warranty does not apply under the following conditions:

• Improper installation.
• Neglect or abuse of equipment.
• Excessive mineral content of water used.

No other Warranty, written or verbal, other than the foregoing, is authorized.

OPTIONAL SERVICE CONTRACTS ON AUTOMATIC URNS:

Period of contract, 12 months from date of installation.(Maximum of 15 months from date of shipment regardless of date of installation.)

Covers authorized field labor (NO TRAVEL TIME) to repair or replace parts or components that show defect in material or workmanship.

Any service contract must be purchased at the same time as the urn to which it applies.

No service contract valid until payment has been made.

SERVICE CONTRACT

Most specification projects and general service policies today require one year service-warranty on equipment including labor and parts. _____ standard warranty does not include any field labor. We strongly recommend your purchase of one year service contract, to include parts and field labor (no travel time).

See price list for cost.

DESIGN CHANGES

We reserve the right to discontinue any model or item or make any changes or improvements at any time, without incurring any obligation to make such changes on products sold previously and in service. It is the policy of _____ to improve its product whenever it is possible and practical to do so.

FIG. 16.5.   An equipment warranty form. Company and product names are to be filled in.

together with manuals of operating instructions. Figure 16.5 is an example of an equipment warranty.

If equipment manuals are not readily obtainable from manufacturers, they may be secured from an equipment dealer, manufacturer's representative, and foodservice or facilities consultant. Multi-unit operations compile manuals for this purpose which are given to each manager. Such manuals are numbered, dated, and coded. When an instructional change occurs, a new page is inserted and the old one is discarded.

Where computers are available, maintenance can be stored in memory and information recalled as required. For example:

(1) Program a computer so that each unit of equipment is inserted showing respective frequency of maintenance, lapse time period, and kind of work required.

(2) Computers also may perform analyses and store maintenance data.

(3) Computers should provide a maintenance printout report at set intervals (daily, weekly, or monthly) as well as type of maintenance needed.

GUIDE FOR PREVENTIVE MAINTENANCE

The following is a selected guide for preventive and corrective maintenance of cooking and other equipment generally found in a foodservice facility. Since many types of equipment are employed, a complete listing of all equipment was not considered necessary within the framework of this chapter. Several items have been selected to illustrate methods and procedures involved. A complete inventory may then be evolved by using the suggested techniques required for this program.

Griddles

Weekly. Inspect griddle for solid residues, hard grease, and loose parts. Check thermostat, signal lights, and other controls for proper working order.

Monthly.

(1) Recalibrate or check thermostat accuracy. Refer to manufacturer's manual for procedures. Use a surface thermometer and check cooking surfaces for cold or unused hot spots (may indicate defective heating elements).

(2) Check level of cooking plate. Plate should tilt forward about 5° toward grease trough (for proper runoff of the fat).

(3) Gas griddles require a check of correct color of flame; check the pilot light and adjust gas-air mixture valve, if necessary.

Convection Ovens

Weekly.

(1) Check oven for loose parts, including handles, control knobs, hinges, and surface exterior walls.
(2) Check alignment and level of each deck.
(3) Check interior for baked-on residues, and remove according to cleaning instructions.

Monthly.

(1) If gas heated, check flame quality (it should be bluish).
(2) Check parts (if clogged, remove material with a round-pointed tool, such as an awl).
(3) Check oven compartment light (if necessary, replace with a high temperature bulb of similar wattage). Check control and signal lights (replace with a similar type of bulb, if required).
(4) Check vent orifice and closure lever (ensure that it does not stick).
(5) Calibrate thermostat by using an oven thermocouple. Make sure that thermocouple bulb is placed adjacent to thermostat. Take several readings: when power is activated, at 15 min, and at end of cycle.
(6) Check oven cavity for uniform heating temperature by moving thermocouple to several locations. Allow at least 5 min for thermocouple to register the temperature at each location.
(7) Check wiring (should not be loose or frayed).
(8) Check doors for alignment and tight closures.

Deep Fat Fryers

Daily.

(1) Skim debris from surface.
(2) Empty strainer, generally located on the bottom of the fryer.
(3) Filter fat or frying medium through mechanical or paper filter device.
(4) Observe signal lights and timing mechanism for proper operation.

Weekly.

(1) Check frying temperatures with deep fat thermometer or thermocouple. Calibrate temperatures against control. Use at least three temperature settings for calibration.
(2) All control switches and indicator lights should be checked for proper working order and sequence.

(3) Follow operator's manual for proper placement for thermostat bulb or tube end.

(4) Inspect fryer for leakage. Tighten bolts and screws, if necessary.

(5) If fryer has automatic lift-out baskets, check for proper timing. Lift-out mechanisms should be lubricated according to instructions listed in equipment manual.

Tilting Skillets

Daily.

(1) Follow manual for cleaning instructions. Proper cleaning will prevent malfunction of the unit.

Weekly.

(1) Temperature gradients must be checked against a control thermometer (use griddle or thermocouple device). Locate the point where the thermostat is activated and place the control adjacent to it.

(2) Follow manual for lubrication of hinges, gears, and other parts.

(3) Check color of gas flame to ensure correct air-gas mixture. Observe height of the flame (should touch bottom of the frypan).

(4) Check all hinges for alignment. Tighten where necessary.

(5) Check cover for proper fit and alignment.

(6) Remove residues formed as a result of water hardness.

Appendix

USDA Standards for Prepared Meat and Poultry Products and Useful Tables

Standards for meat and poultry products are pertinent guidelines to assist in the task of quality interpretation and cost evaluation. To fall into this classification, a food must contain a *minimum* amount of meat or poultry prescribed by the USDA. For example, ready-to-serve chicken soup must contain at least 2% chicken. Condensed chicken soup must contain 4% or more, since it would then contain at least 2% when diluted with water. But chicken-flavored soup, which is not considered a poultry product, may contain less chicken.

The standards for meat ingredients usually are based on the fresh weight of the product, whereas those for poultry are measured on the weight of the cooked, deboned product. Since meat and poultry shrink during cooking, standards take this factor into account. For instance, beef pot pie must contain at least 25% fresh beef. Turkey pot pie must contain 14% or more cooked turkey. Chicken burgers must be 100% chicken; a product containing fillers must be called chicken patties. Following is a current list of product standards.

Red Meat Products

NOTE: All percentages of meat are on the basis of fresh uncooked weight, unless otherwise indicated.

1. *Barbecued Meats:* Weight of meat when barbecued cannot exceed 70% of the fresh uncooked meat; must have barbecued (crusted)

appearance and be prepared over burning or smoldering hardwood or its sawdust.

2. *Barbecue Sauce with Meat:* At least 35% meat (cooked basis).
3. *Beans with Bacon in Sauce:* At least 12% bacon.
4. *Beans with Frankfurters in Sauce:* At least 20% franks.
5. *Beans with Ham in Sauce:* At least 12% ham (cooked basis).
6. *Beans with Meatballs in Sauce:* At least 20% meatballs.
7. *Beef and Dumplings with Gravy or Beef and Gravy with Dumplings:* At least 25% beef.
8. *Beef Burgundy:* At least 50% beef.
9. *Beef Sauce with Beef and Mushrooms:* At least 25% beef and 7% mushrooms.
10. *Beef Sausage (raw):* No more than 30% fat.
11. *Beef Stroganoff:* At least 45% fresh uncooked beef or 30% cooked beef, and at least 10% sour cream or a "gourmet" combination of at least 7.5% sour cream and 5% wine.
12. *Beef with Barbecue Sauce:* At least 50% beef (cooked basis).
13. *Beef and Gravy:* At least 50% beef (cooked basis).
14. *Gravy with Beef:* At least 35% beef (cooked basis).
15. *Breaded Steaks, Chops, etc.:* Breading not to exceed 30% of finished product weight.
16. *Breakfast Sausage:* No more than 50% fat.
17. *Brunswick Stew:* At least 25% meat.
18. *Burritos:* At least 15% meat.
19. *Cabbage Rolls:* At least 12% meat.
20. *Cannelloni with Meat and Sauce:* At least 10% meat.
21. *Campelletti with Meat in Sauce:* At least 12% meat.
22. *Chili Con Carne:* At least 40% meat.
23. *Chili Con Carne with Beans:* At least 25% meat.
24. *Chili Hot Dog Sauce with Meat:* At least 6% meat.
25. *Chili Hot Dog with Meat:* At least 40% meat in chili.
26. *Chili Macaroni:* At least 16% meat.
27. *Chili Pie:* At least 20% meat.
28. *Chili Sauce with Meat:* At least 6% meat.
29. *Chop Suey (American Style) with Macaroni and Meat:* At least 25% meat.
30. *Chop Suey Vegetables with Meat:* At least 12% meat.
31. *Chow Mein Vegetables with Meat:* At least 12% meat.
32. *Condensed, Creamed Dried Beef or Chipped Beef:* At least 18% dried or chipped beef (figured on reconstituted total content).
33. *Corned Beef and Cabbage:* At least 25% corned beef.
34. *Corn Dog:* Must meet standards for frankfurters; batter not to exceed the weight of the frank.
35. *Cream Cheese with Chipped Beef (sandwich spread):* At least 12% meat.
36. *Croquettes:* At least 35% meat.

37. *Curried Sauce with Beef and Rice (casserole):* At least 35% beef (figured on beef and sauce part only).
38. *Deviled Ham:* No more than 35% fat.
39. *Egg Foo Young with Meat:* At least 12% meat.
40. *Egg Rolls with Meat:* At least 10% meat.
41. *Enchilada with Meat:* At least 15% meat.
42. *Frankfurters, Bologna, Other Cooked Sausage:* May contain meat and meat by-products; no more that 30% fat, 10% added water, and 2% corn syrup; no more than 15% poultry unless its presence is reflected in product name; no more than 3.5% cereals and nonfat dry milk, with product name showing their presence. *All Meat:* Only muscle tissue with natural amounts of fat; no by-products, cereal, or binders. *All Beef:* Only meat of beef animals.
43. *Fried Rice with Meat:* At least 10% meat.
44. *Fritters:* At least 35% meat.
45. *Frozen Breakfasts:* At least 15% meat (cooked basis).
46. *Frozen Dinners:* At least 25% meat or meat food product (cooked basis, figured on total meal minus appetizer, bread, and dessert).
47. *Frozen Entrées: Meat and One Vegetable:* At least 50% meat (cooked basis).
48. *Frozen Entrées: Meat Gravy or Sauce, and One Vegetable:* At least 30% meat (cooked basis).
49. *Goulash:* At least 25% meat.
50. *Gravies:* At least 25% meat stock or broth, or at least 6% meat.
51. *Ham, Canned:* Limited to 8% total weight gain after processing; if gain is up to 8%, must be labeled *Ham, with Natural Juices*, if between 8% and 10%, it must be labeled *Ham, Water Added, with Juices.*
52. *Ham, Not Canned:* Must not weigh more after processing than the fresh ham weighs before curing and smoking; if contains up to 10% added weight, must be labeled *Ham, Water Added*; if more than 10%, must be labeled *Imitation Ham.*
53. *Ham a la King:* At least 20% ham (cooked basis).
54. *Ham and Cheese Spread:* At least 25% ham (cooked basis).
55. *Hamburger or Ground Beef:* No more than 30% fat; no extenders.
56. *Ham Chowder:* At least 10% ham (cooked basis).
57. *Ham Croquettes:* At least 35% ham (cooked basis).
58. *Ham Salad:* At least 35% ham (cooked basis).
59. *Ham Spread:* At least 50% ham.
60. *Hash:* At least 35% meat (cooked basis).
61. *High Meat Baby Foods:* At least 30% meat.
62. *Lasagna with Meat and Sauce:* At least 12% meat.
63. *Lima Beans with Ham or Bacon in Sauce:* At least 12% ham or cooked bacon.
64. *Liver Sausage, Liver Loaf, Liver Paste, Liver Cheese, Liver Pudding, Liver Spread, and similar liver products:* At least 30% liver.

65. *Macaroni and Beef in Tomato Sauce:* At least 12% beef.
66. *Macaroni Salad with Ham or Beef:* At least 12% meat (cooked basis).
67. *Manicotti (containing meat filling):* At least 10% meat.
68. *Meatballs:* No more than 12% extenders (cereal, etc.).
69. *Meatballs in Sauce:* At least 50% meatballs.
70. *Meat Casseroles:* At least 25% fresh uncooked meat or 18% cooked meat.
71. *Meat Pies:* At least 25% meat.
72. *Meat Ravioli:* At least 10% meat in ravioli, minus the sauce.
73. *Meat Salads:* At least 35% meat (cooked basis).
74. *Meat Taco Filling:* At least 40% meat.
75. *Meat Tacos:* At least 15% meat.
76. *Meat Turnovers:* At least 25% meat.
77. *Omelet with Bacon:* At least 12% bacon (cooked basis).
78. *Omelet with Ham:* At least 18% ham (cooked basis).
79. *Paté de Foie:* At least 30% liver.
80. *Pepper Steaks:* At least 30% beef (cooked basis).
81. *Pizza Sauce with Sausage:* At least 6% sausage.
82. *Pizza with Meat:* At least 15% meat.
83. *Pizza with Sausage:* At least 12% sausage (cooked basis) or 10% dry sausage, such as pepperoni.
84. *Pork Sausage:* Not more than 50% fat.
85. *Pork with Barbecue Sauce:* At least 50% pork (cooked basis).
86. *Pork with Dressing and Gravy:* At least 30% pork (cooked basis).
87. *Pork and Dressing:* At least 50% pork (cooked basis).
88. *Sandwiches (containing meat):* At least 35% meat.
89. *Sauce with Meat, or Meat Sauce:* At least 6% meat.
90. *Sauerbrauten:* At least 50% meat (cooked basis).
91. *Sauerkraut Balls with Meat:* At least 30% meat.
92. *Sauerkraut with Wieners and Juice:* At least 20% wieners.
93. *Scalloped Potatoes and Ham:* At least 20% ham (cooked basis).
94. *Scallopine:* At least 35% meat (cooked basis).
95. *Scrapple:* At least 40% meat and/or meat by-products.
96. *Spaghetti Sauce and Meatballs:* At least 35% meatballs (cooked basis).
97. *Spaghetti Sauce with Meat:* At least 6% meat.
98. *Spaghetti with Meat and Sauce:* At least 12% meat.
99. *Spanish Rice with Beef or Ham:* At least 20% beef or ham (cooked basis).
100. *Stews (Beef, Lamb, and the like):* At least 25% meat.
101. *Stuffed Cabbage with Meat in Sauce:* At least 12% meat.
102. *Stuffed Peppers with Meat in Sauce:* At least 12% meat.
103. *Sukiyaki:* At least 30% meat.
104. *Sweet and Sour Pork or Beef:* At least 25% fresh uncooked meat or 16% cooked meat, and at least 16% fruit.

105. *Swiss Steak with Gravy:* At least 50% meat (cooked basis).
106. *Gravy and Swiss Steak:* At least 35% meat (cooked basis).
107. *Tamale Pies:* At least 20% meat.
108. *Tamales:* At least 25% meat.
109. *Tamales with Sauce (or with Gravy):* At least 20% meat.
110. *Taquitos:* At least 15% meat.
111. *Tongue Spread:* At least 50% tongue.
112. *Tortellini with Meat:* At least 10% meat.
113. *Veal Birds:* At least 60% meat and no more than 40% stuffing.
114. *Veal Cordon Bleu:* At least 60% veal, 5% ham, and containing Swiss, Gruyère, or Mozzarella cheese.
115. *Veal Fricassee:* At least 40% meat.
116. *Veal Parmagiana:* At least 40% breaded meat product in sauce.
117. *Veal Steaks:* Can be chopped, shaped, cubed, frozen. Beef can be added with product name shown as *Veal Steaks, Beef Added, Chopped, Shaped, and Cubed.* No more than 20% beef or must be labeled *Veal and Beef Steak, Chopped, Shaped, and Cubed.* No more than 30% fat.

Poultry Products

All percentages of poultry (chicken, turkey, or other kinds of poultry) are on cooked deboned basis unless otherwise indicated.

1. *Breaded Poultry:* No more than 30% breading.
2. *Canned Boned Poultry:*
   (a) *Boned (kind), Solid Pack:* At least 95% poultry meat, skin, and fat.
   (b) *Boned (kind):* At least 90% poultry meat, skin, and fat.
   (c) *Boned (kind), with Broth:* At least 80% poultry meat, skin, and fat.
   (d) *Boned (kind), with Specified Percentage of Broth:* At least 50% poultry meat, skin, and fat.
3. *Chicken Cacciatore:* At least 20% chicken meat, or 40% with bone.
4. *Chicken Croquettes:* At least 25% chicken meat.
5. *Chopped Poultry with Broth (Baby Food):* At least 43% meat, with skin, fat, and seasoning.
6. *Creamed Poultry:* At least 20% poultry meat.
7. *Poultry a la King:* At least 20% poultry meat.
8. *Poultry Barbecue:* At least 40% poultry meat.
9. *Poultry Burgers:* 100% poultry meat, with skin and fat.
10. *Poultry Chop Suey:* At least 4% poultry meat.
11. *Chop Suey with Poultry:* At least 2% poultry meat.
12. *Poultry Chow Mein, Without Noodles:* At least 4% poultry meat.
13. *Poultry Dinners:* At least 18% poultry meat.
14. *Poultry Fricassee:* At least 20% poultry meat.

15. *Poultry Fricassee of Wings:* At least 40% poultry meat (cooked basis, with bone).
16. *Poultry Hash:* At least 30% poultry meat.
17. *Poultry Noodles or Dumplings:* At least 15% poultry meat, or 30% with bone.
18. *Noodles or Dumplings with Poultry:* At least 6% poultry meat.
19. *Poultry Pies:* At least 14% poultry meat.
20. *Poultry Ravioli:* At least 2% poultry meat.
21. *Poultry Rolls:* Binding agents limited to 3% in cooked roll.
22. *Poultry Salad:* At least 25% poultry meat.
23. *Poultry Soup:* At least 2% poultry meat.
24. *Poultry Stew:* At least 12% poultry meat.
25. *Poultry Stroganoff:* At least 30% poultry meat.
26. *Poultry Tamales:* At least 6% poultry meat.
27. *Poultry Tetrazzini:* At least 15% poultry meat.
28. *Poultry with Gravy:* At least 35% poultry meat.
29. *Gravy with Poultry:* At least 15% poultry meat.
30. *Sliced Poultry with Gravy:* At least 35% poultry.

Meat Products Having Complete Standards of Identity

Complete standards of identity currently exist for three meat products. These standards require specific ingredients to be present as follows:

(1) *Corned Beef Hash:* Must contain at least 35% beef (cooked basis). Also it must contain potatoes (either fresh, dehydrated, cooked dehydrated, or a mixture of these types), curing agents, and seasonings. It may be made with certain optional ingredients such as onions, garlic, beef broth, or beef fat, but may not contain more than 15% fat nor more than 72% moisture.

(2) *Chopped Ham:* Must contain fresh, cured, or smoked ham, along with certain specified kinds of curing agents and seasonings. It may also contain certain optional ingredients in specified amounts, including finely chopped ham shank meat, dehydrated onions, dehydrated garlic, corn syrup, other chemical substances as permitted in the federal standard, and not more than 3% water to dissolve the curing agents.

(3) *Oleomargarine or Margarine:* Must contain either the rendered fat, oil, or stearin derived from cattle, sheep, swine, or goats; or a vegetable food fat, oil, or stearin; or a combination of these two classes of ingredients in a specified proportion. It must contain individually or in combination, pasteurized cream, cows' milk, skim milk, a combination of nonfat dry milk and water or finely ground soybeans and water. It may contain optional ingredients specified in the standard, including butter, salt, artificial coloring, vitamins A and D, and permitted chemical substances. Fat in finished product may not exceed 80%. Label must indicate whether product is from animal or vegetable origin or both.

TABLE A.1. Boiling Temperatures of Water at Various Altitudes[1]

Altitude		Boiling Point of Water	
ft	m	°F	°C
Sea level	Sea level	212.0	100.0
2,000	610	208.4	98.4
5,000	1524	203.0	95.0
7,500	2286	198.4	92.4
10,000	3048	194.0	90.0
15,000	4572	185.0	85.0
30,000	9144	158.0	70.0

Source: Smith and Minor (1974).
[1] About 2°F or 1°C should be added to the thermometer reading for each additional 1000 ft or 305 m in altitude when frying foods in deep fat.

TABLE A.2. Steam Pressures at Various Altitudes[1]

Temperature		Steam Pressure (psi) At			
°F	°C	Sea Level	4000 ft 1219 m	6000 ft 1829 m	7500 ft 2286 m
228	109	5	7	8	9
240	115	10	12	13	14
250	121	15	17	18	19
259	126	20	22	23	24

[1] When cooking foods at higher altitudes, ½ lb should be added to the gauge pressures for each additional 1000 ft (305 m) in altitude.
1 psi = 6.9 kPa.

TABLE A.3. Cake Recipe Adjustments for High Altitudes[1]

Adjustment	3000 ft 914 m	5000 ft 1524 m	7000 ft 2134 m
Baking powder reduction per tsp in recipe use	1/8 tsp less	1/8 to 1/4 tsp less	1/4 tsp less
Sugar reduction per cup in recipe use	0 to 1 tbsp less	0 to 2 tbsp less	1 to 3 tbsp less
Liquid increase per cup in recipe use	1 to 2 tbsp more	2 to 4 tbsp more	3 to 4 tbsp more

Source: Smith and Minor (1974).
[1] At altitudes above 5000 ft (1524 m), starch gelatinization in a double boiler is impractical. Direct heat and adequate stirring must be used.

TABLE A.4. Approximate pH of Some Common Substances

Apples	2.9–3.3	Grapefruit	3.0–3.8
Apricot nectar, canned	3.8	Grapes	2.8–3.8
Apricots, dried stewed	3.3–3.5	Hominy	6.9–7.9
Asparagus, canned	5.2–5.3	Honey	3.7–3.9
Asparagus, fresh, cooked	6.0–6.2	Jams, fruit	3.5–4.0
Bananas	5.0–5.3	Jellies, fruit	3.0–3.5
Beans, green, cooked	5.7–6.2	Lemon juice	2.2–2.4
Beans, green lima, cooked	6.2–6.4	Lobster or shrimp,	
Beans, homebaked	5.0–6.0	cooked	7.1–7.3
Beans, kidney, cooked	5.9–6.1	Magnesia, milk of	10.5
Beer	4.0–5.0	Meat, cooked	5.6–7.0
Beet greens, cooked	6.0–7.0	Meat, freshly killed	7.2–7.4
Beets, cooked	5.2–5.9	Meat, ripened	5.6–5.8
Blackberries	3.9–4.5	Milk, cows'	6.3–6.8
Blood, human	7.4	Milk, cows', sour	4.7–5.7
Blueberries	3.1–3.2	Milk, human	6.6–7.6
Bread, white	5.3–5.7	Molasses	4.7–5.7
Bread, whole wheat	5.3–5.7	Olives, ripe, canned	6.0
Buttermilk	4.4–4.8	Oranges	3.6–4.3
Cabbage, green, cooked	6.4–6.8	Peaches, raw	3.3–4.1
Cabbage, green, raw	5.8–6.3	Pears, raw	3.5–4.1
Carrots, cooked	5.6–5.9	Peas, cooked	6.2–6.9
Carrots, raw	5.9–6.0	Pickles, dill	3.2–3.5
Cheese, Cheddar, American		Pickles, sour	3.0–3.5
and English	4.9–5.0	Plums, fresh	2.8–5.0
Cherries	3.2–4.5	Potatoes, Irish, cooked	5.2–6.2
Chocolate	5.2–6.0	Potatoes, sweet, cooked	5.3–6.0
Cider	2.9–3.3	Pumpkin	4.8–5.2
Cocoa	6.5	Raspberries, raw	3.5–4.0
Cocoa, breakfast	5.2–6.0	Rhubarb, stewed	3.1–3.3
Cocoa, Dutch process	6.0–8.8	Saliva, human	6.0–7.6
Coffee, infusion, clear	4.7–5.0	Sauerkraut, cooked	3.5
Corn, cooked	6.3–7.0	Spinach, cooked	5.5–7.2
Corn syrups	4.9–5.1	Squash, Hubbard,	
Cracker dough, optimum	7.1	cooked	6.0–6.2
Crackers, soda	5.7–8.5	Strawberries, fresh	3.1–3.5
Dates	4.6–4.8	Tea, infusion, clear	5.8
Eggs, cold storage		Tomatoes, raw or	
whole	7.5–8.2	cooked	4.0–4.5
white	8.6–9.0	Turnips, yellow,	
yolk	6.4–6.9	cooked	5.2–5.8
Eggs, new-laid		Urine, human	4.8–8.4
whole	6.6	Vinegar, cider	2.4–3.4
white	8.0	Water, distilled	
yolk	6.1	CO_2-free	6.8–7.0
Fish, cooked	6.0–6.9	equilibrium with air	5.8
Flour, wheat	6.0–6.5	Water, drinking	6.0–8.2
Gastric contents, human	1.0–3.0	Water, mineral	6.2–9.4
Gingerale	2.0–4.0	Water, sea	8.0–8.4
Gooseberries	2.8–3.1	Wines	2.8–3.8

Source: Smith and Minor (1974).

TABLE A.5. Beverage Sensory Evaluation Chart (Selected Examples)

Beverage	Sensory Defect	Senses Activated (P—Primary) (S—Secondary)				Equivalent Descriptive Characteristic	Sensory Area Affected		
		Sight	Touch	Taste	Odor		Nose	Tongue Mouth	Throat
Coffee	Bitter		P	S	—	Alum, hops, fruit, rind	—	*	*
	Burnt		S	S	P	Charcoal, smoked fish, meat	*	*	*
	Earthy		—	P	S	Soil, earth	*	*	—
	Fermented		S	P	S	Vinegar	*	*	*
	Grassy		—	P	S	Grass, new-mown hay	*	*	—
	Musty		—	S	P	Mold, cheese	*	*	—
	Acid		S	P	—	Lemony, tart	*	*	—
	Dirty		S	P	S	Off-flavor, earthy	*	*	*
Milk	Oxidized		S	P	P	Off-flavor, oily, metallic, cardboardy	*	*	*
	Heat (cooked)		S	P	P	Cooked, burnt	*	*	*
	Sour		S	P	P	Sharp, nauseating, rank	*	*	*
	Feedy		—	P	P	Animal feed, hay	*	*	—
	Barny		—	P	P	Odor of barn, stable	*	*	—
	Dirty		—	P	P	Off-flavor, earthy	*	*	—
	Onion		S	P	P	Onion grass	*	*	*
Imitation dairy beverages	Heat (cooked)		S	P	P	Cooked, burnt	*	*	*
	Oxidized		S	P	P	Off-flavor, oily, metallic, cardboardy	*	*	*
	Sour		S	P	P	Sharp, rank, nauseating	*	*	*
	Greasy		P	P	—	Oily, fatty	—	*	*
	Bitter		P	S	—	Fruit rind	—	*	*
	Sweet		S	P	—	Sugary	—	*	*
	Rich		P	P	—	Nauseating, lingering sweet-ness	—	*	*
Soft drinks (carbonated)	Metallic	—	S	P	—	Iron, sharp, coppery	—	*	*
	Yeasty	S	S	P	P	Bitter, ethereal, foaming	*	*	*
	Musty	S	—	P	P	Moldy, earthy, cheese	*	*	—
	Oily	S	S	P	—	Fatty, greasy	—	*	—
	Turpentine	—	—	P	S	Aromatic, medicinal, spicy	*	*	—
	Chlorine	—	S	P	P	Medicinal, acrid, pungent	*	*	—
	Dirty	—	—	P	S	Earthy, off-flavor, nauseating	*	*	—
	Sour	—	—	P	S	Acidity, vinegar	—	*	—
	Alkaline	—	S	P	S	Limy, chalky	—	*	*

(Continued)

TABLE A.5. (Continued)

Beverage	Sensory Defect	Senses Activated (P—Primary) (S—Secondary) Sight	Touch	Taste	Odor	Equivalent Descriptive Characteristic	Sensory Area Affected Nose	Tongue/Mouth	Throat
Juices	Discoloration	P				Darker than normal			
	Cooked			P	P	Burnt, smoky	*	*	*
	Moldy			P	P	Musty, earthy, cheese	*	*	
	Sour		S	P	S	Sharp, prickling, vinegar	*	*	*
	Earthy			P	S	Soil, fetid	*	*	
	Bitter		P	P		Fruit rind, alum, puckery		*	*
Tea	Astringent		P	S	S	Sharp, acrid, stinging, puckery	*	*	*
	Burnt	S	S	P	P	Charcoal, smoked	*	*	
	Common		S	P	S	Insipid, light	*	*	*
	Harsh		S	P	S	Bitter, pungent, biting	*	*	
	Metallic			P	S	Coppery, biting, sharp	*	*	*
	Musty			P	P	Mildew, cheese	*	*	*
	Pungent		P	P	S	Astringent, puckery	*	*	
	Tainted			P	P	Off-flavor, strange character	*	*	*
	Woody			P	S	Grassy, hay		*	
Cocoa	Bitter			P		Puckery, alum, fruit rind	*	*	*
	Harsh	S	S	P	S	Pungent, biting	*	*	*
	Thin	S		P	S	Watery, insipid	*	*	
	Moldy	S	S	P	P	Musty, mildew, cheese	*	*	
	Brackish		S	P	S	Salty, acrid, nauseating	*	*	*
Water	Oily	S	P	S	S	Slimy, greasy	*	*	*
	Earthy			P	S	Soil, fetid	*	*	
	Alkaline		S	P	S	Lime, chalky	*	*	*
	Putrid		S	P	P	Rotten egg, sulfur	*	*	*
	Floral			S	P	Sweet, nauseating	*	*	
	Metallic		S	P		Coppery, iron		*	*
	Acid			P	S	Sharp, sour, vinegar	*	*	
	Fishy			P	P	Foul, repulsive	*	*	
	Chemical		S	P	P	Pungent, chlorine, puckery	*	*	*

*Indicates positive reaction.

TABLE A.6.   Conversion Factors

Length

1 centimeter	0.394 inch
1 inch	2.540 centimeters
1 meter	3.2808 feet
1 foot	0.305 meter
1 meter	1.0936 yards
1 yard	0.9144 meter
1 kilometer	0.62137 mile
1 mile	1.60935 kilometers

Volume

1 cubic centimeter	0.0610 cubic inch
1 cubic inch	16.3872 cubic centimeters
1 cubic meter	35.314 cubic feet
1 cubic foot	0.02832 cubic meter
1 cubic meter	1.3079 cubic yards
1 cubic yard	0.7646 cubic meter

Capacity

1 milliliter	1 cubic centimeter
1 milliliter	0.03382 ounce (U.S. liquid)
1 ounce (U.S. liquid)	29.573 milliliters
1 milliliter	0.2705 dram (U.S. Apothecaries)
1 dram (U.S. Apothecaries)	3.6967 milliliters
1 liter	1.05671 quarts (U.S. liquid)
1 quart (U.S. liquid)	0.94633 liter
1 liter	0.26418 gallon (U.S. liquid)
1 gallon (U.S. liquid)	3.78533 liters

Mass and Weight

1 grain	0.0648 gram
1 gram	0.03527 ounce (avoirdupois)
1 ounce (avoirdupois)	28.3495 grams
1 kilogram	2.20462 pounds (avoirdupois)
1 pound (avoirdupois)	0.45359 kilogram

PORTION CONTROL DATA

The use of standardized recipes is an important factor in portion control. A recipe, however, can be depended upon to give the stated number of portions only if the servings are of a uniform size. The most dependable method to use when measuring portions is to serve the food with ladles, scoops, and spoons of standard size.

LADLES

Ladles may be used in serving soups, creamed dishes, stews, sauces, gravies, and other similar products.

The following sizes of ladles are most frequently used for serving:

1/4 cup (2 ounces)
1/2 cup (4 ounces)
3/4 cup (6 ounces)
1 cup (8 ounces)

SERVING SPOONS

A serving spoon (solid or perforated) may be used instead of a scoop. Since these spoons are not identified by number, it is necessary to measure or weigh food in the spoons used to obtain the approximate serving size desired.

SCOOPS

The number of the scoop indicates the number of scoopfuls it takes to make one quart. The table below shows the level measures of each scoop in cups or tablespoons.

Scoop Number	Level Measure
6	2/3 cup
8	1/2 cup
10	2/5 cup
12	1/3 cup
16	1/4 cup
20	3 1/5 tablespoons
24	2 2/3 tablespoons.
30	2 1/5 tablespoons
40	1 3/5 tablespoons

Scoops may be used for portioning such items as drop cookies, muffins, meat patties, and some vegetables, salads, and sandwich fillings.

FRACTIONAL EQUIVALENTS FOR USE IN CONVERTING RECIPES

The following chart is designed to help you change fractional parts of pounds, gallons, cups, etc., to accurate weights or measures. For example, reading from left to right, the table shows that 7/8 of

	1 TABLESPOON	1 CUP	1 PINT	1 QUART	1 GALLON	1 POUND
1	3 tsp	16 Tbsp	2 cups	2 pints	4 quarts	16 ounces
7/8	$2\frac{1}{2}$ tsp	1 cup less 2 Tbsp	$1\frac{3}{4}$ cups	$3\frac{1}{2}$ cups	3 quarts plus 1 pint	14 ounces
3/4	$2\frac{1}{4}$ tsp	12 Tbsp	$1\frac{1}{2}$ cups	3 cups	3 quarts	12 ounces
2/3	2 tsp	10 Tbsp plus 2 tsp	$1\frac{1}{3}$ cups	$2\frac{2}{3}$ cups	2 quarts plus $2\frac{2}{3}$ cups	$10\frac{2}{3}$ ounces
5/8	2 tsp (scant)	10 Tbsp	$1\frac{1}{4}$ cups	$2\frac{1}{2}$ cups	2 quarts plus 1 pint	10 ounces
1/2	$1\frac{1}{2}$ tsp	8 Tbsp	1 cup	2 cups	2 quarts	8 ounces
3/8	$1\frac{1}{8}$ tsp	6 Tbsp	$\frac{3}{4}$ cup	$1\frac{1}{2}$ cups	1 quart plus 1 pint	6 ounces
1/3	1 tsp	5 Tbsp plus 1 tsp	$\frac{2}{3}$ cup	$1\frac{1}{3}$ cups	1 quart plus $1\frac{1}{3}$ cups	$5\frac{1}{3}$ ounces
1/4	$\frac{3}{4}$ tsp	4 Tbsp	$\frac{1}{2}$ cup	1 cup	1 quart	4 ounces
1/8	$\frac{1}{2}$ tsp (scant)	2 Tbsp	$\frac{1}{4}$ cup	$\frac{1}{2}$ cup	1 pint	2 ounces
1/16	$\frac{1}{4}$ tsp (scant)	1 Tbsp	2 Tbsp	4 Tbsp	1 cup	1 ounce

FIG. A.I. Portion control data.
Courtesy of Koch Refrigerators, Inc.

FLUID OUNCES	CUPS	#8 SCOOPS	#12 SCOOPS	CONTAINERS	#16 SCOOPS	#24 SCOOPS	#30 SCOOPS	#40 SCOOPS
130	16	32	48	One Gallon	64	96	120	160
					62	93		
120	15	30	45		60	90		150
					58	87		
110	14	28	42		56	84	105	140
					54	81		
	13	26	39		52	78		130
100				One #10 Can	50	75		
	12	24	36	Three Quarts	48	72	90	120
				Two #5 Cans	46	69		
90	11	22	33		44	66		110
					42	63		
80	10	20	30	Three #2½ Cans	40	60	75	100
					38	57		
70	9	18	27		36	54		90
					34	51		
	8	16	24	One Half Gallon	32	48	60	80
60					30	45		
	7	14	21		28	42		70
50				Two #2½ Cans	26	39		
	6	12	18	One #5 Can	24	36	45	60
					22	33		
40	5	10	15		20	30		50
					18	27		
	4	8	12	One Quart	16	24	30	40
30				One #2½ Can	14	21		
	3	6	9		12	18		30
20					10	15		
	2	4	6	One #303 Can	8	12	15	20
8	1	2	3	One Cup	4	6	7½	10

FIG. A.2.   Container portion and conversion chart.
Courtesy of Koch Refrigerators, Inc.

6 oz.	Approximately ¾ cup 6 fl. oz.	Used for frozen concentrated juices and individual servings of single strength juices.
8 oz.	Approximately 1 cup 8 oz. (7¾ fl. oz.)	Used mainly in metropolitan areas for most fruits, vegetables and specialty items.
No. 1 (Picnic)	Approximately 1¼ cups 10½ oz. (9½ fl. oz.)	Used for condensed soups, some fruits, vegetables, meat and fish products.
No. 300	Approximately 1¾ cups 15½ oz. (13½ fl. oz.)	For specialty items, such as beans with pork, spaghetti, macaroni, chili con carne, date and nut bread—also a variety of fruits, including cranberry sauce and blueberries.
No. 303	Approximately 2 cups 1 lb. (15 fl. oz.)	Used extensively for vegetables; plus fruits, such as sweet and sour cherries, fruit cocktail, apple sauce.
No. 2	Approximately 2½ cups 1 lb. 4 oz. (1 pt. 2 fl. oz.)	Used for vegetables, many fruits and juices.
No. 2½	Approximately 3½ cups 1 lb. 13 oz. (1 pt. 10 fl. oz.)	Used principally for fruits, such as peaches, pears, plums and fruit cocktail; plus vegetables, such as tomatoes, sauerkraut and pumpkin.
46 oz.	Approximately 5¾ cups 46 oz. (1 qt. 14 fl. oz.)	Used almost exclusively for juices, also for whole chicken.
No. 10	Approximately 12 cups 6 lbs. 9 oz. (3 qts.)	So-called "institutional" or "restaurant" size container, for most fruits and vegetables. Stocked by some retail stores.

G. A.3.   A guide to common can sizes.
urtesy of the American Can Company.

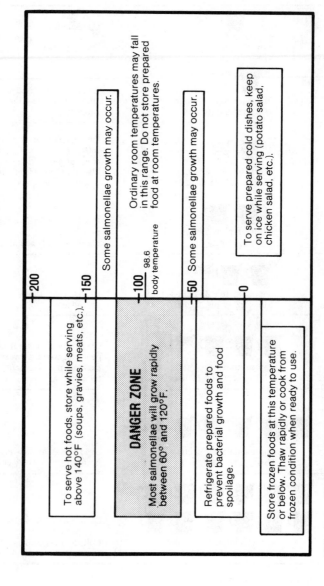

FIG. A.4. Food temperature guide.
Courtesy of Agricultural Extension Service, USDA.

344

Sample	Date Rec'd	Code(s)	Date Exam.	Cont. Size	Cond. of Cont.	Amt. Headspace	Net Wt. Contents	Color	Odor	Flavor	Extra- neous Matter	Consis- tency	Remarks

FIG. A.5. Sample of an incoming supplies receiving form.
From Thorner and Herzberg (1979).

345

Glossary

Acidity (acid condition)   A pH value less than 7.0. In soft drinks, acidity is related to sourness. Pure water has a neutral pH value of 7.0. The lower the pH value the more acid the substance

Additive (food)   A substance or mixture of substances, other than a basic foodstuff, which is present in food as a result of any aspect of production, storage, or processing

Alkalinity   A pH value greater than 7.0. Soaps are alkaline. The higher the number above 7.0, up to 14, the more alkaline the substance

Antioxidant   A chemical compound that retards the oxidation of oils and fats

Antitoxin   A chemical compound that inhibits the action of biochemicals that are toxic to the human body

Aseptic   Characterized by precautions for the exclusion of microorganisms

Aspic   A mixture of foods and gelatin. It may be clear or opaque

Au naturel   Uncooked or simply cooked foods

Bain-marie   A hot water vat, usually equipped with temperature controls, to hold foods prior to further use or service. Often used by chefs as a double boiler

Bake   The application of dry heat performed in an oven; roasting is similar to baking when meat is employed

Baste   To add moisture to food during cooking; to prevent drying or to add flavor. The liquid may be stock, water, a sauce, melted fat, or the fluid recovered from heating meat or fish

Blanch   A heating process used to inactivate enzymes. Performed by precooking or cooking in boiling water or steam

Blend   The mixing of two or more foods by mechanical means or by using a wire whip, fork, paddle, or spoon

Brackish water   Water that contains large amounts of dissolved minerals but is less salty than sea water

Braise   The browning of vegetables or meat in a small amount of fat. After browning, a product is slowly cooked in a small quantity of liquid

Broil   Cooking by the use of a direct or radiant heat source

Browning (enzymatic)   A process whereby food such as fruits turn brown or darken during storage; also similar to nonenzymatic browning, which is not catalyzed by an enzyme

Butterfat   The fat portion of milk

Calorie   A unit used to express the heat-producing or energy-producing value of food. 1 Kcal = amount of heat required to raise 1 kg of water 1°C

Capon   A desexed male chicken weighing about 4 to 7 lb when mature

Carbonated   Denotes the charging of water with carbon dioxide (CO_2) to create soda water

Catalysis   A process whereby a chemical reaction is greatly accelerated by the presence of a certain chemical (catalyst) which is not consumed in the reaction

Chop   To cut food into small pieces with a knife or other implement

Cleaning   Removal of residues of food, dirt, dust, foreign material, or other soiling ingredients or materials

Cloudiness (haze)   A term common in the soft drink industry relating to bacterial contamination or the reaction of a product with unprotected metal

Coddled eggs   Allowing eggs to cook in hot water. Water is boiled and then poured over eggs. The eggs are removed when the desired degree of doneness is reached

Comminuted   A product which is ground up or mashed into small pieces. Hamburger is a type of comminuted product

Compote   A mixture of stewed fruit

Concentrates   Relates to a substance in a strengthened form. More commonly, a substance with reduced water content

Contaminate   To add an impurity or pollute

Cream   To produce a product that has a soft and creamy texture by mechanical or hand mixing

Cut   To add fat into dry products by gentle means. To chop food into small pieces

Deep fat frying   To cook food at a high temperature in a fat medium which completely covers the food

Denaturation   The alteration and/or precipitation by heat or chemical agents of hydrophilic colloids, here referring to food proteins

Destabilization   The alteration and/or precipitation by heat or chemical agents of hydrophobic colloids, here referring to food proteins

Detergents   Cleaning agents such as soaps, synthetic powders, liquids, and solvents

Dice   Cutting of food into 0.25 to 0.5 in. cubes

Doneness   The extent to which a food is heated or cooked

Emulsifiers   Substances used to create and stabilize emulsions

Emulsion   In reference to foods, usually a mixture of fat droplets dispersed in water; an example is mayonnaise

Entrée   Usually refers to the main dish or course

Enzyme   A protein compound that accelerates chemical reactions at a faster rate; an organic catalyst

Fermentation   A biochemical change causing an off-flavor in a food, such as fruit juices

Filet   Boneless meat

Fillet   Boneless fish

Foam   A mixture of air in a solution usually containing protein and fat that produces a fluffy structure

Fold   The use of two motions for combining ingredients, by slowly turning over and across the bottom of a utensil. Usually a hand operation performed with a whip or rubber spatula

Freezer burn   The loss of water from the surface of a frozen food resulting in a darkened area and undesirable appearance and texture

Fricassee   Braising pieces of poultry or meat

Fry   To cook in a fat medium. When using a small quantity of fat, the process is called pan-frying or sautéing. When food is completely covered with fat, the process is called deep fat frying

Grill   Frying food on a griddle; also may be toasted or sautéed

Grind   To grind, crush, or cut into small particles

Hardness   There are two types encountered: carbonate which is due to calcium and magnesium bicarbonates and carbonates; and noncarbonate which is due to calcium and magnesium sulfates, chlorides, and nitrates

Homogenization   The reduction of fat globule size under intense turbulence to produce a stable dispersion

Humectant   Chemical compounds like common sugar, or glycerol, or salt which when added to food helps bind water

Hygroscopic   Having the ability to absorb and hold moisture

Knead   A process usually applied to dough or other dense or thick mixtures wherein a product is folded, pressed, and stretched repeatedly; may also be done mechanically by employing a special kneading attachment to a mixer

Legumes   A category of vegetables that include peas, beans, and lentils

Liaison   Materials which are thickening agents like egg yolks or starch

Macedoine   Composed of a mixture of fruits or vegetables; the latter may be cooked or uncooked

Marinate   The liquid is referred to as a marinade; the process is the immersion of a food in oil and vinegar with the possible addition of flavors, spices, or wine; or in a brine or pickling solution; a process of tenderizing

Mask   To negate, reduce, or cover a food's character; performed by the use of sauces or mayonnaise

Melt   The process of liquefying a solid food like butter or lard

Microorganisms   Microscopic organisms, bacteria, yeast, mold

Mince   Chopping or cutting food into small segments

Mix   To blend or combine foods

Moisture content   The amount of water present in a food

Mold   A cellular growth usually found in moist damp areas. Filamentous on occasion

Mouth feel   The sensory perception in the mouth of the textural character of a food

MSNF   Milk solids not fat; usually pertains to dried skim milk powder

Noncarbonated   Soft drinks without CO_2 gas

Nondairy   Imitation dairy products made without milk or milk products in the formulation. May contain milk ingredients such as casein

Oxidation   The reaction of food compounds with air (oxygen) leading to the production of undesirable flavors, odors, and even toxic materials

Panbroil   To cook food on a grill or in a frying pan with the addition of a liquid medium like fat or butter. When meat is panbroiled, resulting liquid or fat is removed during the process

Panfry   To cook or sauté a food in a small amount of a frying medium

Parboil   To cook food by boiling water for a very short period

Pasteurization   Low heat treatment of a fluid to inactivate microorganisms and enzymes, thereby destroying pathogens and improving keeping quality

Pectin   A thickener or stabilizer used to gel mixtures

Perishable   Subject to rapid deterioration or spoilage

Peroxides   Chemicals which are produced during chemical reactions causing rancidity of foods. These compounds break down and cause destruction of nutrients and production of off-flavors and off-odors

pH   Measurement of hydrogen ion concentration. Relates to the amount of acidity or alkalinity of a food

Pigment   The color material contained in cells and tissues of foods

Poach   Slow cooking at a temperature of 180°–190°F (83°–88°C); to simmer in a small amount of water into which the food is placed

Portion control   Relates to convenience packets of food or liquids in premeasured amounts

Precipitation   The settling out of solid material in a liquid medium

Psychrophilic bacteria   Cold-loving bacteria that survive and grow at refrigerator temperatures

Puree   A process whereby a food is rubbed or worked through a sieve; generally used for soups

Rare   Refers to the degree of doneness of a food that has been underdone or slightly cooked, such as a rare steak

Reconstitute   To add back liquid to a dehydrated or freeze-dried product, such as water to dry milk

Reduce   The removal of a liquid by evaporation with the aid of heat; to concentrate to a denser state

Roast   To bake, usually meats or nuts

Salmonella   A food poisoning organism. There are over 1200 known species of this genus

Sanitation   Consists of two parts, cleaning and sanitizing

Sanitizing   The effective bacterial treatment of clean surfaces of equipment and utensils which shall provide an equivalent effect of a solution containing 50 ppm of available chlorine under use conditions

Saponification   The chemical reaction between an alkali and a fat

Sauté   A rapid frying process employing a small amount of frying medium to prevent food from adhering to a utensil. A food-release agent containing lecithin may also be used

Scald   Cooking or heating a liquid to just below its boiling point; to blanch; to help facilitate the removal of skins by immersion in hot or boiling water which loosens outer surfaces, as with some fruits or vegetables

Sear   The browning of the surface of a food by the application of high heat to improve appearance and flavor

Sediment   Solid matter that has precipitated out of solution, or foreign matter found in the bottom of a beverage container

Senses   The five human senses are: sight, touch, hearing, taste, and smell

Separation   The dividing into two distinct phases of the liquid and solids, often by bacterial or chemical action

Shelf-life   The average life or storage time that a food material will retain its original quality attributes

Simmer   A slow cooking process at temperatures of 180°–190°F (83°–88°C), usually attended by bubbles that form on the surface and break slowly

Slice   To cut food into thin slices with a knife or by a mechanical slicer; carving is a form of specialized slicing

Smoke point   The temperature at which oils or fats begin to smoke. Shortening and frying mediums that smoke above 400°F (205°C) have a high smoke point

Soft drinks   Any nonalcoholic beverages containing syrup, essences, or fruit concentrate that is mixed with water or carbonated water

Spoilage   Deterioration of a product through microbial contamination, addition of chemicals, or neglectful or abusive treatment

Stabilizers   Thickening or gelling agents

Staphylococcus   A food poisoning organism which may produce an enterotoxin; cause of the most common foodborne intoxication today

Sterilized   The absence of viable microorganisms

Stir   To blend or mix foods to a uniform consistency, to prevent burning or scorching by preventing thick-textured foods from adhering to the bottom of a utensil. Performed with a paddle, ladle, or spoon

Suspension   Solids held in a liquid that do not precipitate out, such as colloids

Sweetening agents   Products such as beet or cane sugars and corn syrup, or synthetic agents that impart a sweet character

Thermoduric bacteria   Those bacteria that can survive high heat treatments

Thermophilic bacteria   Those bacteria that can grow at high temperatures

Thicken   To alter the consistency of a food by adding flour, eggs, or starch and then cooking it. Cold foods may be thickened by the use of gelatin.

Toss   A gentle mixing process, like tossing salad segments

Total solids   Food components other than water or the nonaqueous portion of a food product

Toxin   A chemical which when ingested can cause serious illness

Unicellular   Consisting of a single cell, pertaining to microorganisms

Viscosity   The property of a liquid that is characterized by its consistency or flowability. Flow relationships include such terms as plastic, elastic, and pasty and refer to the rheology of foods

Wetting agent   Compounds which by reducing surface tension increase the capacity of water to contact surfaces. Wetting agents assist in the accelerated spot-free drying of dishes and glasses

Yeast   Microscopic round or oval vegetable cells belonging to the fungus class and used in the fermentation of sugars, brewing, and bread making

References

AM. HOME ECON. ASSOC. 1966. Handbook of Food Preparation. American Home Economics Assoc., Washington, DC.

AM. HOSPITAL ASSOC. 1972. Food Service Manual for Health Care Institutions. American Hospital Assoc., Chicago.

AM. SOC. TESTING MATER. 1964. Book of ASTM Standards. American Society for Testing and Materials, Philadelphia.

ANDERSON CLAYTON FOODS. 1971. Frying Facts. Anderson Clayton Foods, Dallas.

ANON. 1975. The Almanac of the Canning, Freezing, Preserving Industries. Edward E. Judge and Sons, Westminster, MD.

AURAND, L.W. and WOODS, A.E. 1973. Food Chemistry. AVI Publishing Co., Westport, CT.

AVERY, A.C. 1980. A Modern Guide to Foodservice Equipment. CBI Publishing Co., Boston.

BOWES, C.G. 1971. A Guide to Profitable Meat Management. Cahners Publishing Co., Boston.

CAIN, W.S. 1974. Odors, Evaluation, Utilization and Control. New York Academy of Sciences, New York.

CASOLA, M. 1969. Successful Mass Cookery and Volume Feeding. Ahrens Publishing Co., New York.

COLL. HOME ECON., KANS. STATE UNIV. 1975. Practical Cookery, 24th Revised Edition. John Wiley & Sons, New York.

CONSUMER MARKET. SERV., U.S. DEP. AGRIC. 1970. Grading America's Foods. Consumer and Marketing Service, U.S. Dept. Agric., Washington, DC.

COPSON, D.A. 1975. Microwave Heating, 2nd Edition. AVI Publishing Co., Westport, CT.

DESROSIER, N.W. and DESROSIER, J.N. 1977. The Technology of Food Preservation, 4th Edition. AVI Publishing Co., Westport, CT.

ECKSTEIN, E.F. 1978. Menu Planning, 2nd Edition. AVI Publishing Co., Westport, CT.

EDWARDS, C.C. 1973. Nutrition labeling. Fed. Regist. 38 (13, Part III) 2125.

ESHBACH, C.E. 1974A. Food Service Management. Cahners Publishing Co., Boston.

ESHBACH, C.E. 1974B. Food Service Trends. Cahners Publishing Co., Boston.

FOLSOM, L.A. 1974. The Professional Chef, 4th Edition. Cahners Publishing Co., Boston.

GARARD, I.D. 1974. The Story of Food. AVI Publishing Co., Westport, CT.

GELMAN, G. and TENNANT, H.R. 1946. Safe Keeping of Subsistence. Inst. Armed Forces, Washington, DC.

GRAHAM, H.D. 1980. The Safety of Foods, 2nd Edition. AVI Publishing Co., Westport, CT.

GUTHRIE, R.K. 1980. Food Sanitation, 2nd Edition. AVI Publishing Co., Westport, CT.

HALL, C.W., FARRALL, A.W. and RIPPEN, A.L.   1971.   Encyclopedia of Food Engineering. AVI Publishing Co., Westport, CT.

HARRIS, R.S. and KARMAS, E.   1975.   Nutritional Evaluation of Food Processing, 2nd Edition. AVI Publishing Co., Westport, CT.

JENSEN, M.W. and FOLKES, T.M.   1973.   A New Era in Consumer Safety. FDA Consumer 7 (1) 10.

JOHNSON, A.H. and PETERSON, M.S.   1974.   Encyclopedia of Food Technology. AVI Publishing Co., Westport, CT.

KAZARIAN, E.A.   1975.   Food Service Facilities Planning. AVI Publishing Co., Westport, CT.

KAZARIAN, E.A.   1979.   Work Analysis and Design for Hotels, Restaurants, and Institutions, 2nd Edition. AVI Publishing Co., Westport, CT.

KERR, R.G.   1969.   Fish Cookery for One Hundred. U.S. Dep. Inter., Washington, DC, Test Kitchen Ser. 1.

KNIGHT, J.B. and KOTSCHEVAR, L.H.   1979.   Quantity Food Production, 4th Edition. Cahners Publishing Co., Boston.

KOTSCHEVAR, L.H. and McWILLIAMS, M.   1969.   Understanding Food. John Wiley & Sons, New York.

KRAMER, A.   1980.   Food and the Consumer, Revised Edition. AVI Publishing Co., Westport, CT.

KRAMER, A. and TWIGG, B.A.   1970.   Quality Control for the Food Industry, Vol. 1. AVI Publishing Co., Westport, CT.

KRAMER, A. and TWIGG, B.A.   1973.   Quality Control for the Food Industry, Vol. 2. AVI Publishing Co., Westport, CT.

LABUZA, T.P. and SLOAN, A.E.   1977.   Food for Thought, 2nd Edition. AVI Publishing Co., Westport, CT.

LEVIE, A.   1979.   Meat Handbook, 4th Edition. AVI Publishing Co., Westport, CT.

LONGREE, K. and BLAKER, G.C.   1971.   Sanitary Techniques in Food Service. John Wiley & Sons, New York.

LUNDBERG, D.E. and KOTSCHEVAR, L.H.   1965.   Understanding Cooking Programmed. Univ. Massachusetts Press, Amherst.

MANUF. CHEM. ASSOC.   1971.   Food Additives—What They Are—How They Are Used. Manufacturing Chemists' Assoc., Washington, DC.

MARIO, T.   1978.   Quantity Cooking. AVI Publishing Co., Westport, CT.

McCLELLAND, N.I.   1965.   Water Quality Considerations and Related Dishwashing Problems. Natl. Sanitation Found., Ann Arbor, MI.

MERKEL, J.A.   1983.   Basic Engineering Principles, 2nd Edition. AVI Publishing Co., Westport, CT.

MEYER, L.H.   1978.   Food Chemistry. AVI Publishing Co., Westport, CT.

NAPLETON, L.   1971.   A Guide to Microwave Catering. Northwood Publications, London.

NATL. ACAD. SCI.-NATL. RES. COUNCIL.   1972.   Food Chemicals Codex. Natl. Acad. Sci.-Natl. Res. Council, Washington, DC.

NATL. ASSOC. FROZEN FOOD PACKERS.   1969.   Frozen food temperatures: Their meaning and measurement. Natl. Assoc. Frozen Food Packers, Washington, DC, Tech. Serv. Bull. 7.

NATL. ASSOC. MEAT PURVEYORS.   1978.   Meat Buyers' Guide. Natl. Assoc. Meat Purveyors, Chicago.

NATL. FOOD PROCESSORS ASSOC.   1968.   Laboratory Manual for Food Canners and Processors, Vol. 1 and 2, 3rd Edition. AVI Publishing Co., Westport, CT.

NATL. INST. FOODSERV. IND.   1974.   Applied Foodservice Sanitation. Natl. Inst. for the Foodservice Industry, Chicago.

NUTR. SERV. IOWA STATE DEP. HEALTH.   1962.   A Guide to Sanitation of Food Service Establishments. Nutrition Service, Iowa State Dep. of Health, Ames.

PAUL, C. and PALMER, H.H.   1972.   Food Theory and Applications. John Wiley & Sons, New York.

PEARSON, D.   1971.   Chemical Analysis of Foods, 6th Edition. Chemical Publishing Co., New York.
PECKHAM, G.C.   1970.   Foundations of Food Preparation. Macmillan Co., London.
POMERANZ, Y. and MELOAN, C.E.   1980.   Food Analysis Laboratory Experiments, 2nd Edition. AVI Publishing Co., Westport, CT.
POTTER, N.N.   1978.   Food Science, 3rd Edition. AVI Publishing Co., Westport, CT.
PYKE, M.   1974.   Catering Science and Technology. John Murray Publishers, London.
RICHARDSON, T.M.   1974.   Sanitation for Foodservice Workers, 2nd Edition. Cahners Publishing Co., Boston.
SCRIVEN, C. and STEVENS, J.   1980.   Food Equipment Facts. Conceptual Design Publishing Co., Troy, NY.
SIVETZ, M. and DESROSIER, N.W.   1979.   Coffee Technology. AVI Publishing Co., Westport, CT.
SMITH, L.L. and MINOR, L.J.   1974.   Food Service Science. AVI Publishing Co., Westport, CT.
STADELMAN, W.J. and COTTERILL, O.J.   1977.   Egg Science and Technology, 2nd Edition. AVI Publishing Co., Westport, CT.
STEWART, G. and AMERINE, M.A.   1973.   Introduction to Food Science. Academic Press, New York.
SULTAN, W.J.   1976.   Practical Baking Manual. AVI Publishing Co., Westport, CT.
SULTAN, W.J.   1981.   Practical Baking, Revised 3rd Edition. AVI Publishing Co., Westport, CT.
TERRELL, M.E.   1971.   Professional Food Preparation. John Wiley & Sons, New York.
THORNER, M.E.   1973.   Convenience and Fast Food Handbook. AVI Publishing Co., Westport, CT.
THORNER, M.E. and HERZBERG, R.J.   1979.   Non-alcoholic Food Service Beverage Handbook, 2nd Edition. AVI Publishing Co., Westport, CT.
TRESSLER, D.K. and NELSON, P.E.   1980.   Fruit and Vegetable Juice Processing Technology, 3rd Edition. AVI Publishing Co., Westport, CT.
TRESSLER, D.K., VAN ARSDEL, W.B. and COPLEY, M.J.   1968.   The Freezing Preservation of Foods, Vol. 4, 4th Edition. AVI Publishing Co., Westport, CT.
U.S. DEP. AGRIC.   1971.   Quantity Recipes for Type A School Lunches. U.S. Govt. Printing Office, Washington, DC.
U.S. DEP. AGRIC.   1971.   Standards for Meat and Poultry Products. Consumer Market. Serv. Bull. 85.
VANEGMOND-PANNELL, D.   1981.   School Foodservice, 2nd Edition. AVI Publishing Co., Westport, CT.
WATT, B.K. and MERRILL, A.L.   1963.   Composition of Foods, Raw, Processed, Prepared. U.S. Dep. Agric., Washington, DC. Agric. Handb. 8.
WEST, B.B., WOOD, L. and HARGER, V.F.   1966.   Food Service in Institutions, 4th Edition. John Wiley & Sons, New York.
WILKINSON, J.   1981.   The Complete Book of Cooking Equipment, 2nd Edition. CBI Publishing Co., Boston.
WOODROOF, J.G. and PHILLIPS, G.F.   1981.   Beverages: Carbonated and Non-carbonated, Revised Edition. AVI Publishing Co., Westport, CT.

Index

Air, effect on food, 88
Air conditioning, 313–314
Air pollution control, 262
Algae, 199, 230
Altitude, cooking adjustments for, 335
Association of Food and Drug Officials of
    the United States, frozen food
    storage guidelines, 82–83
Attributes, for inspection, 60

Bacteria, as spoilage agents, 228
    in cooked foods, 154
    in juice, 212–213
    in milk, 204, 206
    in soft drinks, 199, 200
    in vending equipment, 300
    growth factors, 230–231
Bain-marie, 154
Bake oven, performance evaluation, 101
    sanitizing procedures, 242
Bakery products, from frozen dough, 170–
    172
    mixes, 167, 172
    standards of identity, 55, 171
    storage, 85, 86
    types, 166–167
Beverages, See also specific beverages
    dispensers, 258–259
    hot water systems, 240–241
    poor quality, 173–174
    sensory evaluation, 11–18, 337–338
    vending equipment, 289–290, 294–296,
    297–303
    water content, 265
Blender, 129
Bread, for sandwiches, 138
    standards of identity, 171

Breading, 68–70
Broiler, performance evaluation, 101
    sanitizing procedure, 242
Browning, 108–109, 146
Bulk lot, 61
Butter, sampling, 30–31
    storage, 88, 141

Cabinets, holding, 101
    hot, 153, 154–155
Cacao products, standards of identity, 55
Cafeteria, automated, 292
Cake, handling, 167
    mixes, 172
    quality parameters, 167
    storage, 167–168
Can openers, sanitizing procedures, 129–
    130, 244
Canned food, See also Containers
    can damage, 75
    can sizes, 343
    storage, 80
Carbonated beverages, carbonation of,
    191–192, 197
    categories, 189
    dispensers, 198, 255–256
    sensory evaluation, 14
    syrup spoilage, 74
    syrup-water ratio, 74–75, 196, 197
Carbonated water, 33–34, 189
Carbonation, 191–192, 197
Carbonator, 191, 192, 256
Cereal, standards of identity, 55
Char-broiler, 318–319
Cheese, quality control procedures, 141,
    159–160
    storage, 141, 160

Cheese products, standards of identity, 55
Chlorination, 275, 278
Chocolate beverages. *See* Cocoa beverages
Chronosophy, 100
Cleaning schedule, 241
Clostridium perfringens, 232, 233, 237–238
Cocoa beverages, 222–226
  chilled, 225
  hot chocolate, 223–226
    dispensing of, 223–225, 260, 300–301
    powder spoilage, 225–226
    vending equipment, 300–301
  milk type, 222
  prepared, 222
Coffee, aroma, 73, 174
  chemical composition, 177, 178
  deterioration, 186
  factors affecting character, 175–176
  flavor, 174–175
  grind type, 178
  grinding of, 185–186
  instant, 184–185
  quality evaluation form, 188
  sensory evaluation, 14, 73
  serving containers, 183–184
  storage, 185
  vending equipment, 289, 294–295, 297–300
  water quality effects, 280–281
  whitening agents, 185, 211
Coffee brewing, 175–184
  brew water feed, 180
  coffee clarity, 181
  coffee wettability, 180–181
  cycle, 177–178
  extraction, 176–177, 179–180
  filtering systems, 181, 182
  formula, 178
  holding techniques, 153, 183
  inspection report form, 187
  mixing, 182–183
  problems, 186–188
  repouring, 182
  sanitation, 176
  temperature, 176
  vending equipment, in, 297–299
  water quality, 179
Coffee brewing equipment, 178, 179
  sanitizing procedures, 244–247, 252–255
  timing devices, 100
Coffee serving equipment, sanitizing procedures, 255
Cola, syrup-water ratio, 74–75
Complaint evaluation, 18–19
Computers, for record keeping, 325

Consumers, complaints, 18–19
  interpretation of quality, 2
Containers, drained weight, 66–68
  fill of, 65–66
  maximum headspace, 65–66
  portion chart, 342
  water capacity, 64–65
Convection oven, performance evaluation, 101, 102–104
  prevention maintenance, 326
Convenience food, 5
Conversion factors, 339
Cooler, 78
Corn, grades, 72
Cottage cheese, standards of identity, 45
Cream, curdling, 185
  dispensing, 206–207, 257
  handling, 185
  off-flavor, 202
  standards of identity, 55
Crust formation, 163

Dairy products, shelf-life, 206
  standards of identity, 55
Deep fat fryer, capacity rating, 112
  components, 111
  efficiency rating, 112–113
  frying medium, 114–117
  frying procedures, 117–118, 119–120
  number of units required, 113
  performance evaluation, 101
  preventive maintenance, 326–327
  quality factors, 111
  record keeping, 120–121
  sanitizing procedures, 118–119, 242–243
  timing devices, 100
Defrosting. *See* Thawing
Department of Agriculture, enforcement activities, 41–44
  product inspection procedures, 64–68
  responsibilities, 39
  standards, 40–41, 45–48, 329–334
Department of Defense, 39
Department of the Interior, 39
Desserts, convenience, 165–172
  frozen, 55, 165–166
  postcooking quality control, 153
Detergents, 238–239
Dishwashing. *See* Warewashing machines
Dispensing freezer, sanitizing procedures, 258
Dough, frozen, 170–172

Drained weight determination, 66–68
Dried fruit, 91

Egg boiler, 101
Eggs, boiling, 101, 140
    convenience products, 92, 140–141
    frying, 139
    grades, 44
    omelets, 140
    poaching, 139
    scrambling, 139
    storage, 92, 138–139
Electrical test meter, 33, 96
Electricity cost, 309, 310
Electrostatic precipitator, 319
Energy management, 307–320
    administrative responsibility, 320
    conservation, 309
    costs, 309, 310
    National Restaurant Association
        guidelines, 310–320
        air conditioning, 313–314
        char-broilers, 318–319
        food preparation, 311–313
        heating, 313–314
        lighting, 315–316
        refrigeration, 316–317
        sanitation, 314–315
        transportation, 317–318
        ventilation, 313–314
    supply and demand, 307–309
    survey charts, 310–311
    use breakdown, 320
Enterotoxin, 236, 237
Equipment, See also specific equipment
    manuals, 325
    performance factors, 95–96
    preventive maintenance, 97–98, 321–
        237
    quality determination, for, 11, 19–34, 96
    sanitizing procedures, 241–244

Fair Packaging and Labeling Act, 39
Fat, as deep frying medium, 114–120
    absorption, 115, 116
    deterioration, 115–117
    handling characteristics, 114
    problems in use, 119–120
    quality vs. economy, 115
    smoke point, 114
    in ground meat, 70–71

Fat analyzer, 30, 32
Filled milk products, 209
Fish, cooking procedures, 150–151
    grades, 72
    storage, 86, 92
Fish products, breading, 68, 69
    forms, 48–52
    grades, 53
    serving yield, 54
    specifications, 48–53
    storage, 92
Flavor, 3, 16
Flavoring, standards of identity, 55
Food, See also specific foods
    air effects on, 88
    bacterial contamination, 230–232
    heat effects on, 98
    insect contamination, 71, 92, 232
    issuing procedures, 93–94
    light effects on, 88–89
    pH, 231, 336
    quality, 3–4
    sensory evaluation, 11–18
    storage, 85–86, 93–94
    temperature guide, 344
Food and Drug Administration, breading
        percentage guidelines, 68
    product inspection procedures, 64–65
    responsibilities, 38
    standards of identity, 44–45
Food enzymes, 229
Food grading, 43–44, 71–72. See also
        Grades under specific foods and
        beverages
Food labeling, 39–40, 42–43
Food laws, 39, 46–47
Food preparation, energy management
        guidelines, 311–320
    water quality in, 282
Food standards, See also Standards under
        specific foods and beverages
    preparation of, 40–41
    regulatory agencies and, 38–39
    specifications, 38–55
    standards of identity, 44–45
Food technologist, 4
Food warmer, 102, 153, 154–155
Foodborne illness, 232–238
    Clostridium perfringens infection, 237–
        238
    salmonellosis, 237
    Staphylococcus food intoxication, 236–
        237
Freezer, dispensing, 258
    processing, 78
    storage, 78

Frozen food, drained weight, 66–68
  pre-prepared, 155–156
  receiving procedures, 58, 83–84
  storage, 80–85
  thaw indicators, 75
  thawing procedures, 135–136
Fruit, dried, 91
  frozen, 162
  grades, 53–54
  purchasing, 53
  quality control procedures, 162
  specifications, 53–54
  storage, 86, 89, 90
Fruit products, standards of identity, 55
Frying medium, deterioration, 115–117
  fat absorption, 115–116
  for eggs, 139
  handling characteristics, 114
  quality vs. economy, 115
  smoke point, 114

Gastroenteritis, 237–238
Germicides, 239
Gravy, 157–158, 159
Griddle, performance evaluation, 101
  preventive maintenance, 128, 325
Grill, performance evaluation, 101
Grinder, sanitizing procedures, 244
Ground meat, fat percentage, 70–71
  storage, 92

Heat exchange, 98–99
Heating, energy management guidelines,
  313–314
Holding times, and overproduction, 153–
  156
Hot water systems, 240–241
Humidity, 86–88
Hydrometer, 25–29
  Brix, 26–27, 196, 218
  directions for use, 27–29
Hygiene, 231–232
Hysteresis, 163

Ice, 193–194
  contamination, 261
Ice cream, as convenience dessert, 165–
  166
  flavor defects, 166
  quality scoring, 166
  vending equipment, 291
Ice cream soda, 208–209
Ice making equipment, 194–195
  sanitizing procedures, 261–262
Ice milk, standards of identity, 44–45
Iced tea, dispensers, 221, 259–260
  instant, 221
  preparation, 220–221
Infrared warming lamp, 153, 155
Insect control, 71, 92, 232
Inspection, attributes and variables, 60–
  63
  product control, 63–64
Issuing procedures, 93–94

Jam, standards of identity, 55
Juice, 211–218
  cloud formation, 215
  color changes, 214
  dispensing, 216–218
  flavor deterioration, 214
  frozen concentrates, 215–217
  off-flavor, 212
  oxidative rancidity, 215
  pH, 213
  quality testing, 218
  spoilage, 212–215
  storage, 215

Kettle, performance evaluation, 101
Kitchen, air pollution control in, 262

Leveling bubble, 96
Light, effect on food, 88–89
Lighting, energy management guidelines,
  315–316

Maggots, 71
Maintenance, 97–98, 321–327
  developing the program, 321–325
  equipment manuals, 325
  guide, 325–327
  record keeping, 321–325

Management, energy, 307–320
  interpretation of quality, 3
  quality control role, 2
Margarine, standards of identity, 55
  storage, 88
Measuring, devices, 31, 133, 135
  fractional equivalents, 340–341
Meat, cooking quality control, 146–148
  browning, 146
  dry heat, 147
  frozen meat, 148
  moist heat, 146, 147
  roasting, 147–148
  grades, 43–44
  heat effects, 98
  portion cut, 47
  spoilage, 91–92
  standards, 40, 45–46, 550
  storage, 85, 86, 91–92
Meat products, standards, 329–334
Microorganisms, See also Algae; Bacteria;
  Molds; Yeasts; specific names
  growth factors, 228
  humidity effects, 86–87
  in hot chocolate powder, 225
  in juice, 212–214
  in meat, 91
  in soft drinks, 199–200, 201
  in water, 271
Microwave oven, cooking quality control,
  browning, 108–109
  delayed cooking procedures, 108
  food plating, 106–107
  food positioning, 106–107
  food preparation, 105–110
  meat, 144
  production assembly problems, 107–
    108
  maintenance, 110–111
  performance evaluation, operating
    efficiency, 109–110
  timing test procedures, 101, 104–105
  sanitizing procedures, 110
Microwave radiation leakage meter, 33,
  34, 96
Milk, dispensing, 202–204, 205–206, 256
  flavor defects, 202
  sensory evaluation, 73–74
  spoilage chemical, 205
  microbiological, 204–205, 206
  poor temperature control, from, 206
  test for, 73–74
  standards of identity, 55
  storage, 88
Milk substitutes. See Nondairy products
Mites, 71
Mixer, sanitizing procedures, 243

Molds, as spoilage agents, 199, 214, 229,
  300

National Restaurant Association, energy
  management guidelines, 310–
  320
Nondairy products, 209–211
  characteristics, 211
  definitions, 209–210
  evaluation, 211
  spoilage, 210
Noodle products, standards of identity, 55
Nutrient loss, 144
Nutritional labeling, 40, 41, 42

Occupational Safety and Health Act
  (OSHA), 263
Odor, perception of, 12–14, 16–17
Off-flavor, coffee, 186
  cream, 202
  juice, 212
  milk, 202
  soft drinks, 199, 200, 201
Oil, as frying medium, 114, 115
Omelet, 140
Orange juice, 216
Oven, See also Bake oven; Convection
  oven; Microwave oven
  performance evaluation, 101
  sanitizing procedures, 242
  timing devices, 100
Overproduction, 153, 154
Oxidation, 88, 205, 215

Packaging, inspection control, 75
Pantry operation, 132
Peanut butter, standards of identity, 55
Peeler, sanitizing procedures, 129
Performance evaluation, equipment
  requiring, 101–102
  factors in, 95–96
pH, bacterial growth effects, 231
  meters, 32, 33
  of food, 336
  of fruit juice, 213
  of soft drinks, 199–200

Pie, defects, 170
    frozen, 169–170
    quality characteristics, 169
    shells, 170
Pollution control, 262, 318–319
Portion control data, 340–341
Portioning devices, 132–133
Potatoes, cooking quality control, 145–146
Poultry, age groups, 47–48
    classification, 46
    cooking quality control, 148–150
    cuts, 48
    forms, 48
    grades, 43–44, 47
    specifications, 46–48
    standards, 45–48
    storage, 92–93
Poultry products, standards, 333–334
    storage, 92–93
Poultry Products Inspection Act, 46–47
Pre-prepared food, 5
    distribution, 155
    manufacturers' processing guidelines, 151
    quality checks, 151–152
Pressure cooker. See Steam cooker
Pressure gauge, 33, 96
Product inspection control, 41–43, 63–75
    breading percentage, 68–70
    drained weight, 66–68
    fat percentage in meat, 70–71
    fill of container, 65–66
    insect filth, 71
    maximum headspace, 65–66
    packaging, 75
    sampling techniques, 59–63
    sensory evaluation, 71–75
    water capacity, 64–65
Prunes, standards of identity, 44
Pudding, instant, 172
Purchasing, 35, 53

Quality, interpretations of, 2–3
Quality assurance, 1
Quality characteristics, 61
Quality control, See also under specific subjects
    cooking procedures, 143–152
        fish, 150–151
        heating, 143
        meat, 146–148
        nutrient loss, 144
        poultry, 148–150

    pre-prepared food, 151–152
    seafood, 150–151
    definition, 1
    postcooking procedures, 153–163
        cheese, 159–160
        food distribution, 155
        fruit, 162
        gravies, 157–159
        holding of food, 153, 154–156
        microbiological contamination, 154
        overproduction, 153, 154
        salad dressings, 157, 158–159
        salads, 160–161
        sandwiches, 161–162
        sauces, 157–159
        syneresis prevention, 162–163
    precooking procedures, 131–141
        butter, 141
        cheese, 141
        eggs, 138–141
        recipes, 132, 133, 134
        salads, 136–137
        sandwiches, 137–138
        thawing, 131, 135–136
        weights and measures, 132–133, 135
    projects, 6–7
Quality control laboratory, floor plan, 8
    location, 8–9
    need for, 11
    space requirements, 8, 9
Quality control program, basic components, 5–6
    development, 4
    for efficiency foodservice, 5
    implementation, 11–34
        equipment for, 11, 19–34
        sensory evaluation in, 11–18
Quick bread, 168

Range, sanitizing procedures, 242
Receiving, 57–59
    equipment for, 59, 60, 61
    forms, 345
    procedures, 58
    record keeping, 58–59
Recipes, format, 132, 133, 134, 143
    fractional equivalents, 340–341
Refractometer, 24–25, 196
Refrigeration, energy management guidelines, 316–317
    in storage facilities, 77, 78
Regulatory agencies, 38–39

Risk inspection, 61
Rodent control, 232

Salad, quality control procedures, 136–137, 153, 160–161
Salad dressing, convenience type, 159–160
  quality control procedures, 137, 157, 158–159
  standards of identity, 55
  storage, 157–158
Salmonella, 232, 233, 237
Salmonellosis, 237
Sampling techniques, 59–63
  definition of terms, 60–61
  Department of Agriculture regulations, 62–63
  factors influencing, 62
  nature of material, 62
  sample size, 62
  schedule, 59–60
  small lots, 63
Sandwiches, breads, 138
  fillings, 137
  quality control procedures, 137–138, 161–162
  spreads, 138
  storage, 138
Sanitizer, 239–240
Sanitizing procedures, 231–232, 238–241, See also under specific equipment
  cleaning schedules, 241
  energy management guidelines, 314–315
  preventive maintenance, as, 98
Sauce, convenience type, 158, 159
  functions, 157
  maintaining quality, 159
  storage, 157–158, 159
Scale, 19–21, 132–133
  characteristics, 19–20
  location, 20–21
  maintenance, 21
  number required, 21
  receiving, 60
  sanitizing procedures, 21
Scoop, 31
Seltzer, 189
Semiperishable food, storage, 79–80
Sensory evaluation, 11–18
  factors affecting, 13
  in food grading, 71–72
  in product inspection control, 71–75
  proficiency in, 13

sensory perception mechanisms, 13–15
  techniques, 12–13, 15–17
    by odor detection, 16–17
    by taste, 17
    by visual observation, 16
Shellfish, breading percentage, 68, 69–70
  cooking quality control, 150–151
  forms, 50, 51–52
  grades, 72
  serving yield, 54
  storage, 86
Shredder, sanitizing procedures, 129
Sieve, 30
Sight, in sensory evaluation, 12, 13, 15, 16
Skipper insects, 92
Slicer, sanitizing procedures, 129, 244
Sliminess, of meat, 91
Slush beverages, 208
Smell, sense. See Odor
Soap, 239
Soft drinks, classification, 189
  definition, 189
  dispensing components control, 189–190
  ice in, 193–195
  most popular flavors, 189
  off-flavor, 199, 200, 201
  quality control procedures, 195–198
  refrigeration, 192–193
  specifications, 189
  spoilage, 199–202
    biochemical, 202
    chemical, 201–202
    microbiological, 199–200, 201
    pH, 199–200
    physical, 200–201
  standards of identity, 55
  syrup handling, 190
  syrup-water ratio, 34, 196, 197
  vending equipment, 295–296, 301–303
  water, precooling, 191
    purification, 190–191
    quality, 281
  water cap, 194
Soft-serve beverages, 207–208
Souring, of meat, 91–92
Sparkling water, 189
Specifications, 35–38
  fact form sheet, 37–38
  food standards and, 38–55
  methods of preparing, 36
  product grouping, 36–37
Spoilage, 227–231, See also under specific foods and beverages
  algae-associated, 230
  bacterial, 230–231
  biochemical, 229

chemical, 230
microbiological, 228–229
physical, 229–230
Standards and grades, regulatory food, 38–55
Standards of identity, 44–45
Staphylococcus aureus, 232, 233, 236
Staphylococcus food intoxication, 236–237
Steam cooker, 121–126
    browning and steaming, 124–125
    countertop specialty, 125
    design, 122–125
        compartmented, 123, 124
        high-pressure, 123–124
        steam-jacketed, 122–123
    general features, 121–222
    maintenance, 125–126
    performance evaluation, 102
    sanitizing procedures, 125, 243
    timing devices, 100
Steam pressure, 335
Steam table, 153, 154
Stopwatch, 29, 96
Storage, baked products, 85, 86
    butter, 88, 141
    cake, 167–168
    canned food, 80
    cheese, 141, 160
    coffee, 185
    dried fruit, 91
    egg products, 92
    eggs, 138–139
    fish, 86, 92
    fish products, 92
    frozen food, 80–85
        Association of Food and Drug Officials of the United States, code, 82–83
        deterioration, 81
        intermittent thawing, 81–82
        personnel responsible for, 80–81
        receiving guidelines, 83–84
        stability, 84–85
        temperature measuring techniques, 83
    fruit, 86, 89, 90
    gravies, 157–158
    humidity effects, 86–88
    juice, 215
    margarine, 88
    meat, 85, 86
    milk, 88, 203–204, 205
    poultry, 92–93
    poultry products, 92–93
    salad dressing, 157–158
    sandwiches, 138

sauces, 157–158, 159
semiperishable foods, 79–80
shellfish, 86
soft drink syrups, 190
vegetables, 89–91
Storage facilities, dry, 78–80
    procedures, 78–79
    refrigerated, 77, 78
        coolers, 78
        processing freezers, 78
        storage freezers, 78
        thawers, 78
Storage life, 85–86
Sublot, 61
Supermarket display technique, 79
Syneresis, 162–163
Syrup, handling, 140
    spoilage, 74
    storage, 140
Syrup-water ratio, for soft drinks, 34, 74–75, 196, 197

Tart shell, 170
Taste, in sensory evaluation, 12, 14, 15, 17–18
Taste panel, 17–18
Tea, 218–221
    brewing, 219–221
    hot, 219–220
    iced, dispensers, 221, 259–260
    instant, 221
    preparation, 220–221
    instant powdered, 219, 221
    spoilage, 219
Teapot, sanitizing procedures, 260
Temperature, canned food storage, 80
    control, 98–100
        thermostat in, 99–100
    effect on carbonation, 191, 200
    frozen food storage, 81, 82–83, 84–85
    guide, 344
    time-temperature relationship, 100
Thaw indicator, 75
Thawer, 78
Thawing, methods, 131, 135–136
    microwave oven for, 105–106
Thermometer, 22–24
    accuracy testing, 22
    errors in reading, 22
    requirements, 23–24
    thermostats, in, 23
    types, 22–23, 96
Thermostat, 23

basic design, 99
  specifications, 99–100
Tilting skillet, 126–127
  cooking temperatures, 127
  labor saving device, as, 127
  operating factors, 127
  preventive maintenance, 327
  sanitizing procedures, 127
Timer, 29, 96
Timing, 96, 100–101
Toaster, sanitizing procedures, 243
Tongue, tasting mechanism of, 14, 15
Touch, in sensory evaluation, 14–15
Transportation, energy management
    guidelines, 317–318
Trier, 30–31

Variables, for inspection, 61
Vegetables, classification, 53
  cooking quality control, 144–146
  canned, 145
  dehydrated, 145
  fresh, 144–145
  frozen, 145
  grades, 53, 54–55
  purchasing, 53
  specifications, 53, 54–55
  storage, 89–91
Vending equipment, 287–305
  automated cafeterias, in, 292
  coffee brewing by, 297–299
  coin-operated, 289–292
  design, 288–289
  hot chocolate, 300–301
  inspection forms, 302, 304–305
  operating principles, 288
  operational aspects, 290–292
  quality control, 292–305
  sanitizing procedures, 293–305
    coffee machines, 294–295, 297, 300
    cold food machines, 296–297
    definitions, 294
    hot food machines, 296–297
    sanitation kit, 293–294
    soft drink machines, 295–296
  soft drinks, 301–303
    can and bottle, 303
    premix, 303
    quality control, 303
  types, 289–292
    beverages, 291
    canned food, 291
    cigarette, 290, 291

column dispensers, 290
    cupboard, 291
    drop flap, 290–291
    ice cream, 291
    solid pack, 290
Vending industry, 287–288
Ventilation, energy management
    guidelines, 313–314
Vermin control, 232
Visual observation, in sensory evaluation,
    16
Vitamin loss, 144

Waffle iron, sanitizing procedures, 243
Warewashing machine, 283–285
  cleaning, 284–285
  hot water systems, 240
Warranty form, 324
Water, algae contamination, 230
  analysis report form, 283
  as beverage component, 174, 265
  boiling temperature, 335
  brackish, 267–268
  chemical composition, 265–266, 267
  chlorine content, 190
  for coffee brewing, 179, 280–281
  for food preparation, 282
  hardness, 267, 272–274
  impurities, 267, 268–271
    color, 271
    dissolved gases, 270
    dissolved minerals, 268–270
    free mineral acids, 270
    greases, 270
    microorganisms, 271
    odor, 271
    oils, 270
    organic matter, 271
    suspended solids, 271
    taste, 271
    turbidity, 271
  properties, 266
  soft drinks, for, 190–191, 281
  sources, 266–267
  testing, 282–283
Water analysis test kit, 30, 51
Water capacity determination, 64–65
Water treatment, 271–280
  chlorination, 275, 278
  determining treatment capacity, 279–
    280
  purifiers, 274–275, 276–277, 279
  reverse osmosis, 278–279, 281

strainers, 275, 277
water softening, 272–274, 279
  ion exchange, 272–273, 280
  polyphosphate systems, 273–274, 280
Weighing devices. *See* Scale
Weights, fractional equivalents, 340–341
Whitener, nondairy, 185, 211

Wholesome Poultry Products Act, 47

Yeasts, as spoilage agents, 199, 213–214, 229